HOOVER'S FBI

HOOVER'S FBI

William W. Turner

THUNDER'S MOUTH PRESS
NEW YORK

Copyright © 1993 by William W. Turner

1 2 3 4 5 6 7 8 9 10 / 99 98 97 96 95 94 93

All rights reserved
First edition
First printing 1993

Published by
Thunder's Mouth Press
54 Greene Street, Suite 4S
New York, N.Y. 10013

Revised and updated reprint, originally published in 1970

Library of Congress Cataloging-in-Publication Data
Turner, William W.
　　Hoover's FBI / William W. Turner.
　　　　p.　　cm.
　　ISBN 1-56025-063-1 : $12.95
　　1. United States.　Federal Bureau of Investigation.　I. Title.
　　HV8138.T849　1993
　　353. 0074'09--dc20　　　　　　　　　　　　　　　　92-44099
　　　　　　　　　　　　　　　　　　　　　　　　　　　　　　CIP

Editorial production and text design by Thumb Print
Cover design © The Great American Art Company
Printed in the United States of America

Distributed by
Publisher's Group West
4065 Hollis Street
Emeryville, CA 94608
(800) 788-3123

By William W. Turner

THE POLICE ESTABLISHMENT

INVISIBLE WITNESS: THE USE AND ABUSE OF THE
NEW TECHNOLOGY OF CRIME INVESTIGATION

POWER ON THE RIGHT

THE ASSASSINATION OF ROBERT F. KENNEDY
(with Jonn Christian)

THE 10-SECOND JAILBREAK
(with Warren Hinckle and Eliot Asinof)

DEADLY SECRETS: THE CIA-MAFIA WAR AGAINST
CASTRO AND THE ASSASSINATION OF J. F. K.
(with Warren Hinckle)

To Magdalen and Will,
without whom . . .

And to Margaret
with whom . . .

ACKNOWLEDGMENTS

Few books are one-man enterprises, and this is no exception. To the FBI agents past and present who have contributed in one form or another, my sincere—and discreet—gratitude. To Nelson H. Gibbons, one of the Bureau's best who long ago joined me in letting it all hang out. . . well, thanks again, Skip.

A special note of indebtedness to Karen Kahn, who helped pummel the first draft into final condition. And to editor Shelly Lowenkopf, who wasn't scared off by the treatment.

Finally, my thanks go to Neil Ortenberg of Thunder's Mouth Press and Charlie Winton of Publishers Group West, who realized the current significance of *Hoover's FBI*.

CONTENTS

FOREWORD
TO THE 1970 EDITION

When the history of mid-twentieth-century America is finally written, the Federal Bureau of Investigation under J. Edgar Hoover will go down as one of the greatest of contemporary phenomena. Traditionally, police agencies with their immense powers have been viewed with healthy skepticism by the public. But Hoover and the FBI, propelled by the magic of high-tension publicity into a position of untouchability, have stood immune from the prodding, probing, and at times ridicule that is the lot of the ordinary agency.

The phenomenon is not without potential danger. Maverick industrialist Cyrus Eaton once remarked, "I always worry when I see a nation feel that it is coming to greatness through the activities of its policemen." Centuries ago, the Roman poet Juvenal perceived such dangers when he asked, "Who will police the police?" This question applies with unparalleled force at this pivotal stage in the FBI's history.

For the day that Hoover must turn in his Badge Number One cannot be far off. In 1969, rumors abounded that he had made an agreement with the Nixon administration to step down on his seventy-fifth birthday, January 1, 1970—it was said he felt the Bureau would be in safe hands with Nixon, as opposed to a more liberal chief executive—but he promptly spiked the rumors with the announcement that he had no intention of stepping down and looked forward to many more years in the fight against the "crisis" of lawlessness. Certainly, the FBI Chief's Pharisee-like devotion to the letter of the law rather than the spirit of the law is useful to the administration in the current "law and order" climate. But the indispensable man will some day go. Who will be his successor?

Hoover has made it clear that if he has his way, the next Director will come from the inside. In fact, with his blessing Congressman

H. Allen Smith, a former FBI agent, recently introduced a bill that would have made it mandatory that the Director be appointed from among those who have been on the FBI payroll for seven consecutive years. Hoover's faithful sidekick, Associate Director Clyde Tolson, is aging and ailing, and will probably bow out with the Director if not before. Hoover hasn't groomed anyone for the job, and hasn't indicated his preference. An internal power struggle has produced two major candidates: John P. Mohr, long an assistant to the Director and head of the administrative division, and Cartha ("Deke") DeLoach, the other assistant to the Director, elevated to that post in 1965 by dint of his success in running the FBI publicity and public relations program.

If an insider is named, DeLoach would seem to have the edge by virtue of his personal friendship with Nixon, dating back to the days when the president was in Congress and DeLoach was an FBI liaison man making the Capitol Hill rounds. But there is a compromise candidate who can be considered both an insider and an outsider: former Assistant Director Louis B. Nichols, now an executive vice president of Schenley Industries. When he retired in 1957, Nichols got the hundred-thousand-a-year job through the good offices of Roy M. Cohn, a friend of the Director's who had been Joseph McCarthy's chief inquisitor and later became a Schenley legal counsel. Nichols is an unwavering Hoover loyalist: he named a son John Edgar and got Schenley's board chairman to underwrite the Director's books. He broke into the news in 1969 when, according to *Life* magazine, he stormed into Hoover's office and sought, successfully, the transfer of three New York agents who had furnished the Department of Justice with affidavits adverse to Roy Cohn.

There have been hints, however, that Nixon would like to appoint an outsider. One leading contender is Joseph I. Woods, the sheriff of Cook County, Illinois, and an ex–FBI agent (1951-1961); his sister Rose Mary has long been Nixon's secretary. Another front runner is Spiro Agnew's superintendent of the Maryland State Police, Colonel Carey Jarman. The press has speculated about John Edward Ingersoll, a forty-year-old official of the International Association of Chiefs of Police and director of the Department of Justice's newly created Bureau of Narcotics and Dangerous Drugs. Also mentioned have been Peter J. Pitchess, sheriff of Los Angeles County, who is also an FBI alumnus; Chief Thomas Cahill of the San Francisco police, an old-guard type often praised by Hoover; former Chief Thomas Reddin of Los Angeles, now a newscaster on television; and District Attorney Evelle J. Younger of Los Angeles, still another former G-man.

But the paramount question is: what is to be the shape and dimension of the post-Hoover FBI? Difficult as it is to believe, Hoover took over during the Calvin Coolidge administration, in 1924. So entrenched has he become that he considers presidents mere transients. He was given a free hand in molding his agency, and the FBI reflects to an uncommon degree his own personality. His whims, fancies, prejudices, and idiosyncrasies are stamped on it, and his slightest wish, express or implied, becomes an edict to his subordinates. One amusing but quite true story will illustrate the point. The Director is fond of jotting pungent notations on the borders of memorandums, and the filling of all four borders is known as a "four-bagger." Once, he was irked by a memo that left little room for his scrawlings. "Watch the borders," he wrote in his characteristic green ink. Uncertain of what he meant and afraid to ask, officials carried out the dictum to the letter. For over a week, agents were staked out along the Canadian and Mexican borders, unsure of what they were watching for.

Although such absurdities are commonplace in this super-monolithic organization, the FBI's public image blots them out. Burnished to brightness by publicity techniques that are the envy of Madison Avenue, Hoover has been made to appear bigger than life. By virtue of this mystique he has become one of the most powerful men in America. At the same time, he is personally as much of a mystery as Howard Hughes. So recondite is the flesh-and-blood Director that humorist Art Buchwald was moved to write, in a column that drew a frigid response from the Bureau, "He is a mythical person first thought up by the *Reader's Digest,* and over the years he has become such a legend that no President has dared reveal the truth."

In this book I will attempt to breathe some life into the cardboard silhouette of the old Bureau bulldog, because to fathom the Man, as he is referred to by his underlings, is to understand the organization. Inside the Bureau he is quite real, and his personality diffuses itself into all phases of the operation. Behind the jealously guarded patina of perfection is a very mortal man, one who brought the FBI into unprecedented fame and in the end, ironically, has made it, in the words of the Associated Press, "one of our most controversial" arms of government.

Every story has two sides, and the virtues of the FBI have been recited for years in a Niagara of books, articles, feature stories, movies, radio shows, and TV accounts. Its vices, on the other hand, have remained largely unchronicled. Consider these paradoxes:

• That Hoover, universally regarded as the nation's top law enforcement officer, has never personally investigated a case in the field

• That although the FBI is considered the Nemesis of Crime, it only has jurisdiction over about 1 percent of the serious crimes committed and does not ordinarily handle homicides and other violent and heinous crimes

• That the FBI and organized crime have flourished simultaneously

• That the arbitrarily designated FBI Top Ten Fugitives are for the most part human tumbleweeds of slight menace to society as a whole

• That the renowned "atom spies" case that resulted in the execution of Julius and Ethel Rosenberg was overblown for political purposes, while the truly professional spies, Colonel Rudolf I. Abel and the Peter Krogers, escaped the FBI net and carried on espionage activities for many more years

• That the vaunted esprit de corps of the agent force is actually a self-protective allegiance on the part of the agents, serving to protect them from their employer's excesses

John F. Kennedy once quipped that the "three most overrated things in the world are the state of Texas, the FBI, and mounted deer heads."* That the Bureau is overrated is not very important in

---

*Quoted by William Manchester in *The Death of a President*.

itself; no public agency can function without a broad base of public confidence. What is of concern, however, is that by reason of being grossly overrated the FBI has become, as Senator Eugene McCarthy put it, "a fiefdom."

Rising in Washington is a huge new multimillion-dollar headquarters that will further symbolize the FBI's autonomy and independence from the Department of Justice and its other nominal masters. From the day he took office, Hoover has demonstrated an ambition for his Bureau that matches that of the empire builders of the Old West, and he has run it in the same aggressive and autocratic style. Today, the FBI hardly resembles the modest agency of 1924. Few Americans have any idea of the extent to which the FBI probes our national life, investigating not only violations of law but vague and undefined nonstatutory areas. Because of this accumulation of jurisdiction, contends Arthur S. Miller of George Washington University's National Law Center, "a national police force seems to be either in being or in the making. At some time, the FBI will be recognized as a national police force—in fact if not in theory.*

The idea of the FBI as a national police force, with its connotations of omnipresence and thought control, may come as a shock to many who have been conditioned to believe that Hoover has exercised his powers with restraint. But is it baseless paranoia to look with concern on the vast network of FBI informers and "confidential sources" crisscrossing the nation—on college campuses, in labor and industry, in government, even including airline stewardesses who wait on traveling businessmen? Is it unreasonable to be troubled by Hoover's incessant talk of a foreign-directed conspiracy—the American Communist Party puppeted by Moscow, the Black Panther Party dancing to Beijing's tune, the student radicals inspired by alien ideologies? Is there any possibility that our conspiracy-obsessed FBI chief is champing to implement the Emergency Detention Act (Title II of the Internal Security Act of 1950), which permits the president to proclaim an internal security emergency when, in addition to more explicit situations, there is "insurrection in the United States in aid of a foreign enemy?" After the act became law, Hoover told Congress:

---

*Quoted in the *Wall Street Journal,* October 15, 1968.

"There is a potential fifth-column of 550,000 people dedicated to this [Communist] philosophy"—this when the membership of the domestic Communist Party was fewer than twenty-five thousand and fading. How many political dissidents will be rounded up if the Bureau's "Det-Com [Detention of Communists] Program" is ever activated? No one knows. But some idea can be gained from the fact that nearly seven thousand FBI agents won't be enough to do the job—selected local police and trusted members of the Society of Former Special Agents of the FBI have been deputized to assist.

These are the kinds of questions Hoover's stewardship has raised.

In the first part of this book, I have outlined my own ten-and-a-half-year career as a special agent, because I believe it reveals much about the Bureau. During that career I gradually became disabused of my illusions about the Bureau, and in the end became to the FBI, if such analogies apply, what Ralph Nader was to General Motors. In any event, *you* are the consumer who is paying. You have a right to know what you are paying for. A pamphlet handed to the millions of people who take the guided tour of FBI headquarters begins, "Director Hoover feels the American people have a right to see the FBI in action and to know of its operations." To which I would add: They also have a right to see the other FBI, the one behind the guided tours and the newsprint curtain.

In the second part of the book I have tried to portray the Man hardly anyone knows, and in the third to give an unofficial view of the organization, drawing heavily on my own experiences. True, it has been several years now since I last flashed the credentials of a special agent. But those still in the Bureau tell me that nothing has really changed. For Hoover and his FBI, time stood still that sweltering Chicago evening when John Dillinger fell in a blaze of gunfire.

Finally, there are decisions to be made about the future. Should someone who has been associated with the Hoover era take over, or should the whole structure be opened to the outside? What about redesigning the FBI for the 1970s? I have presumed to make a few recommendations in the final chapter, and one or two may seem radical. But after more than forty-five years of one-man rule, radical changes are in order for the Bureau.

INTRODUCTION

TO THE 1993 EDITION

On the muggy Los Angeles night of July 1, 1968, I arrived at the studios of "The Joe Pyne Show," a nationally syndicated television production, to be interviewed concerning my first book, *The Police Establishment.* Pyne was a contentious conservative, a kind of early-day Rush Limbaugh, who was notorious for verbally mugging guests he disagreed with. It was obvious he thought he had me up a dark alley when he shunned even a perfunctory handshake. Certainly the theme of the book was enough to get his testosterone flowing: the urban police forces across the country were bonded by a powerful lobbying and public relations network presided over by J. Edgar Hoover, then in his forty-fifth year as FBI Director. Hoover gave every indication that he intended to go on, and on, and on, like the Energizer battery. There was an aura of immortality about him.

Before the show began, Pyne huddled in the wings with his producer, giving me a chance to steal a look at his cue cards. Sure enough, he was loaded up for a personal attack on me rather than a discussion of the issues. And the ammunition could only have come from the FBI. I had been a Bureau agent for more than ten years, finally poking the tiger from inside the cage by seeking a congressional investigation of Hoover's foot-dragging on organized crime, his preoccupation with pursuing the human tumbleweeds of crime to pile up statistics, and the cult of personality surrounding him.

When the cameras rolled I answered questions before Pyne could ask them. He became more and more exasperated, until he finally snapped, "A hundred years from now who are people going to remember, Bill Turner or J. Edgar Hoover?"

"Why Hoover, of course," I shot back. "He'll still be Director."

Cut for a commercial.

When I obtained my FBI file under the Freedom of Information Act (FOI) a decade later, the FBI's back-door collaboration with Joe

Pyne was confirmed. Several days before the show, Pyne's producer had called the local FBI office soliciting "any information on Turner" because there were "some derogatory comments concerning the FBI" in the book. The Special Agent in Charge (SAC) immediately sent an "Urgent" teletype to Washington headquarters urging that Pyne be furnished an abstract of my dossier. If this wasn't done, the SAC warned, "IT MAY WRONGLY APPEAR THAT TURNER AND HIS ILK ARE PARAGONS OF TRUTH, VERACITY AND COMPETENCY TO JUDGE."

The teletype touched off a flurry of activity at headquarters. Supervisor Milton A. Jones of the Crime Records Division, as the public relations arm was then called, memoed his boss, Assistant Director Tom Bishop, recommending that an anonymous letter be prepared by his staff for transmittal to Pyne with the understanding "that it is not to be attributed to the FBI." Jones felt secure that the Bureau's hand would not be revealed because "We have cooperated on a confidential basis previously with Pyne." The memo was bumped all the way up to Hoover, who scrawled his distinctive "OK H."

By this time I had become a moving target for FBI COINTEL-PRO, ranking number 3 on Hoover's enemies list. I learned this from Assistant Director William C. Sullivan after he retired several years later. Number 1, Sullivan said, was Quinn Tamm, a former Bureau executive who headed the International Association of Chiefs of Police; he had earned Hoover's opprobrium by resisting FBI hegemony over his organization. Number 2 was columnist Jack Anderson, who frequently knocked Hoover's halo askew. In addition to the enemies list, there were "No Contact" lists maintained in headquarters and each field office on those who had to one degree or another voiced doubts about the agency's invincibility or, worse still, Hoover personally. Agents were under instructions studiously to avoid such persons officially and socially.

But the lists were not as long as they might have been because many would-be critics were intimidated into silence by visits from FBI agents or the knowledge that Hoover was the keeper of the secret files containing data on the dark sides of people's lives. An example of the former occurred in the 1950s in Cleveland, Ohio, when, according to Athan G. Theocharis and John Stuart Cox in *The Boss,* a woman gossiped to members of her bridge club that "the Director was a homosexual and kept a large group of boys around him." Word filtered back to the local FBI with the result that the Special Agent in Charge summoned the gossip to his office and, in the words of his report to Washington, "chastised her most vigorously" and ensured that "she understood the untruth of her statements" and "the serious nature of her action in having made them." And, after a Washington beautician and her assistant asserted that "all the bookies in Washington turned in money to the Director" and that the Director was "a sissy, liked men, and was a queer," Hoover immediately sent two agents "to take this scandal monger & liar on." The agents browbeat the women into submission, threatening to haul them before a grand jury for their capital crime, and they meekly promised never to "be guilty of such statements again."

Over the years the FBI aggressively accumulated every scrap of derogatory and compromising information it could find on politicians, celebrities, and anyone else in a position to exert influence. The data were collected from other agencies, news clips, incidental to Bureau investigations, from bugs and taps, and from informants and confidential sources. Prominent among the targets were the Kennedys, Frank Sinatra, Marilyn Monroe, and, earlier, Eleanor Roosevelt. But there was hardly anyone of note who escaped having a skinny in the Bureau files. The field offices assiduously collected information on the peccadilloes, sexual liaisons, and shady dealings of those with national stature and funneled it to Washington, where it was harbored in Hoover's office in files headed Official & Confidential and Personal & Confidential. The supersensitive ones were stored in the Director's safe without headings. It was undoubtedly the largest collection of blackmail material that ever existed. Anyone pondering a swipe at Hoover had to decide whether it was worth the risk. Most played it safe.

As a result Hoover ran the FBI as he pleased. The checks and balances designed to bridle overly ambitious bureaucrats were neutralized. Representative Emmanuel Celler, chairman of the House Judiciary Committee at the time, asserted that the Director's unprecedented clout derived from "the fact that he was the head of an agency that in turn had tremendous power, power of surveillance, power of control over the lives and destinies of every man in the nation. He had a dossier on every member of Congress and every member of the Senate." In those relatively prudish days politicians had every reason to envision the end of their careers should their dirty linen be hung out in public.

And it was. How this worked was illustrated in the case of Representative Cornelius Gallagher of New Jersey. As recounted by Curt Gentry in *J. Edgar Hoover,* Gallagher, whose committee had oversight on government agencies, proposed to deliver a stinging speech expressing concern over the FBI's excessive surveillance of citizens. He pulled no punches and got a bit personal. "It has been called to my attention," the speech draft began, "that the Director of the FBI and the Deputy Director of the FBI have been living as man and wife for 28 years at the public's expense; as a member of Congress we have an oversight duty and that oversight is to make sure that the funds that go to the FBI are properly spent. . . ." The allusion to the Deputy Director was to Hoover's constant companion, Clyde Tolson.

It should be noted that in the homophobic climate of the times, Hoover and fellow conservatives condemned gays as deviates of the worst kind. The hypocrisy of Hoover's morality play did not come to light until after his death, when details of his own gayness emerged. And it was the same with Roy Cohn, a Red-hunter and faggot-basher who was ideologically and personally close to Hoover. Only after his death due to AIDS was his rip-roaring gay lifestyle revealed.

Gallagher's fatal miscalculation was to furnish an advance copy of the draft to Cohn, whom he and his wife had known for some time. "You'll be sorry," Cohn warned Gallagher. "I know how they work." Cohn tattled to Hoover, who put his publicity chief, Cartha DeLoach, on the case. DeLoach, who had a reputation as a ruthless operator, leaked data gleaned from wiretaps that suggested Gallagher was schmoozing with Mafia figures to *Life* magazine, whose crime reporters were given under-the-table scoops in return for glowing evaluations of the FBI's endeavors against the underworld.

After the *Life* "exposé" ran, DeLoach told Cohn, "If you still know that guy, you had better get him to resign from Congress." If Gallagher didn't resign, DeLoach threatened, a story would be circulated that a minor mob figure in the *Life* story had died of a seizure while making love to Gallagher's wife. It was a sick fabrication, as Cohn would attest on his deathbed. An outraged Gallagher took to the floor of the House and perorated, "I doubt if even Goebbels [the Nazi propaganda minister] had the terrible capacity of a DeLoach to spread the big lie, nor could Goebbels exceed the filthy mind of a DeLoach." But from that moment on, Gallagher's career was in decline.

There are those who date Hoover's decline from November 22, 1963, when President John F. Kennedy was assassinated in Dallas. Up until that awful day Hoover had achieved so much power that he was virtually untouchable. He had catapulted to fame in the 1930s when his incorruptible Bureau had knocked off the Public Enemies—"Creepy" Karpis, "Pretty Boy" Floyd, "Ma" Barker, and John Dillinger come to mind—one by one, usually in a blaze of gunfire. But these were the straw men of crime. What no one seemed to notice lurking behind all the spectacular headlines was the national crime syndicate. Its coffers bulging from the sale of illicit booze during Prohibition, it had consolidated its own power and expanded its rackets, shakedowns, scams, and narcotics trafficking, all the while infiltrating organized labor, politics, and legitimate businesses. A more corruptive influence on a nationwide scale could not be imagined, yet Hoover, for reasons this book will explore, acted as if the crime world were flat. I recall asking Julius Mattson, my supervisor in the Seattle FBI office in 1956, why we were squandering resources on petty criminals while the Mafia went unopposed. "Don't mention the Mafia," he replied. "Hoover doesn't acknowledge that it exists." It will remain one of the ironies of history that Hoover's FBI and organized crime flourished simultaneously.

Coupled with his success against German spies and saboteurs during World War II and relentless "war" on domestic Communism after, the Director became a national icon, the embodiment of the triumph of good over evil. At that point preservation of the image became his prime concern. "Embarrassment to the Bureau" became the cardinal sin, and woe to the hapless agent who happened to commit it; he (there were no women agents while Hoover was alive) was banished to an FBI gulag—Butte, Montana, maybe, or Anchorage, Alaska. Hoover lashed out at the "hoity-toity professors" and "bleeding-heart liberals" he perceived as his most articulate detractors and launched a vigorous campaign to control the fourth estate by rewarding his supporters with inside information and punishing the skeptics by bloodying their reputations.

But it took the epochal event of the Kennedy assassination to kick-start the country's critical faculties about Hoover. In the wake of the shooting I flew to Dallas and wrote a story for *Saga* magazine about the breakdown in security. Seeing the story run in a men's journal of limited circulation was one thing, but having it picked up by national columnist Drew Pearson, Jack Anderson's mentor, was quite another. In his column of January 29, 1964, Pearson reported my findings that the FBI had known Lee Harvey Oswald was in Dallas but failed to notify the Secret Service and that there had been a "lack of cooperation and communication between law enforcement agencies." Hoover was furious and planted rebuttals with *his* favorite columnists, including Ed Sullivan. But when the Warren Commission issued its final report in September 1964, Hoover was stunned. In what was virtually a rubber-stamp of what I had reported, the Commission concluded that the Bureau had taken "an unduly restrictive view of its role in preventive intelligence work prior to the assassination." As the Commission saw it, "A more carefully coordinated treatment of the Oswald case by the FBI might have resulted in bringing Oswald's activities to the attention of the Secret Service." Although it was more a slap on the wrist than a forceful reprimand, Hoover went ballistic. First he severed diplomatic relations with Earl Warren, striking him from the Director's Special Correspondents roster on which he had been enshrined since collaborating with the FBI when he was governor of California. Then he severely disciplined every agent even obliquely associated with the Oswald affair, creating a brisk business for moving-van companies.

The handwriting was on the wall. Hoover couldn't label the blue-ribbon members of the Warren Commission subversive, suspect, or biased. He had been nailed by his peers, even by Gerald

Ford, his informant on the Commission. The myth had been pierced, and fear and loathing in Washington was a thing of the past. The press breathed an almost audible sigh of relief and, tenuously at first, began chronicling the FBI with something short of adulation. The puff pieces became fewer and fewer; open discussion took their place. On September 25, 1965, *The Saturday Evening Post* ran a piece by James Phelan venturing the hitherto forbidden thought that Hoover soon would have to be replaced. And on April 9, 1971, *Life,* which had been virtually a house organ for the FBI, bannered, "After Almost Half A Century In Total And Imperious Charge, G-Man Under Fire."

Yet Hoover clung to power, his megalomania and bulldog determination undiminished. During the turbulent 1960s he became almost slavish to Lyndon Johnson and Richard Nixon, carrying out their every wish, whether express or implied, to avoid a dreaded pink slip. He went past the mandatory retirement age dependent on the presidents like a dog for the bone. His heart wasn't in protecting the civil rights movement, which he viewed as Communist-inspired, but he jumped through LBJ's hoops. But it was not until he branded Dr. Martin Luther King, Jr., "the most notorious liar in the world" in 1964 for daring to question his commitment to civil rights enforcement that Hoover wore his heart on his sleeve. The outburst was regarded as one more sign that he was slipping. The man who had looked on presidents as mere transients in the White House, there for four years or eight at most, was going through the angst of job insecurity.

An element of paranoia seemed to grip Hoover after his Kennedy assassination blunder. On the third anniversary of Oswald's death at the hands of Jack Ruby, a UPI dispatch datelined Dallas crossed his desk. It reported that yellow chrysanthemums had been placed on Oswald's grave with the message "He has left all the world confused." Marguerite Oswald, who had resolutely defended her son as the dupe of an intelligence agency, was quoted as saying the flowers were left by "a former FBI agent." Hoover scrawled an addendum stating, "She's utterly irresponsible although it could have been Turner." It was a sign of the bunker mentality that became more apparent as the years rolled on.

When *Hoover's FBI* was published in its hardcover edition in 1970, J. Edgar Hoover was still very much in charge. But in the foreword I wrote that a changing of the guard was coming closer to reality and described the power struggle going on to succeed him. More important than who would be the new Director was the question of what direction the post-Hoover FBI should take. In this new edition of the book I have left the foreword intact, so that it reads in the present tense even though it was written in 1969. This way, I hope, the atmosphere of that time will be captured. For the same reason, I have also left intact the text of the original edition's eighteenth chapter. That chapter, originally titled "The Future?," reveals my fears and hopes regarding the course the Bureau would take after 1970; for this new edition, it has been retitled "Epilogue 1970." It's followed by a new epilogue, "Epilogue 1993," designed to bring readers up to date on what's happened inside the FBI since this book was first published.

At the same time, I have updated parts of the book proper in the light of the Freedom of Information Act disclosures and events that have occurred in the interim. In doing so I have switched to the past tense in describing persons, places, and things of that era. In this way, I hope, the historical perspective of Hoover and his Bureau will be preserved.

Hoover's FBI was one of the most remarkable—and dangerous—phenomena in recent history. In the strictest sense the organization was the alter ego of the man, mirroring his pride, prejudice, strong points, and hangups with uncanny accuracy. In *Hoover's FBI* I have tried to re-create that accuracy.

PART ONE
PERSONAL FILE

CHAPTER ONE
PERSONAL FILE: VOLUME I

Let it be clear that this administration recognizes the
value of daring and dissent—that we greet healthy
controversy as the hallmark of healthy change.

—*John Fitzgerald Kennedy*
in his inaugural address

During the late summer and early fall of 1961, the lights burned
late in FBI headquarters in the Department of Justice building
in Washington as a special squad, headed by Supervisor
William E. Clark, struggled with one of the Bureau's most difficult
cases. It was not a spreading spy scandal of vicious kidnapping, nor
had it any precedent in the annals of our most publicized agency. A
barrage of letters was being fired off to members of Congress asking
for a *congressional investigation of the FBI*. Worse still, the author
of the letters could not be labeled a Communist, dupe, or sympathizer. He was an FBI special agent with over ten years of exemplary
service.

I was that agent. The affair became celebrated inside the FBI as
the Turner Case.

The letters were not written in a fit of pique or as retribution
for an alleged injustice. During my career I gradually became convinced that there was a vast disparity between the FBI's public
image and its actual condition. Starting in 1924, J. Edgar Hoover
had snatched the Bureau of Investigation, as it was then called, from

the depths of disrepute and corruption and had shaped it into a precision crime-fighting machine. But by the dawn of the space age, the director was still living in the long-faded Dillinger days, when the FBI legend was born. To preserve and protect the G-man legend was his prime concern, overshadowing all others and dictating the policies of the agency. In a letter to Representative Emanuel Celler of New York, chairman of the House Judiciary Committee, I declared: "It is indeed frustrating to work under conditions where every action (or lack of action) is predicated upon the potentiality of embarrassment to the Bureau."

In a letter to Senator Estes Kefauver, I expanded upon the cult-of-personality theme. Embarrassment to the Bureau, I pointed out, was a two-edged sword. If an agent caused adverse publicity, even if he was a victim of circumstances, he was severely disciplined by "the greatest assemblage of Monday morning quarterbacks in the world"—the headquarters executives. As a result, I contended, there was an exodus of the best men, and those who stayed tended to "play it safe." As an example, I said, it was not uncommon to see veteran agents slip out the back door at the sound of the bank robbery alarm rather than risk a bungle in that type of fast-paced investigation.

This narcissism, I asserted, led the Bureau to concentrate on lesser crimes and criminals while ignoring the larger menace. "Most agents would prefer to lock horns with organized crime," I assured Celler, "but are saddled with wresting minor violations from local authorities for the purpose of statistics-gathering."

The language of the letters admittedly was blunt and at times intemperate, but I was in no mood for elliptical prose. Most agents had ambivalent feelings toward the FBI. They were dedicated to the concept of the organization and believe that the agent corps was a superior group of men. But at the same time they seethed in frustration over the state of affairs at the time. For years I had listened to their gripes around the water cooler and to the latest rumors of the Director's impending retirement at forbidden coffee breaks in out-of-the-way cafes (coffee breaks for agents were banned by Bureau regulations). "A San Diego contractor has been given the green light to start building Hoover's retirement home," was one rumor that was based on the Director's annual trek to suburban La Jolla and the nearby Del Mar racetrack. But every year, the reports proved to be baseless.

No agent who valued his career or hoped to avoid being black-balled in private industry dared to speak out. A number, however, chose to vent their feelings by means of anonymous letters, and rare was the member of Congress or high official of the executive branch who did not receive one. In October 1967 and August 1968, for example, unsigned letters typed on the letterhead stationery of the Los Angeles division were sent to then Attorney General Ramsey Clark, with copies to certain members of Congress. One of the authors was in touch with me. He averred that the letters represent-ed the collective thinking of himself and several others presently assigned to the Los Angeles division, and that their main intent was to prevent the naming of Assistant to the Director Cartha ("Deke") DeLoach as Hoover's successor. DeLoach had been prominently mentioned for the post.

The Los Angeles letters were detailed and uninhibited, and amounted to a broadside at Hoover and his top executives. "Hoover lives in the past, dreams of days of Dillinger, Pretty Boy Floyd and others; is surrounded by aged or incompetent men who have spent their careers looking backward and telling Hoover what he wants to hear," the first letter contended. It went on to claim that one high-ranking aide has been "involved in many drunken scenes, including one in Toots Shor's in New York City some years ago and on numerous airline flights and in many field offices includ-ing Chicago, where on one occasion he demanded not one but two prostitutes be provided for his enjoyment by that office." It charged that another top official was a former "juvenile delinquent" whose "emotional instability" and other character flaws rendered him "not qualified mentally or morally for any position in the FBI." The first letter contained eight pages of specifications; the second, five.

Both letters pleaded that Clark, as Hoover's immediate superi-or, personally investigate the validity of the charges. "There is no one in the FBI that is able to furnish any information unless placed under oath and given protection against retribution by Hoover," they emphasized. "There are hundreds of us agents prepared, however, to come forward once an investigation is under way and it is set out that we will be protected." The charges were grave not only because, if true, they constituted serious maladministration of the Bureau, but because "security risks" by legal definition were occupying extremely sensitive positions.

There is no indication, the agent-authors reported, that Clark took any action. One could sympathize with his dilemma. As the agents put it, "Hoover won't hesitate to drop 'leaks' about you, and will do anything in his considerable power to run you out of government if you try to expose him or correct the situation now existing in the FBI."

Because the recipient can easily dismiss them as "poison pen" or crank letters, I have always considered anonymous letters an exercise in futility. Moreover, the author was not guaranteed anonymity. The Bureau was often given copies of them by the recipient, and it went to extreme lengths to discover who was setting the bones to rattling in the closet. Some of the most urgent examinations conducted by the FBI laboratories were handwriting and typewriter comparisons of anonymous letters.

Still the Bureau was plagued by them. When my letter-writing campaign first began, Chief Inspector Roy K. Moore was pulled off a New York City inspection and sent to Oklahoma City, where I was stationed at the time.

"Do you know anything about an anonymous letter postmarked in Chicago?" he asked as his very first question.

"No, I don't," I replied. "I sign my letters."

"That," he said with a wry smile, "is all too apparent."

My personal file, which Moore was thumbing through, held little portent of trouble. My background was the orthodox one that the Bureau looked for in its agents. I was born in Buffalo, New York, in 1927 into a solidly Republican household, and both parental families were well established in the city. At seventeen, I had enlisted in the Navy during World War II and served on board an LST in the far Pacific. Turning down an appointment out of the Seventh Fleet to the Naval Academy at Annapolis—a military career didn't appeal to me—I had enrolled at Canisius College, a Jesuit school, and in 1949 had obtained a degree in chemistry. That I had played semiprofessional baseball and ice hockey would have been a plus factor in the Bureau's eyes.

The business world held little allure, and I soon set my sights on law enforcement. As I was getting ready to apply for the New York state police, the word went around that the FBI had broadened its educational requirements and would accept college graduates other than lawyers and accountants. Like most young men of the time, I regarded the Bureau with considerable awe. The legend of the G-men was part of contemporary history, and J. Edgar Hoover was a household word. Not only had the FBI prevailed over the flamboyant "Public Enemies" of the thirties, it had successfully combated Nazi spies in the Western Hemisphere during World War II.

So it was more in hope than anticipation that I put in an application with the Buffalo field office. It was promptly and politely turned down by the local agent in charge because I was two years under the stated minimum age of twenty-five. Whimsically, I mailed an application to Washington headquarters, and to my surprise a notice arrived instructing me to report to the Buffalo office for written and oral testing. Though everything seemed to go well, I was still skeptical. But when the notice to report for a physical examination came, I knew the corner had been turned. Two weeks later, the coveted probationary appointment as a special agent came through.

On February 5, 1951, I reported to FBI headquarters and swore to uphold the Constitution and investigate violations of federal law and those matters in which "the United States is or may be a party at interest." There followed a ten-week training course at the FBI Academy, situated on the U.S. Marine base at Quantico, Virginia. Then out into the field.

My first office was St. Louis. It was a time of tremendous build-up in the investigation of persons applying for work at sensitive government-sponsored installations, and the bulk of my assignment consisted of background checks on prospective employees at the AEC plant at Paducah, Kentucky. The year's stint passed without incident, but at my second office, San Francisco, I became involved in a bitter flap.

With another agent just transferred in, I reported to Assistant Special Agent in Charge (ASAC) Ralph Bachman, who handled the assignment of personnel. "Which one of you is the single man?" he asked. I nodded. "You'll go on the techs," he ordered.

"The techs" meant technical surveillance installations—the central monitoring plants into which all permanent wiretaps and bugs were fed. Since they were manned twenty-four hours a day, considerable shift work was involved. This was apparently the reason he selected a single man.

As a matter of office policy, tours of duty in the Clubs, as the plants were called, were restricted to six months. Not only was the assignment tedious, but it offered no opportunity for an agent to keep his investigative skills polished. Six months passed, then a year. Finally, the transfer came. Due to the fact that they had acquired a familiarity with the principal security subjects who had been under electronic surveillance, agents ordinarily went from the Clubs to the security squad. But my transfer was to the applicant squad.

There were some agents who preferred "the Apps." They did not pose the risk nor challenge of criminal work or the complexity of security investigation, and night work and weekend duty were infrequent. That the Apps weren't my bag was not particularly relevant, but that the assignment was counter to Bureau regulations was. The manual instructed that agents with less than three years' experience be rotated so as to gain experience in all phases of the work, and I was into my third year without substantial criminal or security experience. Since there were more than two hundred agents in the San Francisco division, I didn't feel it unreasonable to ask for a transfer to another squad. But ASAC Bachman denied the request without explanation.

A few weeks later, at a periodic in-service training session in Washington, I decided to appeal Bachman's decision. Theoretically, Hoover's door was open to any agent who wanted to see him, but in practice supplicants were carefully screened. A number of agents had sought transfers because of family or personal hardships, and the Director had obliged. Mine was a slightly different case. Since the matter merely involved an intraoffice transfer, I elected to see Assistant Director W. R. Glavin, who headed the administrative division. A personable, gray-haired man on the verge of retirement, Glavin was well regarded by the agents. My personnel file was on his desk, and from his remarks it was obvious that he had looked it through. He expressed wholehearted agreement with my position. "By the time you get back to San Francisco," he assured me with a friendly slap on the back, "you'll be on a criminal or security squad."

Glavin was as good as his word—I was on a criminal squad in the Oakland resident agency. But the San Francisco brass were evidently affronted that I had gone over their heads, despite the official option to do so. The wires to Washington hummed. About a month later, a letter of censure signed by Hoover and accompanied by a disciplinary transfer to Seattle was in my mail folder. According to the Director, a stolen car case in St. Louis constituted "criminal investigative work performed." Moreover, he admonished, "You failed to advise the Bureau official to whom you spoke that you had been on annual leave and leave without pay for an extended period during your assignment in San Francisco, thus creating the impression that you had been doing technical work longer than you actually had."

In conclusion, Hoover wrote that "it appears that you were possibly more interested in selecting the assignments that you personally preferred and that you furnished false and misleading information in order to accomplish this purpose. The Bureau expects Agents to accept assignments as the needs of the service require and your actions in furnishing misleading information were certainly most reprehensible."

Since these were my naïve days in the Bureau, I was flabbergasted. The stolen car case cited by the Director consisted of no more than a check of the records of the Missouri Highway Patrol, and being on leave didn't represent experience in anything.* I was indignant, but the intent of the letter was so patently to put me in my place that to contest it would have been as fruitless as a priest in Pawtucket telling the Pope he had erred.

Not yet ready to quit, I packed my bags and headed north.

---

*Leave without pay bears explanation. Periodically, the FBI overtook its budget near the end of the fiscal year. Rather than request a supplementary appropriation from Congress as other agencies did and thus detract from its legend of efficiency, headquarters issued a request for agents to volunteer to go on leave without pay. I had obliged by taking several weeks.

CHAPTER TWO

PERSONAL FILE: VOLUME II

Fidelity—Bravery—Integrity.
—*The FBI motto*

"I know why you're here," greeted Richard D. Auerbach, the special agent in charge (SAC) at Seattle. "Since you're on probation, I'm supposed to watch you closely. But if you pull your weight, I won't be watching you closer than anyone else." Then, as if to indicate I had been right in my stand, he assigned me to criminal work.

Auerbach was a uniquely independent SAC. At one time he had been secretary to Senator Styles Bridges, the influential conservative Republican from New Hampshire. Entering the FBI during World War II, he had been assigned to the bureau's SIS unit countering Nazi espionage in South America. As he rose rapidly through the ranks, he retained his flair for strategic political contacts. At the time, for example, he was assiduously cultivating Edgar Eisenhower, a Tacoma attorney and the brother of President Dwight Eisenhower. So powerful had he become in his own right that he was known to initiates as the Director of the West Coast, and he lived up to the billing by the domineering manner in which he dealt not only with his colleagues on the coast but with high-echelon officials at Washington headquarters as well. In line for an assistant directorship, he diplomatically hedged—no one flatly turned down Hoover's summons—in order to give a wide berth to the power struggle at Ninth and Pennsylvania.

Often blustery and assertive, Auerbach personified more the hard-driving corporation executive than the local G-man chief. He was unconcerned with the grubby realities of investigation. He disdained guns, being rarely seen at firearms practice. The rules obliged SACs to lead major raids and apprehensions of Top Ten Fugitives, and on such occasions he was an incongruous figure in his natty suit and colorful tie. Although he knew how to dispense tongue-lashings, he backed his agents to the hilt—an uncommon trait among SACs. Once, acting on a hunch, I went to a card room and checked the twenty-dollar bills in the day's receipts against a list of marked bills included in a bank robbery take. By the time I had returned to the office, the card room proprietor had called to report that sixty dollars was missing, with the unavoidable implication that I had palmed the money. In the FBI there can be no more serious charge against an agent, and most SACs would have picked up the phone to call Washington. But Auerbach, certain that I hadn't taken the money and just as certain that if it never turned up I would be forever stigmatized in the eyes of the Bureau, launched a quiet probe of his own. Several hours later a sheepish proprietor telephoned to say the money had been found in another till.

Under "Big A," as the agents called Auerbach, the San Francisco unpleasantness was soon a dim memory. On the balmy Friday morning of March 12, 1954, I underwent a baptism of fire when three bandits wearing false noses and spectacles held up the Greenwood branch of the Seattle First National Bank, leaving one police officer dead and two permanently injured in a wild gun battle. Compared to this, the daily routine was pretty tame. The FBI does not have jurisdiction over murder except those on government reservations, and the bulk of my time was spent on relatively minor waterfront thefts, chasing military deserters, looking for fugitives, and developing informants.

Yet life in Auerbach's satrapy was never dull. When the caseload would drop off and there was a hiatus in bank robberies, he would grow increasingly fretful until he made something happen. An ordinary draft delinquency case illustrates the point. The policy was to locate and interview the delinquent, enlisting his compliance with the law, since the object was to fill the Army's ranks rather

than the jails. It was only in the more aggravated cases that offenders were prosecuted.

Leroy Jefferson had been declared delinquent by a Los Angeles
board for failure to advise them of his current address. The case was
assigned to a rookie agent, who traced Jefferson to a transient
apartment building without much difficulty. When the agent
knocked on the door, however, the subject slipped out a back window. The effrontery was too much for Auerbach, and he shifted
into high. One of those infrequent Selective Service warrants was
sworn out, and a full-scale raid was mounted against the apartment.
The gang-busters tableau was straight out of Hollywood. We
parked our easily spotted FBI cars a block away. Then, armed to the
teeth, we closed in on the apartment and sealed off all exits, including the infamous back window. The spectacle quickly attracted a
crowd, which undoubtedly thought a Top Ten Fugitive was at bay.
Led by the ASAC, several agents pounded on Jefferson's door and
demanded his surrender. He complied, incredulous that all the com-
motion was due to his failure to keep in touch with his draft board.
As he was led handcuffed into an FBI car and whisked off to jail, we
swiftly withdrew—so swiftly that the ASAC was left stranded at the
scene and had to call the office to dispatch a car.

The episode had an ironic sequel. Although the FBI didn't know
it, Jefferson had been under surveillance by the Federal Bureau of
Narcotics, which suspected him of being a major figure in one of the
largest dope rings in the west. A few weeks later, while free on bail
on the Selective Service detainer, Jefferson was quietly arrested by
narcotics agents and Los Angeles police on felony narcotics charges.
Later convicted, he was sentenced to twenty years in prison.

The slack periods were perilous for agents as well. On one of
those rare stifling-hot days in Seattle, I parked an FBI car in an
allotted space next to the office. Before long, Auerbach summoned
me to his office, and I knew from the bulldog look that I was in for
an upbraiding.

"You left Car Forty-nine on the street unlocked and with the
windows open," he charged.

"But boss," I argued, "it's ninety degrees out and there's nothing that can be stolen."

"There's Bureau property in it," he shot back.

"Bureau property?" I asked, puzzled.

"The first aid kit and fire extinguisher."

As punishment, Auerbach ordered me not to use Bureau cars for two weeks—in this way I would appreciate them more. So for the next fortnight I walked, rode the bus, and hitched rides on my investigative rounds.

As the years rolled on, no radical change appeared on the FBI horizon, and I started to prepare for another career by enrolling in electrical engineering courses at night at the University of Washington. My aim was to go into electronic sales engineering, but Auerbach assumed it was to ready myself for "sound school," a euphemism for the Bureau's intensive course in wiretapping and bugging, and he put out a memorandum to all agents encouraging such self-improvement efforts.

In early 1957, a major electronics manufacturer, Motorola, made me an attractive offer which would have let me keep one foot in law enforcement through sales to police agencies. Negotiations had reached the point where I was going to make a surreptitious weekend trip to finalize the deal. Leaving the FBI with Hoover's blessing posed delicate problems. To be discovered job hunting while still an agent raised a presumption of disaffection that might result in a forced resignation. Consequently, an agent put out feelers very discreetly, and studiously avoided such companies as Ford and Sears Roebuck, which were known to have close ties with Bureau officials.

Once the job was safely landed, there was a protocol to follow. It is part of the FBI legend that agents do not quit in disillusionment, but rather are lured away by lucrative industry offers. "Our employees are constantly being offered higher-paying positions in business, industry, and government," Hoover puffed in his 1962 appropriations testimony. Letters of resignation were always couched in terms consistent with the legend, and invariably carried a "hearts and flowers" touch, rhapsodizing over Hoover and his organization and promising to be loyal to the Bureau even in civilian life. (The letters were usually ghostwritten by an agent's supervisor, who was presumably a master of the art.) Following an "exit interview" by the SAC or ASAC, the unstated purpose of which was to detect latent gripes or grudges against the Bureau, the departing employee was handed an application blank for the nationwide Society of Former Special Agents of the Federal Bureau of Investigation. By joining, he would continue as a member of "the FBI family," of which J. Edgar was the patriarch.*

Behind closed doors, I told Auerbach, the only SAC I would trust in such circumstances, that I was leaving the Bureau. It had been a disappointment, I said, and I wanted to move on. "Don't worry," he retorted, "the Bureau's going to change soon." Seizing a pencil, he began a point-by-point comparison of the agent position versus the electronics one. The agent position came out on top by his figuring. He buzzed for his secretary and dictated a cordially diplomatic letter to my prospective employer turning down the offer. Then came the kicker. "I'm notifying the Bureau that you are being designated a relief supervisor in this office," he said. A relief supervisor headed a squad of agents during the absence of the regular supervisor, making assignments, approving or rejecting reports, and directing the agents' activities. It was the first step up the ladder, a Bureau version of the junior executive.

I left Auerbach's office in a daze. The whirlwind persuader had scored again.

My career began to move along at a brisk clip. In one three-month period in 1959, I received three personal letters of commendation from the Director. One was for solving a bank robbery, another for making a difficult wiretap installation, and the third for special performance as an inspector's aide—another rung up the

---

*Following the protocol was not complete insurance. In 1961, for example, two East Coast agents quietly sought and obtained job offers from the intelligence division of the Internal Revenue Service, then adding to its manpower for the war on organized crime. The pair gave the Bureau thirty days' notice, but were vague as to their future plans in the exit interviews because of the intense jealousies among the federal investigative agencies. But the IRS routinely sent their names to the FBI identification division for a required criminal record check, which resulted in their immediate forced resignation for "not being candid in the exit interview." Then the IRS reneged on the job offers because they were leaving the FBI under a cloud. With some outside pressure, the contretemps was finally settled when the IRS agreed to stick by the job offers.

ladder. The feat had rarely been duplicated, and in recognition SAC
Earl Milnes (Auerbach had been transferred to Chicago as SAC
some months before) drew up a recommendation to the Bureau for
a meritorious increase in pay. I never received it. An inspection team
arrived in the office unannounced, as usual, and an eager aide discovered an Air France timetable and travel folder in my desk—I was
about to leave for Europe on vacation. He wrote it up as a breach of
regulations, since the manual forbade nonofficial property in official
desks. Milnes was so miffed at the hitch in an otherwise smooth
inspection that he tore up the recommendation.

I had grown used to this kind of pettifoggery in the FBI and
could shrug it off as a petty annoyance, the hallmark of a bureaucracy. But what I had increasingly less stomach for was the vast
cleavage between the FBI reputation and reality. The Bureau
claimed, for example, to be above politics. Yet, as a young agent in
1953, I had watched Hoover appear on national television at the
side of Eisenhower's attorney general, Herbert Brownell, and
posthumously assassinate the character of former state department
official Harry Dexter White. It was a consummate political act. The
evidence against White was gossamer, but the Director went along
with Brownell's attempt to indict the Truman administration as
"soft on Communism." The proper place, of course, for any evidence against White was—or had been—a court of law, but in the
Washington political jungle Hoover was swinging with the apes.

The branding of White was, I knew, a labor of love for Hoover,
for as the paranoia of the McCarthy era subsided, his irrational
obsession with the radical left remained at fever pitch. The Director
had emerged as the nation's foremost theological anti-Communist,
setting the tone at home for the global ramifications of the cold war.
But he would never let the beast die. As the Communist Party USA
dissipated into a negligible political force—it never really possessed
the means of violent overthrow of the government, whatever its
rhetoric—Hoover continued to cry wolf. And the field offices, as
acutely responsive to his dialectics as the Red Guard to Chairman
Mao's, continued to smother domestic Communists and "state of
mind" Reds with attention as if a violent coup were only hours
away. Not all agents were as hung up on the subject as their

leader—they were split on the issue of McCarthyism—but none were foolhardy enough to dispute the Director.

In Seattle, once considered a hotbed of radicalism, the security subjects were an impotent lot. They consisted mainly of middle-aged CPUSA functionaries trying to recapture the glories of the thirties, and enfeebled "Wobblies" (International Workers of the World), the lumber camp firebrands of two decades before, now huddled into the Washington Pension Union. Yet some thirty agents assigned to the security squad made a career out of shadowing them and filling out surveillance logs, penetrating their meetings with paid informants and writing prolix reports, tapping some of their phones, and harassing them with nuisance calls and suggestive remarks to their employers.

The criminal policy, I felt, was a matter of garbled priorities. Organized crime, colloquially known as "the Mob," had long since extended its carcinomatous hand into virtually every area of American life, ulcerating the political, economic, and social strata. Clearly, because of its interstate nature, it was a federal responsibility. Yet the FBI remained inert. "Put it in the GIIF [General Investigative Intelligence File]," a supervisor told me when an informant had reported Mafia activity. The GIIF was a catchall for miscellaneous information. At this late date, 1956, the FBI had not acknowledged that organized crime as such existed, although it was to be rudely shocked the following year when caught napping by the Apalachin, New York, conclave of top Mafia chieftains.

The FBI crime program was double-barreled: it exploited to the maximum headline-grabbing "glamour" crimes such as kidnapping and bank robbery, and it pushed hard for statistics that Hoover could represent to Congress and the public as "new peaks of achievement"—so many convictions, so much stolen property recovered, so many fugitive apprehensions, and so forth, always a mite higher than the previous year.

As the end of each fiscal year neared, the gun would sound for the start of the statistics race. One year, for example, a lag in convictions produced a farce we sarcastically called the Great Brick Caper. Near the Bremerton Naval Shipyard across Puget Sound from Seattle there was an abandoned World War II government housing project, and some local residents were taking bricks from the crumbling wash houses to build barbecue pits and garden borders. As defense lawyers would later claim, the houses were an "attractive nuisance."

A squad of agents was dispatched from Seattle to mine the statistical lode. For my part, I questioned a shipyard worker, a restaurant owner, and a well-digger. The latter fell back on his rights and refused to discuss the matter, which saved him from the net. Those who cooperated by furnishing statements, however, were charged with "crime on a government reservation—larceny." A dozen convictions were quickly rung up.

The Great Brick Caper was not an isolated episode. In 1959, a case that began in legitimate fashion ended as an even more wretched excess. A police officer in a suburban town reported that a man was selling hand tools apparently stolen from McChord Air Force Base near Tacoma. Investigation showed that some airmen assigned to a warehouse were helping themselves to crescent wrenches, screwdrivers, hand drills, and other inexpensive tools and giving them to the man to fence.

The tools were not recognizable as government property, although the fence represented them as military surplus. They were purchased by mechanics, gas station owners and attendants, and other citizens. In retrieving the tools, we did not consider the purchasers culpable and took witness statements, omitting the preamble warning of constitutional rights, for use against the fence. To a man, they were willing to be helpful to the FBI.

They *were* helpful—in a way none of us suspected. The supervisor handling the case, who was feeling the heat on statistics, took their statements to the Assistant United States Attorney (AUSA), tossed them on his desk, and declared, "Here are seven more." The AUSA, assuming the group was knowingly involved with the airmen and the fence already in custody, readily authorized prosecution.

The seven warrants in hand, the supervisor told me to round up an apprehension team. But I was to wait two days before making the arrests so that fugitive form letters could be sent to Bureau headquarters and the men officially declared FBI fugitives. We were low on fugitive apprehensions, too.

Two days later, I gathered a reluctant apprehension team on the outskirts of the town to plan the arrests. One of the agents, thoroughly disgusted with the sham, wanted to resign on the spot but I refused to accept his credentials. None of us were proud of what we had to do. In a small community, the stigma of being arrested by the prestigious FBI could be ruinous; I knew that one of the "fugitives" had applied for a deputy sheriff's commission and this would finish his hopes.

Suddenly, the triple "beep" of the bank robbery alarm sounded over the car radios. To a man, we hoped that it was the real thing— anything to postpone the arrests. But it was a false alarm, and we moved in.

At their arraignment, the seven unexpectedly pleaded not guilty, forcing the AUSA to take a hard look at the statements he had so trustingly accepted as evidence of guilt. He turned livid. Charges against several were immediately dismissed, and the remainder were subsequently acquitted. But the seven fugitive arrests would never be erased, and they were duly added to the total of 9,090 "fleeing felons" Hoover boasted had been apprehended in 1959.

"Fidelity, Bravery, Integrity"—the motto was discordant, mocking. It was clear that no change would evolve. Hoover was in robust health and seemed as determined as ever to hang on. "They'll have to carry me out of here," he assertedly vowed in a gesture of defiance reminiscent of Sewell Avery, the chairman of Montgomery Ward who had to be carried from his office when he refused to cooperate with the authorities during World War II. Even if he did unexpectedly bow out, it was almost certain that he would be able to hand-pick his successor from inside the Bureau, thus perpetuating nepotism and assuring that any change would be superficial. The cult of personality would merely go on and on.*

Once again I resolved to leave. But this time I also resolved to

---

*In 1965, Congressman H. Allen Smith of Glendale, California, who had been an agent from 1935 to 1942, introduced a bill that would have made it mandatory for successive FBI directors to have served in the Bureau for the previous seven consecutive years. It didn't become law, but the Omnibus Crime Control and Safe Streets Act of 1968 provided that the next director be appointed by the president, subject to the "advice and consent of the Senate." Lopped from the act was a clause that would have limited his term to fifteen years. Among FBI reforms adopted after Hoover's death was a ten-year term limit for Directors.

try to do something to bring change. While recuperating from a severe attack of hepatitis, I had ample time to think it over. With ten years of service and an unassailable record, I was well credentialed to speak with authority about the Bureau. For years I had listened to married agents complain that they couldn't afford to speak out because of their families. I was a bachelor. Even if rocking the boat meant that some employment doors would be shut in my face, others would be open.

The question was: how do you come to grips with a myth? One option was to resign in good standing and then try to air the inside story publicly. But I still harbored a hope that change could be brought about without dragging the Bureau's dirty linen into the open. Moreover, a free-form attack launched after writing one of those "hearts and flowers" resignation letters seemed a bit hypocritical.

I decided to poke the tiger from inside the cage.

"Don't try to buck Hoover," a near-retirement agent privy to my plans warned. "He's too powerful. You'll be crucified." Perhaps. But I felt that there were segments of Congress that would respond to revelations on the manner in which a public agency was discharging its public trust. And the prospect of John F. Kennedy being elected president was heartening. Unlike Richard Nixon, young Kennedy was not an unabashed admirer of the FBI chief, and his New Frontier might just come to include the Bureau.*

As I saw it, the uneven odds would make a structured assault from within a very brief affair. So I put out job feelers, registering with a placement agency, filling out several applications, and writing the employment chairman of the ex-agent's society in the San Francisco area where I wanted to locate.

I stated I would be available in about a month. It turned out to be more like six months.

---

*The hope was premature. In his book *Power in Washington,* former presidential assistant Douglass Cater related that on the night of his election, John Kennedy asked two close friends their assessment of the FBI Director. "Both offered unfavorable verdicts," wrote Cater. "Next morning, as the first order of business at his press conference as president-elect, Kennedy announced his intention of reappointing Hoover to his long-time post. Everyone understood that it was a shrewd and power-conscious move on Kennedy's part."

CHAPTER THREE
PERSONAL FILE: VOLUME III

. . . the pride in being a part of an organization
that is held in high esteem.

—J. Edgar Hoover
FBI Notes, May 1961

O klahoma City was one of the key offices in building the FBI legend. On July 23, 1933, one year before Public Enemy Number One John Dillinger was gunned down by G-men in Chicago, wealthy oilman Charles F. Urschel was kidnapped at gunpoint from his Oklahoma City home. Two hundred thousand dollars in ransom was paid, and the victim was released unharmed. He had been held captive, blindfolded, on a ranch. The day before his release, he recalled, there had been a downpour, and he had not heard an airplane that had previously come over the ranch each morning. Poring over airline records, FBI agents determined that on that particular day an American Airlines flight from Fort Worth to Amarillo had detoured around Paradise, Texas, because of a sudden rainstorm.

Agents located the ranch outside of Paradise on which Urschel had been held. It belonged to the stepfather and mother of Kathryn Kelly, wife of the scourge of the plains, George ("Machinegun") Kelly. An alert was put out for Kelly and a confederate, Albert L. Bates. Two months later, FBI agents cornered Kelly in Memphis, Tennessee. "Don't shoot, G-men!" he cried out, creating a nickname for FBI agents that was to become famous.

Fittingly, the climax of my own career was to come in the city where such a large part of the legend was born. While hospitalized with hepatitis, I had received a transfer to Oklahoma City. It had been occasioned, I would learn, by the sudden resignation of the sound man there, who had become fed up after nineteen years of service as a radio technician and special agent. I was a sound man, and single to boot.

I arrived in Oklahoma City in October 1960. Although Machinegun Kelly was quietly serving his life term in Alcatraz, the case had come back to haunt the Bureau. In its zeal, the FBI had also charged Kelly's wife, who had been arrested with him in Memphis, with participating in the crime. At the trial, Kathryn Kelly took the stand and testified that she had begged her husband to release Urschel when she found out about the kidnapping, but that he told her it was "none of [her] business" and that Urschel would be killed if the ransom was not paid.

The prosecution's case against Kathryn Kelly rested almost exclusively on the testimony of a local accountant and self-styled handwriting expert, D. C. Patterson. Prior to the Kellys' arrest in Memphis, Urschel and the *Daily Oklahoman* newspaper had received threatening letters postmarked Chicago, Illinois, that bore the fingerprints of George Kelly. Patterson declared, however, that his analysis of the handwriting had determined that Kathryn Kelly was the letters' author. She vigorously denied it, and her attorney requested a delay in order to have the handwriting independently analyzed. The judge turned down the request—"I am not going to continue this case all fall," he remarked—and Kathryn Kelly was convicted. She was sentenced to life imprisonment.

In his 1938 book *Persons in Hiding*, J. Edgar Hoover portrayed Kathryn Kelly as the mastermind behind the abduction:

> . . . when the ransom letters began to arrive, they carried an atmosphere of imagination and a casual use of hyphenated words entirely foreign to the average gangster.
>
> There were many possible suspects; none of them, however, was of a mental type to write such letters. There was evidence of feminine thought and psychology. There was only one conclusion: that the actual work had been done by

some woman of superior intelligence. That woman was
Kathryn Kelly.

Considering the paucity of hard evidence, this was by any
account a most amazing deduction. In 1958, its accuracy was
thrown into serious doubt. After a quarter-century of imprisonment,
all the while protesting her innocence, Mrs. Kelly obtained the services of an attorney willing to reopen the matter. In an appeal filed
in the U.S. District Court in Oklahoma City, he contended that
compulsory process had been denied her because of the trial judge's
refusal to permit time for her to have the letters examined independently. Mrs. Kelly was ordered freed pending a hearing in which the
FBI was instructed to produce its file on the case.

The FBI never produced the file—for the simple reason that it
contained a document directly contradicting the handwriting
"expert" Patterson and hence tending to exculpate Kathryn Kelly.
The document was an FBI laboratory report, dated September 23,
1933, reporting the results of an examination of the letters by
Charles A. Appel, the Bureau's top expert at the time. Appel stated:

> The handwriting on the letters to the *Oklahomian* [*sic*]
> and to Urschel is not identical with that of Mrs. Kelly.
> There are a great many similarities which on casual exami-
> nation would lead one to think that these handwritings are
> the same. However, detailed analysis indicated that Mrs.
> Kelly did not write these letters.

According to Appel, George Kelly "may have written these letters,"
but there was an insufficient sample to tell for sure.

The discovery of this report in 1958 confronted the FBI with a
monumental dilemma. On the one hand, the Bureau had a reputation for laboring as hard to free the innocent as to convict the
guilty, and simple justice demanded that the report be made available to the court. On the other, disclosure that the long-suppressed
report existed could be a source of extreme embarrassment.

The pivotal question was whether the FBI or the U.S. attorney
at Oklahoma City had done the suppressing. Both the agent to

whom the case had been assigned in 1933 and the U.S. attorney were dead. On October 15, 1959, SAC Wesley G. Grapp of the Oklahoma City office informed Bureau headquarters that a review of both the local FBI file and that of the U.S. attorney (USA) did "not indicate that the USA's office was ever made aware of the fact that the two letters mailed from Chicago on 9/18/33 had been submitted to the FBI Laboratory in 1933 for a handwriting examination or that the FBI Laboratory conclusion was contrary to that of PATTERSON." Ordinarily, FBI files strictly account for documents or information released to outside agencies. Presumably, someone in the Bureau had held back the report.

In his letter to the headquarters, SAC Grapp weighed the possibilities. "Should action be taken at this time to acquaint the U.S. Attorney with these circumstances," he wrote, "it is not improbable he might take the position that he was obligated to acknowledge to the Court and the defendants at this time that the testimony of the Government witness on this particular point of evidence was possibly based on an erroneous conclusion. . . ." In other words, the cat would be out of the bag, and, as Grapp put it, there could well be "some embarrassment to the Bureau."

To forestall this denouement, Grapp recommended that the existence of the laboratory report not be made known to the U.S. attorney. He reasoned that "it is highly improbable that if the question of handwriting is brought out in any further hearing or re-trial in this case, it will necessarily result in a re-examination of this evidence, thus revealing any erroneous conclusions in PATTERSON's examination." By letting events take their course, then, Patterson's conclusion *might* be rebutted by a fresh examination without rattling any bones in the Bureau closet.

It never was, nor was the suppressed report ever produced, despite the efforts of the highly respected SAC Lee O. Teague, who succeeded Grapp at Oklahoma City. In a letter to headquarters dated July 31, 1961, referencing Grapp's earlier communication, Teague declared: "I recommend exactly to the contrary." But somewhere in the Bureau's decision-making process, it was decided to place justice in the status of "pending inactive."

When I arrived in the Oklahoma City office, the Kathryn Kelly case was the subject of whispered commentary. Only a few senior agents were privy to what was actually going on, and the file was kept locked in the SAC's safe. Needless to say, the documents, which are reproduced in the appendix, were obtained in a manner it would be injudicious to divulge.

As documents released under FOI divulge, Hoover was incensed that I dared to expose this FBI chicanery, and he remained ever vigilant for a chance to get even. In 1970, when I was preparing an article on the Kathryn Kelly case for *Scanlan's Monthly* called "J. Edgar Hoover Gets His First Woman," he thought he had me. As part of the article I wanted to update the status of Kathryn Kelly, and to this end retained an Oklahoma private investigation firm. It discovered that in 1959, shortly after the FBI refused to produce its file with the exonerating laboratory report and Kelly remained free as the result, she was given a bookkeeping job at the Oklahoma County Home and Hospital with the promise of a pension after fifteen years. It didn't take much imagination to figure out who was behind that arrangement. And, sure enough, when the private investigator tried to meet with Kelly he was rebuffed by her supervisor, a Mrs. Beulah Pless, who asserted that Kelly had "paid her debt to society" and wanted to be left alone. Even the argument that new evidence might vindicate her employee failed to budge her. Obviously Kelly was in effect being held incommunicado. And perhaps she wanted it that way, since she had only four years to go for her pension.

I have no idea how that investigator introduced himself to Beulah Pless, but when Pless called the FBI to report his interview attempt she claimed he identified himself as "Bill Turner of the FBI." With that the Oklahoma City office teletyped Washington that an investigation would be opened to determine if indeed it was I. If it was, I could be prosecuted for impersonating a federal officer, since I no longer was with the Bureau.

Hoover obviously was delighted. "Press vigorously!" he ordered. The Oklahoma agents showed my photo to Pless and her assistant, but they didn't recognize me. They canvassed hotels, motels, and auto rental agencies, but my name didn't show up. They came up empty-handed. The reason was that I hadn't been in Oklahoma City since I was an agent nine years earlier. After reading the teletype breaking the bad news, Hoover scribbled, "It is a shame we can't nail this jackal."

Wesley Grapp was a household name inside the Bureau. A protégé of the ultraconservative Senator Karl E. Mundt of South Dakota, he was regarded as an iron disciplinarian of the most zealous sort. One hapless, physically ill agent, whose offense is lost to memory, was required by Grapp to check the agents' bullpen each evening and leave a memorandum on the Assistant SAC's desk that he had found it clean and in order, an indignity that may or may not have contributed to the agent's suicide. In internal politics, Grapp was also wired in to Assistant Director Cartha DeLoach, head of the publicity division. So powerful did he eventually become in his own right that in 1967, according to Los Angeles agent-informants, he refused to obey Hoover's order to change places with the SAC in Boston—and got away with it.

My first meeting with Grapp was decidedly cool. As protocol demanded, I presented myself at his office for formal introduction within a few days of my arrival. He put me up short with the command, "You will wait outside until I have finished my business." Once in, I studied the man. He was tall, erect with an almost military carriage. Although he was ruggedly handsome, his eyes were constantly averted. This was the man who a short time before had walked out to accept the surrender of hemmed-in armed bank robbers, yet who had his agent corps uptight with fear. There was none of the usual badinage, just brusque business. My overall impression was one of priggishness. If his later account is any criterion, Grapp was no more impressed with me than I was with him.

During our exchange Grapp had asked the customary question about housing, and I may have signaled that I didn't intend staying too long by saying I was going to get a room in a residence club. In preparing to press a structured assault on the system, I imposed upon myself two rules: (1) to adhere meticulously to the rules of the Bureau system in order to preclude later charges that I had flaunted the rules and regulations, and (2) to seize the initiative and keep it as far as possible.

The manual of rules and regulations clearly permitted an agent to request a transfer at any time; ordinarily, such a request would be simply granted or denied. But I suspected that Grapp might overreact. I mentioned my intention to put in for transfer to Rex I. Shroder, the Assistant SAC with whom I had become acquainted on the Los Angeles inspection the previous year. "Grapp will take it personally," he warned.

When I announced formally to Grapp that I wished to seek a transfer, he had already been advised by Shroder. "Do you realize the consequences of this?" he challenged. I replied that there should be none, since the manual permitted such a request. He stated that he would accompany the request with a special performance rating. I retorted that there was nothing in the manual specifying that a special performance rating be prepared on the occasion of a transfer request. He said he was sending one anyway. On it, he rated the key category of attitude as "unsatisfactory," with the explanation, "he is lacking in enthusiasm for his present assignment."

This was quite obvious. In the course of casual conversation with Shroder—I think it was during a round of golf—I had mentioned that Oklahoma was a bit too frontier for my personal liking. In fact, the offices of preference I had listed over the years were consistently in large metropolitan areas, ranging from Detroit to Tokyo. This was irrelevant: the request was based on official considerations. "When I first came to Oklahoma City," I would later write to the Director in pursuing the matter through channels, "Mr. Grapp informed me that I had been transferred here to fill the need for a Sound-trained Agent at headquarters city. My subsequent assignment to a permanent road trip, involving investigation away from headquarters city, and imposing an inflexible caseload, negates the purpose for which I was transferred. In addition, I have had four years of experience as a Relief Supervisor, which of course was to be wasted in this situation."

Perhaps what rankled most was that I suggested that the personnel department had committed an oversight in the first place due to the size of the agent staff. There was another Sound-trained agent in Seattle who had Oklahoma City listed as his office of preference, I pointed out, and it might have been more logical to send him. (After I left Oklahoma City, this same agent was transferred in as *my* replacement.)

According to procedure, an agent is supposed to read his performance rating in the presence of its author and then sign it. I flatly
refused to sign until Grapp brought it current. It was mid-December
and I had been in the office only two months. By reporting my statistics on stolen car recoveries and the like as of the end of the previous month, he had shortchanged me enough to make it appear that
I was performing poorly. Once the statistics were updated, it turned
out that I was performing above the office as a whole. Before signing, I dictated an insert to Grapp's secretary advising headquarters
that my signature was to be considered no more than an acknowledgment I had read the rating, and that I took full exception to the
"unsatisfactory" mark on attitude.

Although I was unaware of it at the time, Grapp sent a confidential memorandum, dated December 16, 1960, to the Director
with the performance rating. Accusing me of "pouting and sulking,"
he concluded:

> It appears that SA TURNER is a spoiled, self-centered indi-
> vidual who is trying to pick his assignments in this division,
> as well as what division he will work in. In my opinion he
> needs a good "jolt" to enable him to place himself in the
> proper perspective with the Bureau's needs. My recommen-
> dations for administrative action are as follows:
>
> 1. SA TURNER be placed on probation.
>
> 2. He remain assigned to this division for the present and if
> he ever be transferred from this division that he be assigned
> to another rural area, possibly including Alaska. To do
> otherwise would be rewarding him for his poor attitude.

The "jolt" came in a letter from the Director dated December
27 and postmarked Miami—Hoover was evidently on his annual
winter "working vacation" to the racetrack there—placing me on
probation. In an echo of the letter of probation seven years before
when I had asked for an intraoffice transfer, the Director scolded:
"You apparently place your personal preferences and conveniences
above the welfare and needs of the FBI and your conduct in this

matter is definitely not in keeping with the standards expected of Special Agents of this Bureau."

On the SAC's copy of this letter there was an addendum—I didn't know it at the time—that read: "For *your* information, on SA TURNER's anniversary 2/5, no Ten Year Key or letter from the Director will be sent in view of his unsatisfactory attitude. For *your* information only." The ten-year key was no more than a token of ten years' service, and was paid for out of Recreation Association funds to which I had contributed.

Bureau precedent now dictated that I write a *mea culpa* letter to Hoover in the manner of a chastened child, expressing sorrow for the infraction and promising to do better. Instead, on January 4, 1961, I addressed a letter to the Director taking further exception to the performance rating, contending it had been based on "wrong conclusions." I asked to come to Washington for a face-to-face discussion.

This brought up an interesting point. It was said that the Director's door was always open to agent personnel, and indeed one of the first orders of business at in-service training was for agents wishing to see him to raise their hands. But it was not all that simple. Those who did indicate the desire were given a screening interview to make sure they didn't have anything controversial on their minds. And agents on probation or otherwise in the dog house were scheduled for in-service at a time the Director was out of town.

So Hoover's reply was not unanticipated. "Due to previous commitments," he wrote on January 10, "it will not be possible for me to see you." I didn't take him up on his offer to have a designated assistant see me should I travel to the capital on my own time and at my own expense.

In preparing the performance rating, Grapp had made a tactical error. There existed a body called the Performance Rating Board of Review to which an appeal could be made. I had never heard of any agent availing himself of it, possibly because it was composed of three FBI members and one "monitor" from the Civil Service Commission. Nevertheless, that monitor represented a pair of outside eyes that would see some very strange inside goings-on, and I suspected that the Director would pull the shades. By a letter on January 11, in which I expressed dismay that he "could not find the time to talk to an Agent from the field," I signified a wish to appeal. He responded that I had no right to appeal because the performance rating was "an administrative special type of report" rather than an official one.

Off went other letter to the Director asking him to waive the technicality. Set forth was a multitude of reasons I considered Grapp's bastard report "incomplete and slanted." This terminated our correspondence. In lieu of a letter, Chief Inspector Roy Moore was pulled off an inspection of the New York office and sent to Oklahoma City. For by this time I had picked up a staunch and unflappable ally.

Nelson H. Gibbons had been a house hero in the FBI. An ex-marine who had been a New York state trooper for seven years, he had pulled off an unprecedented feat by single-handedly uncovering a Soviet spy. I remember an espionage desk supervisor telling the story at in-service training, holding Gibbons up as the exemplar of an alert and determined agent. Assigned to a rural area in the Detroit division, Gibbons learned about a man who had come to town to obtain a copy of his baptismal certificate at the Roman Catholic church. He sensed something wrong and began to tail the man. The suspect took a bus heading west. Following along, Gibbons telephoned the Detroit office, saying he believed he had a spy in tow and asking for help. The Detroit supervisor laughed. Gibbons kept on it. Finally, his tenacity was rewarded when the man doubled back and made a bee-line for New York City. It turned out that he was Kaarlo Rudolph Tuomi, a Finnish native who had been inducted into the Soviet military intelligence (GRU) some two decades before.

Tuomi, known in the trade as an "illegal," had been assigned to a Soviet espionage apparat centered in New York, and the venture to Michigan was an effort to create a cover identity. New York agents put the squeeze on Tuomi, converting him into an FBI double agent still ostensibly working for the Soviets. Gibbons's feat paid huge dividends in July 1963 when headlines proclaimed: "FBI Smashes Soviet Spy Ring." Acting on information fed back by Tuomi, the G-men had arrested a couple, Aleksandre and Joy Ann Sokolov, who had appropriated the identities of Robert K. Baltch, a Roman Catholic priest of Amsterdam, New York, and Joy Ann Seskin, née Garber, a housewife of Norwalk, Connecticut. Also in custody were Ivan D. Egerov, attached to the Russian United Nations mission, and his wife Aleksandra. Two other Soviet UN attachés who had purportedly doubled in espionage had already returned to Moscow. The Egerovs were later exchanged for two Americans being held in Russia on spy charges. The Sokolovs were brought to trial, but the Justice Department dropped its prosecution rather than produce the addresses of all its witnesses, including Tuomi, and they were deported. According to the FBI, the ring had procured highly classified information relating to military installations.*

But by the time the FBI reaped his harvest, Gibbons was no longer in the service. For his accomplishment, he had received a three-hundred-dollar incentive award and Hoover's congratulations. But shortly thereafter, he ran afoul of the weight program.

The weight program was instituted by Hoover in 1958 when he himself, on medical advice, decided to take off excess poundage. The program was extended to the field in typical arbitrary fashion. Instead of relying on military doctors giving annual physicals or personal physicians to judge whether an agent's weight was medically proper, the Bureau distributed weight charts put out as guidance by an insurance firm and decreed that each agent be within the "desirable" limit for his height and frame.

The result was chaotic and tragic. The hardest hit were muscular ex-football players in reasonably good shape—I would guess that about every pro football lineman would be over the "desirable" limit. A naval doctor who examined an agent subsisting on lettuce and water branded the program "irresponsible." In New York, an agent collapsed and died at his desk while attempting to conform by means of a crash diet, and his widow sued the Bureau, blaming the weight program as a contributing factor in his death. There were

---

*In their book *Red Spies in the U.N.*, Hearst reporters George Carpozi, Jr., and Pierre J. Huss implied that the FBI got onto the ring through surveillance of the departed UN attachés. They reported Tuomi's role as "not clear," but identified him as a GRU agent who several years before gained "a measure of revenge by enlisting in the CIA as a counterspy."

absurdities: one SAC, jittery over the no-excuse implementation of the program, became supercautious and scaled down to the limit for the frame size below his own; in Seattle, an agent was turned down for a recommended promotion because he was one pound over the "desirable" mark and quit in disgust.

Nelson ("Skip") Gibbons found himself initially an unlucky thirteen pounds over the chart's limit. This was ironic, since he was a former Marine Corps boxer and St. Bonaventure University football lineman, and had remained a physical fitness buff. A physician of the Detroit police department who looked him over had recommended no loss of weight. Nevertheless, by the time he took his 1960 annual physical at Selfridge Air Force Base, he had "slimmed down" to only five pounds over the magic number. The doctor checked his weight as satisfactory on the form, with the remark: "Medically I feel that this man's weight is proper."

When the form was returned to him for signature via the Detroit office, however, Skip Gibbons found the "satisfactory" crossed out and a notation added: "Lose 5 lbs." He sent the form back to the office unsigned with the explanation that it had been altered. He was then warned by the Assistant SAC that if he didn't sign, he would be charged with insubordination.

As Gibbons would later put it in a letter to the Department of Justice, "I directed a telegram to Mr. Hoover requesting an interview, and although I did not specify a date, I received the stock answer that he would not be available." So he consulted an attorney—the charge of insubordination is grave—who counseled him to sign the form as merely acknowledging he had read it.

Without a couple of weeks, in September 1960, Gibbons was en route to Mobile, Alabama, a transfer in hand. Accompanying the transfer was a performance rating designating him "unsatisfactory" in judgment because he had contacted an attorney before signing the form. And on the Bureau copy of the transfer, Associate Director Clyde Tolson scrawled the reminder: "Transfer O. C. [Oklahoma City] in November." Skip was on the well-known "Bureau bicycle," on which it was hoped he would pedal himself right out of service.

Gibbons arrived in Oklahoma City on schedule, and his first session with Grapp was electric. "I'm going to give you ulcers," the

SAC is quoted as greeting him. To which Skip's fine Irish wit flashed back, "I don't get ulcers, I give them."

The whole thing was about to plunge into an incredible miasma of pettifoggery, nitpicking, hair-splitting, and bureaucratic rhetoric, and Skip was a welcome addition to the lonely Young Turk brigade. The FBI takes itself with deadly seriousness, and its officials play terribly important games. Only a pregnant sense of humor can provide a frame of reference for reality.

Skip was also a bachelor, and he pledged to go all the way. We agreed on two major points. One, we would always tell the straight truth, which would be doubly frustrating to the Bureau because it would find no conflict in our versions. And two, we would not, for our part, drag any other employee into the battle. We sealed the pact with a handshake.

In early January 1961, Skip received a three-week suspension without pay for assertedly having an "unsatisfactory attitude toward the physical requirements of your position." He hopped in his car and drove to Washington, but again Hoover was too busy. However, he did see John P. Mohr, the rotund assistant to the Director. Mohr warned him that if he was not at his "desirable" weight by the time he returned from suspension, he would be handed another one, this time for thirty days.

On Skip's first day back in the office, Grapp accosted him with an accusation of "sulking," and loudly ordered him into the SAC's office while a phone call was made to the Bureau to report the episode, but the call was never made. Meanwhile, Grapp was inundating me with a sea of paper, requiring the preparation of a daily log as well as a "running log" broken down by cities and towns of contacts with FBI National Academy graduates, law enforcement representatives, civic and business leaders, and a host of other categories in the public relations sphere. He had based this special bookkeeping on the allegation that my work performance was "lackadaisical," which was directly contradicted by the fact that I was handling a larger-than-average caseload with half the number of delinquent cases.

The arrival of Chief Inspector Roy Moore on February 2 was greeted by Skip and myself with relief, since we wanted to end the running skirmish with Grapp and engage Bureau headquarters in combat. Mild-mannered and pleasant, Moore had obtained a measure of fame in the solution of the United Air Lines bombing case in Denver some years earlier, and he would shortly be appointed the first SAC of the new field office at Jackson, Mississippi, a post requiring considerable diplomacy. He was not entirely devoid of a sense of humor. When Skip blithely charged Grapp with "hiding behind the Bureau's apron strings," he couldn't help but laugh.

From the outset, however, it was evident Moore knew what he had to do. "What do you mean by writing a letter like that to the Director of the FBI?" he asked me, introducing a note of hostility. He pored over the files Skip and I had handled and presented me with a morass of trivial errors—he had used an agent-accountant to scrutinize records minutely—plus two substantive write-ups. The first was captioned "Personal Use of Bureau Car" and demanded an explanation for this dismissable offense. I had been out on an investigation, I recalled, when I became ill. Fearing a relapse from the hepatitis recovery, I had driven to a nearby doctor's office. Had I been an SAC and had an agent reported to me following a serious illness, I stated, I would have insisted that he use a Bureau car to see a doctor at any time. The second write-up implied that I had fictionalized an interview with a police captain. I had reported that the captain had denied knowing a suspect in a prostitution case, whereas he had later called the office with information about the suspect. But the file clearly reflected that the captain was using the suspect as an informant at the time of my interview, and had later dropped him. I told Moore I would no more expect the captain to reveal his informants to me than I would mine to him. Moore dropped the matter of both write-ups.

Moore had instructed me to prepare a memorandum outlining my complaints against Grapp. It was a long one, but two points arrested Moore's attention. In rebutting the SAC's contention that at an Oklahoma peace officers' convention he heard numerous laudatory remarks about my predecessor on the road trip (who had been assigned to it for two years) and not one about me, I asserted that in my numerous contacts with Oklahoma law officers "not one has made to me any laudatory comments concerning Mr. Grapp.

One, however, remarked that if Mr. Grapp had been caught speeding in his county, he would not have let him go." The second point was my peroration, expressing the belief that the SAC was not a "fit person to judge attitude, as his own leaves much to be desired." "I feel it my duty to point out to you," I wrote, "that if he is as arbitrary and overbearing in his dealings with persons outside the Bureau, and there is indication that he is, he may well be a source of embarrassment to the Bureau at some future date."

"What do you mean?" bristled Moore. "What evidence do you have?" The inquiry had taken an unexpected turn.

Moore remonstrated with me for not reporting the speeding affair at the time. Grapp had been returning from the Panhandle in a Bureau car after mixing some grouse hunting with official contacts when he was stopped by a highway patrolman. He had gotten out of a ticket by identifying himself as an FBI official. I agreed to furnish additional material concerning Grapp's demeanor if Moore would agree to check it all out. I stressed that I was not making allegations but merely furnishing leads for him to investigate, since I did not have first-hand knowledge. After I had given him the names of an Air Force colonel, a police photographer, a former Bureau contract garage owner, and several others who were in a position to express personal opinions of the SAC and his relations with them, Moore insisted that I divulge the identities of the agents who had supplied me with the information. I flatly refused. But Skip Gibbons gave Moore substantially the same information.

Two days after his arrival, Inspector Moore interviewed me again. Ironically, he remarked that it had been his first visit to Oklahoma City, and while he enjoyed seeing new places he wouldn't want to live there. The conversation was strangely relaxed. What did he think of the new Kennedy administration and the attorney general? "Young," he replied. "They'll have to prove themselves." Pointedly, I said, "Well, I was impressed with the president's state of the union message, especially as it pertained to encouraging daring and dissent on the part of government employees."

Somewhat to my surprise, Moore announced that he was returning to Washington that very afternoon to report his findings. He had been in possession of our leads for only a day, and to check them out thoroughly would have required a good week. The inspector had hardly left the office, and his only visitor had been the Air Force colonel.

As I took my leave, Moore almost apologetically remarked, "There's only one man who makes the decision."

CHAPTER FOUR

PERSONAL FILE: VOLUME IV

Mr. Hoover's reputation and stature have made
the FBI one of the outstanding law enforcement
agencies in the world and the key to this success
has been Mr. Hoover's concern for the personnel
of this Bureau.

— *Assistant to the Director John P. Mohr*
in reply to my charges

Inside of a week, the Director addressed substantially similar letters to Skip and myself. "You have recently made a number of
allegations against your Special Agent in Charge," mine read,
"claiming that he has been at fault in his supervision of you and
asserting that he has been derelict in several other matters in which
you were not personally involved. *A Bureau Inspector has made a
thorough and careful investigation of all your charges and it has
been determined that they are baseless* [italics added]."

For such "inexcusable judgment," Hoover said, we were to be
suspended without pay for thirty days. Accompanying my letter was
a transfer to Knoxville, Tennessee. Skip's was to Butte, Montana.

We had now exhausted remedy within the FBI. It would have
been futile to bring to the Director's attention Section 9-A of the
Manual of Rules and Regulations: "It is imperative that any information pertaining to allegations of misconduct or improper performance of duty coming to the attention of any Bureau employee be
promptly and fully reported to the Bureau." Nor was there any

point in contesting the superficiality and incompleteness of Moore's investigation.

What I had actually hoped for was, in the government's euphemism, an "involuntary separation." Ordinarily, agents had no protection from Hoover's "merit system." But under the Veteran's Preference Act of 1944, a veteran of World War II was entitled to appeal outside the FBI if he was suspended for more than thirty days or fired. By suspending us for just thirty days, the Bureau was circumventing the appeal process. As Assistant to the Director John Mohr would later testify: "If we had enough to fire Mr. Turner in Oklahoma City, we would have preferred charges against him. We did not. We suspended him for thirty days, which was the maximum action we could take at that time."

Suspended agents traditionally atoned for their sins during the purgatorial period by offering to perform menial tasks around the office. Instead, I marched over to the unemployment commission office and applied for benefits. The spectacle of an FBI agent in line created a mild stir, although one claims examiner reminisced about the 1958 purge in the local Bureau office. Then Skip and I drove off for a skiing holiday on the slopes at Aspen, Colorado.

At this point the attorney general, Hoover's titular superior, represented an intermediate appeal step before Congress. Accordingly, before leaving for Aspen, I fired off a telegram to the incoming Robert Kennedy, briefly explaining the situation and requesting to see him personally. There was some reason to be encouraged by young Kennedy's debut as attorney general. Sources inside the FBI had advised us that he was asserting his hegemony, giving orders to Bureau officials without going through the Director's office. Bobby was walking unannounced into Hoover's office and once even caught "the Man" napping on a couch; and he was barging into the Bureau gym, heretofore as barred to Justice officials as a country club to blacks. According to rumor, the new director would be Byron "Whizzer" White. (White was later appointed by JFK to the Supreme Court.)

But the Kennedys, consummate political practitioners, were not about to dump Hoover, at least not until after the 1964 elections. I received a return telegram from Bobby: *"Suggest you contact Direc-*

tor, Federal Bureau of Investigation on this matter." It was sent collect, and I had to pay $1.45 for its souvenir value. Skip fared no better. Upon his arrival at Butte he sent a detailed letter to the employment policy officer of the department that got a brush-off reply. But privately, Bobby couldn't resist slipping his celebrated white elephant the harpoon. He told Hoover that if he couldn't handle his own agents, personnel policies might well be put under the department's wing.

My arrival in Knoxville was attended by more internal fuss than Jimmy Hoffa's trip to Chattanooga. Grapp was instructed to notify Knoxville and the Bureau of my arrival plans within forty-eight hours, and a radiogram went out as I boarded the train. The SAC at Knoxville was advised to keep me under close supervision and after ninety days to submit a performance rating with "recommendations re probation and possible administrative action." Additionally, he was given verbal orders from John Mohr that I was not to be allowed to leave the Knoxville area. I was under a kind of house arrest.

Now that the deck had been cleared, I began the letter-writing campaign described earlier. The first recipients were Senators Warren G. Magnuson and Henry M. Jackson of Washington State, where I had resided for so long, and Jacob K. Javits and Kenneth M. Keating of New York. The letters stated that I also spoke for Skip, who had authorized me to do so. The tone was admittedly iconoclastic. In the letter to Javits, for instance, I described the Bureau as an "autocratic empire isolated by myth from outside inspection." In a letter to Senator Estes Kefauver—I was residing in his state now—I asserted that "morale in the Bureau is at an all-time low" and described aberrations caused by the vanity criterion of "embarrassment to the Bureau." And since Kefauver was quite familiar with the organized crime problem, I pointed up the FBI's inertia in the battle against the criminal syndicates that was compounded by the Director's hostility toward several honest efforts to cope with them. Specifically, I alluded to the case of Richard Ogilvie, former special assistant to the U.S. attorney general, who had termed the Bureau uncooperative in the Department of Justice drive against the Apalachin conferees. In a letter to all agents that had just been circulated, Hoover had bluntly labeled Ogilvie's contentions as unfounded. It would appear, I wrote, that the Director held any statement not serving to perpetuate "the Hoover myth" as an "unfounded allegation."

Meanwhile, Skip and I were in regular touch. The SAC at Butte was piling up enormous phone bills talking to John Mohr in Washington, he said. The Bureau had tried its damnedest to convince him that I was acting as his "attorney" and leading him astray, and that his prodigality would be forgiven if he would turn against me. Failing in that, Butte officials had subjected him to long interrogation sessions, apparently in an effort to draw details from him that would conflict with my letters to Congress, of which the Bureau was now aware. The best they had done in this little exercise was to discover that I had stated Grapp greeted Skip with "I'm going to give you ulcers" on Skip's "very first day in the office," whereas it had actually been the second day.

At this point the situation was incongruous. By day, I was a full-fledged FBI agent working on a wide variety of cases, some of them of considerable importance. The first case assigned me was a fraud against the government complaint against a metals plant that involved a potential recovery of over one million dollars. When a tip on possible espionage came in, I received the investigation. When a lock on the Tennessee River unaccountably collapsed, blocking the passage of a Saturn missile en route by barge to Cape Canaveral, I was designated to confer with General Vogel, head of the Tennessee Valley Authority, and his chief counsel and chief engineer on the possibility that sabotage was involved. When an antitrust investigation of the soft drink industry in the area was undertaken, I was assigned to a special squad handling the delicate and complex inquiries. I also worked on an intensified White Slave Act program and a complaint of a wiretap installed in violation of the Communications Act of 1934. Yet later on, John Mohr would belittle my stint in Knoxville with the claim that I only handled "minor" cases there.

By night I sat in the hotel room typing letters to Congress.

By all odds, I had to be the most "radioactive" agent in the Bureau, and I fully expected that the Knoxville personnel would stay far away in order to avoid contamination. They did not. From the SAC through the ranks, they were cordial and helpful. When Grapp, who was now SAC in Miami, and an inspector took pot shots at me in the form of criticism of the way I had handled specific aspects of cases, both the SAC and his assistant went on record as backing my explanations.

The reaction in Congress was cautious. Senator Jackson, whom I had met some years before when I had investigated the burglary of his automobile, asked specifically what he might do. When I rather baldly suggested introducing a bill to set up the hearing the Bureau was circumventing, he wrote back that he couldn't see such a bill ever getting out of committee, but that in any event Chairman Emanuel Celler of the House Judiciary Committee would be the man to approach. So I wrote Celler, who did not reply.

Senator Jacob Javits was the most responsive. By letter on April 24, 1961, he informed Robert Kennedy that "the specific problems faced by Special Agent Turner. . . are disturbing to me. I believe strongly, as I know you do, that every Bureau of the government must in dealing with its employees follow the basic concepts of fair play fundamental to our American way of life." The senator asked Kennedy to look into the matter. The attorney general replied that he already had, and had found no basis for altering the Bureau's action.

About this time an informant inside Bureau headquarters leaked word of the strategy. FBI officials were going around to members of Congress mollifying them by representing the struggle as an internal matter, and I could expect no further action from that quarter. This was later confirmed by aides to Senator Javits, who advised that when the senator asked to see my personnel file Assistant Director Cartha DeLoach showed up and very curtly declared the whole thing an administrative problem that should not concern Congress.

It was expected, the informant advised, that Skip and I would sooner or later become discouraged at the lack of response and resign, thus sparing the Bureau the chagrin of a hearing. To hasten the process, I had been quarantined in Knoxville.

Determined to regain the initiative, I saw an opportunity in the quarantine order. When a civil rights emergency had arisen in the New Orleans office, I had volunteered to leave immediately for the scene but was turned down. To further demonstrate that such an order was indeed in effect, I twice broached the SAC on the subject of leaving town for the weekend, and twice he prohibited it, finally admitting he had instructions due to my "differences with the Bureau."

So I sent off a fresh batch of letters to Kennedy and Congress protesting my house arrest. My father, a printing executive in Buffalo, New York, joined in. When the attorney general remained silent, he wrote: "Lack of response would seem to confirm that you choose to countenance the unfair, un-American and autocratic disciplinary attitude of the Bureau under your direction. This runs counter to the promises in your speeches." Then a rhetorical poser: "What kind of men do you think would best serve the Bureau and our country? The kind who will stand up for their rights and fight for what they believe in, or the kind who will roll over for the second kick on the other side: What kind do you want working for you?"

This provoked young Kennedy into responding, although he evaded the issue. By letter on June 16, he alluded to my duty to "comply with rules and regulations of the FBI," and to "unusual emergency requirements" in the southern offices that might necessitate a curtailment of my "extraneous travels." In his reply to me, he wrist-slapped me by remarking that I had no authority to speak for Skip. Apparently Kennedy was repeating some Bureau misinformation.

But the correspondence was merely a diversionary strike, for I intended to launch a main thrust in federal court in the form of a suit asking that the Bureau be required to show cause why I could not leave Knoxville. One of the senior agents steered me to a local attorney. The attorney looked somewhat aghast as I related the story, but said he would file the suit. "Hoover puts his pants on the same way as anyone else," he remarked. It would take a few days for him to get the required information from a correspondent firm in Washington, he said, because he knew of no precedent for such an action.

While this was in the mill in mid-June, I received word from an informant at headquarters that the Bureau had prepared a seven-page letter of charges with which they proposed to fire me, and that it was in the mail to Knoxville. Apparently the ruckus over my house arrest had forced their hand. In a manner that must remain untold, I laid hands on the letter, called the attorney, and read him its contents. His emphatic reaction was that the charges represented "quantity and not quality," and he counseled me to fight them under the Veteran's Act instead of filing the show cause suit. "You might look bad filing suit because the question of your leaving Knoxville is now moot," he advised.

In fact, I did now have the dismissal letter that I had sweated it out so long to get. But I wanted to file the suit also, to keep the initiative. It was now the weekend. The attorney agreed to complete his legal work with a call to Washington first thing Monday morning if I could stall off being handed the letter, which I knew the Bureau had scheduled for the opening of business Monday. So I signed in very early before anyone else was at the office, filled out a locator card, and took off in a non-radio car. Ironically, the interviews I conducted concerned an applicant for the special agent position. Everywhere I went there was an urgent message for me to call the SAC.

At eleven I called the attorney. His secretary had just started to type the papers, he said, and it would be a couple more hours. Again he urged me, in what he considered my best interests, to forget the suit. I agreed, thanked him, and told him where to mail the bill. When it arrived, it only covered the cost of the long-distance calls. The least he could do, he said.

Returning to the office, I reported to the SAC. He handed me the dismissal letter. I read it in his presence, as if I had never seen its contents. On the bottom of his copy, I knew, there had been appended instructions to note carefully any comments I might make. While I was reading, the SAC's phone rang, and he asked me politely to leave the room. The call, I learned later, was from Assistant Director Nicholas Callahan, whose Administrative Division had drafted the letter. Evidently Callahan was curious, since the event was three hours overdue. Without comment I handed in credentials number 6627, badge, revolver, and handbook. Then I headed for the airport and Washington.

What I didn't know, and only learned years later through a doc-

ument obtained under FOI, was that the Bureau had already tested
the letter with the Civil Service Commission (CSC), which would
decide my appeal. On June 7, John Mohr directed a memo to Clyde
Tolson informing him that he had gone over to the CSC and personally discussed "the Turner matter" with Edward H. Bechtold, the
Veterans' Service Staff Chief. "After a detailed discussion," Mohr
reported, "Bechtold stated he felt that CSC would sustain our discharging Turner, if Turner appealed such action under the Veteran's
Preference Act." The "discussion" was actually highly unethical if
not illegal, since it was tantamount to a prosecutor going before a
judge and asking how he would rule if charges were filed. Mohr got
the answer he was looking for. "Bechtold perused a tentative draft
of the dismissal charges we would bring against Turner," Mohr
wrote, "and felt they would be satisfactory with one or two
changes." The changes were made, and Mohr sent off the letter to
Knoxville secure in the knowledge the outcome was predetermined.

The first order of business was to retain an attorney. Although
my funds were very limited, I decided to start at the top and work
down. I called the office of Edward Bennett Williams and in his
absence was connected with a member of the staff, Vincent J. Fuller.
We arranged a conference. After I recounted the lengthy story and
laid out the documents, he exclaimed, "It sounds like a Gestapo." A
few days later Fuller called to say that Williams would take the case.
The famous attorney had received a quarter of a million dollars in
defending Teamster President Jimmy Hoffa, and a rumor soon
swept the field offices that contesting the FBI had cost me and my
father fifty thousand dollars. It was more like five hundred, a pit-
tance compared to Williams's usual fees.

Next I contacted the offices of Representative Celler and Senators Kefauver and Javits, since the dismissal letter was based wholly
on statements I had made in letters to them that they had forwarded
to the Bureau for comment. The aging, influential Celler would not
see me; his aides explained that now that I had been dismissed and
had an attorney I should pursue the matter through legal channels.
Kefauver was candid, commenting that "Hoover is more powerful
than the president." Indeed, it was dawning on me that the name of
the game was power, not truth.

A visit to Senator Javits's office was more encouraging. His aides reported that the senator was incensed that his inquiries to the Bureau had been used as a basis for firing me. When Cartha DeLoach had posited the need for tight discipline, the senator had shot back that he and his aides had been in the armed services, but that in this case any such need had been far exceeded. Following his celebrated Berlin speech, Javits called me over to the Senate reception chambers. What had been done? he asked his aides. One replied that he had referred the matter to the Government Operations Committee but had little hope of action there.

"Well," remarked the senator, "let's take it up with Bobby or Jack."

"Sure," quipped the aide. "Maybe we can even include the Pope."

"Why not?" I joined in. "There's that tunnel that leads under the ocean to the Vatican."

Javits again urged Robert Kennedy to delve into the matter. The attorney general replied that he had assigned his top aide, John Seigenthaler, to look into it and there was no change. But there was no evidence that Seigenthaler, later editor of the *Nashville Tennessean,* had conducted the requisite field investigation. In retrospect, it would seem that the Kennedys, having made a political decision to retain Hoover temporarily, felt that they had to put on a public face of supporting him. This is precisely what Robert Kennedy did in other controversies that ensued, even though it became an open secret that his differences with the Director were irreconcilable.

Since the Veteran's Administration did not have the mechanism for conducting appeal hearings, the Civil Service Commission acted as a surrogate. Ed Williams warned me, however, not to expect relief through any administrative process. This ominous note was reinforced by other signs. When I talked with the civil service field examiner who would preside at the hearing, Michael E. Sedmak, he told me that it was strictly a closed-door affair. When I called him back the next day to clarify a point, he said that the chief of the Appeals Examining Office, Stephen L. Elliott, wanted to talk to me. Elliott was plainly antagonistic. "What are you doing in Washington?" he demanded.

"What do you mean about unjustified suspensions?"

Although Elliott later apologized, agent-informants sent out word that the outcome of the hearing had been foreordained—the Bureau had been reassured on this score prior to proceeding with the dismissal—and that the hearing would only resolve certain points. They were right. Documents released under FOI showed that Sedmak, in an ex-parte session with a Bureau official, noted that he had known John Mohr's brother Paul, then an Atlanta FBI agent, at Muhlenberg College and George Washington University law school. In a second such session a few days before the hearing, he reassured John Mohr that there was no way I was going to prevail.

This was confirmed by T. J. Dulski, who represented my home district in Buffalo. The congressman had written to Hoover, characterizing his action as "unfair and harsh" in that an employee "certainly is entitled to confer with his superiors if he is dissatisfied with his assignment." But Dulski privately told me that the case was such a "hot potato" in Washington that the commission could not possibly rule in my favor because of the precedent it would set. I took this as authoritative, because Dulski was a member of the civil service committee in Congress.

Nevertheless, Congressman Dulski notified the Civil Service Commission that he intended to sit in on the hearing. Elliott leaked this to the FBI, and who should show up in Dulski's office but Cartha DeLoach, Hoover's heavy hitter. DeLoach told Dulski that the hearing was none of Congress's business, that it was simply an FBI administrative matter. DeLoach's memorandum, obtained under the Freedom of Information Act, reveals that the purpose of the visit was to intimidate and apparently the message got through. Dulski was a no-show.

There remained one procedural obligation. Under the terms of the Veteran's Act, I had to respond to the Director's dismissal letter within ten days in order to clear the way for a hearing. His letter had directed me to respond to Assistant to the Director Mohr, but I addressed it to him with the explanation: "In view of [Mohr's] remarks to Special Agent Nelson H. Gibbons in January, 1961, to the effect that Mr. Grapp had been in Buffalo and knew how to handle us Buffalo hardnoses, it is apparent that Mr. Mohr had already assumed a prejudicial and retaliatory attitude, which obviously influenced the objectivity of Inspector Moore's subsequent investigation at Oklahoma City."

The rebuttal of a nitpicker's morass was not a task I relished. For instance, in "proving" that I had made "untrue or unjustified statements" to members of Congress, the letter alluded to my claim that a memorandum by Grapp relating to my work performance "is now missing from file." Since it was a field memorandum, I was obviously referring to my field file. I knew it was missing because I had picked the lock on the file cabinet in Knoxville—lock-picking was a skill the Bureau had trained me in—and gone through my personal file. But Hoover pompously declared: "This statement is untrue, as the memorandum in question is in the Bureau's files and has never been missing."

Another example was my statement that the inspector was "obviously sent to Oklahoma City to discredit [me] rather than conduct an impartial investigation." The Director adjudged the statement false. Not so, I said, pointing out that one of the officials whose name I had furnished "has recently reiterated that he has never been contacted. Therefore your statement is false."

But tucked into the semantical mishmash was a very grave charge. In the letters to Javits, Kefauver, and Celler, I had illustrated Skip Gibbons's competency by saying that while assigned to Detroit he had "single-handedly, and despite disbelief on the part of his superiors, uncovered a Soviet spy." Categorizing this as "unauthorized disclosures of information regarding a highly confidential and highly secret investigation," Hoover had branded me a "serious security risk."

Such an allegation, I knew, could stigmatize me forever. Labeling it "a slur on the integrity and loyalty of these responsible members of Congress," I wrote:

> . . . your contention that I made "unauthorized disclosures" is an obvious misrepresentation. You are well aware that this incident was not on a "need-to-know" basis, as it was told to Agents from all over the United States, including myself, at In-Service Training classes. It was presented as an

outstanding example of the results obtained by an alert and
resourceful Agent, specifically Mr. Gibbons, whom you
recently suspended for a total of 7 out of 9 weeks for following the advice of a competent medical authority. Your
reference to me as a security risk is unwarranted, irresponsible, dishonorable and typical of all the flimsy fabrications
contained in your letter.

   Mr. Hoover, you owe me an apology in writing.

   What I received was a letter from the FBI chief—it began "Sir"
and ended "Truly yours"—tersely announcing that the Bureau
intended to finalize my dismissal.

   The security risk matter, of course, came up at the hearing. The
hearing officer demanded to know from the Bureau's chief representative, John Mohr, what this top secret statement was, since otherwise the charge was a faceless one. Mohr hemmed and hawed, but
wouldn't divulge it. The appeals office chief, Stephen Elliott, was
brought in on the basis that he was cleared for top security and
could be confidentially apprised. Still Mohr balked. When I declared
that I would disclose the statement, Mohr threatened to have me
charged with a criminal violation of the Espionage Act of 1918. It
was quite a performance to cover a farcical charge. We brought out
that the Bureau itself apparently never took the statement seriously.
For some two months after headquarters knew that I had made it,
no attempt was made to restrict my duties, which included conducting investigations at the atomic energy installation at Oak Ridge.
And the Bureau had retransmitted the letter containing the supposedly top secret statement to the office of Senator Kefauver via ordinary mail, a clear breach of existing procedures.

   The most damning dereliction of the Bureau was that, had its
charge been bona fide, it could have dismissed me under Public Law
733, which authorizes the separation of security risks without right
of appeal. The Civil Service Commission took note of this in kicking
out the Bureau's "security risk" charge. In my opinion, the charge
was a vindictive and craven misuse of power.

   Despite the dim prospects, I was determined to put on a strong
case at the civil service hearing. This meant securing affidavits and

documents material and relevant to refuting the charges, which were based mainly on the dispute with Grapp. I was not too hopeful for the simple reason that anyone in a position to help me was in the concomitant position of having a continuing relationship with the FBI. Nevertheless, I wrote the two Oklahoma law enforcement officers whom I had contacted most frequently, briefly outlining the situation and the allegation that I had been unable to get along with Oklahomans in general and police officers in particular. In the return mail came a letter from Inspector J. W. ("Bill") Holt on the letterhead of the Oklahoma State Bureau of Investigation saying he had been "talking to some of the other Oklahoma officers about you," and that "you made a number of friends among the law enforcement officers while you were working in Oklahoma, and maybe you will be sent back to Oklahoma sometime." Holt, a graduate of the FBI National Academy, invited: "If you are ever in Oklahoma City drop by the office and visit with us."

Also in the return mail was a letter on official stationery from Chief of Police Homer Gosnell of Ada. I had had a running joke with the officers of this department over my Eastern pronunciation of Ada, which Grapp exploited to contend they were laughing behind my back. "We at the Police Department treated this as a joke and had a great deal of fun out of teasing you about the pronunciation of Ada," said the chief. "But we of the Ada Police Department have a lot of respect for you and enjoyed working with you very much." The letter assured me a warm welcome any time I could manage a visit. The agent who succeeded me in covering the Ada department subsequently wrote to advise that Gosnell had called him into his office, declared that he considered me "one of the best agents that had ever called on the department," and said that if the Bureau held otherwise they were badly mistaken.

As documents obtained under FOI later disclosed, Gosnell's candid letter landed him on the Bureau's blacklist. Orders were forwarded advising the Oklahoma City office "not to schedule any future police for the Ada Police Department" and asserting that "the Bureau will not favorably consider any applications for the [FBI] National Academy from the Ada Police Department."

During this period a number of notes and letters from Oklahoma City agents arrived giving reports and suggestions. Inspector H. Lynn Edwards had been in Oklahoma retracing the steps of Chief Inspector Roy Moore in his "thorough" investigation of our allegations; he learned, it was disclosed, that Moore had conducted practically all of his inquiry by telephone with Grapp at his elbow. Most important, some twenty agents and stenographers had been instructed to prepare affidavits on me; then they were told to rewrite them to include opinions of Grapp; and finally they were told to supply a third set *leaving out* their opinions of Grapp. The communications from Oklahoma all closed with hortatory comments such as "don't let the bastards wear you down."

From these sources I obtained the names of ten former FBI agents who might have relevant testimony. Again, I was not overly optimistic, because few "exes" dared jeopardize their jobs by criticizing the Bureau. Out of the ten, six replied. Two said that because they were still in law enforcement they could not volunteer testimony on my behalf. Both suggested, however, that I have them subpoenaed, in which event they would let it all hang out. But the civil service format did not allow for subpoenas.

The information supplied by a third could not have been used within the somewhat narrow quasi-judicial confines of the hearing.

The remaining three supplied no-punches-pulled affidavits. One had been a thirteen-year veteran with a Bureau-wide reputation for cultivating a network of criminal informants, one of whom had fingered a badly wanted Top Ten Fugitive. So outstandingly had he performed that he had been awarded an unprecedented four meritorious increases in salary plus innumerable commendations from Hoover. But in Kansas City he had run afoul of Grapp and had been transferred to Savannah, where he had resigned. His narration bore striking similarities to my own experiences.

The second had been an agent for five years. He had resisted pressures to resign his Naval Reserve commission. Two days before he was to defy Bureau policy by going on two weeks of annual training duty with the Navy, he was suspended without pay for thirty days on what he claimed was a trumped-up charge of "sending an uncoded radio message." Placed under Grapp in Oklahoma City, he contended he came under a campaign of harassment that culminated in a demand by the SAC that he resign or "something would be found to get me fired on." With his mother in the hospital on the danger list, and on the "verge of nervous breakdown" himself, he resigned. It was accepted *with prejudice,* although congressional intercession later had the phrase deleted.

The third man was the only one I had met personally; the occasion had been an in-service class two years before. He had been a radio technician and special agent for an aggregate of nineteen years, and was a living rebuttal to Chief Inspector Moore's subsequent boast at the hearing that agents who resigned were lured away by offers "two or three times their FBI salary." Mild-mannered and uncontentious, he had somehow incurred Grapp's displeasure to the point where he had quit in disgust with no other job in the offing. It was he, ironically, whose departure created the sound man vacancy that precipitated my transfer to Oklahoma City.

How the FBI discovered that Fred Howell, as we shall call this third man, had sent me a bombshell seventeen-page affidavit is a story in itself. Howell was asked to come into the Chicago office, where he was cordially greeted by SAC James Gale and Inspector Edwards. They informed him that his name had come up with regard to an incident in the contract garage in which Grapp allegedly had insisted upon the same discount for his personal car as had been contractually afforded official cars. Howell calmly informed them, "I have furnished Mr. Turner a seventeen-page signed statement."

Their reaction, according to Howell, was first one of shocked disbelief, then of agitation. "You don't owe Bill Turner anything," Edwards reportedly exclaimed. "But you owe it to the Bureau to inform us of the contents of your letter so that the Bureau can investigate the matter." This was strange, since the Bureau still insisted it had checked it all out "thoroughly." Commented Howell in reporting the incident to me: "It was soon evident to me that his sole purpose was to discount and contradict your allegations against the Bureau and to protect Mr. Grapp." The voluntary visit turned into a three-hour grilling in which Howell "felt like I was being treated as a criminal." He outlined what he had said in the affidavit, which brought a rejoinder from Edwards that he should have reported the information while still in the Bureau. "If I had," retorted Howell, "I would have been fired like Turner."

Edwards admonished Howell not to inform me of the "interview," and demanded that he send the Bureau a copy of the affidavit. Howell obeyed neither demand.

The Bureau privately recognized that Grapp had fumbled the Howell matter. According to the FOI files, it was recommended that, although no disciplinary action be taken against him at the time, "his weakness in handling personnel should be forcefully discussed with him at the conclusion of the Turner case."

On July 20, Edwards took the afternoon plane from Chicago back to Washington. Three days later I received an anonymous letter dated July 21 and postmarked Washington. It was poorly typed on drugstore stationery:

> Have learned of your present situation and as a Friend have a suggestion to make to you —
>
> Write Director letter stating perhaps misunderstanding on both sides and request reinstatement with understanding you will resign 48 hrs afterwards. This would protect your personal record in future years and save time & money.

I doubted that the author of the letter quoted above was any "Friend" of mine. The timing was too exquisite and the terms were too explicit to have been the work of an ordinary agent. I could envision an assistant director pecking away on a typewriter after the stenographers had gone for the day.

After some unaccountable delay—Elliott would only say there were "legal problems"—the hearing began on a hot Monday morning in October 1961. Skip Gibbons had flown in from Butte at his own time and expense. He, attorney Vince Fuller, and I took a cab to the ancient granite-pile building where the hearing would be held. We were a few minutes late, and the Bureau representatives were already sitting stiffly in their seats on one side of a long table. There were eight: Assistants to the Director John Mohr and Cartha DeLoach, an unidentified subaltern who was apparently their walking file cabinet, Chief Inspector Roy Moore, Inspector Edwards,

Grapp, Rex Shroder, and Henry Onsgaard, who had succeeded Shroder as Assistant SAC at Oklahoma City.

There had been a recent article in *National Geographic* called "The FBI, Public Friend Number One" that had carried a portrait of Hoover, Clyde Tolson, Mohr, DeLoach, and the assistant directors, all conservatively attired, sitting primly at a table in the Director's office. Skip nudged me. "Just like *National Geographic*," he quipped.

The hearing went on for four days as the fan droned, moving the air only slightly in the stifling room. As a witness, Skip had to sit outside, and I felt a little lonely against the array of brass across the table. DeLoach stared gloweringly at me, as if to say, "Who are *you* to contest the great FBI?"

It turned out that DeLoach was there to rebut my charge in the letters to Congress that the FBI had been lax in contesting organized crime, as illustrated by the cold shoulder it gave the attorney general's Special Group formed to investigate the mob elite who had attended the 1957 Apalachin conference. In his dismissal letter, Hoover had insisted the FBI had cooperated to an extent "proper and consistent with our jurisdiction," and that I was "impertinent, immature, and indiscreet" in alleging otherwise.

Yet Richard Ogilvie, who had headed the Chicago phase of the Special Group's drive (and was later the governor of Illinois), had publicly declared that the FBI was uncooperative, and added the final indignity that it was "outmoded in its operations." Mohr branded Ogilvie an "enemy of the Bureau." I introduced passages from three articles, "Why the Crime Syndicates Can't Be Touched" by Gerald Goettel, who had headed the New York probe of the Special Group, "The Private Government of Crime" by Daniel P. Moynihan, and "Treasure Chest of the Underworld: Gambling Inc." by Fred P. Cook, all of which supported my view of an FBI laissez-faire policy on organized crime.

DeLoach took the stand in a perfervid denial, citing that the FBI had furnished 1,588 pages of reports to the prosecution of the Apalachin mobsters. But when asked by Vince Fuller if he knew how much of this volume was of actual use, he had to say no. When DeLoach continued to rant about Hoover's impeccable reputation and the FBI's high esteem, Fuller objected. The hearing examiner sustained it, instructing the Bureau official to limit himself to answering the questions.

More fireworks were ignited when we offered into evidence the three ex-agent affidavits. Mohr, acting as FBI counsel, vehemently objected on the grounds they were irrelevant, but he was overruled. Then we requested that the Bureau be ordered to produce the affidavits taken from the employees in Oklahoma City. Mohr seemed surprised that we even knew about them. He argued against it, but was again overruled.

Mohr's consternation was understandable. Here were his own FBI agents flatly contradicting the charge that I was "sulking and pouting" and dragging my heels. All affiants agreed that I had casually remarked that I would not personally prefer the Oklahoma City assignment, which was no secret. But all concurred that this did not impinge on my work. Said one: "I did not receive the impression from S.A. Turner that he was disgruntled or that he did not intend to carry out his Bureau responsibilities to the best of his ability." Another stated: "He always appeared personable and in good humor, and on the few occasions I worked with him, I found him to be a competent agent who created a good impression upon all with whom he came in contact."

So uniformly favorable to me were these affidavits that the Bureau reportedly became concerned that a conspiracy was in the making. Their authors were dispersed via transfer to such widely scattered posts as Minneapolis and New Orleans.

What I didn't know at the time was that the Bureau had also taken affidavits from a number of the stenographic and clerical personnel in Oklahoma City. As revealed by FOI documents, these women without exception agreed that I had been, as one put it, "a fine Bureau representative." I had been upbeat and cooperative, they said, always taking my work seriously. In fact Grapp's own secretary declared, "He never gave any indication to me that he was disgruntled. I never heard him express any dissatisfaction with his assignments. He made a fine appearance, was always pleasant and conducted himself in a gentlemanly manner."

This was not what John Mohr wanted to hear, and he became the disgruntled one. The women were not subject to transfer so he did the next worst thing: he instructed that they were not to be given pay raises or promotions unless personally approved by him.

With the introduction of the letters from Oklahoma law enforcement officers, the Bureau's case started coming apart at the seams. The destruction was accelerated by a set of documents illustrating that the "baseless" charges Skip and I had made against Grapp were not so ephemeral after all. One was an affidavit from Inspector Edwards reporting his interview with the owner of the former contract garage in Oklahoma City. Grapp was known by garage personnel as "Mr. Gripes," the owner was quoted as saying, because he was "overbearing and much too demanding." That Grapp had attempted to secure the government discount for his personal car was confirmed by the owner.

Affidavits executed by the new Oklahoma SAC, Lee Teague, and an agent also verified the police photographer incident. Grapp had been displeased with the quality of a photograph of himself and, one affidavit read, had telephoned the photographer "in what he considered an overbearing, demanding manner inquiring as to why the photograph had not turned out properly." The photographer had reminded the SAC that he was not one of his own employees and therefore did not have to take "this verbal abuse." He said he had known many FBI agents over the years and Grapp was the only one he hadn't liked.

The photograph in question was included by Grapp in his own exhibits for the hearing. Taken in his office, it showed him standing before an American flag and beaming at his mother. All that was missing was a piece of apple pie on the desk.

It also developed that Inspector Edwards had learned a thing or two from the Air Force lieutenant colonel that Inspector Moore had somehow missed. There had been between Grapp and the Office of Special Investigations (OSI) at Travis Air Force Base, which the colonel headed, a dispute over jurisdiction in a base burglary case. According to the colonel, Grapp had summoned him to his office and chewed him out in a manner "that I would never forget about him as a person." Because of this, the officer chose to limit his contact with the SAC, although he continued equitable relations with other personnel of the FBI.

At the hearing, Grapp assumed the stance that everyone else was wrong. He contended that the contract garage owner's "memory is extremely faulty," that statements attributed to him by the police photographer were "in error" or a "figment of his imagination," and that the Air Force colonel had taken a "gratuitous last shot" at him.

As for the bird-hunting expedition in the Bureau car during which he was stopped by the Oklahoma Highway Patrol, Grapp minimized the incident by ticking off the various official duties he said he performed en route. Grapp said he had been doing between fifty and fifty-five miles per hour—the site was a fifty-five-mile zone—and pointed out that he had distinctive antennae on his car, raising the presumption that the patrolman had stopped him for a social visit. But I had sent a telegram to the patrolman, who responded that to the best of his recollection he had clocked Grapp on radar at about eighty-five miles per hour. That he had pulled the SAC over with his flashing light and asked for his driver's license did not indicate that the encounter at least started out on a social plane.

Perhaps the most eye-opening testimony was that of Chief Inspector Roy Moore. On cross-examination, Vince Fuller gradually sketched the token investigation he had conducted of the charges Skip and I had made. Some charges he had merely submitted to Grapp for explanation. Others he had resolved by reviewing files. One concerned a rift between Grapp and an Oklahoma sheriff who had accused him of hogging publicity in a bank robbery case. Fuller asked Moore if "there had indeed been a dispute between the sheriff referred to by Mr. Turner, and SAC Grapp, irrespective of who was right or who was wrong in the dispute." The reply was hostilely dogmatic: "The question as you have framed it, and the use of the word 'dispute' in any technology, is misleading. *The sheriff made a complaint which was unfounded* [italics added]."

Moore admitted that he had taken negative hearsay statements from Oklahoma City agents, for example, that they knew nothing about any demand for discount at the contract garage made by Grapp, but that these agents were "not instructed to conduct the investigation on their own" as it pertained to specific facts. Regarding his own failure to check out all of our allegations, Moore declared that consideration was given to "what embarrassment might ensue in making checks on the heads of an office with outside agencies wherein it was hearsay evidence."

"Do I understand," asked Fuller on a note of incredulity, "that it is not the policy to run out leads in the event action would embarrass the Bureau?"

Hoover, who was closely following the proceedings, noted on a memo from DeLoach reporting on Moore's testimony, "This is exactly what I stated weeks ago would be Fuller's contention but no one believed me."

The tedium of the hearing was broken with Skip's appearance on the stand. His recital of his troubles with the Bureau over the weight program and his run-ins with Grapp, done in his inimitable style, would have brought tears of laughter to a more amusement-minded audience. The climax came with a rendition of the way Grapp, in one of his avuncular moods, had entreated Skip to mend his ways and had repeated a "poem" that preached the futility of trying to change what cannot be changed. Even John Mohr was hard put to contain himself.

But by virtue of his sincere manner and ability to recapture the more ludicrous moments of personnel policy in action, Skip proved a damaging witness to the Bureau. What is more, it must have been excruciating for the FBI officials to see one of their own credentials-carrying agents testifying against them. Skip would obviously have to go. But the thought of another hearing ordeal was apparently more than the Bureau could stand. Shortly after his return to Butte, Skip received a transfer to Alaska. Still he made no move to resign. The stalemate went on for a year, during which Skip advised me that he was being subjected to a campaign of petty harassment.

Skip brought matters to a head by going "over the hill." After what approximated a fugitive hunt, inspectors found him back in Michigan. "What are your intentions?" they asked. "What are yours?" he retorted, forcing the monkey onto the Bureau's back. Someone came up with an ingenious if costly way to get rid of Skip without another hearing. He was given a medical discharge for "nervousness" at a pension of $250 a month. He continued to draw

it for a long time after, while working as a certified ski instructor—
the only officially nervous, government subsidized ski instructor in
the world.

Skip's testimony was the climax of the hearing. That evening we
dined at a restaurant on Pennsylvania Avenue almost across the
street from Bureau headquarters. We felt that we had put on a case
that would have won hands down before a civilian jury, thanks to
the overt and covert assistance of agents past and present and the
sure-handed legal advocacy of Ed Williams and Vince Fuller. Our
only regret was that some agents who had been drawn into the
affair and spoken honestly had suffered retribution. But we knew
that the vast majority of agents were silently behind us. This was
underscored when the waiter informed us our bill had been paid by
a group at another table. Skip had recognized them. "Baltimore
agents," he said.

The summations were anticlimactic. Vince Fuller concentrated
on Inspector Moore's "investigation" at Oklahoma City, punching
out point after point that showed it had not given me "even the consideration afforded a common criminal."

Mohr, for the FBI, opened with the contention that the agency
"would not have taken its action against Mr. Turner had he not
embarked upon this letter-writing career of his," which clashed with
his earlier statement that "If we had enough to fire Mr. Turner in
Oklahoma City, we would have preferred charges against him
then." Without overstatement, the Bureau official declared that I
was "not satisfied with Mr. Hoover as Director of the FBI"—the
unthinkable thought. Then came the characteristic Bureau absolutism: "[Turner] has aligned himself with so-called enemies of the
FBI. There are many, many friends of the FBI but of all the people
he has selected to align himself with are two enemies of ours; name-
ly, Mr. Ogilvie and Mr. Goettel [of the attorney general's Special
Group]; and I think in that respect, that he has demonstrated that
he is unsuitable."

Thus ended the long struggle in which I had forced my own firing in order to secure a forum of reinstatement. Had the commission ruled in my favor, I would have shown up at a field office,
taken back my badge, gun, and credentials, and promptly resigned. I

had made my point, and had no more taste for the quibbling that marked engagements with the Bureau. I headed for San Francisco, where I started in business.

Civil service didn't formally hand down its decision until months later. It threw out nine of the fourteen specifications the Bureau had intended to support its four overall charges. Of the four charges, only two were sustained. But those two, the commission held, were sufficient to warrant the Bureau's action.

The first concerned alleged "untrue or unjustified statements" in the letters to Congress. The commission ruled, for instance, that I had not been untruthful, contrary to the Bureau's claim, in stating that "retaliation" had been taken against me as a result of a request for transfer. Then it turned around and denominated my statement that "morale in the Bureau is at an all-time low" as "irresponsible," as the FBI contended. Since morale is an abstract condition and hence a matter of opinion, such a judgment seemed to me to be beyond definitive bounds. But the overriding point was that all my statements were made in the context of asking Congress to investigate the FBI and see for themselves—not to take my word for it—which the commission apparently missed. Moreover, the constitutional issue I had raised with the dictum that my personal letters to Congress were "none of the Bureau's business" had been deftly skirted with a "short answer" that tenure in government employment is not a right—the old shibboleth of the McCarthy days.

The second sustained charge was that I had "shown a poor attitude toward the Federal Bureau of Investigation and its Director." In other words, I had rocked the boat violently, a cardinal sin in bureaucratic eyes. In my estimation, this was the crux of it, reflecting back as it did to Congressman Dulski's remark that the commission could not possibly rule in my favor because of the precedent it would set. Right or wrong, Hoover was the boss, and it was not my prerogative to challenge the manner in which he was discharging his public trust.

It was not over yet. Ed Williams filed an appeal on my behalf with the U.S. District Court in Washington. Since the courts do not review the merits of the case—the commission's adjudications would remain intact—the brief was confined to the narrow but

immensely important area of constitutional protection. The First
Amendment guarantees the right "to petition the government for a
redress of grievances." This basic precept had been dilated by Title
5, United States Code, Section 652(d), which affirmed that the
"right of government employees to petition Congress, or any member thereof, or to furnish information to either House of Congress,
or to any committee or member thereof, shall not be denied or inter-
fered with."

Our argument was that the FBI's action and the commission's
confirmation of it was not only in clear violation of the First
Amendment and the federal law, but that "the right of Congress to
information without interference from the executive branch" had
been infringed and imperiled. Not unexpectedly, District Judge Bur-
nita Mathews ruled without opinion in the government's favor. The
luck of the draw was not any more auspicious at the court of
appeals level: the panel assigned the case was weighted with two
wizened conservatives, one of whom retired immediately afterward.
They outvoted Judge Charles Fahy, who had been solicitor general
under Roosevelt, again without opinion. In an eight-page dissent,
Fahy concluded that the removal had been effected in a manner
"inconsistent with the protection accorded by Congress in Section
652(d), and by the First Amendment."

During the October 1964 term of the Supreme Court, Ed
Williams petitioned for a writ of certiorari that would permit a full
hearing. Williams maintained that a "substantial question of constitutional and federal statutory law is presented," one that had not
been answered by the mute district and appellate court judges.
"More likely than not," he reasoned, "government employees
would decline under any circumstances either to petition for redress
of grievances or to make disclosures to Congress, for fear of
reprisals from their superiors such as resulted to petitioner herein."

The Supreme Court turned down the petition, which is the case
with the majority it receives. Williams later confided that Chief Justice Earl Warren and Associate Justices William O. Douglas and
William J. Brennan, Jr., wanted to grant the writ, and needed one
more vote. Since the court was divided along conservative-liberal
lines on this issue, the swing vote seemed to be Hugo Black, who

many years before had made the transition from archconservatism to mild liberalism. But this was just at the time that Black began to swing back again, and he finally refused to join in. Yet there had been a technical problem that might have been the cause of rejection. Williams had filed the petition a day late—he had called me and apologized—and the Supreme Court was a stickler on timeliness. According to files obtained under FOI, the Bureau was aware of the tardy filing and considered it entirely possible the victory was a gift.

On the face of it, my whole effort to bring about congressional inspection of the FBI and concomitant reforms seemed to have been futile, indeed counterproductive. The whole stark and vivid transcript of the hearing was put into repose in the musty archives of the commission, and the FBI resumed business as usual. Congress remained supine, the courts deaf. As the *Yale Law Journal* commented on the case in May 1965, the failure of the courts to spell out the restrictions they obviously attached to communicating with the Congress left "uncharted waters" into which government employees could venture only at maximum peril.

On the other hand, Skip and I did succeed in cracking the hermetic seal the FBI had so jealously guarded, permitting some air to rush in. The record was there and available to researchers and Congress. General Billy Mitchell was court-martialed by the Army, but time proved that his version of air power was the right one. James Boyd was labeled a "disgruntled ex-employee" and threatened with criminal action by adherents of Senator Thomas Dodd, but in the end the senator stood convicted of misappropriation of funds by his colleagues. There later were encouraging signs that Hoover's immunity, so absolute in 1961, was beginning to fade. In the context of that time my description of the FBI as an "autocratic empire isolated by myth from outside inspection" seems outrageously impious, but it is really no different in meaning than Senator Eugene McCarthy's 1968 campaign remark that Hoover was running his own "fiefdom," which at that time was a dangerous thing.

PART TWO

THE DIRECTOR

CHAPTER FIVE
THE MAN

There, but for the grace of God, goes God.
— *Sir Winston Churchill*
of a pompous member of Parliament

Who was J. Edgar Hoover, one of the most durably powerful men in America? The press agent's cardboard figure is familiar: the Director who strides briskly to work, greets Boy Scout troops with wholesome clichés, speaks with arcane wisdom on the dangers of crime and Communism, and relieves the pressure of it all with an occasional trip to the two-dollar window at the racetrack.

But who was Hoover the man?

I met the Man, as his subordinates often referred to him, only once. It was toward the end of new agents' training class, by which time the unsuitables had been weeded out. The occasion was attended by all the briefing and preparation once associated with an audience with the Pope. Our counselors from the training division hovered over us like anxious mothers primping their sons for first communion. Grooming and attire were closely inspected. We had heard that the Director considered red ties a sign of insincerity, and none were in evidence. We were cautioned to carry an extra handkerchief—the Director was inclined to distrust those with moist palms—and not to carry on a conversation unless he initiated it. When all was in readiness, we were arranged in order of ascending height and mustered in the anteroom well ahead of the appointed hour.

Although sturdily built with rather short legs, Hoover was not as abbreviated as generally thought. But the bulldog mien, pursed lips, crooked smile, spatulate nose, and fixed brown eyes were unmistakable. So was his brusque, no-nonsense manner. He talked plosively with machine-gun syncopation. It was said that he could be engaging when he chose. Drew Pearson wrote that "he can also be a boon companion who relishes a good joke, a lively conversationalist who can discourse on an astonishing range of topics, a genial host who personally attends to the wants of his guests." A Pittsburgh agent who once had a conversational interview with him came away impressed with his clinical knowledge of martini stirring. But another agent with an impressive personal record was startled when the Director suddenly interrupted the banalities and roared with fire in his eyes, "We've got to get rid of the slackers!"

The office mirrored the man. One traversed some thirty-five feet of deep pile carpet to reach the polished mahogany desk issued by the General Services Administration. Its surface was adorned by a pair of brass pistol lamps, a potted plant, and a brass plaque inscribed: "Two feet on the ground are worth one in the mouth." Flanking the desktop were two small furled American flags with gold eagle standard-tops and, at center, a small replica of the FBI seal. Against the wall to the rear were two large furled American flags with gold eagle standard-tops; a large replica of the FBI seal hung at center.

The anteroom where visitors waited was a storehouse of the artifacts figuring in FBI lore. The most ghoulish was a white plaster facsimile of John Dillinger's death mask, a sort of Kaiser's mustache with the FBI. There was the straw boater Dillinger was wearing when gunned down, and the Corona-Belvedere cigar from his shirt pocket. Also prominent was the roll of martyrs of the FBI. There was a revolving rack containing more than a hundred newspaper cartoons extolling the exploits of the G-men over the years. And covering the walls—space was practically exhausted—were hundreds of scrolls and plaques bestowed by groups ranging from Bible schools to patriotic organizations, heaping praise on the Director. His awards varied from a 1933 Commander of the Royal Order of the Crown of Romania to a 1961 proclamation designating a J. Edgar Hoover Day in the state of Ohio.

Very early in life Hoover exhibited the traits that led him to this veritable throne room. As a boy he was called "Speed" by his companions, and the nickname stuck as he developed into a young man

very urgently on the make. He came from a civil servant family of
modest means—until his death in 1922 his father, Dickerson N.
Hoover, was in charge of printing reports for the Coast and Geodet-
ic Survey. It was his mother, Annie, who was the magisterial figure
in the household, dispensing a dour brand of discipline that rewarded good and punished evil.

The religious influence was strong in young Hoover's life. He
sang in the Presbyterian church choir and taught a Sunday-school
class, dressing in a cadet uniform and enunciating the verities in a
crisp cadence that impressed his listeners. At one point he pondered
the ministry, and the strict moral certitude ingrained in him was one
of the most pronounced traits of his adult life. He was a black-and-
white absolutist on personal conduct, a bit straitlaced and prudish.
If this Calvinistic bent stemmed from his Swiss forebears, it
remained intact in mid-twentieth-century America. Dr. Edward L.R.
Elson, pastor of the National Presbyterian Church, where he wor-
shiped, once reminisced: "His most cherished possessions are the
finger-worn Scriptures of his mother and the New Testament he
won for Bible work."

But piety turned into aggressiveness on the playing fields. He
participated informally in football, and later took up golf and tennis. But he gave up activity in sports when he could not master them
in a minimum of time.

The family was tight-knit. There were a brother, Dickerson, Jr.,
fifteen years his senior, who went on to the Steamboat Inspection
Service and retired in the 1930s, and a sister, Lillian. Lillian's son,
Fred G. Robinette, became an FBI agent in 1942 and stayed just
long enough to win his ten-year key. He left with some sharp words
with his uncle over personnel policies, and became high up in the
inspection division of the Internal Revenue Service. But the quarrel
was patched up, and in 1968 a son, Fred Robinette III, was personally sworn in by Hoover and dispatched to Minneapolis.

Hoover was especially close to "Mother" Hoover and continued to live with her in the modest stucco family dwelling on Seward
Square until her death in 1938. In her declining years she was an
invalid, and he provided her with a nurse. "Yet curiously," wrote
Drew Pearson and Jack Anderson in the January 1969 *True*, "he

never contributed a cent to the care of his sister, Lillian Robinette, who also spent her last years as an invalid. He left all the cost and worry to her son, Fred, then a lowly agent on the FBI payroll. When Fred's wife became pregnant, Fred went into debt to hire a nurse for his mother. The neighbors in Lanham, Maryland, where the Robinettes lived, wondered aloud why Lillian's famous brother didn't help out."

At Central High, young Hoover plunged into his studies with characteristic vigor. He attained high grades and was offered a scholarship by the University of Virginia, but enrolled instead at George Washington University night school so that he could work days as a clerk in the Library of Congress (it has been said that his library experience formed the basis for the FBI's meticulous filing system). In 1916 he obtained a law degree with honors, and a year later took his master's.

In 1917 he entered the Department of Justice as a clerk. In his 1937 *New Yorker* profile, Jack Alexander accounted for Hoover's mercurial rise: "From the day he entered the Department, certain things marked Hoover apart from the scores of other young law clerks. He dressed better than most, and a bit on the dandyish side. He had an exceptional capacity for detail work, and he handled small chores with enthusiasm and thoroughness. He constantly sought new responsibilities to shoulder and welcomed chances to work overtime. . . . His superiors were duly impressed, and so important did they consider his services that they persuaded him to spend the period of the World War at his desk."

This, then, was the ambitious young bureaucrat whom Attorney General Harlan F. Stone tapped for the directorship in 1924 as the Coolidge administration started its cleanup. There was only one thing missing, a prerequisite that, in the light of later events, was sadly overlooked. As the chief of an investigative agency, Hoover had absolutely no investigative experience in the field.

This delinquency was brought home in rather rude fashion by Senator Kenneth D. McKellar in the course of the 1936 appropriations hearings. Was it true, he baited, that Hoover had never personally made an arrest? It was—but not for long. At the time the most irritating burr under the Bureau saddle was Alvin ("Kreepy")

Karpis, dubbed by the Director "Public Rat Number One." Karpis had evaded an elaborate FBI trap at an Atlantic City hotel by scurrying down the fire escape in his underwear, and had slipped another net at Hot Springs, Arkansas. G-men finally pinned him down in a Canal Street rooming house in New Orleans. Agents kept the place under surveillance until Hoover could grab a plane south. While the story of his first "pinch" was widely told, Bureau old-timers could recall that it was Norman H. McCabe who actually put the arm on the fugitive. No one had brought any handcuffs, and Karpis's wrists had to be tied with an agent's necktie. Karpis himself was bemused by the fiction. In his memoirs he recalled seeing Hoover peep around a corner of a building and move in when one of the agents shouted, "Come on, Chief! We got him! You can come out now!"

The same gaucheness marked a later Hoover sally into the field when agents had remnants of the Roger Touhey gang holed up in an apartment. The impulsively courageous chief wanted to rush the stronghold, but was physically restrained by more experienced hands until a more ingenious plan could be worked out.

But if all the gunplay and derring-do that trademarked the G-men of that era now seem a bit camp, it was the stuff that catapulted Hoover into fame. Foppishly dressed, he showed up frequently at Manhattan night spots and sporting attractions such as the Melrose games and boxing matches. Something of a poseur, he was photographed signing an autograph for a curly-locked Shirley Temple, firing a machine gun, biting into a "G-man sandwich" at Lindy's, and chumming it up with such luminaries as ex-Oklahoma bootlegger Sherman Billingsley, maestro of the Stork Club, Toots Shor, Jack Dempsey, and Walter Winchell, who hardly let a column slip by without a Hoover anecdote.

In those days New York was Hoover's playground, a surcease from the deadly routine of Washington. He traveled first class, putting up at the St. Moritz and later at the Waldorf-Astoria, which gave him a free suite. Among his circle of friends were newsmen and Broadway columnists, and they twitted him incessantly on his crime-busting fame. Jack Alexander recounted one occasion when Hoover was holding forth at the Versailles with Quentin Reynolds and Heywood Broun, then in their sportswriting days. "Edgar, I think it's about time you were told that Mrs. Broun has been receiving threatening letters," confided Reynolds. "What!" exclaimed the FBI chief, leaping to his feet. "We'll get right after that. Have you any idea who's sending them?" "Yes," said Reynolds dryly. "The grocer."

Hoover assertedly laughed as heartily as anyone at the joke. In fact, there is evidence that at this stage he didn't take himself or other public personalities all that seriously. In his memoirs, FDR's attorney general, Francis Biddle, told how Hoover used to regale him with gossipy exposés of other cabinet members. "Edgar was not above relishing a story derogatory to an occupant of one of the seats of the mighty, particularly if the great man was pompous or stuffy."

But the Director apparently began to read his own press clippings, for his ego began to dominate. He crossed Toots Shor's off his list because the ribbing there was a bit heavy. He became piqued when after a very social cocktail party his Cadillac was delayed by a line of those belonging to lesser lights. He stalked from a reception given by a wealthy industrialist when informed that the host's nephew, an ordinary FBI agent, was also present.

This snobbishness toward underlings was exemplified in 1955 when the New York office moved into its quarters at 201 East Sixty-ninth. The premises, leased for $325,000 a year, were fitted with a posh office for the Director's personal and exclusive use (although he was rarely seen in it). The landlord threw a housewarming cocktail party, but the agents were cleared out and only Hoover, Bureau officials, and their guests attended. Not long afterward Hoover and Tolson were driving around with the well-known orchestra leader Lawrence Welk in the FBI Cadillac when the guest felt the call of nature. The New York office was nearby. But the only facilities were the men's rooms used by—horrors!—the agents. So Hoover ordered a private toilet built adjacent to his private office (the cost was $3,000), just as he had a private toilet in his Washington office.

(In their turn, the agents delighted in repeating irreverencies built around the Hoover doxologies. Example: *The Director is never wrong.* New York agents cornered a Top Ten fugitive at a subway entrance. A brief skirmish ensued. One agent was grazed in the leg by a bullet and taken to the hospital for observation. The report to Washington got garbled. The next morning, Hoover appeared as scheduled before a civic group. "Gentlemen," he began, "I am with you this morning even though my heart is heavy, for last night in New York one of my agents was killed in a gun battle." The Director's words got back to New York, and agents drew straws to see who would go up to the hospital and finish off the wounded agent. *The Director is superhuman.* Hoover and Tolson were in a beach cabana while in Florida for the winter racing season. It was late in the afternoon. Tolson stuck his head out and peered up and down the deserted beach. "It's all clear, Ed," he announced. "But do you really think you can walk on water?" *In the same vein.* Hoover instructed Tolson to hunt up a cemetery plot for him. Tolson reported back that he had found a beautiful one with a sweeping view of the Potomac. "How much?" "Three thousand dollars." "Too much," snapped Hoover. "You know I'm only going to be there three days.")

Some employees were not above pandering to the Man's vanity. It was common for agents to solicit his autographed picture, send congratulations on his anniversaries, and purchase his books through Bureau discounts. One SAC I knew kept up a steady stream of notes to him, advising him of flattering remarks passed by local citizens. But the prize was the SAC in Miami who had one of his agents, flying to Washington, carry on his lap a birthday cake for Hoover.

Harnessed to this patronage, however, was a tendency toward vindictiveness. An exhibition of this trait took place in a hotel in La Jolla, California, around 1950. The Director arrived for dinner just as the dining room was closing. The maître d' refused to seat him, explaining that he didn't want to keep the help after hours. In a rage, Hoover directed the San Diego SAC to open "security" cases on the maître d' and the help. They were summoned to the FBI office and questioned about their patriotism.

After those careless New York days, the Director's social contact was limited to the political and economic upper crust. Among the Fourth Estate, his friends included Walter Trohan, the venerable

chief of the *Chicago Tribune*'s Washington bureau, columnist and
TV personality Ed Sullivan, and, of course, Walter Winchell. Others
numbered George E. Allen, the self-styled companion of presidents
who was a golfing partner of Dwight Eisenhower, and Charles Edi-
son of New York, a retired power company executive who was an
editorial advisor to the Birch Society's magazine *American Opinion*
and a benefactor of many ultraconservative causes.

Hoover was especially close to Senator Joseph McCarthy. "I've
come to know him well, officially and personally," he said of the
Wisconsin witch-hunter. "I view him as a friend and I believe he so
views me." Although the ardor cooled as the senator's drinking
grew heavier, the Director remained on good terms with Roy Cohn,
McCarthy's boy wonder legal counsel who stayed in the news as a
business wheeler-dealer. Cohn, incidentally, was a lawyer for Schenley Industries, whose chairman of the board and majority stock-
holder, Lewis S. Rosensteil, was an unabashed Hoover fan. Rosensteil's charitable foundation bought 25,000 copies each of *The FBI
Story* and *Masters of Deceit* for distribution to educational institutions, an underwriting worth over $100,000. To complete the fami-
ly picture, Assistant Director Louis B. Nichols was hired by Rosensteil as the firm's executive vice president following his FBI retirement in 1957.

Just how tight-knit this relationship was, was shown when
Hoover transferred three New York agents in May 1969 as punishment for cooperating with U.S. Attorney Robert M. Morgenthau in
his prosecution of Cohn on conspiracy, mail fraud, extortion,
bribery, and blackmail charges. At Morgenthau's request, the agents
submitted affidavits denying any knowledge of an alleged scheme to
entrap Cohn. According to William Lambert in *Life,* September 6,
1969, "The agents' affidavits were filed with the court last April.
Cohn promptly turned his copies over to Nichols, who charged into
the Washington headquarters of the Bureau demanding that the
agents be censured. Hoover personally ordered the three agents
transferred out of New York." Morgenthau was "furious" and confronted John F. Malone, the assistant director who headed the New
York office. Malone, naturally, reported back to Hoover, who then
directed that the wayward agents leave town by midnight the fol-

lowing day. The episode, said Lambert, "thoroughly shook up some of Morgenthau's witnesses" with the idea, "If Cohn, through Nichols, could bring about arbitrary transfer of three FBI agents, what chance had an ordinary citizen?"

On his California swings, Hoover socialized with Alfred Hart, president of the City National Bank of Beverly Hills. Hart was in the liquor business. At one time he was an executive of Gold Seal Liquors of Chicago, which was cited by the Kefauver Crime Committee as mob-dominated by, among others, Charles ("Cherry Nose") Gioe. Hart later formed a liquor distributorship in the Los Angeles area, where one of his partners was State Senator Ralph E. Swing, who figured in the Artie Samish liquor lobby scandal in the mid-1950s.

Proceedings of the New York State Joint Legislative Committee on Crime, Its Causes, Control and Effect on Society raised a serious question as to what influence Hoover's private friendships had on his public duty. Chaired by Republican state senator John H. Hughes, the committee learned that in the trial of an Al Capone lieutenant, federal agents swore that Lewis Rosensteil had been engaged in a liquor "consortium" during Prohibition with Meyer Lansky, Frank Costello, and Joe Fusco, all major figures in organized crime. Fusco had been named by Kefauver as prominent in Gold Seal Liquors along with, as we have seen, Hoover's friend Alfred Hart. Evidence of a continuing Rosensteil-Lansky relationship came from the liquor executive's fourth wife, Susan Rosensteil. She recounted for the committee that in February 1957 she and her husband

> arrived in Havana [this was pre-Castro] and then we went to the Nacional Hotel and we were escorted up to our suite. We had a very big suite and it was filled with flowers. I thought it was more of a funeral, so I looked at the card and the card said: "Welcome, Supreme Commander to Havana. Meyer and Jake."
>
> So I asked my husband who Meyer and Jake were and he said that is Meyer and Jake Lansky, very good friends of his. . . .
>
> So, in about five or ten minutes, we went right down to

the lobby and the gambling room was off the lobby, and
Meyer Lansky was there waiting our arrival. And he was
very happy to see the Supreme Commander. . . .

As reported in *The Nation,* April 5, 1971, by Hank Messick, an
expert on organized crime who testified before the committee, "The
overriding puzzle to the Hughes Committee was Rosensteil. How,
they asked themselves, can a man be a friend of J. Edgar Hoover on
the one hand and a chum of Meyer Lansky on the other? The question is vital."

Indeed it was, and the answer might go a long way toward
explaining why Hoover was as idle as the Maytag repairman when
it came to organized crime. To his dying day he never admitted that
there was a Mafia, although in 1961 when Attorney General
Robert Kennedy put a gun to his head on the subject he suddenly,
in a fit of semantic nonsense, tried to get himself off the hook by
conceding that there was a Cosa Nostra. In fact the Director was
too close for comfort to the mob. Not only were a number of his
rich playmates dealing with the syndicate—construction tycoon Del
E. Webb, who built the Flamingo Hotel in Las Vegas, comes to
mind—but he was on personal terms with one of the Mafia's top
heavies, Frank Costello. The odd couple was introduced by their
mutual Stork Club pal, columnist Walter Winchell. They reportedly
trysted on benches in New York's Central Park and in the Waldorf-
Astoria Hotel, where both had complimentary suites. One of the
great lines about the top cop and Mafia don came from columnist
Earl Wilson, who gossiped that when Hoover invited Costello to
join him in the Waldorf coffee shop, the mobster growled, "I got to
be careful of my associates. They'll accuse me of consortin' with
questionable characters."

Perhaps Hoover's closest friend was Clinton W. Murchison, Sr.,
the Dallas oil Croesus who died in 1969. With a fortune estimated
at a half-billion dollars, the sawed-off Texan contributed generously
to the campaigns of Joe McCarthy and entertained McCarthy and
Hoover at his La Jolla spa. A Washington representative of the
Murchison interests, I. Irving Davidson, had ready access to
Hoover's office. Davidson was one of the capital's more murkily

colorful operators. He was a registered agent of Haiti, where the Murchisons had a venture called HAMPCO (Haitian American Meat Packing Co.) that Bobby Baker helped promote. Describing him as a "Teamster-connected lobbyist and wide-swinging public relations man," *Life* on May 2, 1969, stated that in 1950 Davidson briefly had as a client Ohio Mafia kingpin Thomas Licavoli, whom he induced "to donate $5,000 to the J. Edgar Hoover Foundation, a pet project of Columnist Drew Pearson aimed at furthering research on the sociological aspects of juvenile delinquency."

On his annual sun and fun sojourns in La Jolla with his alter ego Clyde Tolson, Hoover put up in a hundred-dollar-a-day bungalow (#6) at the Del Charro Motel, owned by Murchison and Sid Richardson of Fort Worth, who if not the world's richest oil baron was certainly the crudest. Murchison simply had the bills for the civil servants picked up by one of the companies in his diverse empire, as Richardson did for his special guests.

The FBI chief returned at least one public favor for his Texas pal, in 1954. Murchison held the lease on the Del Mar racing plant, which was more or less a plaything, since he and Hoover were considered track swingers—that two-dollar limit is another facet of the myth—and he once named one of his nags, with pale humor, J. Edgar Mover. It happened that Murchison and his compatriots were regarded as somewhat *déclassé* by San Diego standards, a slight they set about to rectify by devising a plan whereby track receipts on set days would go to a boys' club they had created for the purpose. Hoover, who was a national director of the Boys' Clubs of America and professed a strong interest in well-behaved youth, lent his prestige to the plan. There were "wonderful people" in racing, he told the San Diego *Morning Telegraph,* and the profit to the boys' club "helps directly in making the nation sturdy, for Communist penetration is currently directed mainly at labor organizations and youth organizations." The endorsement evidently lured General "Howling Mad" Smith, the Marine Corps superhero of World War II who had retired in the area, into throwing his weight behind the project. But the general later became howling mad again when he couldn't detect the promised profits flowing into the boys' club coffers.

The scene at the Del Charro during the Hoover-Tolson annual residency resembled a pool party of the rich and infamous. The hotel's manager at the time, Allan Witwer, recalled that there was an annual barbecue featuring chili that had been flown in from Texas on Murchison's plane. At one such event Sid Richardson greedily finished off a bowl and turned to Hoover. "Edgar," he said, "get off your fat ass and get me another bowl of chili." The Director of the FBI complied. There was a ban against Jews, but Barry Goldwater was allowed in because he had turned Episcopalian. Roy Cohn, Hoover's Stork Club buddy, was not. On one occasion McCarthy showed up with Cohn's bright young understudy, G. David Schine, in tow. Schine was shown the gate. An incorrigible boozer, McCarthy jumped in the pool naked and peed outside his cabana. He loved to pose with his arm around the FBI chief.

So wedded was Hoover to his job that he resisted countless lucrative offers from the private sector. He was approached, for instance, to become Commissioner of Baseball and head of the Thoroughbred Racing Association at salaries quadruple what he was making at Level II of the Federal Executive Salary Schedule. He donated at least a portion of royalties from his ghost-written books to the agents' welfare fund, but he did receive such side income as the tax-free $10,000 award from Mutual of Omaha for "contributions to national security and safety." It is said that he did very well in the stock market over the years.

But if Hoover didn't earn all that much, he didn't spend it either. His seven-room home on Thirtieth Place near Rock Creek Park was not pretentious by the section's standards. It was tended by a live-in couple, but the Director did most of the gardening, tending his azaleas in slacks and sport shirt. Each summer when he went to California, the FBI maintenance section gave the house a fresh coat of white paint (one year the agent supervising the painting was given a letter of censure because the paint was slightly off-shade). The section also put in a porch after making full-scale mock-ups of several designs and photographing them so the Director could make a choice.

Once, when Hoover complained that the house had a stale smell when he arrived in the evening, the FBI laboratory custom designed an electronic device that automatically opened the windows after his departure in the morning and lowered them in late afternoon.* It also installed blowers and a duct system to carry away cooking odors. A continuing responsibility of the lab was the television set. One lab man told me that Hoover became impatient because it took time to warm up, so it was altered in such a way that the tubes were always on and the picture leapt instantly to life.**

Hoover's travels, too, drained little from his pocket. In addition to the August "working vacation" in California, he took another with Tolson over Christmas when the Gulfstream and Hialeah parks were in operation. The government picked up the transportation tab. When the Director arrived in his hotel room, there was a bottle of Grant's scotch and two dozen American Beauty roses, courtesy of the local office (the money usually came from the FBI Recreational Association, funded by employees' dues).

It was an unwritten code that the SAC of the office favored by a Hoover-Tolson visit find some way to take care of the hotel bill if the hotel itself was not so gracious. Some years ago in Denver, an SAC inadvisedly assessed the agent corps the price of the bill at the Brown Palace Hotel. When an irate wife wrote the Bureau in protest, a smoking teletype ordered the money returned at once. So literally did the SAC take the order that agents were called down late at night to receive their refunds.

So unrelenting was Hoover's insistence on being comped that agents of the New York office, who knew that he stayed gratis at the Waldorf-Astoria when in town, dubbed him "Freddie the Free-

---

*On February 21, 1966, the Times-Post Service reported that the FBI had installed an automatic window open-and-close device in President Johnson's bedroom. "The rumor is that FBI director J. Edgar Hoover gave the device to the White House some time ago after it was invented by associate FBI director Clyde Tolson. The FBI declined to comment."

**In the fall of 1961, one laboratory agent with a master's degree from MIT returned home late at night from an exhausting assignment in New York only to be called by a Bureau official and told to report to the lab early in the morning. The agent unavailingly pleaded to be allowed to report later in the morning. The urgent matter: Hoover's television set was on the blink. Shortly afterward, the agent left the Bureau.

loader." What galled the agents was that if they did the same, they would be severely disciplined. Notes I took during New Agents Class read: "No employee shall accept any rewards or gratuities."

Another perquisite of the office was a fleet of Cadillac limousines. The one in Washington was an elongated armored black vehicle with the undistinguished D.C. tag 510–563. It could be seen frequently at the Laurel and Bowie racetracks in Maryland, a fact that caused a ripple of amusement in 1963 when the clerk of the House of Representatives, a functionary in his own right, was hauled on the carpet for riding in his government Cadillac on junkets to the racetrack. "Why, I see FBI Director J. Edgar Hoover out there all the time," he alibied. "There's nothing wrong about it at all. A lot of people like to spend an afternoon at the track."

When the Johnson administration began its belt-tightening drive in 1965, the long black Cadillac again became an issue. Many government VIPs were compelled to turn in their limousines for less expensive models. But Hoover kept his, on the basis that the president's directive exempted law enforcement officials in the "direct performance" of their work. But according to the *Wall Street Journal,* White House aides were "wondering aloud whether Mr. Hoover personally uses his big car that way and whether the armored car specified for the FBI chief by appropriations laws couldn't be some humbler model."

What no one seemed to notice was that the Director had not one but four of the wheeled status symbols. The Washington vehicle was annually sent to New York and replaced by a brand new one. The "old" one in New York was chauffeured by a black "agent"— he once moonlighted as a cab driver—as was the one in Miami, which was a familiar sight at the racetracks, the hotel in Key Biscayne where the Director stayed (he used to lodge at the Gulfstream Hotel on Miami Beach), and such eateries as Joe's Stone Crab Restaurant in Miami Beach. More than one Key Biscayne resident was bewildered to view the unmistakable form of the FBI Director only slightly disguised in slouch hat and shorts in a local supermarket, his cart being pushed by a very straight G-man.

The fourth Cadillac was stashed in the garage of the Los Angeles office, where, except for tune-up runs, the tarpaulin came off only once a year when the Del Mar season loomed. Here a black father-and-son team who never quite made it to the FBI Academy kept the limousine polished and in top mechanical condition. As was the case in other cities where the Cadillacs were in mothballs until the Director's arrival, a high-salaried agent from the exhibit section flew out to make sure all was in readiness, including bullet-proof glass. I doubt that it would be extravagant to say that, all costs considered, these Cadillacs purred along at something like fifty dollars per mile.

If Hoover disported himself a bit on the road, he was considered something of a social recluse at home. For years Washington hostesses kept him at or near the top of their most-eligible-bachelor lists, but he kept begging off due to the press of business. His name at one time or another was linked by gossip columnists with Ginger Rogers's mother and Cobina Wright, but there is no evidence he ever dated them or others seriously. In later years in office, he was infrequently seen at social functions outside of semiofficial ones such as the 1965 publisher's party to launch *The FBI's Most Famous Cases* by Andrew Tully. One of the few "to melt Washington's frostiest social iceberg," disclosed *Newsweek,* March 3, 1969, was Secretary of State William Rogers, an attorney general under Eisenhower. The magazine touted Rogers as the only known person "who ever got J. Edgar Hoover to come round to [his] home and sing songs around the piano; he has even smiled at the Rogerses."

Nor did Hoover exactly rate as a Renaissance man. His taste in literature ran to the inspirational, as typified by Ralph Waldo Emerson, Edgar Guest, Norman Vincent Peale, and Robert W. Service, who wrote tales of Alaska. Long ago he memorized Kipling's "If." His magazine diet was restricted to the bland *Reader's Digest* and the even blander *U.S. News & World Report,* written in the economized style Hoover preferred. For the news, he relied on the *New York Daily News,* the *Washington Daily News,* and the *Washington Evening Star,* all with a conservative editorial slant. As for the *New York Times,* he disdained it as "the most anti-FBI paper in the country."

Hoover's musical preferences leaned toward light pop and dance numbers. He enjoyed the newspaper comics, especially Dick

Tracy and the detective comics portraying the inevitable triumph of good over evil. But he shunned cops-and-robbers dramas on TV (except ABC's "The FBI") because he didn't consider them realistic.

The television set, flanked by the two Cairn terriers G-boy and Butch (who wore prestigious low-number dog tags Three and Four), was Hoover's main relaxation. His fare was mostly cowboy shows and sports events. "I like football and baseball as spectator sports," he told a San Diego reporter, "and I even look at the wrestling matches on TV—because it's a good show and that's what I like—a good show." He rooted for the Washington Senators and regularly tuned in the Thursday evening wrestling telecasts from the Washington Arena. He apparently was touchy about wrestling histrionics. On his seventieth birthday, ring announcer Bob Freed extended greetings to "our favorite viewer, J. Edgar Hoover." No sooner had he stepped from the ring than Freed was summoned to the telephone and testily informed by an FBI official that the Director did *not* watch wrestling.

Away from Thirtieth Place, Hoover's inseparable companion was the lugubrious Clyde A. Tolson, of whom one writer observed: "Even when he feels good, Tolson looks worried." He joined the Bureau in 1928 and presumably made an instant impression, for he leaped from agent to assistant director in an unheard-of three years. Also a lifelong bachelor, Tolson tagged along with the Director for lunch at the Mayflower Hotel, dinner at Harvey's, and, of course, the races. Understandably, the two had their spats, and at one juncture Tolson threatened to leave. Instead, he brought in an ex-football player with whom he had gone to college as a sort of third man accompanying them on their outings and trips. The man remained on the payroll for twenty years, yet he was an "unperson" never mentioned in FBI lore.

His name was Guy Hottel, and his triangular presence with Tolson and Hoover fueled speculation about the Director's sexual preferences, if any. I was frequently braced at social gatherings, "Is your boss a homosexual?" It was a fair question considering that Tolson was obviously Hoover's significant other. But lacking solid evidence that the relationship included sex, agents simply termed it "unwholesome." To me it really didn't matter except for the fact that Hoover not only preached family values, he bashed homosexuals with a vengeance. They were barred from Bureau employment at any level, and the few who slipped through the screening process simply disappeared when discovered. I recall a strapping married agent who was a member of a special-assignment team I was on. One morning he didn't show up, and we assumed he was sick. But it turned out he had been caught in a homosexual liaison and was quickly and quietly cashiered. The Bureau didn't want any fuss that would attract publicity.

Hoover was never seen in public with a woman on his arm with the lone exception of Ginger Rogers's mother, but she strenuously denied that there was anything romantic between them. On the other hand Tolson was regarded as less platonic when it came to the opposite sex. One of the more colorful stories that circulated about him concerned a trip he took to Havana, before Castro when Cuba was an anything-goes playground. The purpose was to try to rid himself of a nagging winter cold, and it was one of the rare occasions when he was separated from Hoover. As was expected of him, the head of the FBI delegation in the U.S. embassy went all out to ensure that Tolson's stay was as pleasurable as possible. But perhaps beguiled by Havana's sensuality, he went too far. One night after being wined and dined Tolson returned to his hotel room to find a voluptuous Swedish actress there. Suddenly, the FBI's man in Havana was packing for home.

Guy Hottel was a handsome, rambunctious playboy who definitely didn't fit the FBI's cookie-cutter image. Any question of his sexual persuasion was disposed of by the fact that he married four times. Tolson had him stashed down the street as SAC of the Washington field office, where he was on tap to join the recreational excursions. A journalist briefly related to Hottel through one of his marriages described to me a scene that took place following the arrival of the threesome at their Miami Beach hotel to partake of the Christmas horseracing season. After settling in, Tolson and Hottel announced to Hoover that they had female dates that evening. With that Hoover flew into a tantrum, locking himself in the bathroom and banging on the walls. The burly Hottel had to knock in the door and slap around the FBI Director to bring him to his senses.

The Director was a creature of habit. Each morning he was picked up at his home and chauffeured to the office in the big black Cadillac by one of two black "agents" who didn't go to training school. When the weather was pleasant, the chief might get out a mile or so from the office and stride briskly along with Tolson abreast.

The pair marched into the office promptly at nine. An agent factotum, called the SAC of the Director's office, had laid out the mail it had been decided the chief should see. He was ready to brief Hoover on what important matters were pending. Sam Noisette, an aging black "agent" who served as the Director's receptionist for more than three decades, hovered about.

Every Tuesday morning at ten sharp, Hoover and Tolson held a conference with the ten assistant directors. Questions arose: can the Bureau conduct ten thousand security name checks for the Democratic Convention? The group voted, first the assistants, then Tolson and the Director. "If there are eleven nays and one yea," a former assistant director once revealed, "and the yea is Mr. Hoover's, the answer is yea."

This obsequious relationship often produced ludicrous results. The story is told of the time the Director, after a new agents' class had filed through his office, passed the word to the Training and Inspection Division to get rid of "the one that looks like a truck driver." Officials scrutinized the class, finally firing the one they thought Hoover had meant. But a few days later when the Director dropped in on the peanuts-and-Coke graduation party of the class, he drew an official aside and complained: "That truck driver—I thought I told you to get rid of him."

Another incident involved an agent posted to the Director's office whose appearance was not exactly to Hoover's liking. He was ordered transferred. For good measure, officials sent him across the continent to Los Angeles. There he was assigned as liaison man with the motion picture studio filming *The FBI Story*. When the filming was completed, the producers wrote Hoover praising the cooperation of his liaison man. The agent had a common name, and the Director failed to make the connection, ordering a grade raise. No one dared enlighten the chief or inform him that the goat-to-hero agent had just received a raise. So he was given another one.

One of the few ever to stand up to Hoover was Delf A. ("Jelly") Bryce, once SAC at Oklahoma City. A trick shot artist and ex-state law officer, Bryce was not only known throughout the state as Mr. Oklahoma Law Enforcement but was close to Senator Robert Kerr of the Kerr-McGee Oil Company. Hoover and Bryce had a dispute over the status of the local officers the FBI had recruited during the World War II build-up. The Director wanted them out, since most didn't have college degrees and consequently detracted from the image. Bryce was equally firm in maintaining that college degrees didn't mean that much in law enforcement. Bryce went so far as to toss his credentials on Hoover's desk, but the Director meekly handed them back.

There is an endless store of examples of Hoover's vagaries. For example, an agent assigned to London (as legal attaché to the embassy, the customary title) stopped off in Washington for his periodic briefing and interview with the Director. All seemed to go well. But after he left, Hoover, who suffered from mild xenophobia, complained that he had "gone native" and directed that he be pulled back to the United States. It seems that the agent, originally from Boston, had acquired a touch of an English accent on top of his New England twang.

But the Director gave as whimsically as he took away. Once, an agent assigned to headquarters encountered the Director as he got off the elevator en route to his annual appropriations appearance before Congress. "I hope everything goes well on the Hill, Mr. Hoover," the agent sang out. His alertness evidently struck Hoover's fancy, for the agent suddenly found himself boosted to Assistant SAC of the Puerto Rico office. Similarly, when the New York office moved from Foley Square to an uptown location in 1955, the agent assigned to coordinating the move of furniture received an incentive cash award for his smooth performance, as did another agent who had the elevators properly timed for Hoover's ceremonial arrival.

The Director's arbitrary harshness was legend inside the Bureau. Once, when a teen-age clerk who had pimples got on the same elevator—that five-floor vertical shaft seemed to be Hoover's only point of contact with his employees—the repercussions were felt all the way up the line to an assistant director who was forced into premature retirement. Hoover, in fact, had bitter fallings-out with several of his top aides over the years. To one departing assistant director his parting shot was, "You're sick." Of another, he remarked after the man was gone, "I make few mistakes, but as Fiorello La Guardia said, when I do they're whoppers."

One of the most firmly imbedded legends of the FBI was the reputed absolute lack of venality and corruption. The story of how Hoover accepted the directorship only upon the condition that he be allowed to wield a stiff broom has been told and retold. His policies kept the Bureau relatively scandal free, which could also be said of the chiefs of the other federal detective agencies such as the Secret Service. Only one jolt of Richter-scale magnitude hit the Bureau, and that was in the rather distant past before World War II when New York newspapers luridly described a sex-and-liquor scandal that resulted in wholesale firings, resignations, and transfers.

Yet only the closed nature of the FBI society prevented potential scandals from fouling the image. There was the problem of the New York agent who swiped another's paycheck and cashed it. Ordinarily, the crime would have been one for the Secret Service to investigate, since it involved the forgery of a government security. But the Bureau had the lid kept on by quietly presenting the matter to an assistant U.S. attorney who just as quietly declined prosecution. Once, an SAC beat and abused his wife so severely she called the sheriff and begged for protection. The sheriff, an ex-FBI agent, made sure that the affair was kept hushed up. And according to some agents, one high official coerced a field office into purchasing an engine for his personal boat at a cost of about one thousand dollars out of confidential funds covered by a bogus "blue slip" voucher. Since the official was one of Hoover's favorites, no one seemed to know what could be done about it.

There were some drinking episodes that rivaled the best of W. C. Fields. Once, in New York, one official drove another to the train for Washington after they had had a prolonged drinking session. On the way back the tipsy official drove the wrong way up a street and was stopped by the police. He gave them a verbal lashing, so they took him to the station and booked him. The New York office agent who was on duty arranged for the official to be discreetly released, but the Bureau transferred the agent to North Carolina to make sure he didn't spill the beans. The official didn't tell Hoover about the other official he had delivered to the train in a sodden condition (and who had a track record of drunken scenes from Toots Shor's to airliner cabins). Although he spent time in the Bureau's version of purgatory, his silence was rewarded by the second official, who managed to pull him back up the promotion ladder.

On another occasion an inspector scheduled to speak before a large group of attorneys in a western city got so drunk that he couldn't appear. The SAC filled in for him, but later that night the inspector got into his car and ran several red lights before being stopped by police. Two assistant directors ordered the drunken driving and traffic tickets fixed, but Hoover didn't learn about it for several months. Then he sent out a second inspector to the distant city who returned with a phony story that the allegations were untrue. It seems that this inspector had been primed by one of the assistant directors, who was a patron of the malefactor.

This kind of plotting and scheming always went on in the warren of offices at Ninth and Pennsylvania, and was the reason the agents referred to headquarters as Disneyland-on-the-Potomac, or, in more cynical moods, as the House of Horrors. In the Knight Newspapers series on the FBI in December 1964, John McMullan quoted one former SAC who quit: "To move ahead I would have had to return to that palace of intrigue in Washington, and I didn't want to get mixed up in Bureau politics."

But above it all was the immutable Director. After a day of greeting American Legion delegations, Eagle Scouts, and a group from the Savannah YMCA, scrawling "four-baggers" on memo margins, and conferring with his aides, he and Tolson would abruptly leave. The time was usually around five forty-five. As the elevator descended, the telephone operator would buzz the assistant directors one by one with the word, "He has left." Then they could go home.

CHAPTER SIX
THE POLITICIAN

The Bureau must be divorced completely from politics.
> —J. Edgar Hoover
> *in accepting the post of director in 1924*

President Johnson has declared that he does
not intend to replace J. Edgar Hoover. However,
J. Edgar Hoover has not disclosed whether he
intends to replace President Johnson.
> —*Televison's satirical* That Was
> the Week That Was *in 1964*

When J. Edgar Hoover unburdened himself in November 1964, branding Dr. Martin Luther King, Jr., "the most notorious liar in the country," flailing at the Warren Commission for its temerity in criticizing *him,* and taking a swipe at the Supreme Court, which then had a liberal tilt, many pundits predicted that the FBI chief had exceeded himself and that his long stranglehold on the directorship would at last be broken. By ordinary standards this would have been the case: he would have been heaped with honors and turned out to pasture. But it came as an awakening to those who believe in the division of power that our national police chief possessed the most extraordinary political clout. As he himself put it, as quoted by *Newsweek,* he simply wasn't "gettable."

Why not? What had made one man bigger than his office? In the Washington political jungle, Hoover had survived since the days of Calvin Coolidge because he was the fittest of politicians. For one thing, he spun a myth of efficiency spiced with derring-do that no lesser politician dared poke, for the folks back home were mostly true believers. For another, there were the Files, that massive collection of sweepings from the closets of just about everybody who was anybody.

The power concentrated in Hoover's hands increased incrementally as he expanded the scope of his Bureau, which pried into virtually every aspect of our national life. As usual, the legend ran counter to this overweening ambition. Hoover repeatedly protested that Congress kept piling additional responsibilities upon the FBI despite his wishes to keep the agency trim and within bounds. In June 1961, he told *National Geographic* that he often argued "against bringing the FBI into the picture. Sometimes I win; sometimes I lose."

The reluctance may have been genuine when it came to trivial statutes such as illegal use of the Smokey Bear emblem and interstate transportation of unsafe refrigerators. But the Director never fended off the large blocks of jurisdiction. His political power dated to the day in 1936 that President Roosevelt secretly charged him with investigating "subversive activities," transferring him into the realm of probing what a man thought, not what he did.

When the United States decided it had to stay in the espionage game on a permanent basis, Hoover pushed to take over intelligence activities abroad, citing the success of his counterspy operation against the Germans in South America. But Harry Truman, fearing Hoover's wide-ranging ambitions, established the CIA instead. The Director never gave up, however. After the Bay of Pigs, when CIA stock was at rock bottom, he spread the word through Washington that the FBI could and should take over from the CIA. Then, after the Kennedy assassination, which was the Secret Service's blackest hour, he maneuvered behind the scenes to take over that agency's functions. On the other hand, the FBI chief discouraged a tentative proposal by President Johnson in 1967 that the FBI absorb the anti-narcotics duties of the Federal Bureau of Narcotics (FBN), an arm of the Treasury Department. Johnson had figured that the FBI's immense prestige would diminish public apprehension over the drug problem, but Hoover knew that his apple-cheeked agents couldn't improve on the record of the FBN, which had the highest conviction rate of the federal agencies and accounted for nearly 17 percent of

the federal prison population. Moreover, taking on narcotics jurisdiction would have brought him full tilt into the fight against organized crime and its political allies, a scrap for which he has never
shown much stomach.

The hazards of crossing Hoover's path were demonstrated as
early as the Roosevelt administration. The Director was under fire
from a number of liberals, partially because of a now familiar pattern: when the "bonus army" had marched on Washington, Republican President Herbert Hoover had denounced it as composed for
the most part of "criminals or Communists"—based on inside word
passed by his FBI namesake. J. Edgar Hoover's suspicions focused
on Postmaster General James A. Farley, who, the rumor mill had it,
wanted to install one of his friends in the New York police department as director. In an article titled "FBI Spied on Farley" in the
New York Star, September 28, 1948, Guy Richards revealed one
former FBI agent's account of the Director's reaction:

> A tap was put on Farley's office phones. Others were
> put on his homes in Washington and New York. Not only
> that—on several occasions a rotation of different agents
> was assigned the job of trailing Farley. . . . Of course, in
> those days, agents tapping or tailing big shots like Farley
> often were told that their assignments were for the security
> and protection of the subject—that there had been threats
> on their lives, and stuff like that, and that it was being done
> for their own good.

Another erstwhile agent who shadowed Farley to a New Orleans
convention was under no such illusions of benignity. When he
remonstrated with his boss that Farley was "the most simon-pure
guy in public life and that women were strictly out of his range," he
was chided, "Didn't I understand. . . that it was just as important to
get something on Farley's friends as on Farley?"

In later years, electronic eavesdropping provided Hoover with
some of his most potent political ammunition. Once, when a vocal
"law and order" senator was straddling the fence on whether the
FBI should train local police as Hoover wanted, or whether they

should be allowed to train themselves. Via wiretaps, the Director learned that the senator was receiving payoffs from known organized crime figures. The senator was left with no choice on which way to vote.

Another senator who came a cropper via FBI tapping was Edward V. Long of Missouri. In 1966, Long's subcommittee on administrative practice and procedure held nationwide hearings on government wiretapping, bugging, and other extracurricular snooping. After a kickoff hearing in Washington, the senator traveled to his home state, where he laid bare a maze of FBI bugging and tapping in Kansas City done with the connivance of the telephone company. Assistant to the Director Cartha DeLoach paid the senator a visit, after which Long advised his aides, "I don't intend to take on the FBI." The exposures shifted to the IRS, and the Bureau was hardly mentioned again. When the hearings were over, Hoover, who is attentive to such gestures, sent Long a letter praising him for his work.

But Long was living on borrowed time. The FBI had planted an illegal "bug" in aerospace lobbyist Fred Black's hotel, which although it later imperiled the tax evasion prosecution against Black, provided Hoover with all kinds of juicy dollops concerning Washington personalities. One was that Long was splitting legal fees with St. Louis Teamster attorney Morris Shenker; leaked to *Life* magazine, the information was expanded into a story implying that Long was in the Teamster bag. The adverse publicity this generated undoubtedly cost the senator his bid for reelection in 1968.

With taps installed at one time or another on such disparate targets as the French ambassador's home, the Dominican embassy, and the office of columnist Drew Pearson, and with scores of agents eternally poking into the city's crevices, there was practically nothing of political import escaping Hoover's eye. This made him one of the most formidable power brokers in Washington. One of Lyndon Johnson's first requests upon ensconcing himself in the White House was for 1,200 dossiers on his political adversaries from the FBI's supposedly confidential files, plus the Bobby Baker volumes. Hoover, whose time for mandatory retirement was looming (only the president could extend it), was happy to oblige.

After the initial delivery, Hoover kept up a stream of confidential memos filled with titillating insights into political private lives, which it is said Johnson reserved for his bedtime reading. One concerned the prolonged "illicit love affair" Martin Luther King, Jr., was purportedly having with a Los Angeles woman. The president was spared no detail. "[He] calls this woman every Wednesday and meets her in various cities throughout the country," Hoover wrote, attributing the information to a confidential source that could have been a bug. "The source related an incident which occurred some time ago in a New York City hotel, where King was intoxicated at a small gathering. [He] threatened to leap from the thirteenth-floor window of the hotel if this woman would not say she loved him."

Popular fable has it that the Hoover-Johnson friendship stemmed from nothing more than the fact that they were neighbors when Johnson was in the Senate. There is a trove of homey anecdotes, including how Lynda Bird and Luci would knock on the Director's door when the family dog, Little Beagle, was overdue at dinner time and the wearer of Badge Number One would join in the search.

But it was much deeper than that. In a very real sense, Hoover was part of the Texan's political family. Walter Jenkins's brother had long been an FBI agent in Amarillo, and one of LBJ's shirttail relatives moved from Texas state politics to the FBI (despite the fact that he was slightly under the height minimum), where his rise through the ranks was mercurial. And then there was old Clint Murchison, Hoover's bosom pal, who was one of Johnson's earliest political benefactors.

Perhaps it was not wholly coincidental, then, that some of the FBI's most slipshod work came in cases directly affecting Johnson's political fortunes. The Billie Sol Estes scandal was an exemplar. In the summer of 1961, when Johnson was vice president, the Bureau received the initial complaint and began an inquiry. Then Assistant U.S. Attorney Lawrence Fuller said later that the FBI briefed him on a possible violation of the banking act, but that he was forced to decline prosecution because "a violation of the banking act requires that bank officials or employees be involved. There was no evidence anywhere. Actually, I believe it was presented [for prosecutorial

opinion] prematurely." Asked whether he thought he should have
requested the Bureau to make a broader and deeper investigation
into Estes's fertilizer tank dealings, Fuller rejoined, "No. You don't
tell the FBI what to do. They investigate. You either take a case, or
you decline."

But what the FBI couldn't dig up, LBJ's enemies did, and the
whole mess was exposed. According to the *San Angelo Standard-
Times,* April 21, 1962, Frank Cain of Pacific Finance testified under
oath that when he told Estes that the FBI was checking on him,
Estes replied: "I can stop all that. I will get Lyndon Johnson on the
phone," and that same night added, "I've got that investigation
stopped."

Nor was the Bobby Baker probe a model of supersleuthing. The
deal involving the Murchisons' Haitian meat firm involved a rake-
off for Baker, and the investigation was so superficial that the
Nixon administration ordered the matter reopened. Next the FBI
unsuccessfully "looked all over the country" for a former call girl
the Senate Rules Committee wanted to question, but she was turned
up by private detective Richard Bast. Then the FBI files sprung a
leak, and the contents of a classified report concerning the military
record of insurance man Don Reynolds, who was spilling a story
about kickbacks made to get the business of an LBJ property, found
its way into the press. Senator Hugh Scott demanded to no avail an
investigation of the leakage, asserting it had to occur "at the
instance of some person. . . higher than the FBI in government"—
meaning, of course, Lyndon Johnson.

The assassination of President Kennedy brought out the Hoover-
Johnson team at its precision best. As Congress cranked up to investigate the momentous crime, Johnson took over with the announcement that he was forming his own blue-ribbon commission of
inquiry and had asked the FBI to investigate. Less than three weeks
after the assassination, far too little time to cover all the ground,
Hoover handed the president a confidential summary report that
concluded there was no conspiracy. Simultaneously (as will be seen
in the next chapter), he leaked the report's contents to the press.
Thus was the public inculcated with the "no conspiracy" theory, and
the Warren Commission was handed it as a fait accompli.

However, leaks that might have set back Johnson's cause were tightly plugged. In 1961, in accordance with the policy of an FBI check on all high-level presidential appointments, the Bureau learned about and incorporated in a report a 1959 arrest of Walter Jenkins on a morals charge. This came to light only after Jenkins tripped again in the summer of 1964 and the incident could not be covered up, and it was largely overlooked in the debate over whether the Director had acted prudently in sending flowers to Jenkins in the hospital. And the improprieties of Justice Abe Fortas, who had been the subject of an FBI check when appointed, were surfaced by *Life* magazine in 1969—without help from the Bureau. "Where was the good old FBI when all these appointments were coming off?" rhetorically asked columnist Charles McCabe in the *San Francisco Chronicle*. "Where was that feisty guardian of the morals and politics of the personnel who work for our government?"

Although reports abounded that Johnson was prepared to dump Hoover after his fractious outburst against Martin Luther King, Jr., they eventually became even closer political allies. In the spring of 1965, when Johnson overreacted to the Dominican Republic crisis and sent troops to intervene, it was Hoover, with his agents going in on the heels of the invasion forces, who provided the *pretexte noire* in the form of Reds under the Hispanic beds.*

In fact, declared Robert J. Donovan of the Times-Post Service on May 26, 1965, Johnson had become "personally closer" to the FBI chief than any other president had been, and relied upon him not only for advice on police and security matters but on much broader issues of policy. According to Donovan, Johnson

> . . . talks to Hoover often on the telephone, day and night. Frequently in private conversations with others he sprinkles lofty praise of Hoover, extolling his trustworthiness and recounting how ingeniously the FBI had infiltrated certain questionable organizations.

*The baldness of this stratagem to capitalize on the reputation of Hoover and the Bureau is evident in the fact that the gathering of intelligence outside the continental limits of the United States is the sole responsibility of the CIA.

It has become characteristic of the President to refer to
Hoover in superlatives so much so that at times listeners,
conditioned perhaps by skepticism of experience in Washington, suspect he would not mind if a report on his words
trickled back to the FBI chief.

Two of this capital's shrewdest students of power politics are Lyndon B. Johnson and J. Edgar Hoover. The
importance of what each can contribute to the strength of
the other is well known to both.

As Donovan put it, the Director became "such a politically formidable figure" that presidents had to reckon with the fact that "if
retired to private life unwillingly, Hoover could, were he so disposed, become a political rallying point with awkward implications
for the White House." This undoubtedly was the compelling reason
the Kennedys kept Hoover on. But in deciding to keep him off the
streets, they also resolved to keep him cooped up in his office.
Whereas the FBI chief was accustomed to reporting directly to the
White House, JFK instructed him to report instead to his brother.
Robert in turn put things in proper perspective. When he first
picked up the hot line between the attorney general and the FBI
Director, it was not Hoover but his longtime secretary, Miss Helen
Gandy, who answered. "When I pick up this phone," he said
brusquely, "there's only one man I want to talk to—get the phone
on the Director's desk."

Galling as it was, Hoover had to take orders from the brash
young man who wasn't old enough to play touch football when G-
men were knocking off the Dillinger-era public enemies. And he
must have known that under Kennedy his days as Director were
numbered. In its wrap-up on the FBI, December 7, 1964, *Newsweek*
quoted a Justice Department staffer: "When we had problems with
the FBI, Bob would tell us, 'Take it easy, take it easy,' and you got
the impression that after January 1, 1965, Hoover wouldn't be
around any more. They'd make him an ambassador or something
somewhere." January 1, 1965, was Hoover's seventieth birthday,
and fell, conveniently, just after the 1964 elections that in all proba-
bility would have returned John Kennedy for a second term.

Although publicly Robert Kennedy maintained an air of normalcy, his relations with Hoover were stretched taut. The sniping back and forth is illustrated by the time that Ethel Kennedy, who, according to *Time,* April 25, 1969, was seething at Hoover's "ill-concealed disdain for his young boss," jabbed at his "sorest point, his running feud with Los Angeles Police Chief William Parker. Into Hoover's personal suggestion box one day she popped a note, signed by her, saying 'Parker for FBI Director.'"

But it may have been Hoover who got in the most telling blow. When in 1962 JFK forced Big Steel to roll back its price increases, Robert Kennedy instructed the FBI to expeditiously interview newsmen who had heard remarks passed by Roger Blough of U.S. Steel. Hoover put the most literal construction possible on the instruction, and agents rousted newsmen out of bed in the early morning hours to get their version. The Republicans, of course, cried "Gestapo," not at Hoover but at the Kennedys for using the FBI in such ruthless fashion.

At 12:30 P.M. Dallas time on November 22, 1963, Hoover's job security was assured. According to William Manchester, Robert Kennedy was at lunch at his Virginia home when the Director's cold "metallic voice" on the telephone informed him that his brother was dead. The despised Kennedys were off his back. "Just like that," *Newsweek* reported one Justice officer as saying, "everything went directly to the White House." Later in the afternoon when Robert arrived at his office, he picked up the hot line phone. Hoover was in his office with several aides when it rang . . . and rang . . . and rang. When it stopped ringing, the Director snapped to an aide, "Now get that phone back on Miss Gandy's desk."

With the Nixon administration, Hoover continued among friends. The mutual affinity between him and Richard Nixon dated to the latter's days as an eager young congressman on the House Un-American Activities Committee, egging on Joe McCarthy and prodding Dean Acheson's "form of pink-eye toward the Communist threat in the United States." Nixon was the beneficiary of the selective porosity of FBI files; on one occasion he fed a Republican crony running for Congress in the Los Angeles area data straight from the Director alleging that the Democratic opposition was Red-tainted.

When Nixon ran against Kennedy in 1960, Hoover assigned one of his former college chums at Whittier as FBI liaison, fully expecting him to win, while Kennedy got a rather obscure functionary.

In the 1968 campaign, Hoover couldn't lose. By virtue of his closeness to LBJ, the Director had become chummy with the plastic Hubert Humphrey. During the Miami and Chicago conventions, FBI men augmented both candidates' security forces and shadowed newsmen to learn their activities. These were the kinds of services that Hoover was used to rendering. In 1962, when Robert Kennedy had a special deputy serve William Rogers with an unwanted subpoena to testify at the Florida trial of Jimmy Hoffa, a pair of G-men routed the special deputy out of bed that night to grill him about allegedly misrepresenting himself to Rogers.

But there are indications that in his desperation to cling to his job, Hoover allowed himself to be exploited by the Nixon people. During the 1968 campaign, with its dominant theme of law and order, Nixon's speechwriters quoted the hard-line Director frequently, and when the returns were in the president-elect lost no time in announcing he was retaining the Bureau chief. Then, a few months after taking office, Nixon showcased his prize exhibit by holding a ceremony for one hundred police officers graduating from the FBI National Academy in the White House. Hoover dutifully presented the president with an honorary G-man's badge, which prompted Nixon to reminisce that he had once applied for the FBI agent position but hadn't made it. Haltingly, Hoover explained that he had passed his test with flying colors, but there had not been sufficient appropriations to hire many new men. (Actually, the Los Angeles SAC at the time had evaluated Nixon as lacking in aggressiveness.)

But despite their identical philosophies, there were signs that Nixon would have preferred to replace Hoover. For one thing, there was that preoccupation with the image. The *Wall Street Journal,* on October 10, 1968, claimed that some Republicans wanted to ditch the Director "because they believe the FBI could become an even more effective enforcer of law and order. Among things they would like to change is Mr. Hoover's alleged overcaution in catching crooks. The director is so concerned with the FBI's good name, according to a GOP critic, that he has instructed his agents, when they make arrests, to go even beyond Supreme Court edicts in guarding the rights of suspects."*

Another factor was the FBI's snobbishness in the fight against organized crime—during the Johnson administration Hoover got away with going it alone rather than joining the federal "strike forces" set up for the purpose. According to *Newsweek,* May 26, 1969, Hoover's direct access to the White House had been cut off and he was under orders to deal with Attorney General John Mitchell. "One result of the new state of affairs: the FBI, for the first time, has agreed to join other Federal agencies in the 'strike forces' set up to fight organized crime."

Despite his rigidly doctrinaire aura, Hoover was tractable when faced with political realities. He had, in fact, an uncanny ability to field hot grounders and turn them into double plays. No better example can be found than in his hiring practices concerning minorities. In telling Congress in 1940 that he didn't want a spoils system and that the Bureau's "merit system" was "demonstrably superior to the civil service," he was able to keep it an essentially white Christian operation. There were a few Jews—when pressed the Director would point to the late Harold ("Pop") Nathan, who entered before Hoover, and Assistant Director Alex Rosen—although I never personally encountered any during my ten years in the field. When ex-agent Jack Levine painted the Bureau as a crucible of anti-Semitism, I believe he was exaggerating somewhat, for such bias—and it certainly did exist—was on an individual basis rather than implicit in Bureau policy. In point of fact, Hoover was once given an award by the Washington chapter of B'nai Brith (at the insistence of a liquor dealer member), although other chapters around the country didn't rush to join the ritual, and the organization wasn't exactly a magnet for the Jewish liberal-intellectual community.

But when it came to race, that was something else again. While

---

*Indeed, some civil libertarians held the FBI up as a model in this respect. It should be pointed out, however, that the Bureau could afford to be strictly proper, since its arrests were made only after a thorough investigation, whereas the local police are a patrol force and are confronted with making on-the-spot arrests.

it should be conceded that Asians and blacks might not have been attracted to the special agent position in numbers proportionate to whites, I cannot recall running into any nonwhite in any position during my ten years in the FBI, nor, in scanning through back issues of the house organ for 1952-61, could I find among the field office employees a black or Asian face. Even the steno pools and chief clerk's offices looked like they had been hand-picked by the DAR. There were a few black clerks in Washington and New York—some agents knowingly alluded to them as the "house niggers"—and there were of course the half-dozen black "agents" who never went through training school. But the FBI hardly qualified as an equal opportunity employer.

When Robert Kennedy took over, Hoover bent a bit. "All Bob had to do was ask how come there were no Negro agents," a Kennedy appointee told *Newsweek*. "They got the idea fast." At the same time, pressures were building up from the President's Committee on Equal Employment Opportunity. Deftly, Hoover did a volteface and converted it into a publicity coup. An SAC prominent in the Notre Dame Alumni Association proselytized Aubrey C. Lewis, a black All-American at the school who had gone on to the Chicago Bears. Lewis quickly became the first black agent ever to go through the FBI training academy.

Then, in September 1962, the pages of *Ebony,* the widely circulated black magazine, blossomed with a photo story: "The Negro in the FBI." There was Lewis, in training at the Quantico academy. "The newest Negro fledgling," the article called him, "one of the most promising men recruited for action." There were pictures of the other black "agents" (a departure from the policy of anonymity), all of them, but the reader got the impression they represented only a sampling. "We've paid no attention to race, creed, or color," the Director was quoted as saying. "This has been my strict FBI policy." When the *Ebony* reporter asked where the other Negro agents were assigned, Hoover replied vaguely, "On cases in every part of the country." Pressed as to their number, he hedged by saying he couldn't disclose "the tricks of the trade."

Veteran Hoover-watchers must have been taken aback when he informed *Ebony* that he had been friendly with scientist Dr. George

Washington Carver and NAACP executive director Walter White. "Walter used to visit me any time he was in Washington," the Director observed with first-name familiarity.*

Hoover's blast at Martin Luther King, Jr., was unquestionably the most impolitic lapse of a career marked by few uncautious moments. Possibly he was lulled by the fact that the meeting with the ladies of the press at which he unburdened himself was arranged by Sarah McClendon, who represented safely conservative Texas newspapers. Certainly King was hitting him in his most vulnerable spot—the FBI's unimpressive record in civil rights investigations (in the previous four years there had been only nine convictions in the category). And what the prestigious Nobel Peace Prize winner was saying was difficult to refute. There *were* a lot of native Southerners staffing the Deep South FBI offices, and they *did* fraternize with the redneck cops, and the bombings and murders and brutalities *did* somehow go unsolved. Moreover, Hoover and his aides had a strong personal distaste for King. One Senate counsel recalled that a top aide to Hoover became absolutely phobic when the subject of the black leader came up. After King's assassination, when a Los Angeles area police official proffered information indicating a conspiracy to the FBI, he was politely rebuffed: "We've got our man [James Earl Ray], and that's it. The Director didn't exactly light any candles after King was killed.**

For any less politically adroit and powerful man, the impulsive attack on King would have spelled the end. But Hoover, typically, stuck to his guns. At a Loyola University of Chicago dinner at which he was presented yet another award, he spoke of "zealots or pressure groups" within the civil rights movement that were "spearheaded at times by Communists and moral degenerates." Then Assistant Director William C. Sullivan, the Bureau's short, intense intellectual-in-

---

*As of 1964 the Bureau still wasn't much more than token integrated. "Over 300 of our employees are Negro [about 2 percent]," Hoover told *Newsweek* in late 1964, "and 27 are special agents [about 0.5 percent]." Bureau spokesmen evaded the issue by saying they kept no tabs on race, creed, or color.

**He did send a representative to the funeral, however, in the person of Cartha DeLoach, who had been his point man in the smear of King.

residence on Communism, underlined the smirch by telling the press that some two hundred Communists were among the two hundred thousand civil rights demonstrators participating in the 1963 march on Washington—which had been led, of course, by King.

Then, as the clamor for Hoover's removal persisted, the FBI with exquisite timing arrested a clutch of Mississippi Klansmen for the slayings of three young civil rights workers, the dramatic culmination of an investigation that had stretched over five months. President Johnson went on national television to make the announcement, and there, standing somberly at his side, was J. Edgar Hoover.

The disarming of King had come at a meeting in the Director's office a few days before the arrests. The session was closed, but was later described as "amicable." When he emerged, King read a conciliatory prepared statement that included the phrase "forget the confusions of the past" and flew off to Sweden to pick up his Nobel medal.

In the light of subsequent events, the enigmatic meeting may have amounted to a blackmail session. Writing in the *Washington Post,* May 12, 1967, columnist Marquis Childs alluded to "a rumored FBI report on King's private life derived from an electronic device placed in a hotel room," and paired it with the fact that King had "little to say" when he came out from the meeting "and the report circulated that he had been confronted with the hotel-room recording."

That King was actually under encompassing electronic surveillance came out tangentially during an appeal in June 1969 by ex-heavyweight champion Muhammad Ali from his conviction for refusing to report for military induction. Ali's lawyer drew the admission that his client had been listened in on, but the tap was not on his phone but on the office and New York quarters of King, with whom he had conversed. The disclosure precipitated a bitter battle over who had authorized wiretapping of the nation's most charismatic civil rights leader. Hoover insisted that Robert Kennedy not only authorized the taps but originated the idea. In fact, the existence of taps on King was such an open secret that the Director leaked word during the 1968 Oregon primary (which Robert

Kennedy lost) that his quondam boss had ordered them. During the height of the fuss, on June 19, 1969, he told the *Washington Star* that Kennedy had done so because of concern over King's "Marxist ideas and associations."

Being dead, King and Kennedy were unable to defend themselves. The *Star* story brought out Hoover's version that in the FBI files were two 1963 memorandums from the deceased attorney general that proved he had initiated the taps. President Nixon chimed in with the declaration that he had "personally checked into the matter" and discovered that Kennedy had indeed *authorized* the taps. But neither the FBI nor Nixon's attorney general, John Mitchell, would produce the best evidence: the memorandums themselves.

The memorandums most likely confirmed that Kennedy had merely said yes to the taps after being sold a bill of goods by Bureau officials who claimed King was associating with dangerous radicals (the same guilt by dalliance smear the Birch Society had been peddling for years with a photograph of King sitting next to an avowed Communist at a Tennessee school). This was implicit in statements issued by others in a position to know. Nicholas deB. Katzenbach, who succeeded Kennedy as attorney general (before being kicked upstairs to the State Department after incurring Hoover's wrath over wiretapping disclosures), commented: "To say or imply that this tap was the original conception of Robert Kennedy—that he was the moving force in this situation—or that he had any doubts whatsoever as to Dr. King's integrity or loyalty is false." Burke Marshall, who headed the civil rights division under Kennedy, seethed: "It's outrageous for Mr. Hoover to give characterization of selected documents concerning principally two people now dead in order to deal with adverse publicity to the Bureau." And Ramsey Clark, who took over from Katzenbach, asserted that it was deceptive for Hoover to pose as "a reluctant eavesdropper of Dr. King" because he "repeatedly requested me to authorize FBI wiretaps on Dr. King while I was attorney general. The last of these requests, none of which was granted, came two days before the murder of Dr. King."

It became quite plain, in fact, that Hoover's requests were in the nature of seeking legitimation for bootleg taps kept in operation after April 20, 1965, the date the Bureau contended it discontinued them. In the course of the Muhammad Ali hearings, in which it came out that a tap had also been in on the Phoenix, Arizona, home of black nationalist leader Elijah Muhammad, FBI agent Robert R. Nichols nodded affirmatively when asked if King's home was continually tapped to the time of his assassination. This was affirmed by the disclosure of syndicated columnist Carl T. Rowan on June 15, 1969, that as head of the USIA he had seen FBI summaries of the fruits of the electronic snooping. "For years," wrote Rowan, "the FBI has had a small army of agents and allies roaming the country whispering the dirt about Dr. King." The mongering wasn't aimless: "FBI officials were going before Congressional committees and partly justifying larger appropriations by titillating some Congressmen" with "tid-bits" gleaned through taps and bugs. Raged Rowan in a second column June 20: "I know how much dirt the FBI has dug up, and 90 percent of it is barnyard gossip that has nothing to do with 'internal security' or 'marxist influences.'"

The congressional ears pricked by this lurid stuff all belonged to the southern segregationist–northern reactionary amalgam that long formed Hoover's power base on Capitol Hill. One was John Rooney of Brooklyn, who, as appropriations chairman, handed over the taxpayers' money to the FBI with a chronic lack of interest in where it was all going. Rooney and his colleagues were reportedly so "shocked" by what they heard that they thought the Speaker should have a listen too. With fresh FBI "leaks" in his pocket, Louisiana's flame-tongued John R. Rarick orated the posthumous degradation of Martin Luther King, Jr.*

The mutual backscratching of Hoover and his allies was adequately chronicled. In 1962, after former agent Jack Levine and I criticized the Director's stewardship on the small Pacifica radio network, chairman James O. Eastland of the Senate Internal Security Committee launched a probe of Pacifica that, true to the Mississippian's form, produced nothing except a Red tarring (more will be said later on this score). During the 1966 verbal slugging match between

---

*See the *Congressional Record,* June 16, 1969, p. E4927, and June 18, 1969, p. E5056.

Hoover and Robert Kennedy over who ordered the abortive bugging of Las Vegas casinos, Congressman H. R. Gross of Iowa, who was a reliable pipeline for FBI propaganda, was enlisted to help. Gross, for example, had entered into the *Congressional Record* a put-down of an anonymous letter circulated among numerous members of Congress contending that Hoover was a homosexual, which he referred to as a product of the "Soviet Department of Disinformation." Cartha DeLoach flew from Washington to the Mississippi gulf coast, where Gross was vacationing, to arrange for Gross to write a letter asking Hoover about the "unfounded allegations" (the Bureau's favorite phrase) that he had proceeded without the attorney general's authority. Of course Hoover "welcomed" the chance to reply, and Kennedy was duly rapped.

In 1967, Hoover paid off some political I.O.U.'s by giving the ultraconservative bloc opposing the consular treaty with the Soviet Union an assist. Two years previously the FBI chief had frightened off some of the treaty's supporters by warning that it "would make our work more difficult." During the hearings before the Senate Foreign Relations Committee, Senator Karl Mundt triumphantly waved a letter from Hoover reiterating his stand and stressing that Russian diplomatic posts were "focal points for intelligence operations." Observed Emmet John Hughes in *Newsweek*, February 20, 1967: "The shabbiest part of the whole debate, of course, has been the abject courting—by Administration and opposition alike—of FBI Director J. Edgar Hoover. . . . And if the head of the Soviet secret police wielded such veto power over Russian diplomacy, an Everett Dirksen would hasten to tell his country, sadly and soulfully: this only shows how harshly different is *their* way of life from *ours*."

When FBI partisan Thomas J. Dodd of Connecticut was accused of serious improbities in 1966 (he was later censured by the Senate), Hoover didn't scruple to use his agents as a political police. The white-maned senator was particularly close to the Bureau, having served briefly as an agent in 1934, and thereafter, as one of the Senate's windiest anti-Communist rhetoricians, frequently praised the Director to the skies. Dodd's troubles began when a longtime aide, James Boyd, became disaffected and spirited out of the office documents purporting to show that Dodd had, among other things, pocketed funds from testimonial dinners and acted improperly on behalf of General Julius Klein, an agent of West Germany.

Boyd turned the documents over to Drew Pearson, who invited the FBI to look them over. But instead of investigating the allegations against Dodd, the G-men started in on Pearson and Boyd. In his column on April 25, 1966, Pearson averred that the FBI had called in a dozen or so former employees of Dodd's office, but instead of questioning them about the senator's conduct, cross-examined them about the "theft" of the documents. "As fast as the FBI discovered the identity of the witnesses," wrote Pearson, "they were bullied and badgered, hounded and harassed. One lost his job on a House committee; the news of his dismissal came from Dodd's office. . . . Agents hauled some witnesses right in to Dodd's office for cross-examination and behaved as if they were working for the Senator. Other witnesses were alternately soft-soaped and threatened with Federal prosecution."

Even the private detective that Dodd hired to supplement the FBI's efforts was a former Bureau agent, James J. Lynch of New York. Pearson reported that Lynch tried to intimidate witnesses, hinting to some that he was a federal agent, to others that he worked for Judge Irving Kaufman of the U.S. Court of Appeals in New York. Kaufman, too, was in the FBI family. He was the judge who sentenced the Rosenbergs to the electric chair in the famous Bureau spy case, and Hoover's gratitude was unending. I recall that in 1961, when Kaufman would visit his son at the University of Oklahoma, a senior agent was assigned to chauffeur him around in a Bureau car.*

The most remarkable aspect of Hoover's long crypto-political career was his ability to engage in the rankest partisanship without drawing fire from the opposition. It was a phenomenon perhaps best explained by the old political warrior Alfred E. Smith, who, after a particularly tough campaign, wistfully observed, "Nobody shoots at Santa Claus."

---

*This "courtesy" was extended to many friends of the FBI, from Lawrence Welk to Victor Reisel. Once, when one of Hoover's Texas oilman friends was to visit New York for the first time, the SAC was instructed to have an agent meet him at the airport, be at his disposal during his stay, and show him the sights. The agents selected, the SAC was told, "must make a good impression."

CHAPTER SEVEN
THE PUBLICIST

When other agencies blunder, they make excuses.
When the FBI blunders, it just makes another movie.

—*A Washington aphorism*

While the harsh judgment of history may not record J. Edgar Hoover as a notably effective crime-fighter, it will undoubtedly stamp him as one of the public relations geniuses of his time. Where other agencies were able to establish only a modest base of public support and understanding upon which to operate, Hoover was able to capture the imagination of the populace so thoroughly that the FBI was held in near-universal awe and respect. The image of incorruptibility, of relentless and successful pursuit of criminals and subversives became so indisputable in the public mind that the Director and his G-men seemed virtually untouchable.

The magnitude of the myth can be gauged by the fact that the FBI was generally regarded as the Nemesis of Crime even though it contributed only about 1 percent of the arrests and convictions obtained by American law enforcement. The myth was sustained by a well-financed, Madison Avenue-style publicity campaign waged by the Bureau's publicity department, otherwise known as the Crime Records Division.

It was not always so. When Hoover first became Director, he concentrated on professionalizing his Bureau and even avoided publicity. Thus, when he later came under fire as a publicity-seeker, defenders could recall with all candor that he had not sought out acclaim. "I have on more than one occasion told Mr. Hoover that in his files are many interesting statements that would make excellent material for a Sunday newspaper article, or for a magazine story," attested Alexander Holtzoff of the Department of Justice years ago, "but he has always shrunk, with, I think, unnecessary and undue modesty, from volunteering to give out such data."

Why Hoover abandoned his reticence to seek publicity aggressively is an open question. In his Bureau-blessed *The FBI Story,* Don Whitehead said that it was due to the Director's outrage over the glorification some criminals were receiving and the need for countervailing publicity. Jack Alexander, who did a 1937 *New Yorker* series on Hoover, theorized that the spate of publicity was at first a "spontaneous phenomenon" that the Director did not stimulate, and that in fact he "refused to cooperate with movie companies and fiction writers in the gathering of material or supervising of production." The shock of the Kansas City massacre, argued Alexander, convinced Hoover that "the mere quieting down of the kidnapping and bank-robbery scare was not enough but that an actual crusade was needed. . . . Someone had to become the symbol of the crusade, and the Director decided that, because of his position, it was plainly up to him."

In a *True* article in January 1968, columnist Drew Pearson expanded on Alexander's version. Hoover, he implied, conveyed his thoughts on the subject to Homer Cummings, Franklin Roosevelt's first attorney general. Cummings invited to dinner a small group of Washington newspapermen, including Pearson, and elicited their opinions as to what public relations man was capable of polishing the FBI's image of efficiency to such a glow that no kidnapper would dare challenge it. Their choice was the late Henry Suydam, at the time chief Washington correspondent for the *Brooklyn Eagle* and later chief of *Life*'s Washington bureau. Suydam was appointed a special assistant to the attorney general and, as Pearson puts it, "performed so spectacularly that within a year he had transformed Hoover, previously a barely known bureaucrat, into an omnipotent crime-buster whose name was familiar to every American."

Shortly afterward Suydam was maneuvered out of his job by means of an amendment quietly slipped into the Department of Justice appropriations bill specifying that no salary could be paid a "special assistant to the Attorney General who [was] not a qualified attorney." Suydam, of course, did not qualify. "No one had any doubt regarding the original author," comments Pearson. "J. Edgar

Hoover had learned how to get the publicity and did not need help any more."

Once committed, Hoover plunged into the task with customary vigor and single-mindedness. A torrent of magazine articles, newspaper serializations, books, and movies extolling the heroics of the G-men and preaching the inevitable triumph over evil swept over the American public; some were written in the Crime Records Section and bore the Director's byline; others carried his endorsement or introduction; still others were researched with the cooperation of the Bureau and billed as "inside" stories.

Hoover's principal periodical medium was *American Magazine,* which between April 1936 and June 1938 published seventeen "by J. Edgar Hoover" articles. The sensational tone of the articles can be judged by some of the titles: "King of Bandits," "Gunman's Love," "$200,000 Rat Trap," "Crime's Leading Lady," and "Buzzard in Disguise." Among the book fare were *Ten Thousand Public Enemies* by Courtney Ryley Cooper and *Farewell, Mr. Gangster* by Herbert Corey, both of which bore introductions by Hoover, *Inside the FBI, Our G-Men,* and *Our FBI, An Inside Story.* By way of reciprocation, Cooper wrote a generous introduction to Hoover's *Persons in Hiding,* a melodramatic tome interspersed with didactic interludes. Movies of the era included *G-Men,* with Jimmy Cagney, and a title with a built-in sermon, *You Can't Get Away With It.*

Not everyone was bedazzled by the lionization of Hoover and his minions. In 1936, Senator Kenneth McKellar of Tennessee, a persistent critic of FBI methods, suggested that detailed recountings of how cases were solved worked to the advantage of criminals. In the course of questioning the Director on his publicity policies, he maintained that permitting newsreel cameras inside the Bureau "hurt the department very much, by advertising your methods." Another FBI gadfly, Senator George W. Norris of Nebraska, didn't pull punches before his colleagues: "Mr. Hoover is doing more injury to honest law enforcement in this country by his publicity-seeking feats than is being done by any other one thing connected with his organization. . . . A detective who advertises his exploits every time he gets an opportunity, who spends the public money to see that they are spread over the pages of the newspapers in flaming headlines will in the end be a failure in ferreting out crime. . . ." Even Chief Justice Harlan F. Stone, who as attorney general had appointed Hoover and remained one of his staunchest admirers, had serious reservations about the wisdom of undue publicity. "Personally," he said, "I have been sorry to see the Bureau get the great publicity that it has received. One of the great secrets of Scotland Yard has been that its movements are never advertised. It moves and strikes in the dark and in consequence is more efficient both in its internal organization and its relation to criminals than would otherwise be possible."

The argument apparently failed to convince Hoover, for the aggressive publicity quest continued at full tilt. He seemed to revel in it, posing for an autograph-signing session with Shirley Temple and with a machine gun poised, disporting himself at the Stork Club and other night spots where celebrities congregated, and otherwise catching the limelight. This, combined with his flair for lurid phrase-making, made him an editor's idol.

The attention fed Hoover's never-latent ego to the point that he would brook no competition for newspaper space from underlings. Melvin ("Little Me") Purvis, who headed the Chicago office at the time of the Dillinger chase, was one offender. Short and cocky, Purvis set the trap in which Dillinger was gunned down outside the Biograph Theater and lit a cigar as a signal for his agents to close in. The Chicago newspapers made a local hero out of Purvis, and stories about him flashed across the country on the wire services. All at once the Bureau became too small for both personalities, and it was Purvis who went. (He went to Hollywood to capitalize on his fame, organizing a sort of Junior G-man club sponsored by Post Toasties called the "Melvin Purvis Law-and-Order Patrol.") Purvis' fall from grace was so complete that Whitehead's *The FBI Story* downgrades his role in the case by giving top billing to an agent on special assignment out of headquarters and does not even include his name in the index.

Leon Turreau, who gained a measure of renown for his exploits as agent in charge of the New York office during the halcyon days, was another who incurred the Director's displeasure. Turreau had played a key part in the Lindbergh kidnapping investigation, and later became well-known for leading forays against the German-

American Bund and other Nazi groups in the days before World War II. Leaving the Bureau shortly thereafter, Turreau compounded past offenses by writing a book, *Where My Shadow Falls,* which recounted his experiences. Although there was no law against this, it did violate a Bureau rule that employees not reveal the details of cases they have worked on when they leave the agency. Hoover went to court, seeking to enjoin publication on the grounds that Turreau had no right to cash in on his government employment. The court, however, accepted Turreau's contention that Hoover himself had done this very thing with his book *Persons in Hiding* and numerous articles.

With the Bureau's successes against enemy agents in World War II there came a new wave of headlines and feature stories. The capture of Nazi saboteurs landed by submarine on the Long Island and Florida coasts provided front-page copy for weeks. The arrest of German spy Fritz Duquesne in New York for espionage exploded into the headlines amidst the accounts of battles overseas. The story of how G-men ferreted out the "Doll Lady" of Japanese intrigue, Velvalee Dickinson, was widely told. The operations of the Bureau's Special Intelligence Service (SIS) countering Nazi espionage in South America became the subject of considerable press. In 1945, Twentieth-Century Fox backed producer Louis de Rochemont in making a film called *The House on 92nd Street,* which used the Duquesne case as a theme to dramatize the FBI in action against the spies.

It later came to light, however, that some Bureau feats were purposely overblown to buoy morale on the home front and deter the enemy from sending over more spies. The saboteur coup is a case in point. On the morning of June 13, 1942, eight men trained in demolition techniques in Germany slipped ashore from the U-boat *Innsbruck* near Amagansett, Long Island, and dispersed according to plan. Their eventual targets were a huge aluminum plant, Ohio River locks, and key railroad facilities. Sixteen days later, newspaper headlines blazed: "FBI CAPTURES 8 GERMAN AGENTS LANDED BY SUBS." The accounts heaped praise on FBI prowess, telling how G-men started with the clue of German cigarettes that several of the men left behind as they rode trains into New York City and hunted them down.

The story, it seems, was cut from whole cloth. After the war ended, *New York Daily News* reporter John O'Donnell wrote an article taglined "Truth Will Out! Great Spy Hunt Exploded":

> Last week, Hoover and President Truman's new Attorney General, Tom Clark of Texas, had a violent difference of opinion.
>
> Clark decided that the time had come to open up the files of the secret trial of the eight German saboteurs who were landed from submarines on Long Island and Florida. All were in custody of the FBI within a fortnight of the landings. Within 60 days six had been executed. Two, George Dasch and Ernst P. Burger, are in the Atlanta Penitentiary—Dasch serving a 30-year sentence, Burger life.
>
> Three years ago, when the arrests were announced (the late President Roosevelt was directing the publicity in person), Hoover and the FBI got all the credit for saving the nation from destruction of vital military installations.
>
> The private files now made public by the Attorney General reveal that Dasch and Burger were haters of the Hitler regime, left Germany with the real saboteurs with the determination to expose the plot immediately on arrival, phoned the FBI headquarters in New York immediately on their secret arrival, went to Hoover's Washington office at once, poured out the full story of the plot and the tale of how and why they had led the real saboteurs into the trap.
>
> Now this, of course, spoiled the carefully nursed official story which poured all credit for the outstanding and sensational capture on the FBI and gave full credit to the brilliance, skill, courage, and scientific training of Director Hoover's outfit.
>
> Either unconcerned about or unconscious of Hoover's sensitive feelings for public esteem of his organization, Clark about a fortnight ago agreed with *Newsweek* correspondent John U. Terrell that there was no reason why the story shouldn't be released to the public.
>
> Then, on the eve of publication of Terrell's piece,

Hoover got wind of what was happening. He sounded off his protests vigorously to his new boss. Clark called *Newsweek,* admitted that the story was correct and honestly secured, but pleaded: "Hoover wants to make some changes."

Correspondent Terrell didn't feel like making changes in his story on the official transcript. Department of Justice experts stayed up all night, whipped up their version, and slapped it out to meet *Newsweek* publication—in a version designed to keep up the public prestige of Hoover and the FBI.

A postscript was added in 1962 when George John Dasch, one of the defecting saboteurs, corroborated the O'Donnell exposure in a thin volume called *Eight Spies Against America,* which received no notice and meager distribution. Dasch contended that when he showed up at Bureau headquarters, officials disbelieved his story and decided to check it only when he spilled out some $80,000 in cash the Germans had given him. Since he knew where the rendezvous were to be made, it was a simple matter for the FBI to make the roundup. Dasch claims he was told that he would have to stand trial with his compatriots in order to fool the Germans, but that within six months, after a sham conviction, he would be fully exonerated and freed. But if there was such an arrangement the FBI reneged on it, for Dasch was sentenced to thirty years.

At the end of the trial, Dasch said, he came face to face with Hoover and tried to plead with him:

> He continued on, ignoring me. Again I cried out, this time louder than before: "Mr. Hoover, aren't you really ashamed of yourself?"
>
> An FBI agent walking nearby struck me on the face, sending me sprawling to the floor. One of the army guards helped me to my feet, and through the tears brought on by the hot sting of the agent's hand, I saw the Chief disappear down the hall, seemingly surrounded by an impregnable wall of justice and strength.

It was the FBI's contention (as reported in *The FBI Story,* for one) that Dasch only decided to defect after the landing, when he got "cold feet" and wanted to save his neck. There is no proof of this: on the contrary, circumstantial evidence militates in Dasch's favor. Dasch had stowed away to enter the United States as a boy and taken out citizenship papers. He was caught in Germany by the outbreak of the war during a temporary stay. He did not volunteer for the mission but was forced into it. Once on the beach, he disregarded Nazi orders to kill any witness by allowing a young Coastguardsman to escape; the youth spread the alarm that started the search. Since he spoke fluent English, knew the country, and carried $80,000, Dasch could easily have disappeared without tipping off the FBI.

In prison, Dasch continued to press for the exoneration which, if given, would have branded the FBI account as fiction. In 1948, in a move so swift and secretive that his wife and attorney knew nothing about it, he was whisked from prison and returned to Germany. There, he obtained three sworn affidavits from longtime acquaintances attesting to his anti-Nazi status and his resolve to abort the sabotage mission. But no one in the United States government would listen to his pleas. Today he roams Germany, despised by Germans as a traitor. Ironically, he is most probably an authentic American war hero, responsible for saving many lives. But fate had made him a threat to the FBI's public image.

As the Cold War set in, Hoover and the FBI turned their full attention to Communism. The propaganda apparatus cranked up and churned out material depicting a frightening domestic Red menace directed and subsidized by Moscow. On guard, of course, were the agents of the FBI. "New and more sinister schemes by the various subversive elements operating in the United States faced the FBI in the domestic intelligence field," warned one release. "FBI agents remain on duty around the clock each day of the year to thwart their devious schemes."

It was time to make another movie. In 1952, Columbia Pictures released *Walk East on Beacon,* produced, again, by Louis de Rochemont. Filmed in Boston and Washington, all agent parts in the script were played by Bureau agents with the exception of the

SAC and the inspector, which were played by George Murphy and Karl Weber. The Bureau's own "review" read in part: "This movie, which exposes the innermost operations of a fantastic communist espionage network in America, reveals how seemingly insignificant individuals, apparently above suspicion, fit into the Red web. Many of these Red agents are fanatically dedicated to the cause of Communism. Some are dupes ensnared through youthful indiscretions and forced to render their services through fear of disclosure. The FBI, in slipping behind the scenes to meet the hidden enemy, has employed new and exciting investigative techniques." *Walk* was deemed a "must" for "every American."

In 1958, Hoover came out with a book (actually written by the Crime Records Division, notably Charles Moore) billed as "The Story of Communism in America and How to Fight It." *Masters of Deceit* opened with a chapter simulating a Soviet America and sounding the tocsin "it could happen here." Succeeding chapters bear such titles as "Why Do People Become Communists?," "Infiltration," and "How to Stay Free." The book enjoyed brisk sales and became the conservative bible; it is still to be found in practically every Birch Society and ultra right-wing bookstore.

Hoover's next book on the subject, *A Study in Communism,* did not fare so well. Written in the Bureau's burdensome style and filled with casuistries, it fell flat, helped to obscurity by tart reviews. Harry Schwartz, in the *New York Times,* noted "some disturbing internal evidence" suggesting that Hoover was not "entirely familiar" with the profound changes in the Soviet Union since the death of Stalin, and termed the book not "an adequate introduction to the study of Communism, even at the high-school level." Dick Nolan, in the *San Francisco Examiner,* was blunter, calling it "the worst written hunk of journalese since hungry ghosts first began haunting the marble halls of Government."

A trilogy was completed with the publication of *Communism: 1969,* an anthology arguing that behind the new look of the Communist Party was the same goal of violent revolution. Hardly an eye-opener, the book got wide coverage through a twelve-part serialization in the Hearst press.

By the mid-fifties, Hoover was thinking in terms of a wrap-up volume chronicling the Bureau's lengthening history. "In magazine articles and books, many phases of the Bureau's work have been recorded," he would later say. "Some of those accounts were correct, others were distorted, and some were figments of the imagination." A Bureau-produced book would have been transparently self-serving. So the Director turned to Don Whitehead, a veteran Associated Press reporter. Whitehead was "safe" in that he had established himself as reporting favorably on the Bureau. As Hoover expressed it, "He had written stories on the Bureau and we had complete confidence in his integrity, ability, and objectivity."

The product was *The FBI Story*. In his foreword to the book, Hoover averred that "the full facts were given to [Whitehead] so long as they did not violate security" to insure a "worthwhile, objective result." The book, he said, was an "accurate portrayal" of the FBI and stood in answer to "a campaign of falsehood and vilification [that] has been directed against the FBI by some ignorant and some subversive elements." As has been indicated, however, Whitehead's critical faculties remained suspended during the creative process. He omitted or glossed over Bureau blunders, painted a glowing picture of unmitigated FBI success, and never pointed an admonishing finger at the Director or his charges.

The FBI Story was, perhaps inevitably, made into a movie of the same name. Appropriately, the studio was Warner Brothers, which had done *G-Man* two decades before. Personnel from the Crime Records Division were loaned as technical consultants. I recall that some theaters promoted it by advertising that FBI agents who displayed their credentials would be admitted free. I went, curious as to how Hollywood had treated the subject. The star, Jimmy Stewart, played the role of an FBI agent flitting from case to case, working grueling hours and facing countless dangers, while his wife could only watch and wait. It was so mawkish and overripe that I felt like hiding under my seat, a reaction shared by other agents. But Hoover reportedly was greatly moved, exclaiming that it represented a crowning moment in his career.

When his halo began slipping following the Bureau's monumental boggle at Dallas on November 22, 1963, Hoover found a new way to spruce up the image and defuse his critics—a national television series called "The FBI." Broadcast on the ABC network on Sunday evenings, the series premiered in the fall of 1965 and remained on the air for nine years. It was produced at Warner Brothers-Seven Arts by Executive Producer Quinn Martin, formerly of "The Untouchables," and Producer Charles Larsen. Martin was a unabashed admirer of the Director. "Hoover is a star in his own right," he said upon meeting him for the first time. "I felt much as I did when I met Cary Grant—that this was a special person." Larsen was evidently naïve about law enforcement realities. "Viewers aren't much interested in police cases any law enforcement agency can handle," he told a reporter. "They expect big themes that they consider unique to the FBI. And they prefer current problems. They seem to want to know what great things the FBI is doing right now."

The producers' awe was reflected in the dramas, based on FBI files, in which G-men never slipped and always got their man. A publicity agent connected with the show once asked me what I, as an ex-FBI agent, thought of it. "It's certainly dramatic," I answered, "but it isn't authentic, as Mr. Larsen claims." "What do you mean?" he asked. "Well, for instance, why don't you show the true story of the Young kidnapping in Beverly Hills a couple of years ago? How the kidnapper got away with $250,000 ransom money when FBI agents covering the payoff spot in a taxi couldn't keep up with his high-powered car? How the agent in charge tied up radio traffic with his histrionics, so that other cars couldn't be put on the pursuit?"

"Why, we couldn't show *that*," was the man's subdued reply. Of course they couldn't—and there was nothing in the television code that demanded the series be labeled "a highly romanticized version of the FBI." On the contrary, the production rang with authority. The FBI seal was shown—a rare privilege—and Hoover was occasionally referred to as the occupant of a nearby but off-camera executive suite. At the tag end of the show, a picture of a Top Ten Fugitive was likely to be flashed on the screen with a request for viewers to notify the nearest FBI office if they spot him.

The series was also extraordinary in the degree of control the FBI exercised over it. The Bureau claimed it did not dictate to the producers but was concerned only with being "displayed in the best possible light." However, it commanded veto power over actors and other personnel by insisting on conducting background checks to make sure no one with a potentially embarrassing political or social taint was hired.

The star of the series must have passed the screening with flying colors. Efrem Zimbalist, Jr., who played the briskly efficient Inspector Erskine, was noted in Hollywood for his very conservative political leanings, and in 1964 he campaigned vigorously for Barry Goldwater. (Both the FBI and Ford, the sponsor, asked him to soft-pedal his political activity for fear it would leave the series vulnerable to criticism.) In 1966, Hoover, who had lauded him as show business's "most brilliant star," invited him to speak to police officers graduating from the FBI National Academy, and his comments proved worthy of the occasion. "The doctrine of civil disobedience gathers much of its support from the bigots, the fanatics, the extremists, the emotionally unstable, and the immature," he declaimed. "Contrast their attitude with that of the dedicated police officer—guardian of public safety, friend of the sick and confused, protector of the innocent, nemesis of the criminal, and target for insult and even physical ridicule by any charter or mob which happens to take offense at a particular law."

That the FBI should become intimately and publicly involved in such dollar-oriented enterprises raised a serious question of propriety. Even before the series began programming, New York TV critic Jack Gould questioned whether a federal agency in so sensitive a position should lend its name to so highly commercial a venture as a television series, especially since the series allowed the Bureau to stack the deck in favor of its public image. Quinn Martin brushed off Gould's critique as "a pseudo-intellectual argument" intended to stir up controversy, which was hardly responsive to the issue. But the show went on, viewed by an estimated twenty-five million people who listened in six languages in forty-three countries.

The press conference, a fixture with most other governmental units including the White House, was studiously avoided by Hoover and his officials because of its give-and-take spontaneity. When the Bureau had something to announce—an arrest, the solution of a case, the latest crime statistics—a press release over the Director's signature was handed out to the media. The format had the additional advantage that favored reporters or outlets could be slipped a pre-release, enabling them to "scoop" the competition. Since the FBI disseminated considerably more newsworthy material than most other agencies, the fourth estate was hesitant about offending the Bureau in print.

If there was some question to be asked about a release, or if he wanted to initiate an inquiry, a reporter could submit it to the Crime Records Division. If the Bureau wished to respond, the answer was usually forthcoming quicker than from any other agency in Washington. If not—silence.

One of the trademarks of the FBI was its "no comment" during the course of an investigation that attracted wide attention. The ostensible reason for the secrecy was to avoid jeopardizing the outcome. But there was an attendant advantage. Not only were blunders shrouded, but a successful conclusion implied that the G-men had turned in another outstanding performance in the face of extreme difficulty, which was frequently far from the truth.

Another news management device employed by the FBI was the leak. The assassination of John F. Kennedy provided two insights into its use. On December 9, 1963, less than three weeks after the assassination, J. Edgar Hoover handed to President Johnson a confidential four-volume FBI summary report that concluded that Lee Harvey Oswald was a lone assassin, that Jack Ruby had acted independently, and that there was no conspiracy. Simultaneously, the contents and conclusions of the report were leaked to the *Washington Star,* which along with the archconservative *Chicago Tribune* was long a Bureau sounding board. From the *Star* the wire services picked up the story and it was printed in newspapers across the country.

The effect was precisely as intended: The FBI version was imposed upon the Warren Commission, which at that point had barely begun to formulate its plans. To reach any other conclusions, the commission would have had to overrule the most prestigious investigative agency in the nation. The consternation of the members over news of the *fait accompli* thrust upon them was revealed in declassified transcripts of the executive sessions. On December 16, Representative Gerald Ford told his colleagues:

> I was called by one of the. . . top AP or UP people at Dallas at the time. He said, Jerry, I'm surprised that we got, and the other press services got, stories out the very same day, in effect, he was saying *what they have asked us to do.* The minute he said that it lead me to the belief that he was infer-ring that there had been a deliberate leak from some agency of the Federal Government, and now they *wanted us to confirm by Commission action what had been leaked previ-ously.* [italics added]

Chairman Earl Warren offered that Attorney General Katzenbach had been asked about the leak and had replied, "There is only one source." Senator Richard Russell complained, "Every day there was something." To which Warren agreed: "Yes, until it was all out and I tell you frankly I just don't find anything in that [FBI summary] report that has not been leaked to the press."

The *Chicago Tribune* was the outlet for a leak deprecating New Orleans District Attorney Jim Garrison after he charged that the FBI had prior knowledge of the plot against Kennedy but did nothing about it. In the course of a press conference on December 26, 1967, the free-wheeling DA said that a former security clerk in the New Orleans office, William S. Walters, had reported that early on the morning of November 17, 1963, he "received a TWX message directed to all southern regional offices of the FBI. The message advised that an attempt to assassinate President Kennedy would be made in Dallas on November 22, 1963." Another TWX came in a few hours later countermanding the first one, Walters assertedly revealed. After the assassination, agents "were ordered to resolve the conflicts with new reports and to destroy the old ones."

The allegation must have stung Hoover. Although FBI spokes-men replied "no comment" to press inquiries, an answer of sorts came three days later in the form of an article in the *Tribune* putting Garrison's mental capacity in question. A World War II Air Medal winner and lieutenant colonel in the Louisiana National Guard,

Garrison had been reactivated for the Korean War in 1951 but was soon discharged due to a chronic dysentery condition. The *Tribune* story played up a supposed "anxiety complex" and "psychoneurotic" state army doctors had detected to imply that Garrison was mentally unstable. The author, Russell Freiburg of the *Tribune*'s Washington bureau, admitted when pressed that he had obtained a copy of Garrison's army 201 file. How?—since such records are by law unavailable to outsiders. On a TV program, I put it to Freiburg that his newspaper had never believed that Hoover "put his pants on one leg at a time," and for this institutional act of faith he had been rewarded with the copy. He did not categorically deny it.

Over the years, a number of simpatico members of the press had access to the inner sanctum. In the thirties, Rex Collier of the *Washington Star,* a personal friend of the Director, ran a continuing feature called "War on Crime" which was fed by data from FBI files. In 1968, *Star* staffer Jeremiah O'Leary, drawing on information given him by Crime Records, presented the FBI version of the assassination of Dr. Martin Luther King, Jr., in "The Greatest Manhunt in Law Enforcement History," published in the August 1968 *Reader's Digest.* Writing on the assumption that Ray was a lone killer, O'Leary gave a dramatic if palpably slanted account of the Bureau's far-ranging search for the fugitive.

Others in the favored sanctum included Walter Trohan, dean of the *Chicago Tribune*'s Washington bureau, Ralph de Toledano of the *National Review,* William I. Nichols, editor and publisher of *This Week* Sunday newspaper supplement, and columnist/television personality Ed Sullivan. Walter Winchell was particularly close to Hoover, and hardly a week went by that he did not favor the "G-man chief" with a gossipy bit in his column. By the same token, Hoover had a *persona non grata* list of correspondents representing the "liberal" press—"The *New York Times* is the most anti-FBI paper in the country," he was quoted as saying—and of writers who at one time or another had taken pot shots at the Bureau.

Quite often, Hoover granted interviews in his office to "neutral" editors, publishers, and journalists. These sessions were, to put it mildly, unilateral. The Director fired off his views on whatever he wished to talk about in his staccato style, so that only the boldest

visitor got a word in edgewise. If the "discussion" took an undesired turn, he pressed a hidden button under his desk and within
seconds the phone on his desk rang conveying "urgent" business, an
excuse for the visitor to be ushered out of the room. Journalist
James Phelan recalled his session while doing the *Saturday Evening
Post* cover story: "I had a list of twelve questions to ask. For two
hours Hoover went on and on, covering a range of subjects. I left
with eleven questions unasked and twelve unanswered."

Although Hoover gave lip service to the concept that the press
should call it as he sees it—"There is the press, which stands ready
to warn us if we get off base or fail to measure up to the standards
expected of us," he said—the record shows that he did not hesitate
to attempt censorship. As far back as 1937, Jack Alexander in his
New Yorker piece stated that among the press corps in the nation's
capital there was "an undercurrent of feeling" that somehow
Hoover was "doing something to undermine the citadel of liberty."
Specifically, Alexander said that one correspondent of a midwestern
newspaper

> swears that while he was gathering material for an article
> on Hoover, which Hoover knew would be unfavorable, he
> was shadowed. Another is similarly positive that he, too,
> was followed while he was preparing an article on Hoover
> for a magazine. This one says that a shadower watched him
> post his manuscript in a Washington mailbox and that next
> morning a man purporting to be from the F.B.I. visited the
> office of the magazine, in New York, and asked to see the
> manuscript.

According to Alexander, Hoover hotly denied the surveillance,
pointing out that the morbid fear of being followed is "a classic
instance of pathological behavior." But there was ample evidence to
confirm a continuing pattern of FBI scrutiny and intimidation of the
press.

A case in point involved Drew Pearson and his associate Jack
Anderson, who frequently hauled Hoover over the carpet in their
columns. According to former Washington correspondent William

L. Rivers in his *The Opinion-Makers,* Pearson's telephone line was so loaded with taps that he could hardly hear on calls to one of his assistants. When he wrote a derogatory column on the FBI in the early 1950s, Anderson reportedly found himself the object of a retaliatory investigation in which FBI agents went around questioning his friends. Although the Bureau denied the existence of the probe, Anderson was shown the actual FBI report by a source in the Department of Justice.

I have personally encountered attempts by the FBI to dissuade editors from publishing my articles. In 1963 when President Kennedy was assassinated, *Saga,* a men's magazine of the time, commissioned me to rush to Dallas and do a critique of the security measures that had failed. From inside sources, I learned of the FBI's thick file on suspect Lee Harvey Oswald, the contents of which had never been relayed to the Secret Service. Editor Al Silverman said that no sooner had my manuscript reached his hands than two FBI agents showed up, wanting a look at it. He turned them down and the magazine, unintimidated, ran the article, "The FBI Could Have Saved President Kennedy's Life," in its March 1964 issue. It was left to Hoover to denounce the article in the columns of Ed Sullivan, who printed his "Dear Ed" letter, and Herb Lyons of the *Chicago Tribune.* He was particularly vehement in denying my finding that there was "jealousy and lack of cooperation and communication between law enforcement agencies," but the Warren Commission later ruled that in fact there had been.

Then in 1965 *Playboy* magazine informed my literary agent that it intended to print "The FBI and Organized Crime," a piece dealing with Hoover's history of ineffectiveness against the national syndicate. No sooner had the deal been made than, as editor Murray Fisher put it, "We were visited by a pair of J. Edgar's finest to inquire into our plans, of which they had somehow gotten wind." Exactly how they had gotten wind remained a mystery for years, until I obtained my FBI file under FOI. It seems that Fisher had offered Sandy Smith, a *Chicago Sun-Times* expert on crime, $500 to add his expertise. Fisher didn't have a clue that Smith was an FBI collaborator who, in the words of Bureau documents, was "a great admirer of the Director" and had been "utilized on many different occasions" where his value was "inestimable." To reciprocate, the FBI fed Smith information from its files so that he could authoritatively quote "Justice Department sources" in his stories for the *Sun-Times* and, later, *Life* magazine.

When Fisher gave Smith a copy of my manuscript it was like asking a rabbit to deliver a carrot. Smith hopped straight over to the Chicago FBI office and handed it to the local boss, Marlin Johnson, who in turn notified publicity chief Cartha DeLoach in Washington. Smith told Johnson that he had stalled *Playboy* by saying "he would look over the piece and let Fisher know his thoughts" as a subterfuge for being given the manuscript. But in fact he intended to inform Fisher that he wanted no part of the article because "it is completely ridiculous, inaccurate, and not worth the paper it is written on." Smith practically begged Johnson not to make any contacts in connection with the article because to do so could damage his reputation as a journalist. He stressed that "this article was furnished to him by Fisher in strictest confidence." That he had breached the confidence was only one of his cardinal sins as a journalist. The other, which was more important, was that he had acted as a government censor.

As a result of Smith's treachery *Playboy* killed the article. My agent received a memo from Fisher saying Sandy Smith had claimed my article was filled with inaccuracies and errors, and that in fact the FBI was fighting organized crime. Smith reported to the FBI that Fisher told him *Playboy* "will have nothing to do with the Turner article, will not buy it from Turner, and will not print it under any circumstances in its current or any other form."

But for advocates of a free press there was a happy ending. *The Nation* magazine published the article as it stood under the title "Crime Is Too Big For The FBI," and widely read *Pageant* reprinted it in its May 1966 edition. Hoover could do nothing with *The Nation,* which had long dared to go eyeball to eyeball with him, but he did try to ding *Pageant,* which was strictly mainstream. On the bottom of a memo advising him that the magazine had deviated from the party line, he scrawled: "See that *Pageant* is not on any of our mailing lists and is given no assistance of any kind."

Since I had no inkling at the time that *Playboy* had been duped by an FBI mole, I submitted another article to them a year later that explored gaps in the Bureau's counterespionage operation. The article, which was based largely on the chapter "The FBI As Our Counterspy" in this book, rose all the way up the editorial escalator to the top, only to be turned down. "The magazine is not vulnerable to retaliation," ruled Editorial Director A. C. Spectorsky, "but the [Playboy] clubs are."

The FBI was even more vigilant in trying to suppress books, which after all have a longer shelf life than magazines. Up until 1950 no serious book had been written that was sharply critical of the Bureau. But in that year Max Lowenthal, an attorney and former advisor to President Harry Truman, prepared a manuscript titled *The Federal Bureau of Investigation.* Hoover got wind of it belatedly through an advance notice in the trade journal *Publisher's Weekly,* and Lowenthal instantly became to him what Salman Rushdie is to Iran's ayatollahs. The Director's first move was to enlist Morris Ernst, the ACLU's general counsel, to try to quietly arm-twist the publisher, William Sloane & Associates, into stopping the presses. On the face of it the notion that a high official of an organization devoted to freedom of expression would attempt censorship on behalf of a police agency was boggling. But Ernst not only believed that the ACLU and FBI could coexist, he had an almost slavering personal relationship with Hoover. Still, it was too much for the civil libertarian, and he found no excuse to recuse himself.

Unable to thwart publication, Hoover sicced his press dogs—Fulton Lewis, Jr., George Sokolsky, and Walter Trohan, to name three—on Lowenthal to smear him as a Communist sympathizer, Moscow lackey, and worse. Then the HUAC, which responded to Hoover's every glower, summoned Lowenthal and his publisher for grilling on their putative leftist connections. The FBI finished off the hapless author by slapping a full-time surveillance on him as if he were engaged in subversive activities. He would never publish again.

I entered the Bureau only months after *The Federal Bureau of Investigation* saw the light of print. Although it read like a deadly dull legal brief and its sales were flat, the obsession with Lowenthal lingered. Agents dropped by bookstores suggesting that the proprietor might not want to stock such a blasphemous volume. One SAC came up with the inspiration to steal copies from library racks, but this was rejected on grounds that replacement copies would be ordered and sales would increase. Then an agent invented a twist: relocate the copies out of their Dewey decimal system order in the libraries so no one could find them.

Hoover blamed his publicity arm, the Crime Records Division, for being taken by surprise by the Lowenthal manuscript. (According to Curt Gentry in his *J. Edgar Hoover,* then Crime Records head Louis Nichols sobbed, "Mr. Hoover, if I had known this book was going to be published, I'd have thrown my body between the presses and stopped it.") "After this," the late Assistant Director William S. Sullivan told Gentry, "We developed informants in the publishing houses." Notable among them were Henry Holt, who published Hoover's *Masters of Deceit,* and Bennett Cerf of Random House, who did *The FBI Story.* In 1962 when the manuscript of Fred Cook's critical *The FBI Nobody Knows* was submitted to Random House, Cerf grievously breached publishing ethics by dispatching a copy to Hoover (the book was published elsewhere in 1964).

When I appeared on the Pacifica network in 1962, I mentioned that I was writing a book on the Bureau (which eventually became *Hoover's FBI*). This alerted Cartha DeLoach, who had succeeded Nichols as head of Crime Records, and he tapped the Bureau informants inside the industry. According to his notes, he tried "Random House, Holt Co., Harpers, et al." but was forced to report that "none have heard of it." In fact the manuscript was sitting at Doubleday & Company, which presumably was devoid of moles. But Doubleday sat on the work for over a year, an unconscionably long time to take to make a decision. It finally sent me a rejection slip.

In the meantime I began writing *The Police Establishment,* which took a long, hard look at the nation's metropolitan departments and the way in which they were interlocked through the FBI. The book devolved from a punchbowl discussion with John Dodds, vice president of G. P. Putnam's Sons, who commissioned it off an outline. I had hardly begun the research when the FBI received a tip that Putnam's had bought a book by me on law enforcement. As documents released under FOI disclose, Cartha DeLoach's crew contacted "an ardent friend and admirer of the Bureau" who was close to the publisher, Walter Minton, to find out if it was true. Although the documents black out the name of this informant, John Dodds later told me that it was a longtime friend of Minton who was in the Hearst press. The informant was forced to report that in fact I was working on a manuscript for Putnam's, but he felt he could "pull the rug out from under" it if the FBI fed him "some off-the-record public source data that he could bring to Walter Minton's attention which would show what a low character Turner is. Naturally, he would not identify the FBI as the source." The informant promised to obtain a copy of my manuscript from Minton as soon as it arrived.

As promised, he delivered a confidential copy of the manuscript and it was reviewed by the Crime Research Section in Washington, which predictably took a dim view of it. At the same time John Dodds wrote to me, "It is very impressive. The tone is excellent and generally speaking you are on the right track." In the meantime the informant continued to trash-talk me to Minton, calling me "a thoroughly unreliable character" engaged in "rotten activities." But despite his argument that he strongly doubted "the book is the type that Putnam's Sons wants to be associated with," Minton said he was inclined to go ahead with it because it was under contract.

The Police Establishment was published in June 1968 to favorable reviews, among them pieces in *Newsweek* and *Book World,* where reviewer Nicholas Pileggi saw it as "a comprehensive, well-written book about the entire police system in the United States." But one way to kill a book is to let it die, and this Putnam's did. Although *Publisher's Weekly* had earlier reported that Putnam's intended to back it with heavy "advertising in cities where police conduct is an issue" and an author's media tour, nothing happened. What media appearances I made were on my own initiative. Whether it was Minton who pulled the plug or Lorrie Lewis, the Putnam's publicity director who, the documents disclose, was friendly with the FBI, is not on the record.

When this book, *Hoover's FBI,* was finally published in March 1970, it was fresh news to the Bureau, which had learned about it only two months earlier through a notice in the trade press. Although the New York publishing houses were riddled with FBI informants, the publisher, tiny Sherbourne Press in Los Angeles, wasn't. With no chance of halting the presses, the FBI geared up for a down-and-dirty campaign against it.

As a first step the Bureau ordered each of its divisions to conduct, as an internal memo states, "a review of major identifiable allegations and investigations in captioned book for the purpose of exposing factual inaccuracies worthy of refutation." It had to be one of the most exhaustive book reviews ever conducted, and, considering the number of pages of quibbling and triviality churned out, must have cost the taxpayers hundreds of thousands of dollars in squandered time. For instance, in *Hoover's FBI* I asserted (in Chapter Eleven) that police across the nation griped that "the Bureau tends to be overly secretive with information it collects on criminals—in other words, exchange of information with the FBI is something of a "one-way street." This was a charge that was so well substantiated that it was almost a matter of judicial notice. As an agent I was totally embarrassed by the policy in dealing with the police to the extent that I would hand them an FBI report for return after I had finished going to the bathroom. To knock off this fly the Bureau used an elephant gun: the Training, General Investigative, Special Investigative, Administrative, and Crime Records Division, whose rebuttal was the typical numbers game: "The FBI disseminated 305,545 items of criminal intelligence information to other Federal, State and local law enforcement agencies during the fiscal year 1969, an increase of over 5,000 above the 1968 total." The fact is that most of these items were more fit for a gossip column and had nothing to do with solving crimes. When it was a question of breaking a big case, the FBI played it close to the vest.

Hoover's strategy was not to make a lot of noise about the book right off the bat in the hope that it would go relatively unnoticed and not make the best-seller lists. The strategy was to undertake a kind of COINTELPRO to squelch it. Following a dinner-speech kickoff at the venerable Press Club of San Francisco, the local NBC radio affiliate, KNBR, invited me to tape an interview for the network's "Monitor" program. But within days the interview was canceled "by New York," apparently because "Monitor" was regularly airing the views of Cartha DeLoach.

Then I hit the media circuit in eastern cities to promote

Hoover's FBI. On most of the shows the FBI was invited to send a representative to rebut me, but it flatly declined. When I arrived at the studios of KYW-TV in Philadelphia, host Tom Snyder greeted me, "We even knew what color suit you'd be wearing." It seemed that an agent Larson of the FBI had been in touch with the producer, dropping information that I had been surveilled since my previous stop in Cincinnati (where I appeared on a program with host Nick Clooney, brother of singer Rosemary Clooney, and guest Polly Bergen, the actress, both of whom agreed that criticism of Hoover was long overdue). The program had a call-in format, and one of the callers claimed to be a disinterested party who had just picked a book off the shelf of his home library and found a book critical of me by the Overstreets, who were to education in that era what Pat Robertson is to religion today. In the background I heard the familiar sound of typewriters clacking away in a Bureau stenographer pool and knew this was no average citizen. My deduction was later confirmed by an FBI document in which the local SAC, Joe D. Jamieson, whom I had known and found to be a decent man, boasted, "A pretext call was made by a Supervisor of the Phila. Division" during which "the fact that he [I] was a liar was drawn out." This was the kind of Pollyanna nonsense that officials in the field felt compelled to feed Hoover in order to preserve their careers. In fact all the callers except the FBI plant wanted to know more about what I was saying.

The next stop was Pittsburgh, where I was scheduled to appear on the "Contact" show on KDKA-TV hosted by Marie Torre. According to documents released by the FBI, Torre was "quite pro-FBI" and schmoozed with the local SAC, but she had no control over the selection of guests. When the producer, Mike Fields, called the FBI to offer a place on the show, he was advised that "there was a very simple solution to this—not to have Turner on." Fields argued that the topic of the FBI was of national interest and my book, in fact, addressed issues. With that Bureau headquarters typed up an anonymous letter that an agent hand-delivered to Fields to assist Torre "in defending the FBI against this unwarranted criticism by this completely discredited ex-Agent." When I showed up, Fields, clearly disturbed by such underhanded tactics, gave me a copy. Dated March 23, 1970, the scarlet letter focused on the fact I had been fired by Hoover but omitted that the Civil Service appeal had been rigged in his favor. It alleged I lacked character because, after initially saying there was no evidence of a conspiracy in the John F. Kennedy assassination, I changed position and became "a dedicated supporter" of New Orleans District Attorney Jim Garrison and his theory that the president was the victim of "a highly organized plot." It is true that after a whirlwind trip to Dallas to do a story on the security breakdown, nothing came to my attention indicating a conspiracy. But when I had time to study the evidence I changed my mind, though the always-inflexible FBI never did. Another canard was that I was a "dedicated enemy of law enforcement." At the time I had written numerous articles for the legal press on police science topics and edited a series called *Police Evidence Library* that had been lauded by police reviewers. Hoover was aware of this. In fact when informed about it several years earlier he had scrawled at the bottom of the memo, "What a rat!" My contributions to progressive law enforcement weren't something the Director wanted to hear about.

The anonymous letter was widely distributed to the media, where it wound up in newspaper and television libraries and the hands of reporters and TV hosts. Thus I was hardly surprised when several shows on the remainder of the tour canceled without plausible explanation. Nor were some of the reviews unexpected. In his review of April 7, 1970, Jeremiah O'Leary of the *Washington Evening Star,* who was known to be close to the Bureau, savaged the book with help of the anonymous letter. An FBI memo released under FOI reveals that Hoover sent a laudatory letter to the "quite friendly" reporter the same day, and authorized reprinting a thousand copies of the review for the use of headquarters and all field offices in knocking down the book.

Nevertheless *Hoover's FBI* played to a number of highly favorable reviews. *Publisher's Weekly* called it a "bombshell, a convincing picture" from the inside. The *Denver Post* considered the book a revelation of "the personality cult that surrounds the Director . . . and the reputation of the agency itself." *Playboy* used crisper prose, saying "the message rings out sharply as a rifle retort." *Choice*

Books for College Libraries styled it "an ably written critique of the FBI corrective of the myth" that was "highly recommended for public, high school, and college libraries."

As it turned out, sales of the hardcover edition were modest, and Hoover kept on hold the massive counterattack his staff had laboriously prepared. In part his clandestine campaign to undermine the book had succeeded, but the limited distribution that a small publisher like Sherbourne Press was able to accomplish also was a major factor. But what goes around comes around: Dell decided to issue a paperback edition, and it was an instant success. It went into two printings, but when a third was in the works Hoover suddenly died.

Another instance of attempted suppression involved Mark Lane's *Rush to Judgment,* which in attacking the conclusions of the Warren Commission exposed many sins of omission and commission by FBI assassination investigators. The manuscript had been submitted to Holt, Rhinehart & Winston, into which Henry Holt & Company, publishers of *Masters of Deceit,* had been merged. In this case there is no mystery about how the FBI learned about the submission: as is its custom with influential "friends of the Bureau," it had continued to cultivate publisher Holt, by, for example, taking his son on a personal tour of headquarters and introducing him to the Director. Cartha DeLoach, who headed the Crime Records Division, tried to prevail upon the firm not to publish *Rush to Judgment,* going so far as to proffer a look at the FBI's "Lane file" (presumably, the file was built up in the course of the Bureau's intensive surveillance of Lane in 1964 as he traveled the country speaking against the official version; numerous FBI reports on his activities remain classified in the National Archives). But to their credit, Holt officials disdained the blackmail and published the book, which became a best-seller.

In *Holiday* magazine, Tristam Coffin recounted yet another dissuasion attempt in his article on the Department of Justice. "The care with which the FBI guards [its] image was shown last summer," he wrote, "when a wire-service reporter discovered what he considered a serious FBI blunder in the Billie Sol Estes case. He was asked very earnestly whether he had considered the effect on the 'image' of sending out such a story."

The FBI's diligence in preserving its image through the media was matched by the assiduousness of its public relations program. A highlight of the program was the guided tour of FBI headquarters, which attracted close to half a million visitors each year. Along with the Capitol and other Washington landmarks, it was what tourists talked about most when they returned home. The tours were led by young "special employees," many of whom went on to become agents. There was a touch of the pitchman in their style—"Here, ladies and gentlemen, we have photographs of those individuals currently on the FBI's list of Ten Most Wanted Fugitives"; "We are coming now to what is recognized as the world's greatest crime laboratory"—that was in keeping with the sideshow atmosphere.

The Dillinger exhibit, representing the high-water mark of FBI glory, was a featured exhibit. A duplicate of Public Enemy Number One's death mask was enshrined along with his fingerprint card and an array of weapons including two machine guns. Another display, "Notorious Criminals Captured by the FBI," was a rogues' gallery of such old-time adversaries as Ma Barker and her sons, Alvin Karpis, Frank Nash, and "Baby Face" Nelson that included newspaper clippings telling of their demise at the hands of the G-men. Famous cases cracked by the Bureau were narrated by the guides with a flair for suspense that rivaled Alfred Hitchcock. Some of the displays, which were fabricated by Crime Records' Exhibit Section, were electronically programmed to illustrate with blinking lights the sequential action of a case.

Exemplifying the Bureau's counterespionage work was a tableau captioned "The Crime of the Century: The Case of the A-Bomb Spies." A photograph of a huge mushroom cloud was superimposed with a hammer and sickle, from which arrows lead to the executed Julius and Ethel Rosenberg, her brother David Greenglass, who turned government witness, and other principals in the spy network.

The wonders of the laboratory were impressively arcane to most visitors, and the shooting exhibition brought gasps from young and old alike. The Bureau had a stable of trick shot artists who fired tracer bullets with a machine gun or hit an axe blade head-on, causing the bullet to split and shatter clay discs suspended on each side.

At one time, before the mass influx, visitors were encouraged at tour's end to submit to being fingerprinted, and were given a card bearing one of their prints and the inscription: "Souvenir print. Federal Bureau of Investigation. United States Department of Justice. J. Edgar Hoover, Director. Patents pending." Still, the visitor did not go away empty handed. A booklet, *Know Your FBI*, described the various phases of the operation and acknowledged Hoover's fatherhood of each with such tributes as "a pioneer in the field of scientific crime detection," and "Mr. Hoover always had advocated that an informed public, aware of the danger of communism and threat of the criminal element, is in a position to protect itself from these two evils."

As Tristam Coffin observed, "Most FBI activities revealed to the public, including the director's daily walk to work, have [a] melodramatic air and a slight scent of mothballs—even the FBI reports, which go to a large mailing list and are reproduced in newspapers and over the air." Paradoxically, it was this anachronistic quality that made the Bureau so appealing to many people. In an increasingly complex age, with the nation beset by foreign and domestic crises that seemed incapable of solution, a large segment of the population undoubtedly wished for a return to the simpler times epitomized by the G-men, and wanted in the worst way to believe that Hoover's simplistic answers were relevant to modern America.

Although the exact amount of the taxpayers' money spent by the Crime Records Division on publicity was buried in the Bureau's $200 million-plus annual budget, the extreme importance of the division in the FBI scheme of things was indicated by the rapid rise of its head, Cartha DeLoach. A comparatively young ranking official, he carried the title of assistant to the director, which placed him immediately below Hoover and Clyde Tolson. Significantly, DeLoach outranked the heads of the investigative divisions, who are called assistant directors.

An athletic, sandy-haired Georgian, DeLoach entered the Bureau in 1942 and, after a brief apprenticeship in the field, was transferred to Washington and began his public relations career. Attached to the Security Division, forerunner of the Domestic Intelligence Division, he was once awarded a meritorious increase in salary "for excellent results obtained in connection with liaison duties with other Governmental agencies," which, the commendation read, constituted "a contribution vital to the internal security of the Nation." In 1959, he was named head of the Crime Records Division, automatically assuming the rank of assistant director.

The propriety of a public agency expending large sums of public money on self-promotion is dubious—and, ironically, no holder of the public purse-strings has undertaken to question it because of the formidable image that promotion has generated. Was it proper, for example, to spend $30,000 on printing alone to produce a handout, *The Story of the Federal Bureau of Investigation,* considering that the mass media had more than adequately propagated the FBI story? This was a piddling amount compared to what the total expenditure for publicity must have been, taking into account the hundreds of thousands of man-hours the Crime Records Division burned up.

But cost considerations were secondary to other, more profound ones. As a potential national police force, the FBI was the one agency that should have been subjected to the severest scrutiny, yet the manufacture of a grossly exaggerated image by publicity techniques rendered it virtually immune.

The American people for the most part believed implicitly in the FBI, a trust that was in part misplaced—as I have attempted to show.

Other side effects were less patent. In one, the inflated image created an authoritative mirage that blotted out more sophisticated opinions in the criminology field. The phenomenon was noted early by professionals. In 1938, Newman F. Baker of the American Institute of Criminal Law and Criminology complained that as Hoover "became more and more famous . . . his statements became wilder and wilder," with the result that "to him, one must belong to the machinegun school of criminology or the cream-puff school. There is no middle ground." In October 1937, the American Prison Association, reacting to Hoover's labeling of parole as "one of the major menaces of our country," adopted a resolution regretting "the indiscriminate attacks . . . on parole as tending to inflame and confuse the public mind."

Correctional expert Howard B. Gill nicely summed up the problem several years ago: "Irrespective of all the tested knowledge by students in the field, a tentative and at times raw statement by J. Edgar Hoover in the *Reader's Digest* carries more weight than one hundred research articles in the *Journal of Criminal Law, Criminology and Police Science*."

There is a body of opinion that holds that excessive publicity as practiced by the FBI only incites more crime. Significantly, at least two of Hoover's more notable federal law enforcement colleagues held to this theory. Dr. Harry Anslinger, who for thirty years headed the Federal Bureau of Narcotics, shied away from personal publicity and rejected out of hand countless movie and television offers to glamorize the narcotics agent and his job. "They'd love to make a Dick Tracy out of me," he told one crime writer. "Well—I won't have it. We get our work done without it." And he added: "Any sensational treatment by the movies, on television, or in the press just makes more addicts. We know that."

Chief Postal Inspector D. H. Stevens was of like mind. In his foreword to *The Silent Investigators,* which describes his little-known service, Stephens wrote: "Traditionally, the Inspection Service has sought to avoid publicity because our experience has taught us that undue or flamboyant publicity of criminal matters is not in the interest of the public. . . . Publicizing crime always brings imitators. Criminals, weak-minded persons, and children are prone to imitate the evil acts of others."

No more vivid corroboration that crime publicity begets crime could be found than in the wave of aircraft bombings and bomb scares that followed the 1955 explosion of a United Air Lines flight over Colorado that killed forty-four persons. It was discovered that one Jack Gilbert Graham had taken out life insurance policies on his mother, then planted a bomb in her luggage just before she boarded the plane. This added a new and more horrible dimension to the murder-for-insurance racket, as it resulted in mass loss of life. The FBI assumed jurisdiction, and its investigation was bathed in publicity and recounted in numerous articles as well as Whitehead's *The FBI Story*. A chain of subsequent bombings ensued, as well as more than two thousand false reports of explosives on airplanes.

The television series "The FBI" was viewed in some quarters as a catalyst to violence. Quinn Martin gained a reputation as a "blood and guts" producer with "The Untouchables," and he did not lose the touch. For example, *San Francisco Examiner* critic Dwight Newton, upon viewing an episode called "The Monster," headed his review "Sadism for a Sunday." And Robert Lewis Shayon, writing in the *Saturday Review,* said he was so shocked by several scenes in "The Tormentors," a blood-splashed kidnap story, that he called to complain to the network, the FBI, and the National Association of Broadcasters. Although the treatment may have been standard procedure for the industry, Shayon declared, it was disturbing to have the program "come to us with the approval of a federal agency."

Disturbing it may have been, but it was also free advertising. And that Hoover was not disposed to turn down.

CHAPTER EIGHT

THE CRITIC-FLAYER

Criticism of the FBI may not be treason at first
glance but it is best not to take chances; the
intellectuals whom [Hoover] accuses of having
betrayed us have no loudspeaker in a class with his.

—Historian Bernard DeVoto
in The Easy Chair

On a steamy summer day in 1968 I showed up at the television studios for an appearance on the show "The New Yorkers." The subject for discussion was the police, a rather steamy issue. My sparring partner for the occasion was Edwin Lee, an avowed conservative who had his own family-oriented radio program (and later invited me on it). The bout was hard-hitting but with no low blows. Afterward, Lee invited me for coffee. He never went into the ring, he said, without knowing a bit about his opponent. All he had known about me was that I was an ex-FBI agent, so he had called a highly placed official of the New York office, a friend of his. Come on right over," the official had said, "there's something you ought to see." The "something" was a bulky file on me. The official flipped its pages like a deck of cards; Lee remembered that a number of my magazine articles were there. The official had urged him to attack me personally, to go for the groin with the innuendo that I was a near-Communist. "I deal in issues, not personalities," Lee had cut him off.

One of the most pronounced traits of the Hoover FBI was its tendency to coil and strike back at its critics. To be sure, an agency of government has the right, even the obligation, to set the record straight when it has been unjustly maligned. But with the Bureau, it seemed, no divergent viewpoint, no matter how constructive or well-intended, was considered to be on justifiable middle ground. Having synthesized an image of perfection, the FBI chief was obsessed with putting down anyone who dared to tamper with it.

By dint of his success in mowing down the Public Enemies, Hoover soon came to fancy himself an authority not only on law enforcement but on other phases of the criminal process as well. Although he himself was no more than an armchair investigator, he had no compunction about calling those closer to the action "fiddle-faced reformers" with "mental halitosis." When this brought criticism that he was less than dignified in his speech, he flared, "If it's undignified, then I'll be undignified. I'm going to tell the truth about the rats [criminals]. I'm going to tell the truth about the miserable politicians who protect them and the slimy, silly or sob-sister convict lovers who let them out on sentimental or illy advised [*sic*] paroles. If the people don't like it they can get me fired. But I'm going to say it."

And say it he did. Hooverisms became a byword, if not to the more rational segments of America, at least to the more insecure. But with the Bureau's assumption of national defense responsibilities in the late 1930s, the name-calling in pulp magazines took on a new and more ominous hue. The Communists criticized the FBI, Hoover pointed out, and whoever did the same might just be. . . . The Director was never bashful about attributing ulterior motives to his critics—up to and including a U.S. senator.

The senator was George W. Norris, a Nebraska populist who saw in Hoover's penchant for publicity the seeds of a police state. "Unless we do something to stop this furor of adulation and praise as being omnipotent," Norris predicted, "we shall have an organization—the organization of the FBI—which instead of protecting our people from the evil acts of criminals will itself in the end direct the Government by tyrannical force, as the history of the world shows has always been the case when the secret police and secret detectives have been snooping around the houses of honest men." While acknowledging the "wonderful work" the FBI had done in the past, the senator cautioned that the agency should not be "dominated by any individuals or by any groups who are looking to newspaper advertising for adulation every day of their lives, who arrest men and try them in the newspapers and not in the courts of law."

Judging from the outcry, Norris had hit home. A well-known columnist devoted his entire space to picturing Norris's words as a Communist-inspired smear. Although he was not willing to mention the senator by home, Hoover was unable to desist. In a speech before a women's group shortly afterward, he charged that "the most vicious 'smear' campaign which is being directed against the FBI is a part of the working program of various anti-American forces.... The Communists hope that with the FBI shackled, they can proceed without interference as they go their boring, undermining way to overthrow our Government."

The extremism of the attack on Norris unsettled a number of his colleagues, including Senator Henry F. Ashurst of Arizona, a strong FBI supporter. Said Ashurst: "Charging the able Senior Senator from Nebraska with attempting to smear somebody is about like charging Abe Lincoln with a similar endeavor."

But Hoover wasn't fazed—he went right on implying that critics of his agency were dupes or parties to a Communist-engineered plot. When the *Yale Law Journal* published a fault-finding article, he retorted, "I find such opinions most frequently expressed on the pages of the *Daily Worker,* the publication of the Communist Party."

Although this kind of sniping seemed too palpably irresponsible to take seriously, there had been times when it was wrapped in the cloak of congressional dignity and used for political ends. In 1947, Clifford J. Durr, a Montgomery, Alabama, lawyer and member of the Federal Communications Commission, was on the receiving end. A group of California businessmen had applied for a radio broadcast license, and Hoover had sent over to the FCC, unsolicited, a memorandum alleging that some of the group "are members of the Communist Party or have affiliated themselves with the activities of the Communist movement." When the FCC asked that the information be supplied in evidentiary form—it could not deny a license on the basis of unsubstantiated conclusions—Hoover replied that he could not disclose confidential sources. The FCC then sent staff members to California to look into the matter. "They reported back that it was impossible to guarantee who was or who was not a Communist," Durr recounted, "but that the people referred to were on the whole well regarded and that their main political activity had been in the direction of reelecting Roosevelt."

Still intimidated by Hoover's bodiless charges, the FCC in effect denied the license by the simple expedient of not acting on the application. Durr strongly opposed this tactic. In a speech to members of the press, he asked rhetorically, "Can men be fairly tried when their right to face their accusers, and to be fully advised of the nature and cause of the charge against them, depends upon the 'discretion' of those who accuse them?"

Durr's dissent was finally picked up by columnist Marquis W. Childs. In the *Washington Post,* November 19, 1947, he widened the scope of the discussion by pointing out that there was nothing to prevent Hoover from giving unsolicited evaluations "on the attitudes of those who deal with opinion and news. The mere suggestion of such a step would be enough to frighten the timid into curbing any stray thoughts that could be judged to fall outside the narrowest traditional mold."

The suggestion that Hoover had not been quite a model of rectitude in the license case triggered an angry outburst. Demanding that the FCC "repudiate" Durr, the FBI chief explained that the Bureau did disseminate helpful information to other federal agencies but didn't "evaluate" it or "make recommendations" as to what action if any should be taken. This was a bit short of reality; by labeling people Communists or sympathizers the FBI was consciously making a de facto evaluation, and by distributing the evaluation to other agencies it was impinging in a most potent way on the final decision.

The outrageously biased nature of the information on which the FBI based its evaluation came to light during the FCC's deliberations on Durr's fate. In his own defense, Durr cited some of the criteria the Bureau had used:

> It seems to me that it is of little help to the Commission to be informed that an applicant was, in 1944, at the height of the war, reported by an unidentified source as being in contact with an unidentified individual "who was suspected

of possible pro-Russian activity"; . . . or that "according to an unknown outside source" the name of the applicant "appears" as a member of a committee of an organization of artists and professional people which was active in support of the Democratic presidential nominee in the 1944 presidential elections; . . . or that according to a newspaper account of a speech delivered by vice-Presidential candidate Bricker in the 1944 campaign, the speaker charged that the Democratic party had become the "Hillman-Browder Communist Party" and that the applicant had left his job with the government to support the campaign of President Roosevelt, the founder of this "Communistic Party"; or that the applicant has been reported by an unidentified source to have been a member of the committee to greet the late president of a large labor union.

Although nothing less absurd than this was ever adduced, the FCC wrote apologetically to the FBI director, saying Durr had spoken only as an individual and expressing full confidence in Hoover and his agency. At the same time, Hoover partisans in Congress were filling the air with oratory, led by the reactionary Republican Senator Homer Capehart of Indiana. Chastising Durr, Capehart made the scaremongering statement that "evidence unfolds daily that in our Government household Communists and their New Deal fellow travelers are being harbored in key positions where they can sabotage our Nation's policies." Capehart vowed that there would be a full investigation, but this, too, turned out to be puff.

The Durr affair was only a whisper compared to the din created by Cleveland industrialist Cyrus Eaton when he complained on national television that the FBI was breathing down the necks of scientists. A maverick capitalist who believed in closer bonds with the Soviet Union, Eaton had sponsored the annual Pugwash conferences that brought together nuclear scientists from both socialistic and capitalistic nations in the interests of peace. On May 4, 1958, on the Mike Wallace program, he stated that "Hitler in his prime, through the Gestapo, never had any such extensive spy organizations as we have in this country today." Of the FBI's reputation he said: "I think it's had a tremendous buildup. It has enjoyed wonderful propaganda and sold itself in a marvelous way. But I always worry when I see a nation feel that it is coming to greatness through the activities of its policemen."

A nationwide storm broke. Offered equal time by the network, Hoover remained silent, letting his apologists answer for him. Walter Trohan of the *Chicago Tribune* waded into Eaton. Then Chairman Francis Walter of the HUAC announced that he was going to subpoena the aging captain of industry, which tended to confirm the police state charge. The swell of public opinion began to form behind Eaton, perhaps with the same reasoning the *New York Herald-Tribune* articulated: "We haven't agreed with many of Eaton's positions, but we think it is a very healthy thing, and a heartening affirmation of the pluralistic nature of our society, to have so wealthy a man taking such an unorthodox and non-conformist position. Go right on speaking your mind, Cyrus. Walter is making a fool out of nobody but himself."

Eaton did go on, and Walter backed down. But it was too bitter a pill for Hoover to swallow. Citing what he called the FBI's "magnificent record of accomplishment," he used the *FBI Law Enforcement Bulletin* of July 1958 to berate the "unscrupulous few" who "through studied insults and calculated distortions would besmirch and disgrace this world-renowned record of democratic achievement."

The use of congressional cronies to try to polish off an adversary was illustrated again in 1962 when former agent Jack Levine loosed a broadside of charges against the Bureau. Quoted widely in the press, Levine unhinged Hoover with a potpourri of inside glimpses, ranging from the Director's idiosyncrasies (new men were told to carry an extra handkerchief because "the Director distrusts persons with moist palms, as he considers this to be an indication of weak character") and megalomania ("we were told by our bureau supervisors that it was very difficult to get pay raises and promotions in the bureau unless the Director receives a great number of laudatory letters") to substantive problems ("Mr. Hoover requires that all of the agents work an accepted amount of overtime in order to build up impressive statistics").

My own opinion was that Levine's insights were substantially correct but in some instances overdrawn. For example, fawning letters weren't necessary for routine advancement through pay scales, although they were quite helpful for those with more lofty ambitions, and to be sure once an agent had had an audience with Hoover during a visit to Washington it behooved him to ask for another one next time he was in. But more important were Levine's reasons for sounding off. He had left the Bureau in disillusionment, he said, although he did later apply for reinstatement. An offer to join the Department of Justice's organized crime section was withdrawn, Levine asserted, because in the words of a Justice official, "the FBI was very displeased by my giving information to the Justice Department and my criticizing them, and . . . they didn't feel that they could employ me in the Justice Department because of the estranged relations that might result."

Despite its quaverings, the Justice Department didn't scruple to milk Levine of what he knew about the Bureau. Then Assistant Attorney General Herbert J. Miller, Jr., in charge of the criminal division, asked him to prepare a report. He did, and it must have raised more than one eyebrow within the staid portals of Justice. Dated January 23, 1962, the report argued that the "bold and imaginative movement towards the New Frontier has come to a grinding halt with respect to the Federal Bureau of Investigation." There were three major obstacles to reform, Levine held: "(1) No one will believe it. (2) The majority of people in the country do not want to believe it because the FBI is one of the few remaining unblemished myths in our culture. (3) Past and present employees of the FBI will be reluctant to cooperate in an investigation of it because of the fear of recriminations by the Director."

Searching and well-documented, the Levine report should have been the fulcrum for an intensive probe of the FBI. Miller did nothing but sit on it. Levine then made the rounds of official Washington with similar results. Only then did he take his case to the public.

Large-circulation magazines turned him down, so he wound up in *The Nation* and on the airwaves of WBAI in New York, one of three stations in the small listener-supported Pacifica Foundation network. In an article titled "Hoover and the Red Scare" in *The*

Nation, he contended that Hoover had consistently overblown the Communist threat "to safeguard the stature and autocratic powers he has gained as the country's No. 1 protector against Communism." In the WBAI interview, he repeated the broad spectrum of charges he had made in the report to Miller.

WBAI had contacted the Department of Justice and the FBI to get their versions. "From the very beginning of our investigation of this matter," the station declared, "government officials have attempted to cast aspersions on Levine's honesty, integrity, and motivation." Indeed, as the program went on the air, WBAI received a telegram from Herbert Miller saying that Levine had started a "campaign of vilification" after Hoover had refused to rehire him.

The Levine revelations kicked up a storm and raised a call from many editorial quarters for the department and the FBI to respond to the issues. On October 23, 1962, the *Boston Herald* said: "A statement from Mr. Hoover on Mr. Levine's charges is clearly called for." The same day the *New York Times* demanded: "If his assertions are false, the American people should be told so by a responsible source. If they are true, in whole or in part, the American people should be told what is being done to correct matters."

Only when Milton Freudenheim of the *Chicago Daily News* incorporated Levine's charges in a widely printed article did the Bureau break its silence. Ducking the issues and aiming personally at Levine, Clyde Tolson wrote a letter to the newspapers, including the *Washington Post,* that had carried Freudenheim's article, in effect scolding them for publishing such "irresponsible and unsubstantiated charges." Tolson had no compunction about searing Levine with the "security risk" brand, alleging that he had "utterly disregarded the security of the Nation."

As the word battle raged, I was invited to comment over KPFA, Berkeley, another Pacifica station, on Levine's scathing indictment. From my experience, I said, he was right. The cult of personality did flourish, and there hadn't been any black agents passing through the training. Moreover, organized crime had been left virtually untouched: "I think that one of the things that does frustrate the agents quite a bit is the fact that they hadn't been given free rein to go against the top hoodlums and the big boys in crime. It's been more or less a situation where their efforts are channeled into accumulating quantitatively a large number of statistics."

At this point the Cuban missile crisis monopolized the news for weeks. While it did, Senator James O. Eastland, Hoover's ideological kinsman, quietly started a probe of the Pacifica network under the aegis of his Internal Security Committee. Seven officers of Pacifica were subpoenaed for the closed hearings beginning January 10, 1963. Although there was much ado over the fact that Los Angeles Communist functionary Dorothy Healey had been given air time—Pacifica was noted for its unexpurgated broadcasting—the hearings produced nothing of substance. But they did manage to swipe the network with a Red brush, and very nearly put it out of business because of the cost of defending itself. Hardly anyone mistook the hearings for anything but a symbiotic gesture. As ACLU official Ernest Besig put it, "One of the sacred cows of the Internal Security Committee was sinned against and now somebody's got to pay the piper."

There was a sequel to the affair, Jack Levine joined a well-known Phoenix, Arizona, law firm and applied for admission to the bar in that state. He was turned down by the Arizona Bar Association on the basis of a letter from J. Edgar Hoover alleging that he had made false accusations against the Bureau. Finally the Arizona Supreme Court had to order him admitted to practice with the opinion that holding a view of the FBI contrary to Hoover's was not tantamount to poor character and was in any case irrelevant.

When TWA Captain Donald J. Cook, Jr., sharply criticized the FBI handling of his plane's hijacking in November 1969, the Bureau was temporarily stymied since Cook could hardly be daubed Red. The incident involved the commandeering at gunpoint of the plane by AWOL Marine Raphael Minichiello, who ultimately ordered it to his native Italy. It was necessary to stop for refueling at New York, where, despite the captain's radioed request that the operation go unmolested, a swarm of FBI men in flack jackets and thinly disguised as ground crew members moved in, hoping to make a precipitous move on Minichiello or pick him off with gunfire. Cook shouted out the cockpit window, "We want everyone away from this plane. This boy is going to shoot us," but the agents continued to close in. The young hijacker panicked and fired a shot into the cockpit ceiling. This finally convinced the FBI to back off, and Cook was able to calm Minichiello down.

In Rome after the episode, Cook told the press: "The Rome police put the FBI to shame. The FBI just thought they were playing Wyatt Earp and wanted to engage in a shootout with a supposed criminal and bring him to justice. They would have wound up unnecessarily killing this boy and, probably, completely destroying a $7 million airplane and wounding or endangering the lives of four crew members." And he added with stinging directness that his own course "cost less in gunpowder and more in gasoline."

Asked for comment, New York SAC John F. Malone remained silent. Patently, the strategy of Malone, a former firearms instructor, was a crude and indefensible grandstand play. But Cook's impertinence was not to go unpunished. Through the voice of Albert T. Taub, an assistant DA who worked closely with the FBI, the captain's comments were labeled "irresponsible"—a favorite Bureau operative phrase—and his actions as an attempt to portray himself as "the sole hero of the escapade."

Yet another illustration of the way Hoover struck back at those who disagreed with him was provided by the 1966 furor over the bugging of Las Vegas casinos. It was discovered that the FBI had strategically planted twenty-two bugs and connected them to telephone lines leading to the local Bureau office. The abortive eavesdropping became a major issue in the elections that fall. Democratic Governor Grant Sawyer, running for reelection, took the position that the FBI had committed an unwarranted and dangerous intrusion. In a letter to then Attorney General Nicholas Katzenbach dated September 1, 1966, he called the federal trespasses "a shocking story of espionage and harassment against our gambling industry." Stressing that "no one is more anxious to join you in an effective fight against organized crime than I and the citizens of Nevada," Sawyer complained that the state had been "the victim of silent war by these agencies, who seem determined to damage or destroy the major business of this state—without regard to morality or the law." The FBI's conduct, he told the press, reminded him "of all I have heard and read about Nazism."

Ignoring the person of Sawyer, Hoover used a sympathetic newspaper to launch a counterattack. In this case it was the *Las Vegas Sun*, which had run a pro-FBI editorial on September 25. Complimenting publisher H. M. ("Hank") Greenspun for his "perspective column," the Bureau chief claimed that his agency's action had been under departmental authority rather than free-lance. The governor, he said, had "minimized the critical issue of hoodlum ownership and pirating of funds from Nevada gambling casinos." Without any qualification, he asserted that "funds illegally skimmed from certain Nevada casinos have been used for a multitude of nefarious purposes."

Sawyer fired back that "the truth or falsity of criminal charges in a democracy should be determined by due process in a court of law. Public agencies secretly feeding unprovable and unverified information to news media constitutes blackmail." Said the governor with unassailable logic: "This same process could be used against any person, any group, any industry, anywhere in the United States."

Not unexpectedly, Hoover didn't reply. But the Republican candidate, Paul Laxalt, wired an apology to the FBI chief for the governor's "Nazi tactics" remark and told the voters he would "iron out the differences" with the Bureau because the "war" was one Nevada could not hope to win. Sawyer countered that Laxalt's position was one of "abject surrender." His office brought me to Las Vegas to do spots on statewide television warning of the dangers of unbridled federal police powers. Amusingly, a member of the John Birch Society running for Congress (he lost heavily) challenged me to a debate. He had telephoned FBI headquarters in Washington to get the lowdown on me. But when I accepted the challenge, he backed out with the comment that I was a "carpetbagger."

Sawyer lost the election. Although some blamed his fight with Hoover, other factors were probably more important: he was going for an unprecedented third term, Laxalt was an appealing candidate in his own right, and there was a Republican tide in the west in 1966.

But as with Jack Levine, Hoover wasn't through with Sawyer. After the election Sawyer went to Washington to sound out President Johnson, Hubert Humphrey, and Civil Service Chairman John Macy about a federal appointment. All three urged that he accept one, and Johnson proposed that it be Governor General of the Panama Canal Zone. After some hesitation, Sawyer agreed.

As is routine in such cases, the White House asked the FBI to start its background check of the prospective appointee. Agents made inquiries about Sawyer in Nevada, but somehow the usual discreetness was absent and the news was bannerlined by the newspapers. It was widely known that Lyndon Johnson was stubbornly perverse about making appointments that had been predicted in the press, and Sawyer never got his.

A classic example of Hoover's hypersensitivity to criticism came when historian Bernard DeVoto wrote his "The Easy Chair" column in *Harper's,* October 1949. Entitled "Notice to the FBI," the column expressed DeVoto's uneasiness over the nebulous standards he thought the FBI used in its personnel inquiries. Asserting that much of the information-gathering was done "irresponsibly," he put the agency on notice that he would no longer discuss personalities in private—only in a court of law.

"I like a country where it's nobody's damned business what magazines anyone reads, what he thinks, whom he has cocktails with," DeVoto wrote. "I like a country where we do not have to stuff the chimney against listening ears and where what we say does not go into the FBI files along with a note from S-17 that I may have another wife in California. I like a country where no college-trained flatfeet collect memoranda about us and ask judicial protection for them, a country where when someone makes statements about us to officials he can be held to account. We had that kind of country only a little while ago and I'm for getting it back."

Evidently beside himself, Hoover dashed off a blistering letter to *Harper's* sidestepping the issues but saying he would not "dignify Mr. DeVoto's half-truths, inaccuracies, distortions, and misstatements with a denial or an explanation. Rebutted DeVoto: "That is his habit; he maintains silence by the stickful on every front page. When he wrote to the magazine, he had already not dignified 'my half-truths, inaccuracies, distortions, and misstatements' by denouncing me formally in archepiscopal curse that was carried by every wire service and printed by every daily newspaper in the country. . . . Not dignifying makes a neater game than answering criticism. It is also a form of loud-mouthed personal abuse, which has other names as well, by a man of great power and high public office."

Syndicated columnist John Crosby also felt the fury of Hoover's pique. In a column "The FBI Commercial" that appeared, among other places, in the *New York Herald-Tribune,* October 2, 1961, Crosby deplored the FBI's self-aggrandizement on the one hand and its vacillation against organized crime on the other. "Nowhere in the world is crime more profitable, better organized or less bothered by law enforcement than in the United States," he declared in the form of an open letter to Hoover, "and you have been the top cop in this country for 36 years. . . . Under your benevolent eye the crime syndicates are now rolling in wealth and respectability, . . . and so well organized is your press relations and so docile the press at accepting your word on police matters that all attempts to grapple with organized crime on a national level have been successfully throttled."

Hoover bitterly assailed Crosby in a letter to the *Herald-Tribune* editor published October 6, 1961. Implying that the columnist might have had an ulterior purpose, he labeled Crosby's opinions as "appalling," "invective," and "degrading," and took the newspaper to task for permitting its pages to serve as a forum for "impugning the efforts of the employees of the FBI who day by day loyally and devotedly serve their country."

Evidently perturbed by the unseemly flap, *Herald-Tribune* publisher John Hay ("Jock") Whitney, who had served as ambassador to Great Britain under Eisenhower, paid a diplomatic call on the Director. Lauding him as a great American, Whitney apologized for the column and passed it off as a slight overstatement on the part of a member of the staff. Unmollified, Hoover launched into a tirade against the judgment of the editor in publishing it. At this Whitney's cool vanished, and he tartly reminded the Director that there was such a thing as freedom of the press.

In his 1964 blast at *Newsweek* for its cover story weighing the pros and cons of Hoover's lengthy stewardship, the Director used a standard technique for discrediting critics. In a letter to the maga-

zine's editor that ran front page in the daily press, he branded the
article "a new low in reporting" and cited several purported errors
of fact. This was in accordance with the time-tested technique of
extracting the weak points of an article (every long one has a few),
strongly rebutting them, and then labeling them as characteristic of
the reporting in the article as a whole.

In this case Hoover made much ado about a passage that said he
"never bothered to send [Robert Kennedy] a note of condolence on
his brother's death," and one stating that the FBI had five agents on
permanent loan to the appropriations subcommittee that handled its
budget requests. Hoover produced a copy of such a note, and the
obliging John Rooney of the subcommittee denied borrowing any
agents. Two mistakes in a lengthy article was better than average—
hardly "a new low in reporting." But what may have stung Hoover
to rage was that there were several quotes from unnamed high officials in his own headquarters, and they weren't uniformly flattering.
"The man is intensely sensitive," one aide was quoted as saying.
"Some go so far as to say he's an extreme egotist."

Even an oblique slight might elicit a brusque response. In September 1959, *True* ran an article on CIA Director Allan Dulles in which
he was compared with his FBI counterpart. "Besides jurisdiction,
there are other basic differences between the organizations, some of
which may be traceable to the differences in the personalities of the
men at the top," wrote author William Nathan. "Where Allen Dulles
is considerate of his men, with the idea of keeping them on as career
employees, J. Edgar Hoover is, by all accounts, a driver with the result
that not many FBI agents accumulate much seniority. Where Dulles
has made the CIA publicity shy, Hoover has built the FBI on a solid
base of publicity, public sympathy, and understanding."

It was Clyde Tolson's turn this time. "I am deeply concerned
over the charges leveled against the FBI in the article, 'Allen Dulles:
America's Global Sherlock.' The charge that 'not many FBI agents
accumulate much seniority' is easily disproved. Of our 6,000 Special
Agents 58 percent have from 10 to as high as 48 years of loyal and
dedicated service." Unimpressed, *True* captioned the Tolson letter:
"G (Gripe) MAN." But the FBI had the last word. Upon returning
from a trip abroad, William Nathan was summoned to FBI head-

quarters, where he was given the details of his trip, including the inbound flight number. The lesson was clear: don't write disparagingly of the Bureau.

On occasion Hoover played the martyr role while his national fan club took up the gauntlet. No better illustration can be found than the furor that followed the August 1962 speech of W. H. ("Ping") Ferry, a former newspaperman and vice president of the Fund for the Republic, before the western states Democratic conference in Seattle. Pricking a series of contemporary myths, the bristly liberal described Hoover as "the indubitable mandarin of anticommunism in the U.S." and held him chiefly responsible for "keeping the Red poltergeist hovering in the national consciousness." Ferry rammed home the point that if Communist spying were as epidemic as the Director claimed, it might be that "the country needs a more efficient spy-swatter."

That did it. Richard Nixon, who happened to be visiting the scene of the crime, called upon Democratic leaders to repudiate Ferry's remarks and apologize for them to Hoover. Republican national chairman William E. Miller straight-facedly termed the utterances "virtually traitorous." Columnist David Lawrence verbally spanked Ferry and the "faction" of the Democratic Party that "considers the fight against communism in the United States as just a lot of nonsense." Even Robert Kennedy, a stranger in this company, felt compelled to chime in. "Those who dismiss the problem of Communist espionage perform a disservice to the nation," he said, but added, "I also have said many times that I think those who see a Communist under every chair are similarly misled."

When Loudon Wainwright suggested in *Life* in 1964 that it was time for Hoover to step down, howls were heard from several quarters. Said Wainwright: "In his current report to the House Committee on Appropriations Mr. Hoover points out that the sentences handed down in 1963 in cases where the FBI investigated totaled 37,009 years—and this doesn't include life sentences. That figure represents an awful lot of vigilance, but I think a new man, freed of any cult, could rack up a respectable high of, say, 35,009 years in his very first year on the job." The cultish Society of Former Special Agents of the FBI was outraged, about which more will be said in the chapter on that organization. But from inside came an indignant letter from the SAC to the FBI Academy at Quantico, Henry L. ("Hank") Sloan. "Subscriptions to *Life* have been forwarded to this academy since March 1963, when we renewed our subscription for twenty-five months to expire in 1965," Sloan advised. "Please cancel immediately the remainder of my subscription." Thus the academy reading room, never a storehouse of wide-ranging opinions, was made even more sterile.

In glaring contrast to Sloan's missive was one from former agent Burnett Britton of San Francisco, who had resigned after thirteen years. Britton said he had found that indeed "the puffing of Hoover's image was the first order of business each day." Shortly after the letter was published, Britton was paid a visit by two FBI inspectors. If he had any gripes about the Bureau, they told him, he should convey them to his representatives in Congress rather than air them in the press.

About the only member of Congress in the 1960s who expressed firm and non-adulatory opinions about Hoover was Senator Eugene J. McCarthy. Speaking to a youthful audience during the 1968 campaign, he promised that if elected he would replace Hoover, CIA Director Richard Helms, and Selective Service head General Louis Hershey. In a follow-up television interview he commented that "any police agency in a democracy ought not to be kept under the control largely of one man to a point where it, the agency, develops into a kind of fief, really, which is somewhat beyond criticism and outside judgment."

In the July *Law Enforcement Bulletin* Hoover shot back that the FBI "has always met its responsibilities and discharged its duties without fear or favor, regardless of criticism and attacks, whatever the source." With this impartiality in mind, he said, "all Americans should view with serious concern the announced intentions and threats by a political candidate, if elected, to take over and revamp the FBI to suit his own personal whims and wishes."

McCarthy, of course, lost. The FBI as a whole might solve only a fraction of its cases, but Hoover always got *his* man.

CHAPTER NINE
THE CRIME-FIGHTER

The art of the police consists in not
seeing what there is no use seeing.
—*Napoleon Bonaparte*

"The battle is joined," trumpeted J. Edgar Hoover. "We have taken up the gauntlet flung down by organized crime. Let us unite in a devastating assault to annihilate this mortal enemy."

This ringing call to arms against the most potent and pervasive criminal enemy in the country was not sounded in 1924, when Hoover first took office, or during the four following decades in which organized crime and the FBI flourished simultaneously. As the criminal syndicates struggled, grew, and prospered, finally eclipsing General Motors as the nation's largest "corporation," the FBI was concentrating on lesser crimes and criminals.

By the time Robert Kennedy at last forced the Director's hand in 1961 and the vast resources of the FBI were directed against organized crime, the sapling had grown to a sturdy tree that simply would not be felled. The intricate conspiracy that is organized crime today was described by the President's Commission on Law Enforcement and the Administration of Justice:

In many ways organized crime is the most sinister kind of crime in America. The men who control it have become rich and powerful by encouraging the need to gamble, by luring the troubled to destroy themselves with drugs, by extorting the profits of honest and hardworking businessmen, by collecting usury from those in financial plight, by maiming or murdering those who oppose them, by bribing those sworn to destroy them. Organized crime is not merely a few preying on a few. In a very real sense, it is dedicated to subverting not only American institutions, but the very decency and integrity that are the most cherished attributes of a free society.

The Mob, the Syndicate, the Combination, the Invisible Government, Cosa Nostra, the Mafia—call it what you will—was fathered by a sumptuary law, the national prohibition act. During the law's life, from shortly after World War I to 1933, bootlegging gangs sprang up in almost every population center to deliver to the back door what couldn't go in the front. The gangs were multiethnic, although in Chicago and New York the Unione Siciliano brotherhood dominated. Primary jurisdiction over bootlegging, rum-running, and tax evasion was vested in the Treasury Department, so that the FBI at this stage was more or less on the sidelines. It was Eliot Ness and his T-men, to name the most celebrated of the federal agents, who took on Al Capone, Frank Nitti, and the lot. The epoch provided a preview of the widespread political power the syndicates would ultimately wield when Capone was named a member of the official party greeting Italian round-the-world fliers in Chicago.

By the time of repeal, a shakeout and bloody internecine warfare had left what was called the Mafia supreme. In December of 1928 the Mafia grand council, composed of local overlords from as far away as Miami, St. Louis, and New York, met in Cleveland to iron out intramural disputes. But before long the two most powerful factions were at each other's throats, and the Masseria-Maranzano war broke out. At its end, Charles ("Lucky") Luciano and Vito Genovese were on top. In one fell swoop on September 11, 1931, the opposition was ruthlessly destroyed in what became known as "purge day" inside the outfit.

With immense wealth accumulated from illegal liquor profits, the Mafia looked for new rackets that would give it room for expansion. It got into narcotics, prostitution, loan-sharking (usury), the numbers rackets, labor racketeering, the scam (bankruptcy fraud), and a host of other illicit enterprises. And it financed, set up, or took control of legitimate businesses, fronted by compliant and ostensibly respectable businessmen. Success was assured by the Mafia's muscle, political influence, and financial leverage. The take-over of such enterprises as liquor distributorships, nightclubs, juke-box firms, and linen supply houses was supplemented by thrusts into the stock market and banking.

It was during the formative years of organized crime in the 1930s that the FBI was pursuing the flamboyant Public Enemies of pulp magazine notoriety. No one argues that the Dillinger-style criminals were not genuine desperados, or that the federal laws empowering the G-men to act were not badly needed at the time. Local authorities were not as well coordinated as today and were being constantly outdistanced.

But the G-men's quarry was, essentially, the "few preying on a few." While all eyes were riveted on the blazing chases of Prettyboy Floyd, Babyface Nelson, et al., the Mafia and its allies were quietly building a criminal cartel preying on the nation. Compare John Dillinger with Vito Genovese. Public Enemy Number One was jaunty and dashing with a streak of wildness, a kind of Douglas Fairbanks of the crime stage. The Mafia boss of bosses, on the other hand, shunned publicity, was personally inconspicuous, and lived modestly in the suburbs, his name only whispered among the "soldiers" of the Mafia.

Despite the FBI's preoccupation with the Public Enemies, other arms of government recognized where the priority lay. As early as 1931 the Wickersham Commission had recommended an "immediate, comprehensive, and scientific nationwide inquiry into organized crime," in order to "make possible the development of an intelligent plan of its control." The Bureau of Narcotics, the Alcohol and Tobacco Tax Unit, and the Internal Revenue Service's Intelligence Division all fought a silent war against the crime syndicates. But they did not advertise their exploits, and there was no public mandate of support. Congressional largesse, consequently, was reserved for the FBI. The Bureau had cornered the crime-fighting market.

In 1935 the FBI, perhaps unwittingly, brushed with organized crime when it obtained the conviction of Joseph ("Socks") Lanza, a member of a Lower East Side Mafia "family" for using the protection racket on fishmongers at the Fulton Fish Market. Lanza was prosecuted under a side-door statute: conspiring to monopolize and regulate the freshwater fish industry. Although he was too crude to rise very high in the Mafia hierarchy, he was singled out by the Kefauver Crime Committee in 1951 as a typical lieutenant.

The illusion that the FBI was combating big-time crime was heightened during this time by the capitulation of Louis ("Lepke") Buchalter. One of the most feared Jewish mobsters of the day, Buchalter conducted a huge traffic in narcotics and an extortion ring victimizing labor and management in the New York restaurant, theater, baking, garment, and fur industries. In 1937, while Hoover's men were chasing bank robbers in the rural midwest, crusading District Attorney Thomas Dewey was taking dead aim at Buchalter. When Dewey secured indictments for murder, narcotics, and extortion, the mobster went into hiding, all the while directing the methodical murder of potential witnesses against him. A massive manhunt was mounted that ended abruptly in 1939 when the fugitive negotiated a surrender to the FBI.

The FBI's version of that surrender spun more silk for the legend. It held that G-men were closing in on Buchalter when Walter Winchell broadcast an appeal for him to give himself up. The fugitive got in touch with Winchell through an intermediary and agreed to surrender to the Bureau on the condition that his civil rights would be respected. The surrender was set for the night of August 24, 1939. As *The FBI Story* tells it, "Director Hoover walked along through New York City's streets to the corner of 28th Street and Fifth Avenue. And there the hunted man, Buchalter, surrendered to him. The FBI got Buchalter, and Winchell got an exclusive story."

The book *Treasury Agent* shed a different light on the story. It was not the FBI but the Federal Bureau of Narcotics that was closing in on the fugitive, a logical version since the FBN held a federal narcotics warrant for his arrest. Assertedly, narcotics agent Andy Koehn had put so much heat on Buchalter's underworld associates that they threatened him with sudden death if he didn't turn himself in. Not wanting to face Dewey's murder rap, Buchalter responded to Winchell's appeal. Naturally, the reporter saw to it that his pal Hoover put the cuffs on Buchalter, not narcotics agents.*

World War II was a time of fantastic prosperity for organized crime. Money was in abundance and goods were scarce, just the kind of situation the mob could exploit. The old rackets were implemented with new twists, and a black market in gasoline and food coupons was created. The extent to which organized crime had consolidated its hold on many segments of the economy was demonstrated by a bizarre compact between Lucky Luciano and the U.S. Navy. Luciano was in prison at the time, the first chieftain since Capone to "take a tumble," for multiple counts of compulsory prostitution brought by Dewey. But Luciano still held a tight grip on the New York waterfront, and he was induced to pass the word to his representatives on the docks to assist in countering sabotage and espionage. In 1945, his contribution to the war effort officially acknowledged, he was paroled and deported to his native Italy. From there and Batista's Cuba he continued to direct his U.S. organization.

The war also provided a glimpse of the corruptive powers of the crime bosses. In 1937 Vito Genovese, feeling Dewey's heat, skipped to Italy and managed to ingratiate himself with Benito Mussolini, which allowed the Genovese-Luciano combine to work both sides of the street. When the American forces occupied Italy, Genovese blithely helped them to expose black market activities. A skeptical

---

*There are two postscripts to the story. In *The Valachi Papers,* which drew on the recollections of Cosa Nostra defector Joseph Valachi, Peter Maas added an intriguing twist. Buchalter's underworld associates convinced him that a deal had been worked out with the federal authorities whereby he would serve his narcotics sentence before New York could lay hands on him. This would at least have given him more time. "But Buchalter soon found he had been duped," wrote Maas. "Within seventeen months he was on trial for his life and, doomed by the testimony of one of his own men, received the death penalty."

Years after the surrender, when *Treasury Agent* reopened the matter, Walter Winchell revealed that he, not Hoover, actually made the "arrest" of Buchalter. "I was not waiting in G-man Hoover's car for Lepke to surrender, etc.," he wrote in his column. "Mr. Hoover was waiting at 28th and 5th (in his car) where I brought Mr. Murder, Inc., after he (Lepke) kept a rendezvous with me four blocks south." Thus the story of Hoover walking "alone through New York City's streets" seems to be a fiction.

Army investigator discovered, however, that Genovese was merely letting the Army get rid of his competition—he himself was one of the biggest black market operators in business. When the investigator tried to bring charges, he was met with monumental indifference and outright hostility on the part of American military and civilian authorities. Then he learned that there was a murder warrant out for Genovese in New York, so he slipped his prisoner onto a troop ship homeward bound. But the New York prosecutor was stymied. Somehow or other the key witness against Genovese had been poisoned in jail, and other witnesses had disappeared. The charges were reluctantly dropped, and the Mafia leader smirkingly resumed business as usual in the United States.

This kind of outrageous scorn of the law provoked no righteous indignation from J. Edgar Hoover. Instead, the FBI kept its sights on the human tumbleweeds of crime: bank robbers, car thieves, freight car burglars, the whey-faced little men who passed bad checks in bunches, the hulking waterfront pilferers. These crimes and criminals contributed handsomely to the ever-larger statistics total with which the Director impressed Congress and the nation.

But they didn't make lively newspaper copy. This deficiency was corrected by the ingenious device called the Top Ten Fugitives Program, which designated some of the more grotesque hoodlums as the FBI's "Ten Most Wanted Men." The brainchild of now retired Inspector H. Lynn Edwards, the program was inaugurated in 1950 with much fanfare. It pulled publicity coming and going: when a fugitive was added to the list, his photograph, a brief description, and criminal data were published in most of the nation's newspapers; when he was apprehended, there was a second publicity burst.

The premium placed on the program by the FBI was indicated by notes I took on a 1953 lecture by a headquarters official to our in-service class: "Top Ten—good publicity—Bureau wants to know if certain newspapers' publicity results in apprehension." Indeed it did. In the course of appropriations testimony on March 6, 1961, Hoover revealed that newspaper blurbs had accounted for the apprehension of twenty-two Top Ten Fugitives, and that television, radio, and magazine exposure had led to the capture of ten more.

Undoubtedly, the program netted some fugitives who might otherwise never be captured. In July 1962, for example, a St. Paul, Minnesota, nurse taking the tour of FBI headquarters recognized one of the Top Ten as a neighbor, and within hours agents had in custody Hugh Bion Morse, wanted in Los Angeles for assault to commit murder. On the twelfth anniversary of the program, March 14, 1962, Hoover boasted that it had bagged 154 "dangerous fugitives" since its inception, while eleven dropped from the list had never been found. Many of the Top Ten had been nabbed by local police, which prompted the Director to hail the program as demonstrating "the outstanding effectiveness of public and law enforcement teamwork."

But the program also gave the public a grossly distorted view of the crime picture by arbitrarily elevating to the status of national menace an array of cheap thugs, barroom knifers, psychopathic rapists, wife-beaters, and alcoholic stick-up men—again, the "few preying on the few." This is not to say there haven't been a few colorful and competent neo-Dillingers on the list. There was Frank Lawrence Sprenz, for instance, a master of disguise who would pull a string of bank robberies and disappear into the blue in a stolen airplane (the FBI billed him as "the notorious flying bank robber"). Sprenz led G-men a merry chase. Once a trap was laid for him at a Vermont airport when he notified a girl friend that he would drop in on her, but he landed away from the airport at which the agents were staked out and was gone again by the time they caught on. He finally came a cropper when forced to crash-land on the Yucatan Peninsula; Mexican police hustled him back over the border and into the arms of the FBI.

Bank robbers Albert Nussbaum and Bobby Wilcoxson, who made the list in the early 1960s, carried machine guns and were not reluctant to use them. This trait, coupled with their affection for a blonde "moll," inspired the Bureau to compare them with Dillinger. But they didn't have his staying power. Nussbaum was apprehended after a chase when his mother tipped off the FBI that he was going to visit her, and Wilcoxson and the girl were found on information furnished by Nussbaum.

However, most Top Ten Fugitives committed crimes under the

jurisdiction of local authorities, and were sought by the FBI under the "unlawful flight to avoid prosecution" statute. Invariably touted as being armed and dangerous, most were so unnecessarily flamboyant and unstable that they would be flatly rejected by organized crime's equivalent of an employment department. It was perhaps symbolic of the FBI's perspective that of the hundreds of criminals who made the list, only one, Frederick J. Tenuto, was linked to organized crime. An escapee from a Pennsylvania prison, Tenuto appeared on the list for years but was never caught. According to Cosa Nostra defector Joseph Valachi, he was an enforcer for the notorious Albert Anastasia and was probably eliminated to prevent his talking.

While the FBI was launching its Top Ten Fugitives Program in 1950, Senator Estes Kefauver was beginning his hearings on organized crime in cities across the nation. The parade of surly, contemptuous crime bigwigs invoking the Fifth Amendment provided a spectacle at once fascinating and revolting. With the help of police specialists on the Mafia, the committee was able to draw a dim outline of the organized crime network reaching from New York to Miami, from Chicago to Los Angeles. Summing up on a note of indignation, Kefauver asserted: "A nationwide crime syndicate does exist in the United States of America despite the protestations . . . that there is no such combine."

To Kefauver, it was abundantly clear that the operations of the syndicate transcended the jurisdiction and resources of the local police. Although he called the FBI a "praiseworthy" agency, he stated, "Much of the responsibility for what is going on rests squarely upon federal enforcement agencies."

As a partial remedy, the senator proposed a three-member National Crime Commission to ramrod a concerted effort against organized crime. Its function would have been to keep up a continuing study of the syndicate's activities, ensure proper liaison among federal, state, and local agencies, recommend legislation, and, most importantly, maintain files on the major figures and set up a clearinghouse for intelligence on their movements.

Kefauver got as far as drafting a joint resolution that provided for the centralization of all criminal records possessed by the federal government when he collided with the imposing bulk of J. Edgar Hoover. As he recalled it in his book *Crime in America:*

> Attorney General [J. Howard] McGrath and FBI Director Hoover, in their statements to our committee, opposed creation of a federal crime commission. They felt—and in my opinion it was unfortunate that we could not convince them otherwise—that creation of such a commission might lead to establishment of a so-called national-type police force. I respect their judgment and sincerity . . . but strongly feel that nothing could be further from the mark. There is no connection between a federal crime commission and a national police force. Every Senator I know—myself included —would stand up and fight to the last breath any suggestion that we create anything resembling an American Gestapo.

The spectre of Kefauver's proposed commission turning into a national police was a canard, since it would possess no police power of its own and would function only in a service capacity. In point of fact, the FBI, with its immense powers and huge central file on public figures, was already much closer to what Hoover professed to fear. The liberals in Congress who were traditionally alert to police-state threats voiced no opposition to the commission. But the conservative bloc controlling the committees hearkened, as usual, to Hoover's cry, and the Kefauver bill died in committee. "The one significant bit of legislation that came out of the Kefauver period," wrote Daniel P. Moynihan in *The Reporter,* July 6, 1961, "the requirement that gamblers register with the federal government and pay a fee, is enforced not by the FBI but by the Internal Revenue Service. In fact, the Treasury Department gets most dirty work of this kind."

Many police officials were sorely disappointed by the defeat of Kefauver's proposals. One, the late Captain James E. Hamilton of the Los Angeles Police Intelligence Division, conceived the idea of an interdepartmental hookup that would pass information freely back and forth on the movements and activities of the important organized crime figures. Chief William H. Parker approved of the idea, and the Law Enforcement Intelligence Unit (LEIU) was born.

The LEIU consisted of trusted Mafia specialists on major departments across the country. As a stopgap measure it proved adequate. Mafiosi stepping off a plane in one of the member cities were usually placed under surveillance, and evidence was pooled so that the department with the best chance of successful prosecution was given the cooperation of the entire body. Once, for instance, Tony Accardo and Sam Giancana, then one-two in the Chicago hierarchy, deplaned in Los Angeles after traveling under fictitious names only to find themselves trailed and questioned by the Intelligence Division. "Now that everyone will know I'm here," groused Giancana, "I can't do any business so I might as well go home." But the local departments could do only so much. As Captain Hamilton put it, "The definite lack has been on a federal level in furnishing local departments information as to the movements of national figures."

The accuracy of Hamilton's complaint was demonstrated with stunning impact on November 14, 1957, when an estimated seventy-five Mafia chieftains and their lieutenants from all over the nation converged unnoticed on Apalachin, New York. The summit council, held on the estate of Joseph Barbara, was broken up by Sergeant Edgar Crosswell of the New York state police, who had suspected Barbara for some time. Among those arrested were Vito Genovese; Santo Trafficante, the Havana-Tampa gambler; the late Joseph Profaci and Carmine Lombardozzi, Brooklyn leaders; Joseph ("Joe Bananas") Bonanno, coordinator of the midwest rackets; Simone Scozzari, Los Angeles gambler; and John Scalish, top man in Cleveland.

The Apalachin raid showed the continuity of leadership in the organization. Two of those nabbed had also attended a 1928 meeting in Cleveland described by police there as a conclave of the "Mafia High Council of America." The Cleveland delegates, too, had come from such distant cities as Tampa, Miami, and St. Louis, and, like Apalachin, the meeting was evidently called to settle affairs following the execution of a high leader. Three weeks prior to the Apalachin meeting, Albert Anastasia had been gunned down in a Manhattan barbershop. From the information that was later assembled, he was apparently murdered because he had gotten too big for his boots, poaching on others' territories and ordering unnecessary murders that only drew police heat.

Another urgent item on the agenda concerned narcotics. As early as 1948, according to Joe Valachi, Frank Costello had urged his confreres to withdraw from the trade because of the efficiency of the Federal Bureau of Narcotics. In *The Valachi Papers,* author Peter Maas credited the FBN with being "the first to recognize the existence of an organization like the Cosa Nostra, and no other arm of the law has put more of a crimp in its operations." Thus it was Dr. Harry Anslinger of the FBN, not J. Edgar Hoover, whose name was anathema to the Mafia. *In Brotherhood of Evil: The Mafia,* Frederick Sondern, Jr., wrote that the mafiosi "regard 'that bastard Anslinger,' as he is generally known in the underworld, as their principal and most effective enemy."

However, not all of the "families," as the local Cosa Nostra entities were termed, had heeded Costello's advice. In fact, for Genovese it was already too late by the time of Apalachin—the FBN had put together a narcotics case that in less than two years would confine him to the Atlanta federal penitentiary for the remainder of his life.

Shock waves from the Apalachin episode reverberated through the marble halls of Washington. Attorney General William Rogers responded by forming his own ad hoc Special Group to Prosecute Organized Crime. Outstanding prosecutors were recruited: the head was Milton Wessel, and Gerald Goettel and Richard Ogilvie ran the New York and Chicago phases respectively. Rogers called upon the several federal agencies to join the Special Group in a team effort.

The FBI wouldn't play ball. In an article, "Why the Crime Syndicates Can't Be Touched," in *Harper's* November 1960 issue, Goettel revealed: "The FBI was the coolest agency of all. J. Edgar Hoover at a national meeting of U.S. attorneys decried the need for 'special groups' to fight organized crime." The Special Group was not only brushed off by the Bureau, Goettel said, but frustrated by the Bureau's vacuuming of information. When the Special Group requested copies of the FBI's reports, "the G-men acted as if they had never heard of Apalachin. This aloofness was due in part to their mistrust of us. It also reflected an internal dilemma—the FBI has long taken the position officially that large criminal syndicates do not exist—or if they do, they are a state and local law enforcement problem."

Goettel's views were echoed by Richard Ogilvie. "Hoover was very cool to the whole idea of the Attorney General's special group," he said. "He ordered that the FBI files, containing the very information we needed on organized crime, were to be closed to us. Furthermore, he forbade any agents even to talk to members of the special group. . . . In addition to fighting the syndicates, we had to shove against the dead weight of bureaucracy."

When the Special Group unexpectedly obtained federal convictions of a number of the Apalachin group, however, the FBI's coolness vanished. The Bureau tried to hustle a lion's share of the credit, citing the fact that it had contributed 1,588 pages of reports to the prosecution. "The public was never told that the FBI gave us the cold shoulder," asserted Goettel. "Indeed a recent magazine article attributed the ultimate success of the Apalachin trial to its fine investigative work. The author pointed to the fact that a preponderance of the government's exhibits were FBI reports. What he did not know was that the reports were not produced until the federal court, at trial, *directed* the FBI to do so."

The FBI glory grab also ruffled Harry Anslinger's feathers. He told a congressional subcommittee that "irrespective of what you read otherwise, the New York state police, the New York Crime Commission, the Alcohol Tax Unit and the Intelligence Unit of the Internal Revenue Service, and the Federal Bureau of Narcotics did this whole job." The FBN chief underscored his pointed omission of the FBI by entering into the record a letter from Milton Wessel of the Special Group giving full apology to his agency "because so many other people are trying to take credit for this since this matter has been brought to the public attention."

Wessel's letter acknowledged that Anslinger had "led the fight against syndicated crime for the last 30 years," and stated that it was the FBN "which conducted all original investigative work, and which successfully handled the difficult matter of coordinated nationwide arrests of the Apalachin defendants."

The convictions were overturned on appeal on the basis that the interpretation of law—that the defendants had conspired to remain silent—was faulty. Its task completed, the Special Group was disbanded. Its work was taken up by the existing Organized Crime and Racketeering Section of the Department of Justice. But in its brief life it had turned in a remarkable performance. As the *Chicago Daily News,* for one, expressed it. "The fact that [Anthony] Accardo was acquitted on a second trial does not detract from the demonstration of skill and tenacity on the part of Ogilvie."

But the issue of Hoover's opposition to the Special Group was not closed. When Goettel and Ogilvie wrote their articles, the Director riposted with a vengeance. In a letter to all agents, he labeled their criticisms "unfounded allegations." Then, using the compliant appropriations subcommittee as a forum, he lit into the pair. The stage was set by the chairman, John Rooney of Brooklyn, who is distinguished by his waspish interrogation of the State Department and utter deference to the FBI. Characterizing the Special Group as a "super-duper Dick Tracy outfit," Rooney grumbled that his subcommittee "gave them the money with some misgiving because we thought that they were inexperienced and would not be able to get along with the old line, solid investigative agencies, such as the FBI."

Then, in martyr's tones, Hoover stated that he had extended "complete cooperation that was proper and consistent with our jurisdiction, "but that the Bureau "had some problems with these gentlemen when they wanted to have assigned to them for their individual direction a substantial number of special agents without any specific target in mind, but to be used on 'fishing expeditions.'" The Director declared in an unmistakable put-down: "Obviously we have neither the manpower nor the time to waste on such speculative ventures." He then remarked, "My only conclusion is that some individuals look at 'Mr. District Attorney' on TV too frequently and absorb some of the fantastic panaceas as to how to solve *local crimes*" [italics added].

The "fishing expedition" passage struck me as wryly amusing in the light of an unforgettable scene that had taken place about the time the Special Group was pleading for help. Senior FBI agents had moved up and down the ranks of automobiles in the parking lot of the Seattle-Tacoma International Airport, occasionally jotting down a license number. Their mission was part of a nationwide drive, but it wasn't aimed at organized crime. The agents were recording out-of-state license numbers on the random chance of finding a stolen car that had been taken interstate. If one was found, they would be able to claim a double statistic: one car recovered, plus the recovery value of the car (to be added to the Fines, Savings, and Recoveries category). It would go into the statistical hopper that enabled Hoover each year to boast of "new peaks of achievement."

Nevertheless, the Apalachin bombshell had jolted the FBI at least partially out of its lethargy. An intensive probe of organized crime figures, called the Top Hoodlum Program, was begun. All agents were explicitly instructed not to discuss its existence with anyone, not even the police from whom they would be eliciting information. I suspect the blinds were drawn due to the "internal dilemma" mentioned by Goettel—that the Director over the years had avoided the problem. This way, if the program were a notable success, the FBI could score a publicity coup. If it were not, no one would know of the failure.

In retrospect, the program seems to have been stillborn. The essential problem was just the opposite from the one the Bureau had been used to in bank robberies and other crimes it had investigated; there, the challenge was to identify the subject and garner sufficient evidence to convict him. The organized crime figures were already known for the most part, and the problem was to detect them in a criminal act. This could only be done by a prolonged intelligence effort, not a crash program.

The FBI, of course, had not made such an effort in the past. At headquarters, there was no division devoted purely to organized crime—not even a section. In the field there were no Mafia specialists, no Mafia file. The *Manual of Instructions,* which spelled out methods for investigating everything from theft from interstate shipment to auto theft, was mute on the intricacies posed by organized crime. Data coming in that touched on top crime personnel was funneled into the catch-all General Investigative Intelligence File (GIIF). While the New York waterfront and a few other isolated locales had been the target of antirackets investigations at one time or another, the only continuing nationwide program had been a quarterly GIIF summary submitted by each field office, and there had been no correlation into a total syndicate picture. Richard Ogilvie put his finger on it: "The FBI is still organized to fight a crime pattern of the 20s and 30s. It is not set up to do battle with the criminal syndicate, the organized conspiracy that drains 22 billion dollars a year from the United States."

So the FBI began from scratch with the arbitrary approach that had so long marked its operations. For instance, every field office was required to designate ten men as the top hoodlums in its area and concentrate on them. In New York and Chicago, ten would only be skimming the top, while in such outposts as Butte and Anchorage it might be ten too many.

In October 1959, almost two years after Apalachin, I reviewed the progress of the Top Hoodlum Program in the Los Angeles office as an inspector's aide. There were bulky files on the local top ten. The data had been acquired through surveillance, record checks, plain old footwork, and wiretaps and bugs. But most of the solid information had been lifted verbatim from the files of the Los Angeles police department.

Moreover, the police Intelligence Division had magnanimously handed over to the FBI a case that was courtroom ready. It seemed that Miami Mafia boss Frankie Carbo had tried to grab a "piece" of welterweight champion Don Jordan. Although promoter Jackie Leonard had yielded, Jordan's two managers had balked. "You're going to be hurt," Carbo threatened Leonard on the phone from Miami. "And when I mean hurt, I mean dead." This was followed by a series of meetings in Los Angeles in which Mafia figure Blinky Palermo of Philadelphia and a local enforcer, Joe Sica, intimidated Leonard and the managers. However, Leonard was wired for sound, and the police listened in on the threatened mayhem.

My recommendation was that the local FBI office concentrate on this case before the rest, since it seemed to offer the potential of a stunning blow against the syndicate. Two years later, Carbo, Palermo, and Sica were convicted in federal court of extortion and conspiracy. The sentences were stiff.

The year 1959 was the high-water mark of the Top Hoodlum Program. Despite the good fortune of the Los Angeles office,

progress was not the FBI's most important product. The rush for
statistics and neatly packaged crime solutions took precedent, and,
with the spur provided by the Special Group gone, the program
began to limp badly. A measure of how badly is provided by the
fact that on December 8, 1959, what state investigators have termed
a "Little Apalachin" was held in a Worcester, Massachusetts, hotel.
Some 150 delegates and their lieutenants from the northeastern
states occupied fifteen rented rooms overnight and made numerous
calls to New York City. The next day they dispersed as unobtrusive-
ly as they had gathered. When state attorney general's investigators
got belated word, they dug up enough about the deliberations to
conclude that certain territories had been reallocated and two "hits"
(killings)—one in Hartford, Connecticut, the other in Youngstown,
Ohio—had been authorized.

It was little wonder that the FBI had been caught napping again.
At the time of the Worcester conclave, the New York office had
only four agents assigned full time to the Top Hoodlum Program,
barely enough to keep up with the paperwork. On the other hand,
more than four hundred were assigned to tracking down putative
Communists.

In 1960, a renewed push for the national nerve center envisioned by Kefauver began to form. The McClellan Senate Rackets
Committee listened to an array of expert witnesses and submitted
plans for a National Crime Commission. In its report issued in
March 1960, the chairman, Senator John F. Kennedy, and two
other senators were in favor. Kennedy noted that local departments
were "powerless to deal with the interstate aspects of the problem,"
and that some "are either unable or unwilling to do any kind of a
job on racketeer control." Robert Kennedy, then chief counsel to
the committee, anticipated Hoover's objection by stressing that the
commission "would not be a national police, but a national information service for police."

But the proposal was stalled by Senators Karl Mundt, Barry
Goldwater, Carl Curtis, and Homer Capehart, who picked up
Hoover's earlier remark that the FBI disseminates numerous "items
of interest" to the police and argued that this indicated sufficient

existing cooperation. They also objected on the grounds that the commission would be an embryonic national police.

Then, in October of the same year, the matter came up before the convention of the International Association of Chiefs of Police (IACP) in Washington. The IACP's committee on organized crime recommended that such a federal nerve center be established. The chairman of the committee, Chief Edward J. Allen of Santa Ana, California, was no stranger to the problem. As chief in the rackets stronghold of Youngstown, Ohio, he had waged a relentless and successful campaign against the mobsters, who represented Mafia "families" in Detroit and Buffalo. He had also written *Merchants of Menace: The Mafia,* an authoritative book published by a criminology house. Appearing in support of the resolution were Milton Wessel of the Special Group and Captain Hamilton, the founder of the LEIU. "A national clearing house for information about the organized underworld would provide us with a weapon to strike a real blow at this nation's organized criminals," urged Hamilton.

But it was not to be. FBI lobbyists buttonholed delegates, talking the resolution down. Then the Director took the rostrum. Denouncing "outside theorists" and "alleged friends" who were "blinded by the urge of empire building," he declaimed:

> The persons who endorse these grandiose schemes have lost sight of some very basic facts. America's compact network of state and local law enforcement agencies traditionally has been the nation's first line of defense against crime. Nothing could be more dangerous to our democratic ideals than the establishment of an all-powerful police agency on the federal scene.

The IACP took the cue. The resolution was tabled, and its prime mover, Allen, was virtually drummed out of the lodge. Allen offered to resign as chairman of the committee but pleaded that its work go on—to no avail. A few weeks after the convention, the IACP board pulled the rug out from under the doughty chief and his supporters by dissolving the committee. After a decent interval it was reinstated under the chairmanship of Chief Thomas Cahill of San Francisco, who was known to be more responsive to Hoover's wishes.

I once talked with Chief Allen about the situation. "Hoover controls the IACP," he affirmed. "I respect him, but on this score he was dead wrong. I admire a man who could admit he is wrong, but Hoover wouldn't do it."

But by 1960 no one could pass off the Mafia as mere Sicilian folklore, so vividly had its presence in this country been documented. So Hoover passed the buck by portraying organized crime as primarily the responsibility of local police, a position contradicted by every authority from Robert Kennedy to James Hamilton. The FBI? It didn't have "jurisdiction in each and every facet of organized crime," he alibied.

It couldn't control "each and every" facet of the problem—no one agency could—but the Bureau could do an awful lot. Among the statues under the FBI's wing were acts relating to the kickback rackets, extortion, antiracketeering, labor-management relations, unauthorized publication or use of communications, obstruction of justice, bankruptcy (the scam has long been a favorite Cosa Nostra fraud), the white slave traffic, perjury, misprision of felony, trust formation, interstate transportation of stolen property, interstate transportation of gambling devices, lottery tickets and wagering data, hijacking, bribery, fraud by wire, and federal firearms control. This amounted to considerable firepower, but it had never been used in any concerted way.

It would have been no trick for Hoover to have filled the jurisdictional gaps if he had really wanted to. He always got what he wanted from Congress; for instance, he got the waiting period shortened in kidnappings and the statute of limitations extended as a result of the Brinks robbery. But kidnapping and bank robbery were pet Bureau crimes.

After Apalachin, the *New York Herald-Tribune* assumed that the FBI's prior inertia was due to a lack of proper tools. "Congress has never yet refused anything J. Edgar Hoover said he had to have," it editorialized. "Let him demand the funds to take on this job. Let Congress provide them, plus stronger laws on national crime." But there was only silence at Ninth and Pennsylvania.

When he became attorney general, Robert Kennedy insisted that the FBI join fully in the drive on organized crime. At first, Hoover resisted. In May 1961, hearings were held by the House Judiciary Subcommittee on new laws to curb the crime syndicates, and Chairman Emanuel Celler asked the Director to testify. Instead, a general statement was submitted in the FBI chief's name generally backing the Kennedy proposals. Celler appealed to Kennedy to try to "change Mr. Hoover's attitude," stressing the importance of a personal appearance and pointing out that the hearings would continue for more than a week. Hoover never did find the time.

As a showdown loomed—some insiders in the department say Kennedy was on the verge of firing Hoover—the Director yielded. For the first time in the lengthening history of the FBI, a division was set up to deal with the major hoodlums. The Special Investigative Division was headed by Courtney A. Evans, who had been FBI liaison representative with the Kennedy campaign.

Kennedy also set up what amounted to a Special Group and a national clearinghouse of intelligence on organized crime, but he did it in such a way that Hoover was powerless to object. The already existing Organized Crime and Racketeering Section was beefed up to include sixty attorneys with field offices in New York, Chicago, Miami, and Los Angeles. The section's field attorneys functioned as investigative prosecutors, just as the Special Group had done. Within the section was an intelligence unit that acted as a central clearinghouse. After only two years, the section had compiled dossiers on 1,100 of the country's leading organized crime figures. "We never had a decent intelligence picture before," said William G. Hundley, the section's chief, in explaining why it had been necessary to create an intelligence unit separate from the FBI. "We're positive now who the real overlords are. We've gotten some of them, but only some."

Once engaged on a full-scale basis, the FBI quickly learned that the organized mobsters were a far more potent foe than the Top Ten Fugitives. On April 3, 1963, a team of New York agents photographing mourners at the funeral of the father of Carmine Lombardozzi, an Apalachin delegate, met with near-tragedy. Without warning, four members of the funeral party pounced on veteran agent John P. Foley, whipped him with his own pistol, and left him critically injured.

Then in July 1963, Sam Giancana filed a lawsuit against Hoover et al., in which he sought to enjoin agents from harassing him. In a move that caused many a seasoned cop's jaw to drop, the plaintiff showed in court colored motion pictures of G-men closely tailing him wherever he went—to his home, cocktail lounges, church, his late wife's mausoleum, even the golf course. The diminutive SAC at Chicago, Marlin W. Johnson, was ordered by federal judge Richard B. Austin to respond to questions about the surveillance. "With the air of a man citing the Fifth," reported *Newsweek,* "he intoned: 'I respectfully decline to answer on the orders of the Attorney General of the U.S. and pursuant to Department of Justice Order 260-62.'" Whereupon he was cited for contempt of court, arrested by a deputy U.S. marshal, and fined five hundred dollars.

Judge Austin ordered the FBI shadowing curtailed, cutting the parade of cars following Giancana to one and dropping the agent-golfers at least one foursome behind. "I feel certain," commented the judge, "that based on my background [as a former state's attorney and criminal court chief justice] that a different type of surveillance must have been conducted previously and failed to achieve results. The switch to harassment," he declared, "was an admission of ineptness and a confession of failure to obtain the information sought by methods normally used."*

If the Giancana debacle was mildly embarrassing, the discovery of a plethora of FBI listening devices in Las Vegas casinos was a major disaster. The bugs were planted to glean data supporting suspicions of skimming operations. But because they were illegal, their taint spilled over on a number of cases the department had in a prosecutive status.

---

*When Giancana could not be nailed on a substantive charge, he was eventually hauled before a grand jury and granted immunity under the new anti-organized crime statutes. When he still took the fifth amendment, he was imprisoned for contempt of court. He left the country, and, reportedly, the Cosa Nostra ruling body was not at all distressed by his absence, since his habitual disporting in the nightclubs of the world only drew unwanted attention.

Why did the FBI resort to such an illegal shortcut? In an interview in the *Boston Globe,* December 13, 1966, William Hunley was of the opinion that the widespread electronic eavesdropping was due primarily to the FBI's failure before 1961 to develop an adequate intelligence system on organized crime.

The concerted drive by Kennedy, called Operation Big Squeeze, produced impressive if not conclusive results. For its part, the FBI began probes that would eventually put big names on the blotter, among then Paul ("The Waiter") Ricca and Murray ("The Camel") Humphries of Chicago, and Johnny Dioguardi of New York.

But the most significant breakthrough of the Kennedy period was on the intelligence front. The Kefauver hearings had stripped the mask from the carcinomatous face of organized crime, but its power structure and inside workings were unknown. This was due in large measure to the fact that it was an essentially clandestine group whose members were held in line by a loyalty oath, *omerta,* that carried a penalty of death. There had never been a defector who knew much who was willing to tell all. Joe Valachi changed all that.

Joseph Valachi was a longtime "soldier" in the Vito Genovese family. In 1960, he entered the Atlanta penitentiary on a fifteen-year sentence obtained by narcotics agents. That was the year that Genovese himself came to Atlanta courtesy of the FBN. Somehow the word had been spread through the prison grapevine that Valachi had "spilled his guts" to the FBN, a rumor that obsessed the Mafia underling with the idea that Genovese had marked him for death. In 1962, Valachi fatally clubbed a prisoner he mistakenly took to be his assigned executioner and found himself facing a death sentence. Seeing nothing to lose, he traded off the murder charge for what he knew about his former bosses.

When the FBN began its lengthy interrogation sessions to pump Valachi dry, the FBI heard about it and put in a strong pitch to the Department of Justice (which had custodial authority over the prisoner) to allow the Bureau to take over, saying that what the defector had to divulge "transcended" the traffic narcotics. The Bureau's almost desperate interest in Valachi puzzled the Department, but it is explicable by the fact that Valachi, like bugs and wiretaps, could produce instant intelligence. Hoover was still seething over the humiliation of being practically empty-handed when the new attorney general had demanded underworld intelligence data from the FBI.

Ironically, the fact that the FBN had put Valachi away worked in the FBI's favor, for he was naturally hostile toward those responsible for his predicament. In time the Bureau got its way, and agent James P. Flynn of the New York office slowly extracted the story from Valachi.

Naturally, Hoover was anticipating breaking the story, but Kennedy upstaged him. In August 1963, the Department let it out in a series of carefully timed leaks, and Peter Maas wrote the wrap-up account in the *Saturday Evening Post*. With the Department billing the disclosures as "the biggest intelligence breakthrough yet," the McClellan Committee put Valachi on public exhibit at its hearings.

Obviously nettled, Hoover denigrated the disclosures as not quite "the major intelligence breakthrough" touted by the Department. In the September FBI *Law Enforcement Bulletin* he downgraded Valachi's importance by saying his tales "corroborated and embellished the facts developed by the FBI as early as 1961 which disclosed the makeup of the gangland horde." He went even further before the friendly appropriations subcommittee on February 10, 1966, claiming that "all the Valachi information was known to the Bureau or had been obtained from informants of the Bureau."

After Kennedy left the Department there was a determined effort to suppress publication of Maas's *The Valachi Papers*. Although Hoover's role, if any, is obscure, it is clear that he was dead set against publication, as this scenario with Chairman Rooney at 1966 appropriations testimony shows:

> MR. ROONEY: There is pending for decision the matter of permitting Valachi, this murderer, to write a book from which he would possibly obtain hundreds of thousands of dollars. What is your feeling with regard to permitting such a thing as this to happen, which would also cause reflection upon the good name of a great many Italian-Americans in this country?

MR. HOOVER: My feeling is that no person who is incarcerated in a penitentiary, particularly a Federal penitentiary, should be allowed to write and have published any book, whether for money or not, while he is incarcerated. I think this is highly improper.

It was not Valachi but Maas who was writing the book. Three months later, the Department for the first time in its history went to court to attempt to ban a book. Maas ultimately won.

Hoover's own words, of course, belie his devaluation of Valachi. Before the disclosures, he evidently conceived of organized crime as confined to metropolitan enclaves with little or no national interconnection. As late as January 1962, he declared in the *Law Enforcement Bulletin* that "no single individual or coalition of racketeers dominates organized crime across the nation." After the disclosures, the Director began referring to the Cosa Nostra as a "criminal cartel" that "operates on a nationwide basis, with international implications."

All the fuss over Valachi had obscured the fact that the FBI had let slip another Cosa Nostra "soldier" who wanted to inform. Several years before, James V. Delmont of the Buffalo "family" had, like Valachi, fallen from grace. On the run, he had showed up at the FBI office in Miami on June 25, 1959, offering to divulge secrets in exchange for information about anyone who might have been hunting for him. When the Bureau proposed that he reenter the Mafia as an informant—an incredibly naïve suggestion—he fled in horror (the Miami FBI later said it had no record of his visit). On May 25, 1960, Delmont materialized in the Los Angeles FBI division with the same offer, but was written off as a nut. Ten days later his body was found in a field in east Los Angeles, the victim of a classic Mafia execution.

The Intelligence Division of the Los Angeles police department launched an intensive probe into the murder. The murderers were never positively identified, but in his flight Delmont had left an intriguing legacy. "If any police officer still doubts the existence and power of the Mafia, the Cosa Nostra, or whatever you want to call it," Mafia specialist Sergeant Peter N. Bagoye remarked afterward, "just let him read this case. This man Delmont spent a year and traveled thousands of miles trying tò escape the vengeance of the Mafia. He left a trail of letters and conversations behind—the first known case in which there is any existing blueprint of how the Syndicate works." Captain Daryl Gates, head of the Intelligence Division, classified the Delmont case "a more penetrating insight into the operations of the Mafia than any of the Joe Valachi disclosures, which were mostly confined to one area."

Within hours of the assassination of John Kennedy, which relegated Robert Kennedy to the role of lame duck attorney general, the FBI reverted to its old ways. "The next day we stopped getting information from the FBI on the Bobby Baker investigation," a Department organized crime section lawyer told the *New York Times*. "Within a month the FBI men in the field wouldn't tell us anything. We started running out of gas." The *Times* article, by Fred P. Graham of the Washington bureau, reported that Department sources had complained that the FBI had "virtually pulled out of the effort," which only limped along on the momentum supplied by the Kennedys.

Hoover bristled at the *Times* piece. If there was any tapering off after the president's death, he retorted, it was "because hundreds of FBI agents were assigned to the assassination." But the recession was not temporary. Agents to whom I spoke regretted that the program was throttled back, and one wrote to Attorney General Ramsey Clark in 1967: "Vast segments of our agent personnel must be switched from non-essential counting of meaningless statistics to matters involving top Mafia so their power can be broken." A Tucson agent apparently became completely frustrated with watching the grass grow and took matters into his own hands. According to testimony in open court in 1969, a series of bombings of the premises of Mafia figures in Tucson was the handiwork of this agent, who was bent on a personal clean-up campaign.

In 1967, Ramsey Clark organized a "strike force" concept for dealing with the Cosa Nostra. When a pilot operation iñ Buffalo was a success, the attorney general coopted federal agencies to supply manpower and resources that would focus on target cities for a specific length of time. The FBI balked. Clark, undoubtedly realizing

Hoover's coziness with Lyndon Johnson, didn't press the matter, and the Bureau's participation was limited to furnishing file material.

Nixon's attorney general, John N. Mitchell, signaled that he would brook no reticence on the part of Hoover. Shortly after taking office, he announced that the fight against organized crime would be one of his top priorities. At first, Hoover sought to bypass him and go directly to the president, but that was abruptly ended. Then Mitchell made it plain to the FBI chief that the "strike force" had proven successful and would be continued *with* full FBI cooperation. To the surprise of many longtime observers of the Justice scene, the number of agents assigned to organized crime work in some of the major centers began to multiply. "If the trend of recent weeks continues," wryly commented the Times-Post Service on March 27, 1969, "the enlisting of the FBI in this cooperative anti-crime venture could become one of the memorable achievements of the Nixon Administration."

A month later a hint surfaced that the FBI had again fallen behind in organized crime intelligence. In hearings before a house committee, it was revealed that the Small Business Administration had lent $560,000 to a trucking firm headed by two men linked to organized crime (the loan had come into default) after the FBI had reported "negative" findings, in effect clearing them. An SBA internal memorandum dated January 25, 1967, blamed the agency's New York office for failing to press further and stated that "moreover, it appears that the FBI missed the boat on name checks."

Even had the FBI poured all its resources into the fight, it is doubtful whether total success could have been achieved. Organized crime was too well entrenched, and with its tight organizational charts was not about to be destroyed by the jailing of a few executives, any more than General Electric and Westinghouse skidded with the jailing of their executives for price-rigging. The Nixon people realized this. In his statement announcing the anti-syndicate crime drive, Nixon conceded that despite past efforts, "Not a single one of the twenty-four Cosa Nostra 'families' has been destroyed; they are more firmly entrenched than ever."

Thus it ranks as one of the great derelictions of law enforcement history that Hoover, who had the manpower, prestige, and jurisdic-

tion to crush organized crime in its formative stage, looked the
other way.* There was no use seeing the invisible government when
the neo-Dillingers were highly visible.

---

*Peter Maas calculated that if Cosa Nostra's illegal profits were reported, the
country could meet its obligations with a 10 percent tax *reduction*. Why was
Hoover relatively uninterested? In his book *Theft of a Nation*, criminologist
Donald R. Cressey, who was a consultant on organized crime to the president's
Crime Commission, offered several hypotheses. One had it that Hoover was
jealous of Harry Anslinger of the FBN and perversely denied that the Mafia
existed because his opposite number insisted that it did. Another was that
Hoover was simply astigmatic until Apalachin. Still another went along with the
notion that the FBI didn't have sufficient jurisdiction until Kennedy pushed for
it. This last was decidedly specious. Most of the convictions secured by the FBI
were gained under laws over which it had held domain for many years.

CHAPTER TEN
THE RED-HUNTER

J. Edgar Hoover, head of our thought police—
a martinet, a preposterous figure, but not funny.

> —the late American poet
> Theodore Roethke

ew questioned J. Edgar Hoover's status as the father figure of theological anti-Communism. In the Bible Belt of the American heartland, where atheistic Communism was as fearful an enemy as crop pestilence, within the superpatriotic milieu, among the well-to-do elite who see unfettered free enterprise as the cornerstone of "the American way of life," he ranked as a prophet whose words were inspired, the savior of the chosen people.

In recognition of this role, he was showered with honors. In 1961, the Valley Forge Freedom Foundation gave him its annual award for "writings alerting the American people to the dangers of Communism." In 1964 he was named "American of the Year" by the Americanism Educational League, a right-wing organization based in Southern California. The ultimate accolade came in 1968 from the Cuban Anti-Communist Journalist Association in Miami, an exile group that was violently anti-Castro. It named him "The Man of the Century." The list went on and on.

Hoover's anti-Communism seemed to be a gut-level rather than a deeply reasoned conviction. According to Richard Harwood in the *Washington Post,* June 28, 1966, a former JFK staff member recalled that the late president "was appalled at Hoover's obsession with 'Reds under every bed' and was unable to carry on a coherent conversation with him." The Director's pontifications on the subject betray a dire lack of sophistication. In reviewing *A Study in Commu-*

nism when it was published in 1962, Harry Schwartz of the *New York Times* allowed that the book gave "a good description of the horrors of the Stalinist era" but failed to throw much "light on the many and important changes that have taken place in the Soviet Union since Stalin's death." In fact, Schwartz found evidence that Hoover was not entirely familiar with such changes. Or, as Emmet John Hughes once put it, the "FBI chief's knowledge of Communism is roughly as sophisticated as Dean Rusk's knowledge of ballistics."

Yet Hoover did once take a stab at exploring what made Communism go. In 1919, he was appointed head of the General Intelligence Division (GID) in the Department of Justice, which had been created to cope with the wave of bombings attributed to anarchists and radicals. It gave him a chance for an almost clinical study. As James Phelan recounted it in the *Saturday Evening Post,* September 25, 1965:

> Since his young manhood, Hoover has been outraged, baffled and fascinated by the Communists, who typify everything that he is not. As a young Justice Department assistant he was active in the deportations that followed Attorney General A. Mitchell Palmer's "Red raids" after World War I. He interrogated and argued with many of the "bolsheviks," studied their manifestoes and writings, and tried to understand what made them tick. He finally concluded that there was something psychologically wrong with them.

The Palmer Red Raids were one of the most shameful chapters in the American democratic experiment. A Senate investigation of them revealed that in late 1919 and early 1920 some ten thousand persons were caught in nationwide dragnets, that in some cities ninety-seven out of a hundred were arrested without warrants, and that the overwhelming majority were never successfully prosecuted. Many were beaten, manhandled, and abused; all were crammed into detention cells that within a few days became stinking cesspools. A few notorious radicals of the day were netted, and some not so notorious. But most of the victims were non-English-speaking

aliens, simple working people, and American citizens—as one
reporter observed, "a tame, unterroristic looking crowd."

The excesses of the raids, so starkly reminiscent of European
police states, provided a backlash of revulsion. They were called
"government by hysteria" and "Palmer's reign of terror." And
Hoover's role in them was much more prominent than he later
cared to admit.

"Under the general guidance of bureau chief [William J.] Flynn
and through the unstinting zeal of Hoover," historian Robert K.
Murray has written in *Red Scare, A Study in National Hysteria,*
"this unit [the GID] rapidly became the nerve center of the entire
Justice Department and by January 1920 made its war on radicalism the department's primary occupation. In fact, there are indications that both Flynn and Hoover purposely played on the attorney
general's fears and *exploited the whole issue of radicalism in order
to enhance the Bureau of Investigation's power and prestige*" [italics
added].

If Murray was correct, Hoover virtually from the start of his
career displayed a remarkable talent for synthesizing dragons and
then acting out the role of St. George. In any event, he exhibited
here for the first time an adroitness in shifting or diminishing the
blame when things went wrong. The record shows clearly that he
was instrumental in the raids. It was he who drew up the briefs
upon which the warrants were based. It was he to whom agents
were instructed to communicate "any matters of vital importance or
interest that may arise" during the raids, and, afterward, "a breakdown of the affiliations involved."

This was only consistent, for it was under Hoover's direction
that the GID had compiled within months, according to evidence
presented to the Senate investigators, "a more or less complete history of over sixty thousand radically inclined individuals." By the
time of the raids, the GID card-index system held the staggering
total of four hundred and fifty thousand names. In other words,
Hoover was the father in 1917 of the massive dossier file that even
today is the wellspring of the FBI's political power.

When the cell doors clanged shut, Hoover lost none of his
enthusiasm. He told the *New York Times* that approximately three

thousand of the aliens made "perfect" cases for deportation and that others could be proved (only 446 were ultimately deported). "Deportation hearings and the shipment of the 'Reds' from this country will be pushed rapidly," he said. "Second, third, and as many other 'Soviet Arks' as may be necessary will be made ready as the convictions proceed." The press had dubbed the vessels carrying deportees to Russia "Soviet Arks," and Hoover, with bureau chief Flynn, had shown up at the pier to see the first one off.

The proceedings gave disturbing hints of contempt on Hoover's part for due process and civil liberties. He insisted that the simple presence of a person's name on a radical organization's membership list was sufficient evidence for deportation as a dangerous alien—it should not be necessary to prove that the person was cognizant of and subscribed to the views of the organization. He exerted pressure for high bails—ideally ten thousand dollars—which would have assured that practically no one got out of jail until his case was disposed of. He contended that it was "of vital importance" that no arrested person be admitted until he had agreed to answer questions put to him, that is, until he had testified against himself. Again he was behind an order from the bureau to all field offices that "persons taken into custody are not to be permitted to communicate with any outside person [including an attorney] until after examination by this office and until permission is given by this office."

When it got to the hearing stage, the Senate investigating committee hauled Attorney General Mitchell Palmer on the carpet. While taking ex officio responsibility for the raids' conduct, he was hazy on the details of their planning. When pressed as to details, he replied: "Mr. Hoover was in charge of this in the Bureau of Investigation." He gave a similar response when asked why prisoners were held incommunicado and why warrants were not obtained in all cases. In his turn, Hoover passed the buck to the Department of Labor, which at that time held jurisdiction over immigration matters, and to the bureau field offices.

Although the GID was abolished, Hoover emerged almost unscathed. Within a few years his role in the sordid affair was so thoroughly buried that incoming Attorney General Harlan Fisk Stone, who had branded the raids an "arbitrary exercise of power," saw fit to appoint him FBI Director. In 1947, Hoover piously told the *New York Herald-Tribune,* "I deplored the manner in which the raids were executed then, and my position has remained unchanged." In *The FBI Story* Don Whitehead rewrote history, casting Palmer in the role of mastermind and relegating young Hoover to the part of theoretician and brief-writer. In Whitehead's view, the important thing to know about the Red Raid era was that Hoover was the first to perceive Communism as an international conspiracy of dangerous portent.

For fifteen years following the demise of the GID, Hoover and the G-men concentrated on crime-busting. Then, in 1936, Roosevelt put the FBI back in the antisubversion business on an unofficial basis. In 1939, with war imminent, FDR publicly announced that he had instructed the Bureau "to take charge of investigative work in matters relating to espionage, sabotage, and violations of the neutrality regulations." In 1949, Hoover reactivated the GID, renaming it the Security Division (it is now called the Domestic Intelligence Division). The huge dossier system was enlarged, along with the informant program that the FBI chief had pioneered with the old GID.

One month after its reactivation, in February 1940, Hoover gave the Security Division a shakedown cruise. In what amounted to a small-scale Red Raid, agents armed with warrants made predawn knocks on the doors of eleven persons in Detroit and one in Milwaukee. The nominal charge was violation of a federal law forbidding recruitment of personnel for a foreign army on U.S. soil—all were members of the Abraham Lincoln Brigade that had fought on the Loyalist side in the Spanish Civil War. But the war had been over for years, and the belated punishment was obviously for political unorthodoxy.

The transparency of the motive precipitated a storm of controversy. The *Milwaukee Journal,* hardly a radical organ, asserted that the tactics of the G-men were "to be outright condemned." The liberal *New Republic* labeled the FBI "an American OGPU" and declared that the "glamour that surrounds [Hoover] conceals the growth of a power inconsistent with our conception of democratic institutions." Senator George Norris charged that the prisoners had been subjected to "third-degree methods" and with considerable prescience warned, "unless this is stopped, there will be a spy behind every stump and a detective in every closet." New attorney general Robert H. Jackson moved to quash the indictments secured by his predecessor, with the sharp reminder that "some degree of amnesty at least is being extended in Spain." There had been no prosecutions, he noted, of those who had aided the Franco forces.

But Roosevelt, who had anointed Hoover and admired his aggressiveness, gave him a pointed gesture of support at a correspondents' dinner. The storm spent itself, leaving the Director only slightly dampened.

With the end of World War II and the beginning of the cold war, the FBI renewed its passionate crusade against Communism. The opening salvo was fired on December 10, 1945, when Hoover warned the International Association of Chiefs of Police in convention that national law enforcement would be hard put to halt the advance of the enemy. "Panderers of diabolic mistrust," he said, "already are concentrating their efforts to confuse and divide by applying the Fascist smear to *progressive police departments like the FBI* and other American institutions to conceal their own sinister purposes" [italics added].

This kind of phillipic became Hoover's trademark in his relentless talk about Communism. Powerful forces were at work to convert "our haven of liberty" to a "Godless, totalitarian state," he would say, and those who opposed the endeavors of the FBI and "patriotic organizations" in their efforts to avert the millennium were rankly unwholesome, if not downright subversive. The theme was sounded, for instance, in a speech before the Daughters of the American Revolution on April 22, 1954: "It is an established fact that whenever one has dared to expose the Communist threat, he has invited upon himself the adroit and skilled talents of experts of character assassination."

The allusion to character assassination by Communists was in a way a case of reversing the magnetic field, for it was very doubtful whether Senator Joseph McCarthy would have long survived in his reckless smearing campaign without the ammunition provided him by Hoover. FBI agents put in long hours poring over Bureau security files and abstracting them for Roy Cohn, McCarthy's chief inquisitor during the hearings in the early 1950s. Moreover, it was the alarums of the Director, who spoke with the ring of authority, that helped spin the legend of a clear and present domestic danger that was an extension of a conspiracy hatched in Moscow. Without this legend, the Wisconsin demagogue could not have claimed his victims.

When the incoming Eisenhower administration started to make political hay out of the claim that Harry Truman was "soft on Communism," it was the ubiquitous Hoover and those files again. In 1945, the Director had communicated to Truman the names of several administration officials who were suspected of furnishing data to persons relaying it to the Soviets. One so named was Harry Dexter White. In 1947, the FBI's information on White was presented to a grand jury, which refused to indict on grounds of insufficient evidence. Eisenhower's attorney general, Herbert Brownell, decided to convict the since-deceased White in the court of public opinion. Standing before network television cameras brandishing the letter Hoover had written to Truman, Brownell sought to persuade his millions of viewers that a Democratic president had consciously employed Soviet spies in his executive departments. And there at his side, standing in mute affirmation, was J. Edgar Hoover. "These viewers were ignorant of judicial procedure," wrote Roger Burlingame in *The Sixth Column*, "and as far as they are concerned communications from the FBI are, on the face of them, damning. Such was the effect of the publicity build-up achieved over the years by J. Edgar Hoover."

Protagonists of this kind of extremism in the guise of national security habitually exploited the prestige of the FBI in order to further their ends. For example, J. Parnell Thomas of the HUAC used a confidential letter from Hoover to Commerce Secretary Averell Harriman that contained part of an FBI loyalty report on scientist Edward U. Condon in hearings that resulted in Condon's expulsion from government. There was no disavowal of the tactic from the FBI. Bragged Thomas: "The closest relationship exists between this committee and the FBI. . . . It is something, however, that we cannot talk too much about."

During the most virulent stage of the Red phobia, the FBI files piped a steady flow of information not only to the committees but to anti-Communist groups with no official standing. One beneficiary was American Business Consultants, formed by ex-FBI agents to clue in employers on prospective employees who might be left of center. The firm put out a newsletter, *Counterattack,* that incorporated file data, much of it raw. "Leaks which occurred through this medium were hard to spot," averred Roger Burlingame, "as they were usually presented in the form of innuendo, suggesting that named persons were being watched by the FBI without revealing the specific accusations in the dossiers."

The FBI's most perceptible role in the McCarthy epoch was as investigator for the loyalty program begun under Truman and brought to full blossom under Eisenhower. Aimed at supposed "interlocking subversion" in government, the program as finally set up allowed for the removal of an employee without appeal when there was "reasonable doubt as to loyalty." When a cry arose that the program mocked the Constitution and the "beyond reasonable doubt" standard of guilt, Hoover defended it with the words: "A government job is a matter of privilege and not a right. Misunderstanding of this point has led to much of the current nonsense voiced about the program."

Actually, much of the misunderstanding has revolved around the FBI role. Bureau spokesmen have repeatedly emphasized that the agency merely reported the results of its inquiries and made no evaluations—this was the function of the employing agency. But the gathering of "raw" material involved a certain selectivity, and the refinement of that material into a finished report was per se an exercise in evaluation. Obviously the political views and prejudices of the investigator and his superiors were bound to have an influence on the report—and it was upon that report that the employing agency had to depend.

Very many agents in the FBI, I learned, were hostile not only to avowed Communists but to the entire left-of-center spectrum. The typical agent came from a white Christian culture that was politically conservative and behaviorally orthodox. There were, for example, disproportionate numbers of eastern seaboard Irishmen, graduates of Deep South universities, and western Mormons. Once inside the Bureau subculture, the agent was indoctrinated in the belief that only J. Edgar Hoover's early recognition and exposure of the Communist menace had preserved the American way of life. The enemy was not only Communists and socialists, but "those liberals" and "dangerous-thinking one worlders."

Some idea of the extreme tone of this indoctrination can be gained from a passage in the report agent Jack Levine to the Department of Justice. Describing a lecture to new agents in 1960, it said: "A Bureau official commented that it was very fortunate that Adlai Stevenson did not receive the Democratic nomination for the Presidency. He stated that if Stevenson was ever elected President the Bureau's security problems would be staggering because his close advisors and supporters were Communists, Communist sympathizers, and pseudo-intellectual radicals. This official further commented on how easily 'eggheads' like Stevenson had been duped by the Communists."

My own initial inculcation in 1951 included rather convoluted views of certain events. I can recall, for instance, that the Peekskill riots of a few years before, in which the police were as club-happy as Chicago's force in 1968, was portrayed as a staged disorder by Communist leaders designed, as my notes read, "to array [rank and file CP] members against law enforcement officers as their bitterest enemies." Nothing changed; Hoover still blamed cunning Reds as the planners, *provocateurs,* and catalysts behind contemporary disorders and as the engineers of all criticism of the police and the FBI.

Agents who carried these demon beliefs into the field were plainly predisposed to slant reports, subconsciously if not deliberately. At the height of the controversy over McCarthy, it seemed to me that the agents were split on the issue, but many of those who disapproved of him rejected his methods, not his politics. Some agents evidenced a near-pathological hatred of leftists. On the evening in 1953 that the Rosenbergs were executed (it was shortly after five P.M. on the Pacific coast), a knot of San Francisco agents stayed on after quitting time, their ears glued to a radio. When the bulletin came that the couple was dead, they let out a cheer. This antipathy found expression in the daily routine. A few agents delighted in harassing security subjects by making telephone calls to them giving false information and telephoning their employers—

anonymously, of course—with the tidings that they were Communists and ought to be fired. One agent I knew made a practice of "shadowing" subjects by practically stepping on their heels. Once, when one turned to protest, the agent punched him in the face and sent him reeling. This was COINTELPRO in its nascent stage, before it was refined in the 1960s.

The confidential informant was the Bureau's most effective tool for penetrating "the opposition." Since American jurisprudence requires that a person bearing witness against another do so by confrontation in court so that his reliability can be gauged and his testimony subjected to cross-examination, informants were only occasionally "surfaced" in cases under prosecution. But no such troublesome procedures were necessary under administrative rules. Under the loyalty program, the government had it both ways—it could introduce an informant's allegations without revealing his identity. This Kafkaesque device became known as the "faceless informer" system.

Informants' accusations were incorporated into FBI reports disseminated to employing agencies and the government security apparatus. They were attributed only to, say, Confidential Informant T-3 (his identity was recorded on the Administrative Page of the report, which was not circulated outside the FBI). The only way to weigh his credibility was to accept the Bureau's characterization of him as "of known reliability," "of unknown reliability," or "who has furnished reliable information in the past."

The "T" symbols concealed not only regular informants but anyone who didn't want his identity divulged—former employers, acquaintances, business associates—and information from banks and the like that was legitimately available only upon the issuance of a subpoena duces tecum. Or they might hide a wiretap, bug, or "black bag job"—a break-and-enter venture. These latter sources were, of course, paraphrased to preclude their being pinpointed, but invariably they were described as "of known reliability." They were kept in a "Do not file" file, then periodically destroyed.

The celebrated Judith Coplon spy case of 1949 provided an unsettling insight into the miasma of raw data FBI report writers were expected to transmogrify into a finished product, the tenuousness of some informant allegations, and the use of "T" symbols to cloak wiretaps. The disclosures would never have occurred had not the government elected to prosecute Miss Coplon criminally rather than dismissing her, thus bringing into play evidential standards. In what evidently was a showcase trial, she was charged with passing classified data obtained through her position as a Department of Justice employee to a paramour, Valentin Gubitchev of the Soviet United Nations delegation.

A first trial was held in Washington on the actual theft charge. The defense requested that the entire FBI file be made available so that the competency and accuracy of the testimony could be tested. Judge Albert L. Reeves so ordered, provoking a crisis at Ninth and Pennsylvania. Hoover adamantly opposed producing the file on the grounds that the integrity of FBI files would be jeopardized. The decision belonged to Attorney General Tom C. Clark. "He was naturally aware," the *Washington Post* stated on June 15, 1949, "of the embarrassment to the Government—especially to the work of the FBI—which revelation of these voluminous documents, filled with gossip, hearsay, and innuendo against innocent citizens would entail." But he was also aware that to drop the prosecution would bring down the wrath of Red-hunters riding high in the saddle.

Hoover's worst fears were realized. Introduced at the trial was a Bureau report stating that a confidential informant had advised that Frederic March, Canada Lee, Norman Corwin of CBS, and Daniel L. Marsh, president of Boston University, were "outstanding Communist Party fellow travelers." Another informant was said to have been "satisfied" that a number of Hollywood actors and writers were card-carrying Communists. Still another—perhaps a wiretap—alleged that the name of Florence March was "mentioned" in a conversation between two putative Communists.

The standard of guilt by association, a fixture of the McCarthy era, was prominent in the reports. The Marches were so affixed, as was Mrs. Edward U. Condon. Actress Helen Hayes was informed on as having performed in a 1945 skit for the benefit of the American Society for Russian Relief. An informant had submitted a list of speakers at a 1945 meeting in New York called "Crisis Coming, Atom Bomb—for Peace or War" that was duly entered into the file;

the list numbered Colonel Evans Carlson of Carlson's Raiders, Senator Charles W. Tobey, Helen Keller, Danny Kaye, sculptor Jo Davidson, Henry Wallace, and Frederic March.

The revelations dealt the FBI what the *Washington Post* termed its "worst legal smashup in 25 years." Much of what had found its way into the files was as patently unsavory as the notes in a gossip columnist's hatband. In the *Boston Sunday Post,* June 12, 1949, John Griffin aired a common anxiety: "If the FBI accepts and makes a record of every name that is being given by anyone, then nobody in the United States is protected against abuse. What is there to prevent a person sending the name of someone he doesn't like into the FBI as a possible Communist?"

In a memorandum to his field officials, Hoover denied responsibility for the disaster, saying he had "urged the Attorney General to seek a mistrial or a citation for contempt rather than produce these reports with consequent devastating harm to the FBI's responsibility for internal security, as well as the disclosure of as yet uncorroborated information in our files concerning individuals." Not a word about the ludicrous nature of most of the information, or the need to purge it from the files. And no reevaluation of the entire informant program.

The program was badly in need of severe measures, for the creation of information was becoming standard procedure among informants paid on a C.O.D. basis. The most notorious case of fabrication involved Harvey M. Matusow, a Communist Party dropout who became an FBI informant in 1950 and was subsequently used by Senator McCarthy. In 1955, Matusow "got religion" and confessed that he had given false testimony in two trials and several hearings. Other informants, paid over four hundred dollars per month for their "continuing productivity," turned out to be singularly unreliable and were prone to embellish their reports. Noting that one well-paid informant "has testified under oath that he would lie under oath, if directed to do so by his present employers," columnists Joseph and Stewart Alsop argued that putting political informers on the government payroll "has been regularly denounced as pernicious and dangerous since the time of the Roman historian Tacitus."

But pay wasn't the only motivation. Many informants held political views so far to the right that they were nearly hysterical in their accusations against "the Communists." Many of these veterans of the "age of suspicions," as James Wechsler called it, were busy on the right-wing lecture circuit and publishing network. Among them were Herbert A. Philbrick, the Boston CP infiltrator who wrote *I Led Three Lives*; Matt Cvetic of Pittsburgh, author of *I Was a Spy for the FBI*; Karl Prussion, a West Coast CP defector whose lectures expose such secrets as how Communists "planned the San Francisco riots"; and Marion Miller, a Los Angeles housewife who wrote *I Was a Spy* and branded a prominent rabbi as Red. In 1967 there were so many speakers billed by the John Birch Society as "ex-FBI undercover agents" that Hoover felt compelled to disavow the description as "an improper attempt to capitalize on the name of the FBI."

•

By 1953, the Communist Party USA was in eclipse. Notes I took at in-service training that year show that by the FBI's own reckoning, the membership had skidded from half a million before World War II to a paltry twenty-four thousand. By the early 1960s, its strength had dipped below ten thousand. With an aging leadership decimated by the Smith Act trials and ranks thoroughly penetrated by FBI informants, the CPUSA was an echo of the past.

The moribund state of the CPUSA was apparent to most insiders. In an article "Hoover and the Red Scare" in *The Nation,* October 20, 1962, former FBI agent Jack Levine asserted that there was a ratio of one informant for every 5.7 Party members, which made the FBI, through its dues-paying contingent, "the largest single financial contributor to the coffers of the Communist Party." The coffers were hardly bulging. Labor columnist Victor Riesel disclosed on March 29, 1963: "After a little footwork and a lot more pencil work, I can report that the Communist Party of the U.S.A. has collected and effectively funneled a minimum of $10-million in the past decade." This is an average of a million dollars a year, most of the amount having been collected in the early part of the decade. It was pitifully meager compared with the three million a year the Birch Society was taking in.

In 1962, Robert Kennedy made the distinction that Soviet espionage, not the domestic Communist Party, posed a viable threat. The problem "doesn't lie with the Communist Party here in the United States," he said, adding that "what is almost hysteria about the activities of Communists within the United States is misplaced apprehension."

The CP's former general secretary, Earl Browder, told the FBI in 1963, "The Communist Party is completely a waste of time in this country. . . . Communism would not work here. Its theories don't fit America." To the man who had guided the CPUSA for fifteen years before being ousted by order of Stalin for preaching coexistence, the 1960s edition was no more than a "weak nuisance."

Yet even as the ghost shrank, Hoover continued to inflate its image as a threat. In appropriations testimony on March 6, 1961, he intimated that a numerically small Party was deceptive, for the front was everywhere: "Some two hundred known, or suspected, Communist front and Communist-infiltrated organizations are now under investigation by the FBI. Many of these fronts are national in scope with chapters in various cities throughout the United States. They represent transmission belts through which the Communist Party furthers its conspiratorial designs." And there were always those dupes and fellow travelers: "Some celebrated, self-styled pacifists and some men of wealth and prominence have sometimes been unwitting—but sometimes knowing—political shills and stooges of deceitful Communist manipulations."

But Hoover had cried wolf once too often, and the public wasn't going through nightmares over domestic Communism. Then came the campus demonstrations and a new opportunity for the same brand of scaremongering. One of the radical groups on campus was the W. E. B. DuBois Club, named after the black leader who at age ninety-three had announced he was taking up Communism. "The W. E. B. DuBois Clubs are new blood for the vampire of International Communism," cried the Director, keynoting his crusade against university dissidents.

The DuBois Clubs, too, were small and ineffectual, but they held tremendous propaganda potential because the Communist taint could be attached to them. Wasn't Bettina Aptheker, the daughter of Communist theoretician Herbert Aptheker, touring the colleges with Free Speech Movement leader Mario Savio? And wasn't Miss Aptheker a leader of the Berkeley DuBois Club? "One of the most effective means utilized by the Communist Party to reach the hearts, minds, and souls of young people is through its 2-year-old youth front, the W. E. B. DuBois Clubs of America," Hoover told congressional appropriators in 1967. "This group, together with other so-called 'new left' organizations such as the Students for a Democratic Society, work constantly in furtherance of the aims and objectives of the Communist Party throughout the nation."

In point of fact, the CP had by 1967 become disenchanted with the Clubs, which had failed to hew to the Party line, and was looking for some other group to help sponsor. By 1968, the Clubs were just about dead, but Hoover gave them artificial respiration. "This Communist front continues to receive practically all of its financial support from the Communist Party," he said.

Since his intelligence couldn't have been that faulty, the Director seems to have been playing propaganda games with a ghost. He had portrayed the Clubs as working "hand in hand" with the SDS, which he described as "the primary spokesmen of the new left." And the New Left, he warned, was "a new type of subversion and their danger is great."

So there it was in one simplistic package—the New Left in general and the SDS in particular, with the DuBois Clubs a Red albatross around their necks.*

Hoover's puerile conception of the youthful left was reflected by many of his minions. At a briefing for the Chicago police department Red Squad in April 1968—the FBI had been mentor to police anti-subversive units since the McCarthy days—G-man David Ryan declared that John Abt, an "attorney for the Communist Party USA," had been "able to put across the idea [to the National Conference for New Politics (NCNP)] that the best way to force the

---

*Interestingly, Karl Hess, who had helped draft the 1960 and 1964 Republican platforms and was chief speechwriter for Barry Goldwater, told the press in January 1969 that he was sympathetic to the New Left because of its stand against authoritarianism. "That's why I'm fond of the New Left," he said. "This is one of the reasons I find many of the statements and actions of the SDS very satisfying. Because they're following the precept of the Declaration of Independence."

withdrawal of the United States from Vietnam was to embarrass the administration by causing a disruption of the Democratic National Convention." But, as the *Chicago Journalism Review* elucidated in its February 1969 issue, the NCNP at its conference had hardly discussed the Democratic convention, and in any event had planned to hold its own convention and nominate Dr. Martin Luther King, Jr., and Dr. Benjamin Spock. "Ryan sought to explain the nature and personnel of the New Left in complete ignorance of both," asserted the *Review*. "In discussing the New Left as though it were a federation of organizations instead of simply a journalistic convenience, and in placing Old Left leaders at the helm of the New, the FBI man drew for his country cousins in the Red Squad a frightening picture of Communist ideologues, black militants and revolutionary youth undermining the foundations of the Republic."

In raising the specter of bomb-throwing bearded anarchists in a sort of throwback to the Palmer Red Raid days, Hoover was not above playing fast and loose with the facts. In 1968, he described the SDS as "anarchistic and nihilistic," a generalization that doesn't remotely apply to several of the factions composing the division-ridden group. A few weeks later SDS held its annual convention at Michigan State University, and an episode there gave him the chance to complete the picture by placing a bomb in the SDS hand. In a disclosure that alarmed newspaper readers across the country, the Director reported that during the convention a workshop was held on "Sabotage and Explosives." The implication, of course, was that terrorism by firebombing and demolition had become an integral part of SDS operations.

The truth was considerably less sensational. Such a workshop was not originally on the agenda; in fact, the delegates were on their best behavior because they knew the convention would attract a swarm of police spies. It was SDS policy, however, to permit delegates to set up their own workshops on any subjects they wanted. One devil-may-care delegate did conduct an impromptu demolition "workshop" in one of the classrooms, with crude drawings on the blackboard. Five persons attended. The hundreds of others gave it a wide berth.

In switching the limelight from the decaying CPUSA to student radicalism, Hoover stepped up the tempo of FBI on-campus activity. Since the early days of the loyalty program, the Bureau had cultivated close relations with university administrations so that it had virtually unrestricted access to student records (although many professors, disgusted with the FBI's zeal during the McCarthy days, declined to supply it with personal data). Few college officials questioned the purpose of FBI inquiries. In 1967, at the University of California, for example, admissions officer David Stewart conceded that in "three or four cases in the last few months" he had given the FBI records on students who had neither applied for government jobs nor consented to such an examination.

Campus security police are a prime source of information for the FBI, whose political orientation they largely share. In fact, many of the campus "fuzz" were former FBI agents. This was true at California and Illinois, where the chief security man, W. Thomas Morgan, kept extensive files on purported leftists. *Newsweek* quoted one of Morgan's employees as saying, "Anyone who belongs to a liberal organization goes in. They keep clippings and reports on student demonstrations, arrests, traffic tickets, everything, with elaborate cross-references."

A comparable setup at Yale spawned a controversy. The campus police chief, John W. Powell, a seventeen-year veteran of the FBI, became the target of the *Yale Daily News* for keeping "subversive activities" files into which were funneled the most trivial items. The snooping presumably ended when the university provost ordered the files destroyed.

Generally it was the multiversity dependent upon government research contracts that cooperated most open-handedly with the FBI. At the forefront were Duke, Illinois, Indiana, Texas, Kansas, Michigan State, and Ohio State. It took tiny Wesleyan University of Connecticut to give the Bureau an emphatic no. Following a 1966 SDS peace demonstration, Dean Stanley J. Idzerda refused an FBI request for the SDS membership list. "We keep no such lists of any organizations," he stated. "We consider the student's activity his own affair." And the dean added: "At the same time, it's unfortunate that a climate of suspicion can be created by such activities that might lead some students to be more circumspect than the situation requires. Things like this can be a danger to a free and open community if men change their behavior because of it."

In the resultant furor, the FBI agent who had made the request explained to Dean Idzerda that no probe of the SDS had been contemplated, just "possible infiltration of the SDS chapter by Communist influence." When a student committee wrote Hoover that the investigation constituted an infringement of academic freedom, the Bureau chief replied that such a charge was "not only utterly false but also is so irresponsible as to cast serious doubt on the quality of academic reasoning or the motivation behind it."

The informant system that Hoover had devised during the old GID days was transplanted to the campuses. So uptight was the aged Director about youthful radicalism that he apparently had no misgivings about introducing this kind of cynicism and duplicity into student life. Nor did he evince skepticism over the reliability of student informers, as did, for one, Chief Arthur Beaumont of the University of North Carolina police. "I wouldn't use an informer if I had to," the chief was quoted as saying by *Newsweek,* March 27, 1967. "If they'll lie for you, they'll lie to you."

In recruiting campus spies, the FBI generally used an appeal to the prospect's patriotism coupled frequently with a hint of trouble with the draft board if cooperation—the word "informing" was studiously avoided—was not forthcoming. Agents got their foot in the door by saying they were checking on an acquaintance who had applied for a job, but their attention soon turned to the interviewee.

Some FBI informants were sincerely disillusioned members of target groups, but their information tended to be colored by their vengefulness and bitterness. And money was a common motive for informing. The Bureau paid well for part-time work, even for passing on what one saw and heard in the course of a day. A stipend of $200 a month was not uncommon, and a draft deferment might be tossed in. In 1963, when the government was trying to force the small Advance Youth Organization to register as a Communist front, no less than eleven collegiate informants testified that they had received an aggregate of over $45,000 for brief stints as informants. One Aaron Cohen, an officer of the AYO, netted $6,371.65. During the 1965 trial of three youths who had visited Cuba in violation of passport regulations, informants from San Francisco State and Columbia admitted they had received generous pay; one said the FBI had given him a $300 bonus for accompanying the accused to Cuba.

A look inside the student informer's world was given by Robert Harris, an electrical engineering student at the University of Illinois who spied on the SDS for the FBI, then told the local press about it. Originally, Harris' concern had been over the militant right, but agents argued that the SDS was equally dangerous and talked him into infiltrating it. Harris claimed he had done it for patriotism's sake, that over eight months he received only seventy-five dollars in expenses even though the agents offered him pay. To help indoctrinate their informant, the agents gave him a reprint of testimony by the Director. ("The Director should be printed in capitals," Harris told reporters, "because it's said in the same hushed tone that the word God is mentioned.") Harris gradually formed the conclusion that the G-men honestly believed that the SDS "is a conspiracy of wild-eyed radicals being manipulated by former members of the Communist Party who have decided to go behind the scenes and control SDS to destroy our democracy by violent revolution in the shortest time possible."

Harris found the SDS to be far from that kind of monster, and decided to quit informing because "when carried to this extreme it created a much greater monster than this so-called conspiracy they're looking for."

The extent of the FBI's scrutiny of the campus scene was suggested by a 1963 incident at Carleton College in Minnesota. A student organization had invited Communist editor Danny Rubin to speak as part of its series of controversial presentations. On behalf of the organization, student John F. McAuliff mailed an honorarium check to Rubin. Soon the FBI was investigating McAuliff, possibly having learned his identity through surveillance of the mail. A friend who was quizzed later reported that an agent had "asked him if John would have an academic or serious interest in communism," and other questions designed to catalog his political beliefs. Although cautioned not to mention the interview, the friend tipped off McAuliff, who fired off an irate letter to Hoover saying he had

had "a quaint belief that to be a free man means to be able to write whomever one pleases without having the government investigating you." He charged that the Bureau was failing in its responsibility of "keeping track of potentially treasonous people" without acting "as a brake on the free and fearless expression of all ideas." The *Minneapolis Tribune* broke the story with the comment: "The possible implications of such visits [by the FBI] are too potentially serious in contemporary American society to be handled as 'routine' matters."

Yet a repetition was disclosed in 1965 when Harvard student Aggrey Awori, a Nigerian track star, wrote a letter published in *The Crimson* that was sharply critical of U.S. military intervention in the Congo. Two agents arrived and questioned him for two hours. "If you speak your mind," Awori commented, "the FBI comes to speak to you."

The 1967 exposure of an FBI informant ring on the State University of New York's Brockport campus led to tragedy. In the ensuing controversy over whether such activities were justified or not, the name of Dr. Ernst A. Weiner, who had openly participated in civil rights and antiwar movements, was bandied about as a "subversive" suspect in the local press. When the American Association of University Professors condemned the spying as "faculty intimidation" and "thought control," Hoover retorted vigorously in a letter to Chancellor Samuel Gould of the University system: "I would never permit the FBI to shirk its responsibilities. I feel certain that you, as a responsible educator and citizen, would never condone this Bureau's failure to handle its obligations in the internal security field, or that you would have us ignore specific allegations of subversive activity in any segment of our society, including college campuses."

Engaging in dissidence is subversive? Dr. Weiner was devastated. He wrote a moving letter to the school paper, quoting from Socrates: "For of old I have had many accusers, who have accused me falsely to you during many years. . . . Hardest of all, I do not know and cannot tell the names of my accusers, . . . and therefore I must simply fight with shadows in my own defense and argue when there is no one who answers." A month after the letter was published, Dr. Weiner committed suicide.

If Hoover had his way, the campuses would have been stripped of their traditional function as marketplaces for ideas and become institutional preserves of orthodoxy. The Director long held that students had to be shielded from radical viewpoints. "Youth is unable to evaluate such theories properly," he told Jack Alexander of *The New Yorker* in 1937. He continued to sound that note. In 1969 appropriations testimony, he observed that Communists had made fifty-four campus appearances the previous year—a list was entered into the record each year—while the FBI's "limited staff" could only present "the true facts about Communism" at a few universities such as West Point, Annapolis, the Air Force Academy, and the Naval War College. "I do not feel this should be permitted as I do not think the students should be confronted by individuals as liars," Hoover complained.

Whether the FBI was ever meant to become a promotional organ for its director's political views was dubious. But the larger question was its intimidating presence in force on the national university scene. Despite bleats to the contrary from Hoover and other anti-intellectuals, the protests of student militants were legitimate ones in the eyes of the majority of the academic community. "Those who comfort themselves that the trouble on the college campuses of America is caused by only a 'handful of students' and that the majority are completely out of sympathy with the goals of the militant few," a May 1969 Gallup Poll revealed, "would be disabused of this view if they were to talk to students across the nation." The poll found that while many students disagreed with the tactics used, most desired the reforms being sought.

•

While Hoover has thundered against the militant left and committed considerable manpower to probing it, the militant right flourished under his benign eye. To be sure, he on occasion denounced extremism of any form, and the Ku Klux Klan received his special investigative attentions. But the KKK was the whipping boy of the radical right, so much so that even the benighted HUAC undertook a much-publicized probe of it. As violent and fanatical as it is, the KKK was one of the most bizarre and overrated segments of the ultraright as far as national importance was concerned. Its members tended to be poorly educated, raffish, and unstable, and the organization was faction-ridden and underfunded. Far more potent were the Minutemen, whose importance Hoover consistently downgrades in his appropriations testimony.

Formed in 1960, the Minutemen subscribed to a revolutionary manifesto holding that a "pro-American Government can no longer be established by normal political means" and that "the objectives of the Minutemen are to abandon wasteful, useless efforts and begin immediately to prepare for the day when Americans will once again fight for their lives and their liberty." Paramilitary in design, the organization drilled its members in guerrilla warfare and had arms and ammunition caches deployed around the country. More than any other group, the Minutemen were capable of implementing their rhetoric by force of arms.

A few Bureau field offices perceived the potential of the Minutemen and took it upon themselves to try to penetrate the group. After a number of Congressmen who had voted against funds for the HUAC received notices signed "Minutemen" telling them they were marked for death—"Traitors beware! Even now the cross hairs are on the back of your necks"—Hoover took official notice. On May 19, 1965, he informed Congress, "We have long been aware of the Minutemen organization and our investigation is continuing." He briefly described the organization: "Our investigation indicates that this organization is a loose federation, with each unit acting independently and lacking any real central control," he said. "Its numerical strength is probably greatly exaggerated."

When reporter Harry Jones, Jr., of the *Kansas City Star* read the FBI chief's testimony, his eyes bugged. It had been lifted practically verbatim from an article he had published in the *Washington Post* on November 18, 1964, some six months before. Jones wrote in his book *The Minutemen:* "Somehow, after comparing the *Washington Post* story and Mr. Hoover's words, I was not as overwhelmed as I perhaps should have been by his assurance at the end of his statement: 'We have penetrated this organization and our sources are keeping us advised of developments.'"

Some admirers of Hoover and the FBI postulated that since the shrillest criticism of the Bureau came from extremists of both left and right, the agency had to stand squarely in the middle. Indeed, the left was as hostile to the Director as he was to it. But the extreme right was not so simply categorized. Usually the two exceptions were cited: the KKK and the Minutemen. Klan members contemptuously alluded to the FBI as the "Federal Bureau of Integration," and the Minutemen saw the Bureau as just one more tentacle of a socialistic central government. But a spinoff group that called itself The Real Minutemen and considered regular Minutemen leader Robert B. DePugh entirely too tame regarded Hoover as a towering hero. So did the later assassinated George Lincoln Rockwell of the American Nazi Party. He wanted to "set J. Edgar Hoover loose to round up all the Jews," with the explanation, "J. Edgar Hoover is our kind of people. He talks like a pink but when he acts, he acts like a white man!"

Certainly the Director's words were grist for the right-wing propaganda mills. In trying to illuminate Hoover's stature in the eyes of the radical right United Automobile Workers president Walter Reuther pointed out that his overblowing of the Communist menace at every turn "contributes to the public's frame of mind upon which the radical right feeds."

A case in point was the John Birch Society. Although Hoover mildly disowned the society and declared that he had "no respect" for the views of founder Robert Welch, he was nevertheless one of the society's idols. "We still have high regard for him and the FBI," national public relations director John Rousselot insisted, and, indeed, the Director's portrait once adorned the cover of the Birch monthly, *American Opinion*. Had the society been investigated as its counterparts on the left had? "Regarding your request concerning the John Birch Society and 'Minutemen'," read a letter from the director of the Warren Commission, "this is to advise that this Bureau did not conduct any investigation of those organizations or its [*sic*] members in the State of Texas during 1963."

Although Hoover fulminated against the left and the Bureau kept a stock of published material on the subject, the right was left untouched. Citizen inquiries about such groups as the Birch Society and the anti-Semitic organ *Common Sense* were given the stock answer that the Bureau "does not make evaluations nor draw conclusions as to the character or integrity of any organization, publication or individual." Lest the inquirer jump to the conclusion that the SDS was the sole object of the Bureau's attention, Hoover expressed the hope that "you will not infer in this connection either that we do or do not have data in our files relating to the subject of your inquiry."

Invoking Hoover's magic name was standard procedure with right-wing propagandists. In his tract *None Dare Call It Treason,* widely distributed by the hard-core elements behind Barry Goldwater, author John A. Stormer reverently quoted the Director on Communism no less than seventeen times, and on the jacket is his summons to arms: "We are at war with Communism and the sooner every red-blooded American realizes this, the safer we will be." *Fi-Po News,* the periodical of a reactionary group within the Los Angeles police department, likewise called on Hoover's authority. "FBI Chief J. Edgar Hoover's warnings that this nation's youth is the number one target of the Communist Party have been confirmed by accelerated Party activity, coupled with recent arrests in Hollywood," a 1963 issue said. The article, written by Sergeant Norman H. Moore (who also served as chairman of the subversive committee of the California American Legion), tried mightily to implicate folk music as a Communist plot, a canard so ridiculous that the wire services played it for laughs.

Some phobic anti-Communists even tried to coax Hoover into running for national office. During his 1968 campaign, American Independent Party candidate George Wallace solicited the Director as a vice-presidential running mate, finally settling for the superhawkish General Curtis LeMay. In 1964, Edgar Eugene Bradley, West Coast representative of the anti-Semitic and anti-Catholic Twentieth Century Reformation Hour, was involved in a J. Edgar Hoover–for–President drive that never got off the ground.

In the course of drumming up more men and money for 1970, Hoover came up with a new Red bugbear. On the evidence of "the blatant, belligerent and illogical statements" of Red Chinese leaders, the Director concluded that the United States is beyond doubt China's "Number One enemy." Dredging up the yellow peril scare, he saw fit to mention that there were "over seven hundred desertions by Chinese crewmen in the United States in fiscal 1967," some of whom may "have served as couriers in intelligence operations"; that the entrance of some twenty thousand Chinese immigrants each year "provides a means to send agents into our nation"; and that "there are over three hundred thousand Chinese in the United States, some of whom could be susceptible to recruitment either through ethnic ties or hostage situations because of relatives in Communist China."

The indiscriminate and xenophobic nature of this indictment was intended to make every person of Chinese ancestry suspect. Remonstrated the *San Francisco Chronicle*, July 13, 1969: "He is irresponsibly slurring a large and substantial segment of American citizens and he ought not to do it. The Japanese American Citizens League was even more outraged. Asking that the testimony be stricken from the record, it declared: "Similar unfounded and biased statements were made against the Japanese preceding World War II and were used to foment hatred and suspicion, contributing in 1942 to the incarceration without charges of 110,000 Japanese, 70 percent of whom were American citizens."

The damage that Hoover caused with his hyperbolic and self-serving alarms was incalculable. The Joe McCarthys destroyed themselves in the end by their flagrant excesses. But the Director, cloaked with the mantle of FBI prestige, was able to give the appearance of temperance. By raising time and again the illusion of an all-powerful internal Communist threat, he divided our society and sowed the seeds of suspicion in the land.

CHAPTER ELEVEN

THE TITULAR HEAD OF AMERICAN LAW ENFORCEMENT

The reason why a great many Americans (including some newspapers) associate all Federal law enforcement with the FBI is that the FBI has been more widely publicized, glamorized, idealized and advertised than any other government crime-fighting bureau. . . . It is important, however, to point out that the FBI, Treasury agents and other federal enforcement groups owe much of their success to state and local police departments, and although the police are really the first line of defense against crime, they frequently get little or no public credit for their participation in many important criminal cases.

—*Harry E. Neal retired Assistant*
Chief of the U.S. Secret Service

There were in the 1960s close to four hundred thousand law enforcement officers in the United States, of which fewer than seven thousand were FBI agents. Yet J. Edgar Hoover had long been regarded as the titular head of American law enforcement and his agency as the paradigm of the profession.

The police had ambivalent feelings about the relationship. On the one hand, the immense prestige of the FBI had generally lifted the status of law enforcement in the public mind. And when Hoover

spoke, it was the police cant down the line: the courts are handcuff-
ing the police, overly lenient parole authorities are returning rapists
and muggers to the streets, campus radicals are tearing at the fabric
of conventional society, Communism looms. The dual menaces of
crime and subversion, exploded to scary dimensions by the Director's voice, contributed to the legend of the Thin Blue Line.

Then, too, the police were beholden to the FBI for its "cooperative services"—the laboratory, fingerprint division, police training
program, crime records-keeping—services that many financially
strapped departments could not provide for themselves.

On the other hand the Bureau's tendency toward high-handed-
ness was a constant source of irritation. In the early days, an FBI on
the make repeatedly upstaged local police in making newsworthy
arrests and raids, a policy that was not entirely abandoned. The
supposed exchange of information between the Bureau and local
police was not an exchange at all, but, as the Kefauver Committee
put it, a "one-way street" in the FBI's direction. And resentment
over the FBI's super-image and untouchability—did anyone ever
propose a civilian review board for the Bureau?—smoldered silently
in the police breast.

Police officials rarely complained in public. The law enforcement brotherhood was notoriously reluctant to air its differences in
the press, and its dependence upon FBI services was a definite deterrent. For years, the International Association of Chiefs of Police
passed resolutions heaping praise on Hoover while many members
quietly seethed. Only when the issue of whether the FBI should
completely dominate police training came to a head, was there any
viable move toward emancipation.

The supplying of police services that led to the FBI's hegemony
began practically with Hoover's appointment as Director. Acutely
aware that local law enforcement had neither the funds nor the
expertise to handle it, the IACP had for years been trying to persuade the federal government to establish a bureau of identification
that would provide a centralized fingerprint service. To this end it
had created its own National Bureau of Criminal Identification in
1897, while continuing to lobby for a federally supported bureau. In
1922 a Special Committee on Law Enforcement of the American

Bar Association recommended that a Federal Bureau of Records and Statistics be established within the Department of Justice. This bureau would not only maintain the fingerprint collection but compile and disseminate criminal statistical data as well.

It wasn't long before Hoover took over both functions with his FBI. In 1924, when he was appointed, the International Police Conference (IPC) headed by New York Commissioner R. E. Enright was battling with the IACP over where the fingerprint service should be housed. The IPC favored the Department of Interior, while the IACP, of course, opted for the Justice Department. By this time the IACP had dissolved its own National Bureau and turned the collection over to a reluctant Department of Justice, which was using prisoners at Leavenworth Penitentiary to process them. The situation was highly unsatisfactory.

Marshaling support from Attorney General Stone and sympathizers in Congress, Hoover obtained funding for the project and moved it in-house. There was no objection from the IACP. In fact, recounted an IACP historian, "members, especially those who had fought for the Central Bureau for more than a quarter of a century, took just pride in the knowledge that their fondest hopes were now a reality."

For some time the IACP had been perfecting a statistical system called Uniform Crime Reporting that would provide an overview of the national crime picture. In 1927, it formed a committee, to which Hoover was appointed. By 1930 he had taken over the crime reporting function also, and the ABA's earlier recommendation for a separate bureau was forgotten. Congress passed a law authorizing a permanent FBI Division of Identification and Information to handle both functions. The police were in a position of having to rely on the Bureau.

For years Hoover had used the dry Uniform Crime Reports as a shocker to awaken the public to an awareness of an onrushing "crime menace." Periodically, the Bureau issued press releases disclosing the latest stark statistics. "Serious crime increased seventeen percent in 1968 throughout the United States, FBI director J. Edgar Hoover reported yesterday," went a typical wire service dispatch in early 1969 that included a rough breakdown in categories.

Armed with these quick-draw statistics, the Director fired away at the crime monster. In 1962, for instance, he saw a "massive avalanche of crime" thundering over the land, placing every citizen "in greater danger than ever before of becoming a victim of this criminal onslaught." In 1963 he predicted a "tragic breakdown of law and order" unless crime was curbed. The doomsday tocsins went on and on, magnifying the importance of the police and the FBI. "Public apathy and the lack of citizen cooperation with law enforcement agencies," Hoover said, "is one of the shocking great weaknesses in the fight against crime."

Since only a small fraction of the crimes reported were within FBI jurisdiction, the FBI put on a diligent program to ensure cooperation. "Contacts by Special Agents of the FBI are utilized to enlist the cooperation of new contributors and to explain the purpose of this program and the methods of assembling information for reporting," a preface to the reports related. "When correspondents including specially designed questionnaires fails, Special Agents may be directed to visit the contributor to affirmatively resolve the misunderstanding." I can recall once making a special trip to a small town in Oklahoma on instructions from Washington because the three-man force there hadn't broken down arrest totals according to race. "Well sir," remarked the chief, obviously impressed with FBI thoroughness, "about all our arrests are drunks in overnight, but we'll sure break it down in the future."

Unfortunately, there was no warning label attached to the statistical packages prepared for public consumption, an oversight that left some ill effects. The experience of Chief Thomas Cahill of San Francisco in 1962 illustrated the point. The newspapers were sensationalizing a series of street muggings and assaults. With the glee of one quoting an unimpeachable source, they reported, "Crime in San Francisco, the FBI has confirmed, is up 15.5 percent, as compared with a 1 percent increase in other cities on the average, and a DROP of more than 4 percent in Oakland and Los Angeles." The chief was on the spot. In a television interview, he struggled to explain that figures could be deceptive. The 20 percent rise in homicides, he pointed out, represented only two more than the previous year—there simply weren't many homicides. "Where does the FBI obtain these statistics?" the interviewer asked. "From the San Francisco police department," answered Cahill, perplexed by the irony of it all.

In New York several years ago, FBI figures showed felonies up a whopping 59.9 percent. But as clarified by Chief Inspector Sanford D. Garelik of the New York police, the surge reflected not a crime wave but a crackdown on precinct officials who had been downgrading or pigeon-holing reported crimes. "All statistics in corporations and bureaucratic organizations tend to be self-serving," asserted Garelik, "and the police department is not that different."

Sociologist Albert Biderman attacked the FBI Uniform Crime Reports as conjuring up a false image of crime waves and grossly distorting both the rate and distribution of crime, and Professor Marvin Wolfgang specified many instances in the reports of "error, omission, inconsistency, contradiction, deficiency, and bias." Both were consultants to the President's National Crime Commission, which concluded in its 1967 report that "fears of crime were magnified by lumping statistics for all crimes together and then using violent crimes (the majority) as a stereotype for crime in general."

When the 1965 reports stated that Negroes outnumbered whites in arrests in three of the five "violent crime" categories, even though blacks represented only 11 percent of the population, the NAACP's Roy Wilkins fired back that "records show the Negro is more easily arrested than a white person. Dragnet arrests for a crime committed by one or two persons frequently haul a dozen Negroes to jail and into the record books."

Dr. Sophia M. Robison, regarded as a leading expert in the field, condemned the FBI releases as "not worth the paper they are printed on" and speculated, "It's budget time and they probably want more money." Former federal prosecutor Robert M. Cipes, in *The Crime War: The Manufactured Crusade,* ventured that Hoover "has a vested interest in maintaining the crime wave," not only for larger appropriations but "to sustain a constant state of emergency in which he can serve as national savior." Cipes agreed that it was the Director's "control of crime statistics, as much as any other factor, which has accounted for his phenomenal dominance of American law enforcement."

The President's Commission recommended, in an echo of the long-ago ABA suggestion, that a separate bureau handle the statistics and publish the results with objective interpretations. With his usual slam-bang language, Hoover mocked "the shallow pronouncements of that 'select' group of impractical theorists who would 'define away' and reduce the crime problem by wielding a heavy eraser on statistics."

The FBI laboratory was another "service" to law enforcement, but the trend was toward the establishment of police laboratories at the local level. Contrary to popular belief, the FBI laboratory was not the first in the United States; that honor goes to the Los Angeles police lab, founded in 1929. The Bureau billed its facility, opened in 1932, as "the world's greatest scientific crime laboratory," a superlative not uniformly subscribed to by police. Many police users felt that the FBI lab was unduly timid in its conclusions, while others believed it lagged behind the scientific times. Indeed, it was the Los Angeles police lab and the Internal Revenue Service laboratory that pioneered forensic applications of nuclear activation analysis, the latest wrinkle in identifying unknown substances. It was mostly the smaller departments and those close to Washington that relied on the FBI lab.

The issue of police training eventually became a bone of contention. Over the decades, the FBI field offices supplied instructors in such fields as firearms, arrest techniques, and defensive tactics upon the request of the police. The service was free, and some five thousand training schools were held annually around the country. Again, it was the smaller and more rural departments that most frequently availed themselves of the sessions. The urban departments had their own training academies and teaching staffs, and quite often felt that the FBI, which was not on the front line of battle in the asphalt jungle, was too bookish in its approach.

The pride of the Bureau's police training program was the FBI National Academy, which Hoover termed "the West Point of law enforcement." Founded in 1935 and quartered at Quantico, Virginia, it ran two twelve-week sessions each year. The officers who attended were nominated by their chiefs and screened by the local Bureau offices. Although there was no tuition, the students had to pay their own expenses.* The curriculum ran the gamut of police skills, from the processing of latent fingerprints to investigative methods and defensive tactics. At the conclusion of each session, a formal graduation ceremony was held in Washington—as a new agent, for instance, I was pressed into service as an usher at a graduation featuring the sonorous oratory of Senator Everett Dirksen.

However, the Academy was more highly rated outside police circles than in. It was criticized on several counts: that the techniques were not always the latest; that it was less than a "West Point" because of a lack of command level instruction; that it fell short on the human aspects of enforcement. When a Baltimore policeman who had attended suggested areas of improvement, Hoover's reaction was to threaten to suspend classes.

Well over five thousand graduates returned to their departments imbued with the spirit of FBI-police camaraderie, and they diffused this spirit as well as their training throughout those departments. But the FBI didn't just turn a graduate loose—it considered him an adopted member of the family. He was inducted into the FBI National Academy Associates, which held its own conclave each year in conjunction with the IACP convention. In all FBI reports and correspondence he was distinguished by "NA" after his name. Within two weeks of his graduation, the police officer was contacted by a field office agent and within thirty days by the SAC; thereafter contact had to be made with him at least once every thirty days. Thus the graduate might become, perhaps unwittingly, a source of information for the FBI concerning the internal affairs of his department. This grated on some police executives. "The FBI doesn't realize that National Academy graduates aren't FBI agents," a California chief told me, "but that their first loyalty is to the department."

With the completion of expanded facilities at Quantico, the ranks of National Academy men were multiplied. Congress appro-

---

*The Veterans of Foreign Wars annually bestowed a $1,000 grant to attend the academy to the police officer winning its J. Edgar Hoover Award as "the outstanding law enforcement officer in the United States." The winners of the award usually turned out to have already attended the academy, in which case they were allowed to designate a brother officer.

priated fifteen million dollars for the project in 1965 as part of the
Law Enforcement Assistance Act, and the Marines chipped in with
an additional eighty acres of land. The new complex boosted the
yearly capacity from over two hundred to over twelve hundred and
enabled an additional one thousand policemen to take short specialized courses.

To help bind together the far-flung law enforcement brotherhood, the Bureau published the *Law Enforcement Bulletin*, a
monthly slick mailed to some fifty-seven thousand police officers,
sheriffs, and prosecuting attorneys. In addition to articles by the FBI
staff, the *LEB* contained contributions from police authorities, such
as "Marihuana—A Calling Card to Narcotic Addiction," by Henry
L. Giordano of the Federal Bureau of Narcotics, in the November
1968 issue. Needless to say, police experts with pronouncedly progressive views, and there were a few, didn't see the light of print.

But the *LEB*'s main function seemed to be as a pulpit for
Hoover's homilies. The opening pages were set aside for him, and
he used them to take swipes at everything and everybody from
Eugene McCarthy to capital punishment abolitions. He panned Barbara Garson's off-Broadway play *MacBird* in the April 1967 issue
with the admonishment: "We should be alarmed when widespread
recognition and monetary awards go to a person who writes a
'satirical' piece of trash which maliciously defames the President of
our country." In his lurid style he attacked crime in general: "We
have on the loose in our country today a predatory monster called
crime. . . . Its far-reaching forages threaten every city and hamlet in
the Nation, and it strikes fear in the hearts and minds of the law-
abiding public" (June 1968). He matched hyperbole with the
despised campus radicals: "They regard themselves as the nucleus of
an elite dictatorial ruling class of the future" (September 1968).
Advance copies of the *LEB* were sent to the wire services, which
then disseminated the Director's pronunciamentos across the land.

Despite an air of magnanimity, the FBI's "cooperative services"
were in fact contingent upon the recipient's being in a state of grace
with the Bureau. For years Hoover and Chief William Parker carried on a feud, and for years the Los Angeles police were turned
down for the National Academy with the excuse that quotas were

filled, although applications from neighboring departments were regularly accepted. When a rift developed between the Dallas police and the Bureau following the John Kennedy assassination—a main agitant was a police intelligence officer's insistence that an FBI agent had remarked, "We knew he [Oswald] was capable of assassinating the president," in the face of heated denials by the agent and Hoover—that department was likewise cut off (the rift was healed a bit in 1966 when a new chief was appointed). In 1961, when the chief of the Ada, Oklahoma, force went on record as supporting me against Bureau officials, his department was left out in the cold.

When a 1965 *New York Times* article alleged that the FBI's participation in the Department of Justice drive on organized crime had been grudging, Attorney General Nicholas Katzenbach rose to the Bureau's defense by explaining that when law enforcement agencies "think they can make a good case by doing it alone," they sometimes try to do so because of "professional pride and organizational jealousy." The suggestion of interagency jealousies nettled Hoover more than the original charge. He indignantly declared that there was not "a scintilla of truth in that as pertains to the FBI."

His acute sensitivity on this point was understandable, for it was one of the Bureau's more vulnerable spots. Although the FBI paid lip service to local enforcement as the backbone of the counter-crime effort, the Bureau managed to alienate many police officers with its imperious attitudes and predilection for glory-grabbing.

One of the most serious complaints against the FBI was that it wouldn't share information with other agencies. The Kefauver hearings found police across the nation griping that "the Bureau tends to be overly secretive with information it collects on criminals—in other words, exchange of information with the FBI is something of a 'one-way street.'" And Burt Turkus, the former New York prosecutor instrumental in breaking up Murder, Inc., observed that "the bleat of police departments across the country is that the FBI too ardently guards many of the things it learns on a local level—and which could aid the local officer. The FBI on the other hand has indicated more than once, that it is not too impressed with local efficiency or honesty. This cleavage, the mobster always enjoys."

Naturally there were valid reasons why information could not be passed on in specific instances. Yet Bureau policy was unilateral. Although agents frequently called on police officers for such assistants as witnessing a signed statement, they were not allowed to reciprocate. And although police files were ordinarily open to the FBI, the reverse wasn't true. It was a strict rule that no one, police included, was to see an FBI report. Some agents would read off passages they knew police were interested in. I always considered this a bit degrading and handed the officer the report to read, provided it didn't contain sensitive information, while I went to the bathroom. A New York agent who ran afoul of this rule was dealt with harshly, however. He had let a Pinkerton detective read a report, and the man had copied part of it. The Bureau learned about the incident. Not only was the agent's career ended, the FBI attempted to prefer criminal charges against him and successfully blocked his application for a state private investigator's license.

In cases of dual jurisdiction the FBI and police worked together smoothly enough. But when the publicity stakes were high, the Bureau had a propensity to hog the limelight. This happened following a 1956 gun battle in Flint, Michigan, between a bank robber and a police office. The police conducted an intense search for the man they believed to be responsible. The FBI knew they were on the wrong track but didn't say anything. When agents located the actual robber, they made the arrest single-handedly and scooped the police.

The publicity-grabbing was repeated on a larger scale in the 1960 kidnap-murder of Denver brewery scion Adolph Coors, Jr. Scores of FBI agents poured into Denver when the family received a ransom note. The big break came when a neighbor handed over the license number of a yellow Mercury that had been driven suspiciously in the neighborhood prior to the abduction. The number checked out as belonging to one Joseph Corbett, Jr., a convicted murderer who had escaped some time before from a California penal facility. Corbett had been living in Denver under an assumed name and had vanished the day of the kidnapping.

The Bureau played this development close to the vest. It instructed field offices throughout the country to display Corbett's photograph to local police and to indicate that he was wanted as a federal fugitive, and not to give the reason why. Then a "wanted" flyer was issued, again with no reference to the kidnapping. If Corbett were to be taken into custody, the locals would merely notify the FBI, when then could make the grand announcement.

Many local officers saw through the ruse and resented not being cut in. As one Oklahoma prosecutor groused to me, "This is another example of the one-way street."

When Coors's body was found on the outskirts of Denver, the FBI's kidnapping jurisdiction ceased, since he had not been taken interstate. But the fugitive felon act still applied, and the Bureau continued its manhunt. Almost a year after the crime, Corbett was traced to Vancouver, British Columbia—Hoover subsequently said it was through a tip from a *Reader's Digest* article—and was apprehended by G-men and Royal Canadian Mounted Police. He was placed in jail in Seattle pending extradition to Colorado for prosecution under state murder statutes. Ordinarily, this would have ended the FBI involvement, since no federal prosecution was in order and the U.S. marshal was responsible for the custody and transportation of prisoners. But this was no ordinary case. A squabble developed between the marshal and a Colorado sheriff over who should have the distinction of conveying the prize prisoner to Denver. The FBI upstaged both by hustling Corbett from jail and flying him to Denver to the accompaniment of intense press coverage.

Although the celebrated Boston Brinks robbery was billed as a cooperative venture between state and federal authorities, it, too, was marred by hard feelings. The acclaim waiting for whoever solved this one was high, since the Halloween-masked bandits had escaped with a record $1.5 million. Without consulting its partners, the FBI broadcast the serial numbers of the stolen bills, advising anyone who spotted any "bait money" to notify the nearest Bureau office. This move upset local authorities, who had hoped to trace the bills quietly and feared that the publicity would alert the bandits. It may have done exactly that. The federal statute of limitations expired before the case was finally solved because of a falling-out among the thieves.

The December 1963 kidnapping of Frank Sinatra, Jr., saw the FBI act so secretly that some police officials angrily charged it was needlessly jeopardizing lives. Young Sinatra was abducted at gunpoint from his Lake Tahoe motel straddling the California-Nevada border. The FBI immediately took over the investigation, with the Director issuing progress reports from Washington. The exclusion of local police was more complete than usual, possibly because of the bungling of the Dallas police during the assassination aftermath two weeks before, but more likely because the Bureau was still smarting over its own boggle in Dallas and was trying to recoup a measure of prestige.

The first friction came when a local sheriff released to the news media a sketch of one kidnapper drawn by an artist of the California Bureau of Criminal Identification and Investigation from a witness description (the sketch bore a remarkable likeness to one of the men later convicted). The FBI hadn't wanted the sketch given out—as the *San Francisco Chronicle* pointed out, "It was possible for any alert policeman to make the jackpot arrest if he spotted the man in the drawing."

Then the sparks really flew when a California Highway Patrol officer routinely cited a driver for not having snow chains. When the same car arrived at a nearby lodge, some twenty agents of the FBI who had staked the place out arrested the driver and five occupants as suspects in the kidnapping. The Bureau had acted on information from Los Angeles police that the six were suspected of bank robberies in Southern California and just might be capable of the abduction (they turned out not to have done it). Upon being searched, one of the six, an escaped convict armed with two guns, was found to be carrying the CHP officer's citation. "This potentially tragic situation by some quirk did not explode into violence," raged the local CHP commander, his memory still fresh with the murder of another CHP officer a month before who had unwittingly stopped a carload of armed bank robbers. "How many more times will similar circumstances be repeated to sustain the legend of the FBI with the life of one lone CHP officer hanging in the balance?"

When the scene shifted to Los Angeles as the result of traces on phone calls originating there, resentment flared anew. As it closed in on the kidnappers, the FBI left the Los Angeles police totally uninformed. Chief Parker was outraged. Accusing the Bureau of being "unnecessarily secretive," he chided: "This is the first time that we were faced with a problem where there was criminal activity in the City of Los Angeles that was known to a law enforcement agency where we were not permitted to participate." Inspector Edward Walker of the LAPD charged the FBI with "poaching" and argued that the police should at least be given descriptions of the suspects.

Fortunately, the ransom payoff went off without a hitch—that time. But what if police on patrol had noticed the kidnapper's car behaving erratically or suspiciously and halted it? Exactly five years later this situation presented itself, and tragedy was only narrowly averted.

The case was the December 1968 abduction of Barbara Jane Mackle, daughter of millionaire construction man Robert Mackle. The ransom payoff instructions to the father warned that any deviation from the instructions would result in his own death as well as that of the victim. Mackle obeyed, dumping a suitcase stuffed with $500,000 cash into Biscayne Bay off Miami just before dawn on the specified day. Two men in a motorboat fished out the suitcase, landed, and headed for a car. Unaware of what was going on, a Miami policeman and Dade County sheriff's deputy became suspicious and accosted the pair. There was a gun fight, and the two men fled, jettisoning the suitcase and some scuba gear. "Please don't harm her," the anguished father pleaded in the newspapers, saying that it hadn't been a trap. Acting Miami police chief Charles Price issued a statement that the foul-up had occurred because his department had not been forewarned and "there was no coordination between us and the family and others"—the "others" obviously being the FBI. Fortunately, the victim was not killed.

Although relations between the FBI and the New York police were publicly proper, there was no love lost between the two agencies. The strain dated all the way back to the Lindbergh kidnapping. Following the arrest of Bruno Richard Hauptmann, FBI versions of events depicted a Bureau coup. Visitors touring headquarters, for instance, were regaled with tales of how "we" solved the case and were shown a large map of New York City on which agents had kept track of the spent ransom money with colored pins. But as Jack Alexander revealed in his 1937 *New Yorker* article, no mention was "made of the fact that New York police kept a similar map, or of the fact that Treasury agents really set the trap which caught Hauptmann. Perhaps few of the tourists realized that the ransom packets as originally made up by J. P. Morgan & Co. contained no gold notes, and that it was only because Treasury agents insisted that the packets were remade to include $35,000 worth of them. The passing of one of the gold notes at a filling station led directly to Hauptmann's arrest."

Relations were hardly improved by the 1936 affair surrounding the arrest of desperado Harry Brunnette. The fugitive and a partner, Merle Vandenbush, were being sought for a series of daring bank robberies and the kidnapping of a New Jersey trooper. New Jersey police had traced the suspects' car to New York City, where New York detectives took up the hunt. They found that Brunnette and a woman were living in an apartment on West 102nd. Hoping to catch Vandenbush also, the police set up an elaborate stakeout. At this point they informed the FBI of the situation, a courtesy they would soon regret.

A conference was held between the FBI and the police. It was agreed that the apartment would be raided at two the next afternoon, an hour at which Brunnette was usually asleep. It was hoped that Vandenbush would show up in the interim.

Shortly after midnight, however, two New Jersey troopers taking their shift on the stakeout watched in disbelief as Hoover himself appeared on the scene with a squad of G-men and prepared to mount a raid. According to the *New York Times* account, the troopers rushed out and asked the Director what he was doing, but "he merely shrugged his shoulders." The chief had hurried to New York and was staying at the St. Moritz Hotel; he had taken a cab to the scene to size up the situation and had decided it called for an immediate raid.

The raid resembled a Hollywood combination of Gangbusters and the Keystone Kops. A G-man attempted to shoot the lock off the apartment door and Brunnette returned the fire. Unable to dislodge the fugitive with bullets, the FBI men lobbed gas grenades, one of which set fire to the building and necessitated the summoning of the fire department. "Amid the hubbub," *Newsweek* reported, "a flustered G-man poked a submachine gun at a husky fireman. 'Dammit, can't you read?' growled the fireman, pointing at his helmet. 'If you don't take that gun out of my stomach I'll bash your head in.'" After the destructive siege Brunnette was finally captured, but Vandenbush remained at large.

The next day, Police Commissioner Lewis J. Valentine and his New Jersey counterpart expressed outrage at what they considered to be an FBI double cross. If Hoover hadn't jumped the gun in his grab for glory, they charged, Vandenbush might have been taken, too. Back in Washington, the FBI chief haughtily remarked that everyone should have been relieved that the dangerous Brunnette had been caught. "Hindsight is better than foresight," he replied sententiously, and chided that what was needed was less "unjustified and petty criticism" and more wholehearted cooperation.

Two months later, the police arrested Vandenbush without gunplay. He told his captors that he had been on his way to see Brunnette at the apartment and had watched the excitement. He was so close, he said, that he could have reached over and touched Hoover on the shoulder.

•

The great pursuit of John Dillinger in 1934 perhaps epitomized the one-sided relationship between police and the FBI that endured throughout Hoover's directorship. Lost to history is the fact that the frightening image of Dillinger, whom the FBI called "Public Enemy Number One," was the original creation of the commander of the Indiana State Police, Captain Matt Leach. In prison, the then-obscure Dillinger had met and admired Harry Pierpont, a tough and talented gang leader. As far as Leach was concerned, it was Pierpont who was the scourge of the Midwest. So he tried to stir dissension in the gang after Pierpont and Dillinger got out by inflating the importance of Dillinger. Whenever the press was around, Leach would portray the newcomer as king of the desperados, an image the FBI would later preserve by dubbing Dillinger "the most brazen killer this nation has ever known."

Even though Pierpont didn't fall for the trick, Dillinger's immortality was soon assured. Robberies were blamed on him when he was nowhere in the vicinity, and the legend grew. Although the police wanted him for such serious crimes as robbery and murder, the FBI took charge of the chase for the prize trophy when he happened to take a stolen car across a state line. "Act first, talk afterward," commanded Hoover, telling his men to "shoot straight and get the right man."

But the FBI got the wrong man first in a memorable blunder that was glossed over in later accounts of the chase. Agents raced to the Little Bohemia Lodge in northern Wisconsin after receiving a tip that Dillinger and his cohorts were holed up there. As they ringed the building, three men came out the front door and started off in a car. They ignored shouted warnings to stop, apparently because their car radio drowned out the shouts. Ten agents opened fire, killing one man and wounding the other two. Tragically, the men were simply guests and had no connection with the fugitives.

Alerted by the gunfire, Dillinger and his men slipped out the back way, which had been left unguarded because the agents had been told the lodge backed on a lake. But there was a high bank that provided perfect cover, and at daybreak when the G-men rushed the lodge it was too late. The agents fanned out. At a farmhouse not far away was Lester Gillis, better known as "Babyface" Nelson, who had gotten lost in the woods and had completed his escape. He opened fire with a machine gun, killing agent W. Carter Baum and wounding two other officers before being shot himself.

The toll in the abortive raid was two dead and four injured. Had the G-men bothered to consult with local law enforcement, the raid might have been bloodless and successful, for they might have found out more about who was in the lodge and possible escape routes.

The Bureau's determination to get Dillinger by itself had caused rash moves even earlier. Dillinger had once been cornered in an apartment in St. Paul, Minnesota, and he had somehow gotten away after a furious gun battle with the G-men, although a companion had been mortally wounded. The Bureau's lone-wolf tactics had hardly won the hearts of the local police. Captain Leach was outspoken on the subject, recounting that on one occasion a report came in that Dillinger and his gang "were bound for Moorseville in two machines. Those machines were found loaded with armed members of the Department of Justice." Leach fumed that these and other "foolhardy methods by J. Edgar Hoover made it necessary for me to lodge a formal complaint with Governor Paul V. McNutt against the policies of the Department of Justice."

The climax at the Biograph Theater in Chicago was doubly ironic, for although a local policeman's informant revealed the whereabouts of the fugitive, the local police were kept in the dark about the setting of the trap. This secretiveness nearly brought disaster. As FBI agents furtively took up positions around the theater, the manager began to suspect that a holdup was in the offing and called the police. A patrol car swung into the alley next to the theater and one of its occupants trained a shotgun on an agent. When the agent identified himself, the car left hurriedly, but on the other side of the theater Chicago plainclothesmen accosted other loitering agents. Just then, Dillinger emerged. As luck would have it, he turned toward the alley and didn't see the agents flashing their credentials to the plainclothesmen. But he smelled trouble and ducked into the alley. Agents blasted away, and "Public Enemy Number One" went reeling to his death.

A footnote to the case was written by Captain Leach. So incensed was he by the Bureau's recklessness that he prepared a book manuscript contending, among other things, that the bullets in Dillinger's body were from police, not FBI, guns. But by this time the idea of FBI supremacy had so gripped the nation that other versions were doomed. Three years afterwards, Leach was fired as commander of the Indiana state police. The action was taken, the State Police Board announced, at the insistence of Hoover, who had sent over two agents to notify the board members that the Bureau was severing relations with the state police. According to the announcement, the FBI chief had charged Leach with refusing to cooperate with the Bureau in the search for an Indiana bank robbery gang. Leach countered that the FBI had intimidated witnesses so that they would not talk to the state police about the gang, and he outlined to the board the FBI's miscues during the Dillinger hunt.

It was Hoover, not Leach, who prevailed. Leach had been the victim of the Dillinger legend he had created himself, a legend Hoover had used for his own purpose—to acquire formidable personal power. Within months, the defeated captain was killed in an auto wreck while returning home from New York, where he had been trying to convince publishers to print his book.

As the United Press put it, the axing of Leach was "the first result of a drive" by Hoover to secure the cooperation of local law enforcement. As such, it was an object lesson that the police would not soon forget.

•

The Washington-based International Association of Chiefs of Police claimed more than sixty-two hundred members as of 1970. Police officials from the rank of captain up were eligible, as were industrial security men, many of whom were former FBI agents. With a staff of eighty-two headquartered in an elegant mansion near DuPont Circle, the IACP was local law enforcement's strongest and most articulate voice, as well as its very potent congressional lobby.

For years the IACP-FBI relationship was incestuous. On Hoover and Associate Director Clyde Tolson was bestowed the honorific title of life member. Year after year, in ritual symbolism, special resolutions—usually written by FBI personnel and approved by the Director—lavishly praised the FBI chief and were unanimously passed. Hoover's nod or frown could make or break proposals under consideration. At the conventions, FBI officials were invited as keynote speakers. In an unforgettable 1948 speech, then Assistant Director Hugh N. Clegg portrayed the ideal police chief as a man "who cooperates with the FBI in such a generous manner that he has earned our undying gratitude." Such a chief, Clegg orated, sent fingerprints to the FBI, sent his "laboratory problems" to the FBI, and had his men trained by the FBI.

By the late 1950s this kind of supercilious canticle was beginning to sound sour to many police ears. It had dawned on many of the chiefs that the Bureau's "cooperative services" carried a high price tag in terms of Hoover's domination of their affairs, and that some of the services were blatantly turned to self-advantage by the Bureau. The cooling of their ardor began to show itself in subtle ways. The resolutions lauding the Director became less fulsome, the appearance of FBI speakers on the programs less frequent. Then, in

1959, came what seems to have been a bold attempt on the part of an IACP faction to liberate the organization from FBI influence.

The attempt was in the form of a campaign to elect Chief William H. Parker of Los Angeles to the vice presidency, from which he would progress automatically to the presidency. Despite his reactionary political views, Parker was an outstanding administrator, and his department had a national reputation for mechanical efficiency and a lack of corruption. He was the selection of the nominating committee, which rather pointedly explained its choice by saying that the IACP had been "a fraternal brotherhood, but now we glimpse an opportunity to enter into real professionalism through the development of our field service, research and other activities." The committee expected that Parker would do "the best job in realizing the objective of the IACP."

Parker's nomination represented a dual threat to Hoover. To see his archenemy ascend to the presidency of the organization he had dominated for so long would have been insufferable. And the language of the committee's explanation clearly indicated its feeling that Parker was the man to lead the police in developing their own facilities and thus decreasing their dependence on the FBI.

The next day, when the nomination came to a vote, it become evident that FBI lobbyists had done their job well. Unexpectedly, the name of Chief Philip Purcell of Newton, Massachusetts, was entered into nomination from the floor. Even in police circles, Purcell was not widely known, and his chief qualification seems to have been that he was a graduate of the FBI National Academy. When the vote was in, Purcell had trounced Parker 319 to 109. Later, Purcell confirmed that he was the FBI's favorite son candidate in 1959. "Oh, yes," he said. "Hoover poisoned Parker."

At the 1960 convention, Hoover "poisoned" another chief who held views opposite to his own. As we saw in a previous chapter, the Director managed to sabotage a recommendation to the convention from the IACP committee on organized crime that a federal nerve center be set up to disseminate intelligence on major hoodlums to the various police departments. The chairman of the committee and inspiration behind the recommendation was Chief Edward J. Allen of Santa Ana, California. Allen was an acknowledged expert on the

Mafia, having fought it successfully in the rackets stronghold of Youngstown, Ohio, and written *Merchants of Menace: The Mafia.* Allen's position was that the Mafia was very much a reality and was flourishing in the United States. This, of course, ran counter to Hoover's contention that the Mafia was a myth.

After his recommendation went down to defeat, Allen was virtually ostracized by his fellow chiefs. A few weeks after the convention, the IACP board of officers pulled the rug out from under him by deactivating the committee. After a time it was reactivated, but with Chief Thomas Cahill of San Francisco, a Hoover favorite, at its helm. Predictably, the new committee was not overly aggressive and did not espouse the notion of a federal information center.

When I talked to Allen, he flatly asserted that the FBI had torpedoed him. "Hoover controls the IACP and used his influence to abolish the committee," he stated matter-of-factly. He didn't seem bitter over being done in by parliamentary maneuvers, but he did resent the fact that after it had happened a high Bureau official stopped by his table and ridiculed him in front of his colleagues about his belief in the Mafia.

The spectacle of Hoover undercutting Parker and Allen in their own organization evidently produced a backlash, however. A renewed drive for autonomy began. The first step was taken in 1960, when the IACP constitution was amended to strengthen the hand of the executive director hired on a permanent basis. The second step, on the surface paradoxical, was to hire former FBI Assistant Director Quinn Tamm as executive director. But Tamm had retired prematurely from the Bureau after a falling-out with Hoover, and he assured his prospective employers that he had no intention of knuckling under to his erstwhile boss.

In his maiden speech to the membership at the 1962 convention in St. Louis, Tamm made what was tantamount to a declaration of independence. Recalling the organization's early history and achievements, he declared that the IACP was once and should have remained "the dominant voice in law enforcement." Without specifically referring to Hoover, he maintained that the president of the IACP "must be the spokesman for law enforcement in this country," adding that the IACP was "moving in that direction."

The movement consisted of a buildup in the size of the IACP permanent staff, enabling it to furnish many of the services (such as management consulting and police training) the FBI had heretofore provided. This growth in staff could be traced from the six employees working out of a modest office in the Pennsylvania Building in 1962, when Tamm took over, to the large staff that in 1970 functioned on an annual budget of $2.3 million and had outgrown its DuPont Circle quarters. A major impetus in the expansion was the Law Enforcement Assistance Act, which funded police training and other services. The act was administered by the Department of Justice, which under Ramsey Clark was conspicuously generous in allotments to the IACP. Clark, of course, was not enamored of the FBI chief, and Tamm acknowledged his support by commending Clark as having "done more to help local law enforcement than any other Attorney General."

Hoover didn't take all of this lying down, and in 1966 the battle lines were drawn. In that year Chief Purcell progressed to the IACP presidency. But in an editorial in the IACP magazine *Police Chief,* Purcell made it crystal clear that he was no longer the FBI's pawn. Extolling the "vigorous administration of Executive Director Tamm," he in effect handed out a challenge with the words, "We constitute a formidable organization capable of withstanding any onslaught."

Retaliation was swift. A Newton police sergeant who had been accepted for the FBI National Academy was cancelled out, and other "cooperative services" suddenly became unavailable to the Newton force. Purcell became an "unperson" in the FBI's book. When the 1967 edition of *National Academy Associates* came out— the publication is a yearbook of the FBI's "most exclusive alumni association"—Purcell's name was missing from the roster of past graduates.

The Hoover-IACP power struggle centered on the issue of who was to train the police. In earlier days, the police yielded to the Bureau on this point, mostly because the local departments didn't have the funds or personnel to do the job themselves. But times changed. The New York and Los Angeles departments, to name two, opened academies that could offer all the FBI could and more.

In 1952, Joseph Lohman, a former Chicago sheriff who became dean of the criminology school at the University of California, helped found the Southern Police Institute at Louisville, which stressed the humanistic side of police work. By 1970 there were a number of comparable institutes, and the larger states had inaugurated their own training programs (the one in New Jersey featured mobile classrooms). The universities kept pace with police science and public administration courses leading to degrees. Perhaps the most salient point is that the police themselves had substantially more experience in police-type work than the FBI, which did no patrolling.

The IACP's Quinn Tamm believed that the police should train themselves, especially since the Omnibus Crime Act of 1968 made federal funds available for the purpose. He brought over to his organization the capable Jeptha S. Rogers, who for the better part of his career was an inspector in the FBI division maintaining liaison with police academies.

But Hoover used his political power to try to hold on to the right to train the police. In 1967, he went over the head of Ramsey Clark in an attempt to insert a provision in the pending crime bill that would have put all police training in the cities under the FBI; cities that refused would obtain no federal monies for their police programs. Two FBI lobbyists made their familiar rounds on Capitol Hill in an effort to put this proposal through.

Clark sided with the IACP, arguing diplomatically that the FBI was already overloaded with work and its participation should be confined to certain specialized instruction. And he added, showing no little courage, that placing all police training under the FBI might well set the stage for a national police force. Tamm chimed in with a letter to Senator John McClellan, chairman of the subcommittee drafting the crime bill, which put the IACP on record as opposing Hoover's plan to "centralize police training in the hands of the director of the FBI." Such a step, he warned, "could become the first step toward a national police."

Hoover struck back with his customary alacrity. In an Air-Tel (an air mail communication in teletype format) to appropriate field offices, he instructed that members of the IACP's board of officers be contacted and urged to oust Tamm at their next meeting; with unmatched gall Hoover offered several candidates to replace him. But the Director lost this skirmish when the board voted overwhelmingly to express confidence in Tamm, and he lost another when the crime bill rider that would have thrust police training into the hands of the FBI went down in defeat despite the support of McClellan, the aging chairman of the House Judiciary Committee, Emanuel Celler, and a number of conservative legislators.

The war was far from over, and Hoover had no intention of being deposed from his eminence in the IACP. He retained staunch allies inside the association, one of whom was the influential Thomas Cahill of San Francisco. The irony of Cahill's prominence paralleled that of Hoover's. He was catapulted into national fame in the early 1960s because of the outstanding success of his department's avant-garde community relations unit, whose formation he had resisted and which he emasculated in favor of rather hard-nosed tactics. But this ex officio feat earned him a seat as the only police executive on the President's National Crime Commission—he performed as possibly its most reactionary member—and, in turn, the vice presidency of the IACP. Thus he became the organization's 1969 president.

At the 1968 IACP convention in Honolulu, at which Cahill was invested, there was intense politicking. For Cahill, it was nearly an empty honor, for only a few months before a move had been afoot to dump him as San Francisco's police chief. What may have saved him was the improbable combination of a black supervisor's premature demand that he resign and Hoover's strong endorsement from Washington. Hurriedly inviting Cahill to address the October graduating class of the FBI National Academy, the Director raved that he was "the best police chief in the country." Then, at the convention, an FBI delegation led by Cartha DeLoach tried to outflank Quinn Tamm by lobbying for amendments that would have shifted power from the executive director to the president, in this case Cahill. The ploy would have had the effect of muzzling Tamm and designating Cahill as the IACP's official spokesman. It was not adopted.

So the struggle went on, with the stakes transcending the interests of the protagonists. When Tamm and Ramsey Clark cautioned against an incipient national police, they were not, in my opinion, indulging in idle rhetoric. To allow national police powers, including police training and de facto control of the IACP, to remain in the FBI's hands would have been to play with fire.

PART THREE
THE ORGANIZATION

CHAPTER TWELVE
THE CULT OF PERSONALITY

The big Shakeup in the local FBI office is now over,
and the Big Shaker who flew here to do the dark deed
is returning to Washington. Casualties: Ten transfers,
one agent suspended for 30 days (but not by the
thumbs). Shocker: The Washington Wheel came here
as the result of a tip from someone inside the FBI
bureau here. Frevvinsakes. They turn each OTHER in?

> —*Herb Caen in the* San Francisco
> Chronicle, *March 15, 1963*

In the reception rooms of the Bureau's fifty-six field offices a portrait of J. Edgar Hoover was prominently displayed—stern, tight-lipped, the eternal watchdog. Among the agents who passed it daily, there were those who swore they saw the eyes move.

This dark humor reflected the somewhat paranoiac relationship between the Director and his minions in the field. In the early days, when the Bureau was small, Hoover had personal contact with most of his men. But as the agency burgeoned and the relationship became impersonal, he grew distrustful of the faceless employees distributed in outposts around the country, remote from his scrutiny. So he devised an elaborate system of accountability, of inspection and surveillance, and of discipline. And he became obsessed by the notion of loyalty. In practically every field office there hung a framed print of one of Hoover's favorite quotations, taken from

Elbert Hubbard's *Get Out or Get in Line*. It was for all practical purposes the FBI loyalty oath:

> If you work for a man, in heaven's name work for him! If he pays you wages that supply you your bread and butter, work for him—speak well of him, think well of him, stand by him and stand by the institution he represents.

For their part, the agents viewed the Man with ambivalent feelings. They realized that he himself had created the strong image that lent prestige to each of them, and had installed pay scales and retirement benefits unparalleled in government. They saw him in the role of benevolent patriarch of the FBI family, helping when tragedy struck an agent or his family. But they were also aware of a darker side: of the martinet whose system was a masterpiece of quibbling, the supreme leader consumed by megalomania, the insecure celebrity infuriated by specks of dust on his trophies.

The atmosphere generated by this cult of personality was immediately sensed by incoming agents. Although I had no premonition, it was perceptible my first hour in the Bureau. Our new agents' class was assembled in a classroom in the Department of Justice Building when, promptly at nine A.M., the door was flung open and a portly man strode purposefully to the lectern. He introduced himself as Hugh H. Clegg, assistant director in charge of the Training and Inspection Division. This was the official who had co-led the Little Bohemia raid and, only a year before, questioned "atom spy" Klaus Fuchs in custody in England. Round-faced, with abbreviated features, Clegg looked more like a small-town banker than legendary G-man.

Clegg's word of welcome on behalf of the Director was brisk, almost curt. Then he got down to brass tacks. Much was expected of us, he said, and there could be no leeway for those who failed to measure up. We should dress and act like young businessmen. The watchword was "Be a gentleman," and the alternative was dismissal. Clegg recited a litany of rules whose infringement brought heavy penalties. He warned that intoxication was cause for instant dismissal with—he emphasized the word—prejudice. No drinking was allowed on or before duty, misconduct and immorality were forbidden, and information in FBI files was strictly confidential. There was to be no gossiping. (I got the impression, later confirmed, that drinking, philandering, and loose talk were recurring problems in the Bureau.)

In the didactic, clipped style that Hoover made famous, Clegg explained that "firm but fair" discipline was necessary to preserve the FBI's reputation. He darkly related several "incidents" that showed the pitfalls awaiting the unwary agent. One concerned a rookie who one evening left his FBI agent's handbook in his locked car on a downtown street; a prowler broke in and stole the handbook. "That agent is no longer with us," Clegg intoned with graveyard seriousness. "Besides," he added, hanging on each word, "he . . . didn't . . . even . . . look . . . like . . . an . . . agent."

The class stirred uneasily at this rather intimidating introduction to Bureau life and was quite apprehensive about it afterward. Some of the members had been Bureau clerks and special employees (a semi-investigative status), and privately filled us in. Disconcertingly, their first counsel was in the nature of a warning: never confide in Bureau officials, no matter how friendly and sympathetic they might appear to be. Since Hoover had designated them—including SACs—as his personal representatives, they risked their careers by not reporting any deviation from the book or any untoward incident.

Our informants also defined loyalty for us. Criticism of the Man or his policies was looked upon as a sign of disloyalty. Every agent was expected to tattle on anyone who broke the rules, and each office had a few "submarines" who would "torpedo" their colleagues, but they were well known and avoidable. The majority of the agents were bound by a self-protective allegiance that Bureau spokesmen preferred to call esprit de corps.

The cardinal sin, we were told, was to make an error that resulted in "embarrassment to the Bureau." As an example, it was pointed out that the agent whose handbook had been stolen from his car might not have been fired had not the Washington Mounted Police recovered it from a suspect. The police and the FBI had not been on the best of terms, and return of the handbook had been a humiliating loss of face for the Bureau.

My first reaction was that these warnings were laying it on a bit thick, but I soon had reason to change my mind. The breach between the image and the reality began to show. The fabled hard-hitting G-men were really just bureaucratic employees doing things by the book in order not to affect the status quo. Some of our class began to have misgivings about their choice of a career, and one was indiscreet enough to write home saying so, then tear up the letter and toss it in a wastebasket in his room at the FBI Academy. The next day he was summoned to the office, and there was his letter, neatly reconstructed. He was given the opportunity to resign.

It turned out that the surveillance at Quantico and Washington was not hit and miss. The word was passed that the men's rooms were monitored to try to detect latent homosexuals. In 1959, an agent attending in-service training at the Academy stumbled upon a tape recorder hidden in the basement linen closet; it was hooked up to microphones concealed in the living quarters. Although an official dismissed the mikes as a security measure to protect important visitors, no one believed him.

Nor was the field free of surveillance. In 1957 in Miami, for instance, a single agent was dating a vocalist on one of Hoover's favorite network radio shows. Apparently out of jealousy, the wife of a man associated with the show complained to John Mohr that she didn't think a Bureau agent should be in such company. Before long, the agent spotted a tail. Trapping his shadower in a dead-end street, he hauled him to the office, thinking he might be a Communist. Instead, he was a private detective—with Mohr's home and office telephone numbers in his wallet. "They're an awful lot of smart alecs in Miami," Hoover reportedly said.

One either adjusted to this kind of existence—or got out. "After a few years you have to make up your mind whether you're an organization man at heart and you're going to settle in and go for that twenty-year retirement," an ex-agent in law practice was quoted by reporter James Phelan. "The fear of 'embarrassing the Bureau' gets oppressive at times. Personally, I resented the requirement that you write a memorandum whenever you observed a violation of the rules. If a fellow agent goofed off, and you knew about it, you were held responsible if you didn't tag him out. I understand the reason for this. It kept the Bureau well disciplined, but it went against my grain. I didn't like the Big-Brother-Is-Watching-You atmosphere."

•

"Not only do we have to be right at all times," Hoover stressed, "we have to give the appearance of being right." Appearances were everything with the Bureau. To ensure good appearances, the premium was placed on orthodoxy, conformity, and playing as a member of the team rather than as an individual, which might not have been the best way to solve crimes. Hoover encouraged his men to marry female employees, and outside fiancees were investigated to make sure they measured up to FBI standards (one senior agent who married a woman whose brother was considered leftist was suspended and transferred).

Individual performances didn't go unrewarded, however. The SAC might write a commendation for the agent's file, or recommend that the Director personally issue a citation. On occasion, commendations were accompanied by cash awards or raises in pay. The recipients of these "meritorious awards" were listed in the house organ *The Investigator* under the heading "So Proudly We Hail."

But commendations were merely helpful toward promotion, while letters of censure for blundering could be downright disqualifying. For this reason, the tendency was toward caution. I saw supercautious agents disappear out the back door of the office when bank robbery alarms sounded rather than take chances by being in on the start of the investigation. In his 1962 report to the attorney general, ex-agent Jack Levine recounted a similar experience. In July of 1961, he was driving in an FBI car with three other agents when a bank robbery was announced over the radio. Although they were close to the location, Levine said, the driver accelerated away from the bank:

> My companions explained that several years ago an agent in another field office was the first to arrive at the scene of a bank robbery and thus became in charge of the investigation until the bank robbery specialist arrived. The second and third agents to arrive at the bank in attempting to lift

possible hand prints of the robber, smudged them and as a result, the FBI's laboratory was unable to develop them. The two agents who bungled the prints were very severely disciplined. The agent who was innocent of any misfeasance was equally disciplined by the Bureau because, theoretically, he was in charge of the case.

This "horror story" touched upon another feature of Bureau discipline—that it was seldom an individual matter. This was the case in a shooting scrape in Los Angeles. A motel manager reported that a man resembling a fugitive on a wanted bulletin had checked into one of his units. Under cover of darkness, agents deployed in front and back of the unit, then rapped on the door. As it was opened a crack, an agent shoved his arm through to display his credentials. The door was pushed against his arm. The agent shot through the door, the bullet taking the tip off the man's nose. It turned out that he wasn't the fugitive at all, but an innocent party afraid that robbers were trying to force their way in. The affair hit the newspapers, and the Bureau was embarrassed. The agent was punished with suspension and a disciplinary transfer to Seattle. And the supervisor of his squad was also demoted and transferred—even though he was at home when the incident happened.

Another example occurred in Chicago in 1960. A new agent was cleaning his pistol at home when it accidentally discharged, wounding him in the foot. Firearms accidents are not unknown in the FBI, but in this case the admission of the agent to the hospital tipped off the press and the Bureau was embarrassed. The injured agent was denied advance sick leave—ordinarily it is extended—and upon recovery was censured, placed on probation, and shipped to Oklahoma City. His pistol, it turned out, was non-issue, so the headquarters instructor who had helped him obtain a discount in its purchase was "busted" and transferred to New Orleans.

When things went wrong, a scapegoat was usually found. In New York City, an agent driving a Bureau car piled into another car at an intersection, seriously injuring its occupants. The master brake cylinder on the FBI vehicle had failed, causing the accident. When the injured parties brought suit, the U.S. attorney, representing the

Bureau, decided that the government position was indefensible and settled out of court. The settlement had to be paid out of FBI funds. Angry, the Bureau censured and transferred to Chicago the agent involved in the accident, on the irrelevant grounds that he hadn't been wearing his glasses at the time as required.

Still another sampling of Bureau discipline was found in the matter of the New York agent who, in 1960, became involved in a tavern brawl. He had stopped at the tavern for a beer after coming off surveillance duty at midnight. Three young hoodlums entered and provoked a fight. The agent defended himself, but the revolver under his coat was jostled loose and clattered to the floor. The trio fled. Well aware of the whims of the disciplinary machine, the agent didn't report the incident in the hope that it would pass unnoticed. But the three hoodlums, unemployed and with bad conduct discharges from the Army, sensed a chance for easy money. They filed an assault with a deadly weapon complaint against the agent as a prelude to a civil suit. When brought before a Nassau County grand jury, the complaint got short shrift: the jury deliberated but a minute before asking the district attorney what could be done about indicting the three complainants for perjury.

The jury and the local police were shocked to learn that the FBI had already suspended the agent for thirty days and had transferred him to Knoxville, Tennessee. "Even before we considered the case?" asked the perplexed jury foreman. But the agent hadn't reported the fight, and the fiddler had to be paid. Leaving his family in New York, the agent reported to Knoxville rather than resign under a cloud. The perversities of the system hounded him. With another agent, he spotted and arrested an FBI fugitive. The other agent received a letter of commendation from Hoover; he got nothing. And when the Knoxville SAC rated him "satisfactory" on judgment in his performance rating, the SAC received a letter of censure. Finally, after six months in limbo, the probation was lifted, and the agent promptly resigned.

This hypersensitivity to criticism, even of the mildest sort, was exhibited in 1958 when a Washington agent interviewed a well-known scientist, Edward Teller, about one of his colleagues who had applied for an AEC-sponsored project. "Don't you know who I

am?" demanded Teller after the agent had displayed his credentials
but had failed to acknowledge the man's status in the scientific
world. When the agent left, the scientist called the field office and
complained that the agent had not acted in a properly deferential
manner. The upshot was a disciplinary transfer to Indianapolis.

When I met him some time later, the agent told me that he had
known full well who the scientist was but did not feel inclined to
cater to his ego. Nevertheless the Bureau, in a characteristic overre-
action, sent out a memorandum admonishing all agents that they
must be familiar with current events, and agents at in-service sessions were buttonholed in the halls by Bureau officials and given
impromptu grillings on who was who among the luminaries of the
world. When word got around, subscriptions to *Time* and *Newsweek*
skyrocketed.

The one occasion on record in which Hoover did stand behind
an agent was during the hearings of the Warren Commission on the
assassination of JFK. The Dallas office, it turned out, had a thick
file on the putative Marxist and Russophile Lee Harvey Oswald
assigned to James P. Hosty, Jr., of the security squad. Hosty was on
the spot for not having furnished the substance of the file to the
Secret Service beforehand, as the vague instructions in effect at the
time might have required. Hosty explained that there was no reason
to believe that Oswald represented a threat to the president. Testifying before the commission, Hoover concurred: "There was nothing
up to the time of the assassination that gave any indication that this
man was a dangerous character who might do harm to the President
or Vice President." It was a self-serving statement.

Yet several months later, when the eyes of the world were averted, Hoover suspended the agent without pay for thirty days and
transferred him to Kansas City. Members of the church congrega-
tion to which Hosty belonged took up a collection to help tide him
over—he had seven children. But he had no time to negotiate the
sale of his home, since he had to pack and leave town within a matter of days.

Other agents touched by the hand of fate fared no better.
Hosty's supervisor was suspended and transferred to Seattle. A New
Orleans agent who had interviewed Oswald three months before the

assassination was suspended and sent to Springfield, Illinois, but he had enough time in to retire instead. In all, more than thirty agents were snared in the disciplinary machinery set in motion by the Bureau's most embarrassing moment.

Although Bureau spokesmen insisted that all transfers were in the "needs of the service," sudden uprooting to an undesired location was the ultimate punitive weapon. Certainly when the three New York agents who supplied the federal prosecutor with affidavits detrimental to Roy Cohn were given thirty-six hours to get out of town by Hoover, the personal desires of the Director alone were involved. Transfers were also used to retaliate against agents insisting on their legal rights. One agent, who had been a "legal attaché" to the Havana embassy and was forced to leave when Castro took over, was transferred to his office of preference, San Francisco, which is the usual courtesy in such instances. However, he was dropped from Supergrade GS-14, which is that of agents on overseas assignment, despite a regulation that such agents be kept in the grade for one additional year when pulled back through no fault of their own. He pointed this out to a Bureau official. The supergrade was restored, but the Bureau got its revenge by handing him a transfer to Seattle.

The pattern was repeated in the case of a near-retirement firearms instructor in the Seattle office. He had applied to the Department of Labor for disability payments because of a hearing loss suffered through years of exposure to gunfire. Although the Bureau looked dimly on such claims, it couldn't stop him from filing. But it could transfer him, and did—to Chicago.

The transfer ploy was also used on military reservations who refused to resign their commissions. A question of organizational loyalty was involved, since the Bureau realized that those who stayed in the reserves would opt for active duty in case of emergency rather than stay with G-man status. One headquarters supervisor I know who insisted on retaining his naval reserve commission was demoted and transferred to Savannah, Georgia, far from his office of preference on the West Coast. A veteran agent assigned to his office of preference, Salt Lake City, didn't succumb to pressure to give up his air force colonel's commission, so he was sent a transfer to Newark. He managed to have the transfer killed by agreeing to resign from the air force, but a few months later he was transferred to San Francisco, where he arrived without either his rank or his office of preference.

Still another agent who refused to resign from the Naval Ready Reserve was banished to Oklahoma City from Washington. There, he claimed, SAC Wesley Grapp threatened that if he didn't resign from the Bureau he would "find something" on which to fire him. The agent wrote a letter of resignation, and he also wrote one to the American Legion, to which he belonged. "Why does the American Legion insist on embracing Mr. J. Edgar Hoover?" he asked. "Does not the Legion realize that under Mr. Hoover's administration the veteran and the military reservists especially have and are undergoing severe harassment?"

•

In 1959, a conscientious young agent from Detroit was routinely interviewed by an official of the Training and Inspection Division. Was there anything on his mind? Well, yes, there was, he conceded. It seemed a shame that hard-working agents who refused to pad their "voluntary overtime" figures weren't given raises, while those who did were. That *was* a shame, agreed the official. And did the agent pad *his* overtime? Yes, he did—he wanted very badly to get along.

The young agent's naive admission earned him instant dismissal. And it touched off a typical chain reaction. Inspectors descended on Detroit, and when they were through the SAC had been demoted and transferred, a fate that also befell several supervisors.

The trouble stemmed from the fact that the so-called voluntary overtime (VOT) program was actually mandatory. Despite Hoover's contention that all overtime was necessitated by "occasional emergency conditions," the agents were coerced into putting in a certain amount of VOT whether the workload justified it or not. Hence they are sorely tempted to tamper with the records.

Occasional unforeseen demands on time—a spurt in bank robberies, a major case, a surge in applicant inquiries—could require periods of overtime work. Prior to the inauguration of the VOT program in 1954, the average overtime level of slightly over one hour per day accurately reflected those demands. But some agents were unhappy that they received no compensation for this hour-a-day-plus, and a few wrote letters (to be quoted anonymously) to the *Washington Post* saying so. Largely as the result of an editorial campaign by the *Washington Post,* Congress enacted Public Law 763, which gave overtime pay to federal employees whose duties required unscheduled extra work. Statistics revealed that in the previous year the overtime average had been one hour twelve minutes per day per agent, so this became the minimum amount required to qualify for the fringe benefits.

Soon the VOT average began a steady climb. The initial thrust was the result of a Bureau edict that every agent qualify by putting in at least the minimum amount. Then headquarters began to use the monthly "office averages" as gauges of field office workloads and to shuffle personnel accordingly. To protect against loss of manpower, the SACs put the pressure on their supervisors to exact more VOT from the agents. In turn, the supervisors had a vested interest in keeping the rate up in order to avoid intra-office transfers.

So the monkey climbed on the agents' backs. Those who were consistently below the average, even by a minute or two, were required to explain why they weren't "sharing the workload." An ultimatum to that effect from the Detroit SAC to Jack Levine dated May 18, 1961, was typical:

> The following is a comparison of your overtime during the past five months with the office average overtime of Agents assigned Detroit:
>
> | | 12/60 | 1/61 | 2/61 | 3/61 | 4/61 |
> |----------------|-------|------|------|------|------|
> | **Office Average** | 2.57 | 3.05 | 2.58 | 3.05 | 2.45 |
> | **SA Levine** | 2.01 | 2.27 | 1.58 | 2.26 | 2.37 |
>
> You are one of the eleven Agents whose overtime has been consistently below the office average during the past five months. It is apparent that you have not performed your share of overtime during the above period.
>
> Please submit a memorandum reflecting your explanation for your low overtime, and indicating your intentions with respect to overtime in the future.

Of course, Levine may have been performing his share of the work but doing it more efficiently. But any agent receiving such a warning knew that if he didn't boost his average above that of the office, his chances for promotion were in jeopardy and disciplinary action might ensue.

As can be seen from the averages cited, the VOT had doubled and almost tripled in some months from its amount when spontaneous. If an agent put in a normal eight-hour day one day, he had to run up nearly six hours of VOT the next just to hold to the average. Such an investment of time was rarely justified by the "occasional emergency conditions" alluded to by Hoover, and other means were resorted to.

Agents were prone to stretch out the day—the premium was on inefficiency—by carrying on protracted bull sessions, shuffling paper, sitting idly in cars, and otherwise going through the motions. All kinds of time-killing pursuits were common, including going to the movies, ball games, or horseraces, browsing in the library, and even stopping in a bar. Rare was the agent who got caught, since accountability was inept, particularly in the large offices. In 1960, for example, it was discovered that a New York agent had been conducting an almost full-time private law practice while on the FBI payroll and that another agent had attended law school and graduated while satisfying the record that he was "sharing the workload."

In desperation, some agents did falsify the records. I recall a Seattle agent caught in flagrante delicto by the SAC signing the register as arriving at 6:30 A.M. when it was actually 7:30; he was disciplined and transferred to Detroit, narrowly averting being fired. The locator card also provided an opportunity to cheat. Originally designed to list contact points an agent expected to make during his rounds each day, the card was later also used to record times in and out of the office, plus such items as VOT. An agent finding himself low toward the end of the month might pull his cards and erase or kite the VOT entries. In 1959 in San Francisco, sharp-eyed inspectors noted a pattern of erasures on the cards of two veteran agents. One admitted he had made the alterations because he didn't have enough work to keep his VOT level legitimately high. He was fired.

Hoover wasn't aware of what was going on. For instance, two Los Angeles agents wrote virtually identical letters of resignation. However, one, in his exit interview, told the SAC he was leaving to go into another field. The other declared that a major consideration in his decision to quit was the phoniness of the VOT program. The first agent received a flowery letter from the Director saying how much he would be missed. The second got only a curt acknowledgment. At that, he was fortunate. One Los Angeles agent who resisted the fraudulent aspects of the program was forced to resign, which meant he carried the stigma of being "not eligible for rehire."

In early 1961, when I began writing to Congress, I included mention of the abuses of the VOT program. So did my father, William P. Turner, who asserted that agents "have told me that they do not object to putting any amount of time in when necessary, but it's humiliating for dedicated men to feel they must waste up to ten hours a week reading newspapers or otherwise filling in time just so they may record so many hours of 'volunteer' overtime in the office." When I mentioned that an Oklahoma City agent had been denied a raise because he had been only a few minutes under the office average over a period of several months, the Director felt compelled to respond. In a memorandum to all agents dated March 3, 1961, he said, "Any overtime performed must be necessitated by official business, must be essential, productive, not tailored to individual convenience, and must be equitably shared by all personnel." And he added, "Variation of a few minutes in overtime performance is not considered to be significant."

In an attempt to exercise stricter control, all agents were required to fill out daily report forms, an accounting heretofore demanded only of those on duty outside headquarters cities. But so inherently ersatz was the program that within months the Los Angeles and Detroit offices were rocked by incidents in which agents were logging VOT while bowling and playing tennis and basketball.

Yet publicly the VOT program was presented as a selfless contribution to the national treasury. In 1962, for example, the Director puffed to the appropriations subcommittee that the previous year his agents had logged 3,547,697 hours of VOT, which, had it been necessary to employ the 1,706 additional agents this total represented, would have cost the taxpayers another $18,276,442. Year after year, the "value" of this "cost-free service" hardly varied.

•

The enforcement arm of the FBI disciplinary apparatus was the inspection section of the Training and Inspection Division. The staff was composed of young executives on their way up, who first served as permanent aides to an inspector, then went back to the field as assistant SACs, and finally returned as inspectors. If the aspirant's star was still rising after this somewhat hazardous cycle, he moved on out as SAC of a field office.

Each field office was inspected at least once a year, more often if trouble was brewing. The time of the inspection was supposed to be a surprise, although most field offices were tipped off as to when the "goon squad," as the inspectors were known colloquially, would arrive. This advance word was the signal for a "self-inspection" that frequently rivaled the actual once in thoroughness. Cases that were not pressing were temporarily shunted aside while locator cards were combed for errors, pending files were reviewed for mistakes of form such as misserialization and misspellings, the physical condition of the office and cars was brought up to par, and desks were cleaned and polished.

With all the preparation, most inspections were fairly hitchless. For instance, the inspectors invariably tested agent availability by phoning down the roster one evening, but the agents knew this and baby-sat their telephones. On occasion, however, the inspection team came in with an express or implied order to "get" an SAC who had fallen from favor. This happened once in San Francisco, where agents were "written up" for the most trivial of offenses and the office was placed on probation. As a result, the SAC was downgraded by being put in charge of a much smaller office. He got the message and retired.

Every once in a while, an inspection would start out smoothly and explode into a "bloodbath." This was the case in the 1959 inspection of the Los Angeles office in which I was an inspector's aide. It was after one uneventful week that it happened. An itinerant dishwasher had been arrested for illegally wearing a military uniform. Unable to make bail, he languished in jail for some three weeks before being brought before a judge, who asked the U.S. attorney the reason for the undue delay. The USA alibied that he had just received the FBI report. So the judge chewed out the FBI, the newspapers played it page one, and the Bureau was embarrassed. The answer was simple: it was a minor case, and the agents to whom it was assigned had handled it in a perfunctory manner. The heads began to roll—suspensions, transfers, letters of censure. And another rule went into the books: reports must be in the hands of the U.S. attorney within three days of an arrest.

With the surfeit of paperwork, inspectors could always find countless minor errors to magnify into a major fault. One source of misfeasance was an item called TIO, for Time in Office. As the paperwork accumulated, agents became increasingly desk-bound. Obviously, crimes weren't to be solved from a desk. So the Bureau decreed that the TIO average should not exceed 15 percent of the work day. Confronted with another dilemma, agents took to doing their paperwork in libraries and tinkering with the TIO figures. One agent was suspended for not keeping his handbook insertions up to date. Others were criticized for unshined shoes, wearing sport coats, and not wearing hats. During every inspection agents were put on the scales to make sure they are "desirable"—or else.

Occasionally, Bureau discipline cut such a wide swath that whole offices were nearly wiped out. This occurred in 1958 in Oklahoma City after a series of personnel incidents capped by an embarrassing unsolved bank robbery. A suspect in the robbery held in the local jail had undergone extensive FBI grilling without breaking. Then the police gave it a try—and he confessed. Professional jealousies being what they are, the contretemps was unbearable. An inspection team descended, and when their orgy was over most of the office complement of forty was under transfer. One of the few supervisors reminisced, "For weeks, until replacements came in, our desks were piled high with case files we couldn't possibly handle."

Wholesale discipline hit Detroit in 1962. That office, too, had incurred a series of mishaps beginning a few years previously when

an SAC had dragooned agents to paint the office space, thereby out-
raging the painters' union. The already-mentioned VOT incidents
added fuel to the fire, and a budding sex scandal was apparently the
clincher. A female clerk had allegedly been dating some dozen married agents and at the same time carrying on a serious romance with
a Mafia figure. When the Bureau got wind of what was going on, it
threw the book not only at the philanderers but at anyone suspected
of misprision. In a short space of time the office underwent five
inspections.

At least one Detroit agent evidently felt that justice Bureau-style
had gone too far. The inspection party headed by an assistant director had no sooner boarded its airliner for the return to Washington
than an anonymous phone call warned of a bomb on board. The
plane had to be grounded and searched. When it was learned that
the call had been placed from a coin phone virtually in the shadow
of the FBI office, the inspectors turned livid. In a frenzied investigation, the coinbox and its contents were examined for latent fingerprints, and the agent staff was interrogated as suspects. It was even
proposed that the polygraph be used, but cooler heads finally prevailed. The case remains one of the most frustrating of the FBI's
unsolved crimes.

•

Despite the Pollyanna picture painted in public of soaring morale
and a backlog of eager applicants, the personnel situation in 1970
had been steadily deteriorating. The FBI's own figures, while super-
ficially convincing, betrayed the real state of affairs.

"Over the years, the rate of personnel turnover in the FBI has
been traditionally low," Hoover said in 1962. "The esprit de corps
which exists throughout the service today is evidenced by the fact
that turnover for our special agent staff now averages only 0.4 percent and for the Bureau as a whole it is 1.6 percent." The rate for
the federal service was given as 1.8 percent and for the manufactur-
ing industries as 3.7 percent.

The figures cited were monthly, so that the annual agent
turnover rate was 3.6 percent, representing 281 men in whom a
heavy investment in training and selection had been made. More-

over, the rate was not unusually low for detective-type government agencies. The same year, in comparison, the intelligence division of the Internal Revenue Service, which has been at the forefront of the war on organized crime, reported a rate of only 4.4 percent. Comparison with industry was unrealistic, since the main allure of federal employment is job stability and security.

The figures also revealed a startlingly high turnover rate among nonagent personnel; 30 percent, as compared to about 22 percent for the federal service as a whole. Since the FBI paid as well as or better than other agencies, the rate was probably due in part to the regimentation and intrusion into private affairs that was so integral a part of the operation. Take the case of a young air force veteran, Thomas H. Carter, who was fired from his clerk's position in 1965 for "conduct unbecoming an employee." A tipster had told Bureau officials that a young lady from his home town had stayed two nights in his apartment. Although nothing more improper than bundling of the kind condoned in Puritan New England was ever charged or admitted, the FBI defended its action by contending that its standards must be lofty enough to inspire the trust of "the little old lady from Dubuque." Such trust presumably would not be placed in an agency that permitted its employees to "sleep with young girls and carry on."*

By 1964, with the turnover still accelerating, Hoover omitted the figures from his testimony and in their place introduced charts showing the length of service of those in the agency. In 1961, 63 percent of the agent corps had put in ten years or more; by 1967 it was 70 percent. The Director's interpretation was that this experience factor contributed materially to the "growing productivity of our staff."

Looked at another way, however, it meant that the bulk of the turnover was among the younger agents who didn't have a large

---

*Carter sued for reinstatement to clear his record. The suit was turned down by a federal district court on the grounds that he had been indiscreet, at least, and that since the FBI was immune from civil service rules, it could fire at will. However, an appellate court ruled that Carter was entitled to a jury trial on the basis that the FBI handbook for employees instructed that they must maintain "ordinarily expected standards of personal conduct"—not extraordinary standards.

investment in tenure. Most young men who chose the FBI did so because of the relatively high pay and unsurpassable prestige. Once they neared the ten-year mark, the incentive to stay on was almost irresistible. The Bureau had perhaps the most generous retirement plan in government. An agent could retire after twenty years at one-third pay and after thirty years at two-thirds pay. From his first day in the Bureau, the agent was presented with the retirement lure, and once he has set his sights on it he was not likely to rock the boat.

In attempting to rebut my claim that many of the more junior G-men were quitting, some "after a few days in a field office," Hoover stated that over the previous five-year span "only 2.7 percent resigned voluntarily during their first six months of service." Three months later, in September 1961, he contradicted himself when he issued orders to all SACs that prospective appointees were to sign an agreement in writing to remain with the Bureau at least three years. The reason: too many new agents, in whom there was a large recruiting, investigating, and training investment, were resigning after only brief service.

The recruitment pinch had first begun to be felt about 1960. The cause was not additional manpower requirements—in 1961 Hoover requested only fifty more agents than had been authorized for the previous year—but a dearth of suitable applicants. Despite John Mohr's insistence that the Bureau was receiving "numerous applications from persons desiring to become Special Agents," the promise of an FBI career no longer cast a magic spell over young law graduates. And the shortage would become more acute in the next few years as the bloc of agents who had entered during the expanded manpower days of World War II became eligible to retire—and did so to the tune of twenty to thirty a month.

The crisis became so sharp during the fall of 1960 that new agents' classes had to be postponed three times for lack of recruits. As an emergency measure, the Bureau was tapping a readily available reservoir: the clerical force. In the two-year period between mid-1959 and mid-1960, 61 of the 349 men who entered agent training were former clerks, or about one out of five.

The Bureau was forced to broaden its admission standards progressively. First, those with any college degree plus foreign language fluency were deemed eligible. When quotas still went unfilled, science majors were proselytized. I remember that Oklahoma City agents were assigned to telephone the graduating geology class at the University of Oklahoma to try and interest members in an FBI career.

In the spring of 1961, the qualifications were further loosened to include those with three years of either substantial business experience or investigative experience such as insurance adjusting and military policing. The memorandum to the field authorizing these liberalizations cautioned: "This modification of qualifications for the position of Special Agent is *temporary*. It will remain in effect only long enough to implement the Bureau's investigative staff with men in possession of all types of business experience. As these qualifications are temporary, *there should be no publicity nor public announcement.*"

The desire to keep the public in the dark was understandable. At about the time the memorandum was issued, Assistant Director Nicholas Callahan was quoted in *National Geographic*: "An applicant for appointment as special agent must be . . . a graduate of a State-accredited resident law school or a four-year resident accounting school with at least three years' practical accounting experience." And while Callahan was telling the readers that "the selection and training of special agent is a process designed to weed out the faint of heart and discourage all but the most delicate," the Bureau memorandum advising of the "modification" admonished SACs that the training academy "was not to be considered a rehabilitation center for marginal applicants."

As it turned out, the "temporary" relaxation was permanent, and additional measures were taken. Each field office was obligated to obtain at least one recruit for each of four training classes scheduled for the remainder of 1961. The urgency of the situation was evidenced by the requirement that all leads for investigation be sent out by teletype, that the investigation be completed in three days, and that a teletype summary be sent to Washington in order that acceptable applicants could be immediately tendered appointments. At the same time, inducements were offered to retirement eligibles to stay on and to resigned agents to come back.

In letters to Congress, I had attributed the exodus and the

recruiting problem to the fact that morale was at "an all time low," largely as the result of neolithic personnel policies and the Bureau's cult of personality. In answer, Hoover insisted that "any difficulty experienced in obtaining new Special Agents in the FBI is due to the high standards and qualifications upon which this Bureau insists and is not due to poor morale as you have alleged."

An appropriate commentary was delivered by the Civil Service Commission a number of years ago when Hoover complained of a high turnover among Identification Division personnel, who in those days were hired through the civil service system. "An abnormally high rate of turnover," asserted the commission, "is commonly regarded as a reflection upon the working conditions or personnel policies of the employing agency rather than on the source or character of the personnel."

CHAPTER THIRTEEN
THE STATISTICAL G-MEN

Crime, in general, has spawned a wide
range of phony statistics, of all varieties.

—*Daniel Seligman*
in Fortune, *November 1961*

The post-Dillinger reputation of the FBI was sustained largely by "front page" crimes such as kidnapping and bank robbery, coupled with statistical "achievements" that gave the impression of relentless efficiency. In point of fact, however, the detective squads of big city police departments investigated more violent crimes in a week than the FBI did in a year, and the other federal investigative agencies consistently performed on a par with their more celebrated counterpart.

Such was the public's misconception of the FBI's role and accomplishments that it was not unusual to hear someone assign the Bureau narcotics jurisdiction while crediting it with a "conviction rate" of 96 percent and a "profit" to the taxpayers in the form of nearly $1.50 returned from fines, savings, and recoveries for every dollar spent.

Narcotics matters were, of course, within the primary jurisdiction of the Federal Bureau of Narcotics, an arm of the Treasury Department.* The counterfeiting of U.S. currency and securities was all along the charge of the Secret Service, also part of the Treasury

---

*In recent years the FBI has been charged with narcotics investigations.

Department. In his memoirs, former Secret Service assistant chief Harry E. Neal recalled that acquaintances would mistakenly introduce him as "an FBI man." Conceding that the FBI had obviously "accomplished a great deal in the law-enforcement field," Neal contended that "man for man, agents of the Secret Service and of the other Treasury enforcement agencies have made greater inroads against crime and criminals and have accomplished more for the American taxpayer."

While at first glance this may seem an extreme statement, a longer look reveals that it has considerable merit. Indeed, one of Hoover's most persistent claims to distinction was a conviction rate approaching perfection. "Convictions were obtained against 96.1 percent of the persons brought to trial," the Director declared in his 1964 appropriations testimony. In 1962 he reported 96.5 percent; in 1968, 96.7 percent; in 1969, 97.4 percent. Over the years the rate hardly varied by one percentage point.* By the same token, this rate was not, despite inferences to the contrary, the highest among federal detective agencies. The Secret Service repeatedly surpassed the FBI's figure but took no special notice of it. In 1962 testimony, for instance, the Secret Service chief didn't mention his rate of 98.5 percent; it was brought up by a member of the subcommittee.

Lest the conviction rate mislead the reader into believing that the FBI nearly always got its man, it should be pointed out that the rate was calculated against the number of persons arrested and charged, not against the total number of criminal cases received for investigation, a figure that was not announced. We can arrive at an approximation, however, by starting with the number of "investigative matters received exclusive of reimbursable applicant work." In 1968, there were approximately 725,000. Since roughly one-third of the Bureau's work is in security classifications, this works out to about 483,000 criminal cases. Out of this imposing number of cases, only some thirteen thousand convictions were secured.

---

*The conviction rate is figured against "persons brought to trial," which is a somewhat misleading phrase, since it includes those who plead guilty. In fact, somewhere around 90 percent do plead guilty, so that when the FBI has to prove its case in court, the conviction rate drops below 70 percent.

There were a number of reasons for this low ratio. Some of the reported violations turned out not to be a crime, as when a shipping company reported a shipment missing and presumed stolen that later turned out to have been misrouted. Many technical violations were so petty they hardly warranted investigation, but cases were opened in order to help boost the caseload. Agents were rated on how many cases they opened and closed—in Seattle, we would open a case simply on the apparent theft of one bottle of whiskey from a ship's cargo. Before Congress, Hoover presented this "increasing volume of work" as one more justification for more money. In testimony for fiscal 1968, he pegged the caseload at twenty-six cases per agent, which he described as "excessive but we have to bear that additional burden." The Secret Service caseload stood at over one hundred per agent.

Certainly the FBI's performance—or more accurately, lack of performance—in civil rights cases would tend to lower the true conviction rate. Since the Bureau did not publish the percentage of those tried or convicted in separate categories, the exact figure is a mystery. But some indication can be gained from the fact that during the five-year period between 1960 and 1964, when an aggregate of 11,328 cases were handled, only fourteen convictions were obtained—a yield of barely one tenth of 1 percent. Even given the myriad obstacles to convictions in the South, this still represented a meager harvest for justice against the backdrop of the most sustained epoch of violence since the Klan rode high in the 1920s.

Paradoxically, it was the Bureau's appetite for statistics that created one major impediment to successful prosecution. A large proportion of the civil rights complaints stemmed from "police brutality" and alleged that officers acting under the protection of the law denied the victim his civil rights (i.e., physically abused him) because of his race, creed, or color. The FBI was extremely dependent upon local police for "statistical accomplishments" in the form of help in solving cases and in turning over credit for recovering stolen cars and other property, a dependence that constituted a sharp conflict of interest with its statutory duty to police the police. The problem was not limited to the South. Following the 1967 Patterson, New Jersey, rioting, a citizen's committee with evidence against eight police officers who had wantonly damaged Negro business property was forced to go directly to the civil rights section of the Department of Justice for action after local authorities and the FBI had proved inert.

Many FBI cases—perhaps a majority—were stamped "closed" with the crimes still unsolved. This was called an administrative closing, and was accomplished with the declaration: "No suspects developed and all logical leads exhausted." The Bureau did not keep count of unsolved cases, nor of those in which the U.S. Attorney's office declined to prosecute because the evidence was insufficient. Thus the true conviction rate was anybody's guess. Mine was that it was somewhere in the neighborhood of the police rate of serious crimes "cleared by arrest"—25 percent.

The category of fines, savings, and recoveries was similarly inflated. "The $253,634,881 in fines, savings, and recoveries recorded in FBI-investigated cases during 1966 is an increase of nearly $18 million and a half over the 1965 total," the FBI chief asserted. "The 1966 total averaged out to $1.50 for each dollar of direct funds appropriated to the FBI during that year." This was up from the "equivalent of $1.25 returned to the taxpayers of the country for each dollar expended by the FBI" in 1960.

An appreciable amount of the savings category accrued from accounting cases under the Renegotiation Act pertaining to government contracts, and from the Tort Claims Act involving civil suits against the government. The majority of the latter were personal injury suits resulting from accidents involving government vehicles. The Bureau claimed the dollar difference between the amount of the original suit, which was frequently grossly out of line, and the final settlement.

The most lucrative source of "monetary accomplishments" in the recovery category was stolen automobiles—their reported values made up nearly one out of every five dollars of the total in all categories. Like other property in the total, the recovery values claimed were consistently higher than fair market value. Moreover, the overwhelming majority of the vehicles were physically recovered by local law enforcement, and their values then appropriated by the FBI. As Hoover carefully phrased it in his testimony, the monies were "recorded in FBI-investigated cases."

What this meant can be illustrated by a typical stolen car case I handled while at the Knoxville office. Early one morning, an off-duty sheriff had spotted a car whose occupants, four youngsters, were behaving suspiciously. The car bore North Carolina plates. The deputy stopped the car, and one of the youngsters admitted it had been stolen a few hours earlier in Asheville. The deputy took the four into custody and impounded the car at a service station. Papers in the glove compartment disclosed the name of the owner in Asheville, who was promptly notified of the recovery.

Since the car had been transported interstate, the sheriff's office notified the Knoxville FBI. I drove out to the town where the youngsters were in custody. The two boys gave signed statements admitting stealing the car, and the two girls similarly admitted riding interstate, knowing the car to be stolen. The agent on duty in Knoxville obtained telephone authorization for prosecution from the U.S. attorney, and the four were ordered to be taken to the federally approved jail in Knoxville. I expressed misgivings about prosecuting the girls. They claimed to be eighteen, but looked awfully young and frightened (it would develop that they were only seventeen, juveniles under federal law), and I was reluctant to throw them in with older, hardened criminals. "We need the convictions," the SAC insisted. "Besides, they won't be there long."

Later, the four pleaded guilty. The convictions were included in the total presented to Congress. So were the "automobile recovered" statistic and the "recovery value" of $1,500. All three categories, Hoover would say, had attained "new peaks of achievement."

As I have mentioned earlier, the acquisition of statistics was an end in itself. A memorandum from the Knoxville SAC to all agents dated five weeks before the end of the 1961 fiscal year is revealing on this score:

The statistical accomplishments as of April 30, 1961, reflect that we continue to be below the statistical accomplishments for the preceding year in the categories of fines, savings, and recoveries. We have already exceeded our accomplishments in the fugitive category for the entire fiscal year, and in the field of automobiles recovered, we will need five additional recoveries to equal the accomplishments of the preceding fiscal year. . . . [The memorandum goes on to compare the figures in each category for fiscal 1960 and 1961, denoting the percent of change as a plus or minus number.] For your information, for us to equal our accomplishments in the field of convictions, it will be necessary that we report an additional 47 convictions between now and the end of June. In each instance wherein you have a conviction to report, such reporting is to be afforded preferential treatment. In the event final disposition is made in a case during the early part of June [the fiscal year ends June 30], you must insure that such conviction is reported as early as possible, as the cut-off date for reporting statistical accomplishments at the Bureau is usually between the 20th and 25th of each month.

An agent receiving this kind of memorandum realized that he must immediately readjust his priorities. Fugitive cases could be temporarily put aside, but cases with the potential of supplying convictions by the deadline were to be vigorously pursued. Hopefully, there would be a windfall of fines, savings, and recoveries.

The whole point of this annual contest was to exceed the previous year, if only by 1 percent. Remarkably, even in years when the crime rate has climbed steeply, convictions were up only 2 or 3 percent. I knew supervisors with a pre-deadline surplus in some categories to slip cases into their bottom drawers in order to get a head start on the new fiscal year.

As the countdown began for the end of the fiscal year, any number of ingenious—and desperate—schemes were proposed. One year in Seattle, a supervisor seriously suggested that the FBI take over traffic patrol duties from the military police at Fort Lawton and arrest persons exceeding the 20 mph speed limit. Such minor offenders would be haled before the U.S. commissioner, who would levy a nominal fine. With a minimum of fuss, the supervisor reasoned, the FBI could claim convictions for Crime on a Government Reservation, plus the amount of the fine.

This scheme wasn't implemented, but another that matched it in pettiness was. An obscure section of federal law permits a district judge to empower U.S. commissioners to accept guilty pleas and pass sentence in certain cases punishable by not more than six months in jail and a modest fine. The section was created to help lighten the heavy calendars in some courts, but the Seattle FBI office recognized it as a potential gold mine of quick conviction statistics. Arrangements were made to so empower the commissioners in the western district of Washington. Whereas it had previously been necessary to process such petty offenders as, say, a longshoreman caught stealing a bottle of whiskey through the normal federal court procedures—if, indeed, the U.S. attorney would even agree to do so—it now became possible to log the conviction on the day of the theft.

How well the system worked is illustrated by the case of two young brothers who lived near the old harbor defense facility on Puget Sound at Port Townsend. I drew admissions from them that they had torn out a quantity of copper flashing from the abandoned gun emplacements and sold it as scrap for fifteen dollars. Two ferry rides later, they were in Seattle before a U.S. commissioner, pleading guilty and receiving probation. Two convictions were immediately recorded. But until they were informed of this streamlined system in which they wouldn't even need an attorney, the brothers had been reluctant to admit anything. Word of the system's success spread, and other field offices began to adopt it.

As related in an earlier chapter, the statistical imperative even encouraged outright fraud in reporting, as illustrated by the seven hand-tool purchasers whose arrests were delayed so that they could be listed as FBI fugitives—"the fleeing criminals" whose apprehension Hoover reported to the appropriations subcommittee. On another occasion, I identified from latent fingerprints a longshoreman who had stolen a few dollars' worth of merchandise from a ship's cargo. I arrested him on a misdemeanor warrant at his home—he had lived there for years, and had been regularly employed on the waterfront—and turned him over to the U.S. marshal. Returning to the FBI office, I discovered that an alert supervisor had already forwarded a fugitive form letter to Washington. Without knowing it, I had apprehended an official "fleeing criminal"—in his home. I promptly dispatched word to the Bureau that the "fugitive" had been captured.

The supervisory desks in Washington also kept an eagle eye on the field offices' statistical positions, issuing reminders if they were behind the pace in particular categories. They also reviewed incoming case reports from the field for indications that statistics were slipping off the hook. In the Oklahoma City office, I handled a case in which a car stolen in Houston was abandoned out of running condition in Sayre. The subject had actually "bought" the car with a bad check in an amount well in excess of what the car was worth. The U.S. attorney declined to prosecute in view of the circumstances and the subject's dubious mental state. I submitted a report advising of the declination and claiming the inflated sale price as a recovery value (even though the car had been recovered by the sheriff at Sayre and I had never laid eyes on it). However, a diligent supervisor in Washington, apparently seeing an easy conviction slipping away, pointed out that a Houston policeman had indicated a desire that the subject be prosecuted federally and demanded an explanation of the reason he was not. I replied that it was the U.S. attorney, not a Houston policeman, who decided whether a case would be prosecuted.

The culmination of this obsession with statistics came on that annual spring day when the Director journeyed to Capitol Hill to deliver his appropriations pitch. Of all the federal investigative agency heads, Hoover was the only one whose presentation was heavily laden with statistics, punctuated by claims of "all-time highs" and "new peaks of achievement." By his criteria, an indigent car thief who blundered across a state line was just as important as a Cosa Nostra chieftain running a multimillion-dollar crime empire. In contrast, the testimony of the Bureau of Narcotics chief, for one, was low-key and substantive, consisting for the most part of synopses of major cases solved during the preceding year. Yet if the Bureau of Narcotics had a fetish for statistics, it could have taken just two 1960 cases, in which it confiscated pure heroin valued at over $40 million retail, and boasted of a "monetary accomplishment" of $10 for each dollar appropriated.

The appropriations subcommittee chaired by John J. Rooney of Brooklyn perennially accepted Hoover's statistics at face value. Rooney, who was noted for his waspishness where the Voice of

America and other agencies were concerned, once bragged that his subcommittee "never cut one penny" from the FBI's requests. Indeed, in the long history of this yearly waltz behind closed doors invariably ending with expressions of gratitude to the Director for his "interesting and informative" testimony, I can find only one colloquy that might be termed salient and probing. During the 1962 hearings, Frank T. Bow of Ohio pointed out the seeming contradiction in the fact that Department of Justice case filings and terminations had declined somewhat, while FBI records reflected an abrupt increase in reported crime. In reply, Hoover launched into his spiel: "I do know in the cases our agents have handled during the previous fiscal year, we obtained 11,914 convictions, the largest number of convictions for any peacetime year. Also, as I have previously testified, our receipts of investigative matters have been increasing sharply since 1955." When Bow persisted that "someplace, somewhere, somebody is not doing his job," the Director passed the buck by saying there were "many violations" the FBI did not handle. Perhaps what the congressman was driving at was that while felonies had climbed 12 percent, the Bureau's "largest number of convictions" amounted to less than a 2 percent increase, an appreciable lag.

The FBI's statistics orientation in reality amounted to the same kind of quota system that many policemen are burdened with. And it produced the same kind of computer enforcement, often with serious consequences for the technical offender. The public expected bigger things from the Bureau and it was entitled to them. But the agency was so programmed for statistics priority that it ran almost automatically in that direction.

CHAPTER FOURTEEN

STOCK IN TRADE: BANK ROBBERIES AND KIDNAPPINGS

Kidnapping is largely an amateur sport. Unlike
bootlegging, it is desperate and dangerous. It attracts
two kinds of men: nuts and the kind of person who
shoots up banks. It does not attract the kind of man
who peddles illicit goods or murders fellow hoodlums
for hire under the tolerant eye of both police and
public. "Good" criminals, the foundation blocks of the
underworld, avoid it because it's a one-shot racket.

—*Milton S. Mayer*
in Forum, *September 1935*

Bedazzled by the annual statistical extravaganza, Congress didn't
look searchingly into whether the FBI measured up qualitative-
ly in the crime investigation field. If the FBI was all that it was
cracked up to be, one might ask, why did robbers victimize banks in
record-breaking numbers? The fact was that the FBI warning decal
on bank doors hardly proved a deterrent. In 1950, there were 248
reported violations of the federal bank robbery statute; in 1960
there were 753. The count brushed the 2,000 mark by 1970. If the
G-men were deadly efficient, one might expect robbers to give federally insured institutions a wide berth.

The answer was not that simple, for in large measure the G-men
themselves were victims of the changing times. Bank robberies illus-

trated as well as any crime category how radically conditions changed over the years, while the FBI role remained unreviewed and unaltered. In the early 1930s, gangs of gun-slinging bank robbers terrorized the rural Midwest, easily outdistancing the local police. By 1933, banks were being robbed at the rate of nearly two a day, and the public clamor began to be heard by Congress. After the "Kansas City Massacre," in which three lawmen were shot to death and three injured in an abortive attempt by gunmen to free desperado Frank Nash, Congress acted. In 1934, a federal anti-bank-robbery law was enacted using the technical excuse that the Federal Deposit Insurance Corporation insured many banks. At the same time FBI agents were authorized to carry guns.

In many cases the FBI was up against a truly professional operation. Some gangs might spend weeks "casing" a bank and planning a robbery, and there were even specialists in engineering the jobs. As Willie Sutton, possibly the most ingenious of them all, once put it: "I studied crime the way an honest man studies law or accounting."

With this thorough approach, bank robbing was a lucrative enterprise. In 1932, 554 robberies netted a total of $3,384,117—an average of about $6,000 a job—and the record endured for decades. The FBI kept a relentless pressure on bank robbery gangs, and the trade went into eclipse. Lamented Sutton in 1951: "There are fifteen good bank men left in the country."

During the prosperity of World War II, bank robbery frequently hit bottom. Then, in the 1950s, it began a comeback, but with a distinctly amateur cast. I recall investigating several bank robberies in Seattle that would have provided excellent material for a Mack Sennett comedy. In one, a nervous young man held up a bank in the heart of the city but forgot to bring a container for the loot. Frantically, he stuffed his pockets with loose bills, grabbed two fistfuls, and fled on foot. His escape path took him through a crowded department store, where he bounced off customers like a ball in a pinball machine and left a trail of dropped money. He vanished out the revolving door, heedless of the cries of sales clerks trying to return his cash.

Another amateur was literally caught with his pants down. He had dashed from the bank to a nearby pawn shop and was in the act of changing from his "hot" suit to a newly purchased one when a sharp-eyed agent walking by spotted him. Still another made the mistake of celebrating a good-sized haul by buying drinks for the house in the Yankee Doodle Tavern, a gesture that quickly attracted two sober-faced agents.

This zany pattern was nationwide. In San Francisco, three Skid Row inhabitants who sallied across Market Street to rob a bank in the financial district were collared by bank clerks as they sought to pile into the "getaway car," a dilapidated 1946 model outfitted with a wine jug and a collection of girlie magazines; a police lineup had to be postponed because two of the suspects were too drunk to stand. In the same city, a service station attendant robbed a bank in order, he said, to pay back alimony. As he ran out the door, he pulled a gun and almost shot himself in the leg when it accidentally discharged. Then his getaway car wouldn't start, and he was captured sitting in it. Dejectedly, he heard a judge call his bungled robbery "one of the clumsiest I have ever encountered."

Today's robbers come from all walks of life. In Los Angeles, a little old lady pulled a string of holdups by brandishing a vial she claimed contained nitroglycerine. In San Francisco, two car wash employees pulled a bank job on their lunch hour, but made the error of bragging to their boss about it. In New York, a fifteen-year-old girl wanted $2,000 for a trip to Paris and tried to get it by leveling a toy gun at a bank teller. In San Francisco, an eighteen-year-old bride held up a bank and used the money for a fling on the beach at Waikiki, after which she surrendered to Honolulu police.

Paradoxically, one of the largest bank robberies in history was perpetrated by three racetrack characters straight out of Damon Runyon. Encouraged by a previous robbery in which their $97,000 loot was sufficient to buy a racing stable, the trio struck again at a drive-in bank at Port Chester, New York, and escaped with $188,784.51. However, a witness remembered that their license began with "WAS 45." Incredibly, they had used one of their own automobiles, and the FBI had little difficulty in tracing it. In the trunk of the car was most of the loot.

As former SAC Curtis O. Lynum of the San Francisco office noted somewhat wistfully before a 1963 bankers' symposium, "The robber today is not necessarily a hoodlum." The truth of this was confirmed by the salesman who explained his robbery of an Oakland, California, bank by saying, "I was determined to protect my credit rating," and the unemployed New York City clerk who declared indignantly when caught, "Everybody's robbing banks these days—I'm an honest, law-abiding citizen."

Indeed, the low estate to which bank robbery fell is indicated by the fact that in 1964 there were 1,014 robberies, or almost twice the 1932 number, while the average loot came to a paltry $200.

It was quite evident that the conditions of the 1930s no longer existed by the 1950s. True, the type of gang that plundered the hinterlands in the 1930s was not wholly extinct. The three tough, quick-draw Canadians who shot and killed one police officer and wounded two others during the robbery of the Greenwood branch of the Seattle First National Bank in 1954 were reminiscent of the old Brady Gang in Indiana. Certainly Bobby Wilcoxson and Albert Nussbaum, who used machine guns in committing a string of robberies in the early 1960s, were throwbacks to the Dillinger days; and in 1966, the FBI arrested five New York men it said were members of Cosa Nostra for a wide-ranging string of bank robberies.

But for the most part the field belonged to the dilettante, who instead of fleeing across state lines repaired to his neighborhood bar for a bracer. He probably had no prior criminal record, and his most common modus operandi was to stand in line, thrust a note at the teller, settle for what was in the cash drawer, and walk out and blend with the crowd. Consequently, the FBI's standard detection methods—showing the Bank Robbery Album of known bank robbers to witnesses, comparing fingerprints left at the scene with known robbers, and planting informants in the gang—had become practically obsolete. In fact, four out of five bank robberies were being pulled by a lone bandit, and four out of five were going unsolved. Most robbers who were apprehended were caught in the vicinity of the bank by employees, spectators, or police patrols.*

---

*In San Francisco, an agent grabbed a man in front of him who was staging a holdup. However, the report to Washington had to be paraphrased to conceal the fact that the agent had been in the bank on personal business during working hours.

Since bank robberies are violations of state armed robbery statutes, the FBI could, as a matter of policy, yield primary jurisdiction in most cases to the local authorities. This would have freed hundreds of thousands of agent manhours for more serious pursuits, such as the war on organized crime. But Hoover displayed no disposition to quit making a federal case out of the more farcical and inconsequential bank robberies.

•

Of all the crimes on the statute books, kidnappings command the most public attention. Since the victim is usually an infant or a member of a prominent family, the crime arouses intense indignation. The human interest drama unfolds on page one across the country in arresting sequence: the abduction, the ransom demand, the family's attempt to meet the demand, the payoff, and the safe return of the victim—or the discovery of the body. And of all the crime categories, kidnapping undoubtedly contributed the most to the legend of the FBI.

As in the case of bank robbery, the FBI was given jurisdiction as the result of a sustained outcry over a rash of sensational kidnappings capped by the Lindbergh kidnap-slaying of 1932. Three months after the kidnapping, Congress enacted the Lindbergh Kidnap Law awarding the FBI jurisdiction in those cases in which the victim had been taken across a state line. The Bureau joined the New Jersey state police and New York police department, which had handled the case from the start. But it was not until two years later that the suspect, Bruno Richard Hauptmann, was arrested. As we have seen, the breakthrough came when a gas station attendant jotted down the license number of a car whose driver had paid with a gold certificate. The certificate, it developed, was part of the ransom money, and the car was registered to Hauptmann.

Despite the fact that another agency had suggested that the ransom packet contain the outlawed gold certificates, Hoover claimed a lion's share of the credit for the FBI. In appropriations testimony in 1934, he recounted: "We started in on a very diligent check . . . in New York City, over a period of months [and] ran down every one of the ransom bills that we could, until September of this year, when we were able to run down a particular bill that had been passed in

New York at a gas station, and the rest is now public knowledge. Bruno Richard Hauptmann was apprehended, and in his house was found quite a large amount of the ransom money." Two years later, Senator McKellar, at the time the Bureau's one-man "truth squad," challenged this artful version. "Now take the Hauptmann case, concerning which so much has been said," the senator twitted. "That man was turned in by a filling-station agent."

The Lindbergh case established a pattern that, with few exceptions, held true over the years. Hauptmann was an almost illiterate carpenter who committed inexplicable blunders. The overwhelming majority of kidnappers in the major cases that followed were similarly erratic and unstable: Henry Seadlund, whose victim was Charles S. Ross of Chicago in 1936, was a psychopathic killer; Carl Hall and his paramour, Bonnie Heady, kidnap-slayers of little Bobby Greenlease in Kansas City in 1953, were in almost continual alcoholic stupor; Angelo John LaMarca, who in 1956 held infant Peter Weinberger of Long Island for ransom, then killed him, was desperate for money; Joseph Corbett, Jr., the kidnap-slayer of Adolph Coors in Denver, was a brilliant loner; the oddly assorted trio that pulled off the 1963 kidnapping of Frank Sinatra, Jr., hardly rate as criminal geniuses; and so on down the list. Only Machinegun Kelly and Alvin "Creepy" Karpis, who took an abortive fling at the game by abducting banker Edward G. Bremer in St. Paul, Minnesota, possessed any criminal stature.

The blanket of secrecy thrown over kidnapping investigations hides the fact that they are among the easiest crimes to solve.* For one thing, the public's cooperation is unstinting. The 1936 abduction of Mrs. Alice Speed Stoll, which received intense coverage in the newspapers, provides one example. After a nationwide hunt, G-men arrested Thomas N. Robinson, Jr., in Pasadena, California. In his announcement, the Director gave no details but disclosed that

---

*The secrecy also conceals blunders. Leon Turreau, former SAC of the New York office, recalled that his men once recovered the wrong baby in the Lindbergh kidnapping. "Naturally, all of us on the Lindbergh Squad took special pains to keep these blunderings out of reach of the reporters," he said. "The FBI was still struggling for recognition and respect, and couldn't afford the public's horse laughs."

agents had followed a trail of spent ransom money across the country and had nabbed the fugitive without the aid of outside tips. However, the United Press located one Lynn Allen, a lunch-counter manager, who had strongly suspected that a "woman" customer was actually a man. "I remembered a description of Robinson," Allen told UP. "This man filled the description even to the dimple on his chin and a disfigured ear." Allen called Pasadena police, who showed him more photographs of Robinson. He made a positive identification, and the police notified the FBI.

The kidnapper of George Weyerhaeuser, Jr., of the Tacoma, Washington, lumber family was apprehended in an almost identical manner the same year. The FBI had circulated the serial numbers of the ransom money. A saleslady in a Salt Lake City, Utah, department store checked her receipts against a serial number list published in the newspaper and made a match. She advised local police, who arrested the woman who had passed the money. She was the wife of one of the kidnappers. The Bureau took it from there.

The riskiest factor for the kidnapper is the fact that, unlike robbers and burglars, he does not make his "profit" on the spot but must establish contact with the victim's family to arrange for ransom and thus expose himself to capture. The Sinatra kidnappers successfully negotiated this critical stage—with the victim still in their custody, they picked up the $240,000 ransom on the grounds of the Veterans' Administration Hospital in Los Angeles and got away—but one of their number, John W. Irvin, afterward turned himself in and laid bare the plot. The money was recovered.

The kidnapper(s) of Kenneth John Young in Beverly Hills, California, in 1967, however, got away with $250,000 in ransom payment. It had been arranged that the victim would be released immediately upon transfer of the money. The FBI staked out the payoff site, intending to follow the kidnapper's car discreetly until word was radioed that the boy had been freed and then close in. As a cover, Bureau officials decided upon a borrowed taxicab for the surveillance vehicle. But when the intermediary made the money drop as instructed, the kidnapper's car took off at such a high rate of speed that the underpowered taxicab could not keep up with it. As of this writing, the case remains unsolved. The Los Angeles SAC frantically denied agents' contentions that he had blown it.

Those cases the FBI cracked exclusively by its own efforts manifested its strong suit—"the painstaking sifting of clues," as Hoover called it. The Bureau could mobilize an army of agents for major investigations, enabling the kind of fine-tooth combing that more often than not produced a vital clue. In the 1936 Ross kidnapping, for instance, some two hundred and fifty agents saturated a Chicago neighborhood in a successful canvass for the typewriter on which ransom demands had been written. And in the 1956 Weinberger abduction, a special squad of agents spent thousands of man-hours poring over public records to come up with a signature bearing the same handwriting characteristics as the ransom notes. The FBI reputation for tenacity was justly earned.

In the more delicate phases of kidnap investigations, however, the Bureau stumbled more than once. In 1938, young Peter Levine of New Rochelle, New York, was abducted, and a ransom note received by his parents warned against notifying the authorities. The FBI was quietly alerted. "Within a few hours two youthful G-men were clambering over a wall and setting up headquarters in the house; window shades were pulled mysteriously up and down; linemen began installing special telephones; guards skulked on the terraces of the residence. . . . G-men's automobiles roared through the little city." So went a later account by Lou Wedemar of the *New York Daily News,* who broke the news silence on the case. The Levine boy was beheaded by his captor, who was never found, prompting Hoover to blast the press for publishing the news. Retorted Wedemar: "Confusion and hysteria were so evident that the news reached the press within a short time. Even before it was published, however, the kidnapper could not have failed to know that his injunction had been disobeyed."

The 1936 kidnapping of little Charles Mattson in Tacoma, Washington, also seems to have produced an example of FBI overeagerness. The abductor forced the French doors on the Mattson mansion, held a teenage babysitter at gunpoint, and made off with the boy. After several false starts, the family arranged a ransom payoff at an intersection on Seattle's Beacon Hill. At the appointed time a car drove slowly toward the spot, then suddenly veered and sped off. There was no further contact, and shortly thereafter the boy's body was found in a field north of Seattle. An oldtimer in the Seattle office told me he believed that the kidnapper spotted a rather conspicuous FBI stakeout at the payoff site.*

History very nearly repeated itself at the payoff spot in the 1968 kidnapping of four-year-old Stanley Stalford, Jr., of Beverly Hills. The victim's father, a wealthy banker, had arranged for the delivery of $250,000 through an intermediary, Harold Tracton. Following instructions, Tracton parked his car at a dumping ground near the coastal town of El Segundo and began walking down a dirt road in the early morning semidarkness. Suddenly a car pulled up, and Tracton, assuming it was the kidnapper, dropped the money bag. But the car was occupied by FBI agents, who drove off. Within seconds, the kidnapper drove up, the boy in the car with him, but apparently alerted to the trap, he abruptly sped off. FBI cars took up pursuit. During the twenty-eight-block chase, in which speeds hit 100 mph on the straightaways, the kidnapper and agents exchanged shots. Finally, one agent rammed his car into the kidnapper's, sending it slamming into two vehicles at an intersection. Although the shootout and crash injured five other persons, the boy miraculously escaped both with only minor abrasions.

Fallible as it was in the kidnapping field, the Bureau habitually shoved local law enforcement aside when a major case broke. When the FBI was searching for Joseph Corbett, Jr., in the Coors abduction, it circulated a request for a notification flyer among the nation's police agencies listing Corbett as a fugitive from a California penal institution but not pointing out that he was the kidnap suspect, a transparent deception that caused hard feelings among some officers. In the Young case, Bureau officials kept the Beverly Hills police in the dark—Los Angeles agents claim the officials were

---

*Under the code name "Matnap," the Mattson kidnapping is still a pending case in the Seattle office. The prime suspect is a drifter whose true identity has never been established but about whom many details are known. He had lived in one of the squatters' shacks on the Tacoma tideflats shortly before the kidnapping. He was suspected of several bank robberies in the Pacific Northwest and escaped the FBI trap by minutes following a bank robbery in Seattle shortly after the kidnap-slaying.

"hoping for a quick solution and a grab of all the publicity"—with the result that Chief Clinton H. Anderson refused to touch the case until after the victim was released unharmed and FBI jurisdiction ceased because he had not been taken across a state line.

In fact, in the overwhelming majority of cases the victim was not transported interstate, leaving jurisdiction legally in the hands of local enforcement. From Bruno Richard Hauptmann, who was tried under New Jersey murder statutes, to Gary Steven Krist, convicted under Georgia law for the 1968 kidnapping in Atlanta of Barbara Jane Mackle, this had held true.* Only Machinegun Kelly and his confederate, who took their victim from Oklahoma to a Texas ranch, and the Sinatra kidnappers, who brushed the Nevada line in driving the victim from Lake Tahoe to Los Angeles, were prosecuted in federal court.

This chronicle of disappearing jurisdiction did not diminish the FBI's enthusiasm for kidnapping investigations. The Lindbergh Law empowering the Bureau to enter such cases operated on a rebuttable presumption that the victim *was* taken across a state line. At first it required that, in the absence of solid evidence of a crossing, the Bureau sit on the sidelines for one week before entering a case. Following the Weinberger tragedy in 1956, Hoover successfully promoted a reduction to twenty-four hours. Finally, the waiting period was eliminated altogether.

As was true of bank robberies, the times changed with regard to kidnappings. The detective forces of modern big-city departments became entirely capable, in both investigative acumen and skill in the use of modern scientific equipment, of handling these investigations. Since it was in the local courts that kidnapping dramas were almost always played out, it would have been more logical to invest, as a matter of policy, primary responsibility in state and local law enforcement. The FBI could then have played an auxiliary role, utilizing its manpower and facilities to supplement the investigation, particularly in its interstate phases.

---

*Federal charges of extortion, a crime under FBI jurisdiction, were filed against Krist because the ransom note threatened death if instructions were not followed. However, the U.S. attorney yielded to the state's graver kidnapping charges, which carried a possible death penalty.

CHAPTER FIFTEEN

THE FBI AS OUR COUNTERSPY

Many Americans believe that only Hoover stands
between them and Communism. As many others are
convinced that he has personally wiped out organized
crime in the United States. A relentless advertising
campaign has created the image of an ideal and infallible
FBI. While it is far from that it is no closer to the Soviet-
style secret police. The FBI does not solve the problem of
an effective police force in an open society. Rather, it is
the product of a given society, dependent on its myths
and failings. There is a wide breach between the FBI's
public image and its reality.

—Sanche De Gramont
in The Secret War

C onon Molody was a professional soldier fighting in the Secret
War—a trained Soviet spy. Masquerading as Gordon Lonsdale,
a debonair Canadian bachelor, he ran a prospering London
coin machine business by day and a busy espionage ring by night. In
1960, British counterspies closed in and Molody was handed a stiff
prison sentence. Four years later, he was exchanged for a British
businessman held in Moscow on espionage charges. Ordinarily, an
exposed spy was heard from no more. But in March 1965, in a
series of articles in the popular British weekly *The People* (whose
reporter met with Molody somewhere in Eastern Europe), he set
bones to rattling in several closets, including the FBI's. For five
years, Molody claimed, he had operated in the United States, col-

lecting intelligence on rocket development as well as industrial and commercial secrets.

Molody taunted this his disclosures would "cause some very red faces in America's Federal Bureau of Investigation," and indeed his account, while patently embellished, was sufficiently detailed to ring true. This case and others I shall discuss reveal that the FBI's reputation as our counterspy, established through successes against Nazi agents during World War II and solidified by the so-called Atom Spies case in the early 1950s, was dangerously inflated. A veteran of guerrilla operations against the Germans in World War II and later trained in a Soviet espionage school, Molody arrived in the United States in early 1951 aboard a Dutch airliner using a fictitious German identity.* He was assigned, he said, to collaborate with "Alec," the code name of Colonel Rudolf I. Abel, at that time the resident director of Soviet espionage in this country. (The most versatile and accomplished Soviet agent uncovered, Abel was arrested in 1957 and exchanged in 1961 for downed U-2 pilot Francis Gary Powers.)

At considerable length, Molody sketched in *The People*'s series his work in the United States; the detection of possible tails, the selection of dead-letter boxes where messages were hidden, and clandestine meetings with fellow agents. He claimed to have traveled to San Francisco to brief an agent on the surveillance of three men "deeply engaged in America's military program," and told of driving a few miles outside New York City to send precoded messages from a transmitter he carried openly in his car. He met regularly with Abel in Central Park and Washington Square, he said, and received data on the passing of messages and courier movements.

After five years in the United States, Molody was promoted to resident director of espionage in Great Britain. On March 3, 1955, he sailed aboard the liner *United States* for his new assignment. *The People* published a photograph of him purportedly taken aboard the

---

*A seemingly conflicting version has Molody slipping ashore from a Soviet grain freighter in Vancouver, Canada, in 1954, residing in Toronto for several months, then entering the United States at Niagara Falls, New York. Even if accurate, however, this version does not preclude his having set up shop initially in 1951 and then having left the U.S. for an interval.

vessel. Wearing a broad grin, the Statue of Liberty visible in the background, he looked for all the world like an ordinary tourist.

It was precisely this inconspicuousness, this ability to merge into an alien milieu, that distinguished the professional Soviet spy from the Nazi agents of World War II against whom the FBI had had so much success. "Where the Soviet spies carried briefcases," wrote Nathaniel Weyl in *The Battle Against Disloyalty*, "the Nazi agents affected sword canes. The former were often unobtrusive, mild-mannered men, who impressed their neighbors as model fathers and husbands and their associates as superlatively competent scientists. The latter tended to be human tumbleweeds—unstable, flamboyant, and frequently alcoholic." The Nazis were amateurs, contended Weyl, while the Soviets were "men of a different stamp and of a different order of intelligence and capacity."

In a way, then, the Nazi operatives were the Dillingers of the spy trade—rakish, egocentric, and rambunctious. Ironically, Franklin Roosevelt undoubtedly had in mind the FBI's immense popularity earned by conquering the Dillinger-era desperadoes when, in 1936, he bestowed on Hoover overall responsibility for counterespionage in the United States. There is no evidence that the FBI chief balked at accepting. "[It] was a responsibility which Hoover welcomed," wrote H. Montgomery Hyde in *Room 3603,* the story of a British intelligence unit that collaborated with the FBI in the Western Hemisphere during World War II, "since it represented a considerable addition to the prestige and influence of the F.B.I., whose interests its ambitious Director was always most zealous in promoting."

Despite heady victories over the Germans, the adaptation of criminal investigative techniques to counterspy activities was not an unqualified success. In *Room 3603,* Hyde recounted the case of a rather urbane Yugoslavian who, having been recruited by the German *Abwehr,* secretly got in touch with British intelligence and became their double agent. In 1941, the Germans sent the agent, code-named "Bicycle," to the United States. Notified of his transfer by the British, the FBI insisted on taking him over and running him themselves, scorning friendly advice. According to Hyde, "Hoover's men were unable to shed their original gang-busting methods in handling 'Bicycle.' For instance, when the Germans sent over some money for him, instead of allowing it reach him without interference the F.B.I. attempted to draw the courier into a trap, which would of course have notified the Germans that 'Bicycle' was at least under the gravest suspicion." The G-men finally gave up on the double agent, branding him as unreliable. But in fact, maintained Hyde, he was "an extremely intelligent as well as courageous agent and it was somewhat unfortunate that he should have been spoiled in this way."

After the war, Hanson Baldwin, the seasoned military affairs editor of the *New York Times,* cautioned that the FBI's performance should not be viewed as flawless. The Bureau, he asserted, "still has much to learn about counter-espionage. Its wartime capture of the saboteurs landed on our coasts inflated its reputation as a security organization without good cause, for in nearly every case the FBI was first informed of the presence, actual or impending, of the saboteurs by citizens or by other government intelligence agencies. Counter-espionage, counter-sabotage, and anti-subversion are delicate and specialized roles. They call, when captures are made, for less publicity than J. Edgar Hoover has usually given them."

But Hoover, proud as a peacock, had boasted that his Bureau had espionage under control from the outset. "Foreign powers tried to steal not only the atomic bomb but other military secrets," he told the IACP at the convention in Miami in 1945. "The counter-espionage program which we developed did more than encircle spies and render them harmless. It enabled us to learn of their weakness and their aims."

Even as the Director spoke, the Soviets had consummated an espionage coup that the FBI would not learn about for four more years. In *The FBI Story,* Don Whitehead melodramatically describes the moment of truth: "At his desk in the Department of Justice Building on Pennsylvania Avenue, FBI director J. Edgar Hoover studied a top-secret report—and his face flushed with shock and anger. Here was information, reliable beyond doubt, that agents of a foreign power had stolen the very heart out of the atomic bomb, stolen the secret of its construction and detonation." Hoover issued a series of rapid-fire orders, says Whitehead, and the vast machinery of the FBI spun into action.

What followed was transformed by the magical touch of FBI publicity from the worst counterintelligence defeat since the Trojan Horse to an FBI coup. It became part of American folklore how the Bureau doggedly tracked down the Atomic Spies, as Hoover referred to them. The first to be unmasked was atomic physicist Klaus Fuchs, a refugee from the Nazis and covert Communist who had worked on the program developing the atom bomb. One of the more colorful anecdotes told how Fuchs, upon his arrival in New York in 1943, strolled down the street in the dead of winter carrying a tennis ball as a recognition signal for his espionage contact. For nearly two years, Fuchs periodically passed data to this contact, whose identity he did not know.

The FBI, in belatedly seeking the intelligence leak, conducted one of its hallmark inquiries—a massive review and collation of records, in this case those of installations that had figured in the bomb's development. It became evident that the man being sought had worked on uranium processing and bomb assembly and was most likely a physicist. Suspicion began to center on Fuchs. With what must have been considerable surprise, the Bureau discovered that the name had already been twice entered into its files: captured Gestapo records listed one Klaus Fuchs, with an identical birthdate, as a German Communist. And in 1946, when he made good his defection from the Soviet Embassy in Ottawa, Canada, cipher clerk Igor Gouzenko brought with him a notebook from the safe containing among others the notation: "Klaus Fuchs, 84 George Lane, University of Edinburgh, Scotland." The Royal Canadian Mounted Police had duly turned over a copy of the notebook to their FBI colleagues.

Fuchs had long since returned to England. Interrogated by MI-5, he confessed his role in the theft and transmission of atomic secrets. As for his contact in the United States, the scientist could only describe him in broad terms and suggest that he was a chemist. The story was told and retold of how the G-men pored over the records of thousands of firms and institutions employing chemists, gradually whittling down the field to several possibilities, one of them a diminutive Philadelphian named Harry Gold; and how, when Gold gave permission to search his house, they found a street map of Santa Fe, New Mexico, a city hard by the atomic plant of Los Alamos where Fuchs had been posted.

Once again the FBI must have been surprised, for Gold, too, was in the files. In 1947, G-men had brought him before a federal grand jury in Philadelphia investigating espionage. He and an associate, an engineer, had fabricated the story that they had passed on to the Russians only harmless material. Gold had sobbed that he was only a "small, timid, frightened man who in some manner was involved on the fringe of espionage but who never had committed an overt act and who now was completely aghast at what he was on the brink of."

Put on the spot by the discovery of this incident, Gold turned government witness and steered the FBI to David Greenglass, an Army sergeant who had been stationed at Los Alamos. On one of his trips to New Mexico, Gold said, he had been instructed by his Soviet superior in New York to contact Greenglass. As a recognition device, he had been given a torn half of a Jell-O box that fit precisely with one in the sergeant's possession.

More worried over deals he had made in stolen property than espionage, Greenglass agreed to cooperate with the FBI. The Jell-O box half had been given to him by his brother-in-law Julius Rosenberg, he said. His work at Los Alamos had provided him access to restricted data, and he had given to Gold and Rosenberg (while home on furlough) sketches of the bomb's lens mold and triggering device. In keeping with the pattern, Julius Rosenberg had also been entered previously into the FBI's files. In 1945, while employed as an engineer at the Army Signal Corps Fort Monmouth installation, he had been investigated and questioned by the FBI, which had gotten wind of his Communist leanings. But although the Bureau had dug up enough to cause his dismissal, it had failed to detect any indications of spy activity.

Julius and Ethel Rosenberg were arrested and tried under the Espionage Act of 1917. Greenglass and Gold, who hoped for leniency, were the crux of the government's case, which does not seem to have been without taint. Not brought out at the trial was the fact that Ruth Greenglass had told her attorney that David had a "tendency to hysteria," exhibited suicidal impulses, and "would say things were so even if they were not." Gold, who had fed the FBI a concocted story in 1947 and had, admittedly, supplied phony data to the Soviets, was likewise of dubious credibility. G-men spent a marathon four hundred hours with him going over and over his allegations, and by trial time he had become one of the most thoroughly coached witnesses ever to take the stand.

To prove Gold's presence in Albuquerque on the occasion of the meeting with Greenglass—this was crucial in order to prove that the Rosenbergs were implicated in a conspiracy that had actually passed data to the Soviets—the prosecution introduced a photostat of a Hilton Hotel registration card bearing Gold's name. The registration clerk's handwritten entry showed the date as June 3, 1945, while the automatic timer's printed entry was June 4. Oddly, the FBI agents who purportedly found the card in dead storage at the Hilton failed to initial and date it as required to preserve the chain of custody.

In their book *Invitation to Inquest,* Walter and Miriam Schneir disclosed that a second Hilton registration card in Gold's name existed, this one dated September 19, 1945, by both clerk and the timer. It also bore the initials of three FBI agents and the date they acquired it. This card was not introduced at the trial for the simple reason that on September 19, Greenglass was in New York on furlough. But for the Schneirs it provided a presumably authentic sample against which to test the authenticity of the June 3 card.

Mrs. Elizabeth McCarthy, a handwriting and document expert who regularly conducted examinations for the Boston police, compared the two cards. She concluded that the handwriting on both was probably Harry Gold's, which did not rule out the possibility that Gold had executed one or the other post facto. Since the initials of the same Hilton registration clerk appeared on both, Mrs. McCarthy compared known specimens of the clerk's handwriting with the cards. Her conclusion: it was "highly probable" that the clerk had executed the September 19 card, but there were "very real doubts" about the June 3 card. Finally, she found a number of anomalies in the June 3 card that indicated it was not printed in the same format as the later one. "It would be most unusual to set up for one hotel two formats within a few months," she commented.

Coupled with the fact that Gold had not initially mentioned to his attorneys the supposed meeting with Greenglass but only brought it up on their second meeting as "an extra added attraction," the June 3 card appears highly suspect. In order to conduct a detailed microscopic study of the two cards with a view toward a more conclusive opinion, Mrs. McCarthy required the originals. Attorneys wrote to Hoover requesting them but were told, "Due to the passage of time the cards are no longer available." This was strange, since the Bureau did not ordinarily dispose of such exhibits, as the retention of the suppressed laboratory report in the Kathryn Kelly case demonstrates.

When sentencing the Rosenbergs to death, Judge Irving R. Kaufman intoned, "Plain deliberate contemplated murder is dwarfed in magnitude by comparison with the crimes you have committed." The judge accused the Rosenbergs of "putting into the hands of the Russians the A-bomb," and thus causing the "Communist aggression in Korea." Such hyperbole could only have sounded sane in the phobia of the times. In retrospect, the crude sketches made by Greenglass and admitted at the trial seem worthless as scientific knowledge. As the eminent scientist, Dr. Harold Urey, commented after the trial, "[A] man of Greenglass' capacity is wholly incapable of transmitting the physics, chemistry, and mathematics of the atomic bomb to anyone." And as the Joint Congressional Committee on Atomic Energy reported in 1949, there existed "an unfortunate notion that one marvelous 'formula' explains how to make bombs and that it belonged exclusively to the United States. . . . The Soviet Union, for its part, possesses some of the world's most gifted scientists, . . . men whose abilities and whose understanding of the fundamental physics behind the bomb only the unrealistic were prone to underestimate."

If anyone had been capable of passing on information of value to the Russians it would have been Fuchs. But the scientist was far beyond the pale of American justice, and the Rosenbergs were not. Although Greenglass testified that Julius Rosenberg was making preparations to flee after Fuchs was exposed, it turned out that he was actually making long-range plans for his machine shop business. The Rosenbergs became the defendants in what the *Columbia*

Law Journal termed America's "outstanding political trial." As Pulitzer Prize winner Sanche De Gramont expressed it, "The Rosenbergs were guilty, but they were guilty at the wrong time. In a way, they were the victims of catharsis—their death sentences served as atonement for thirty years of official neglect." The fact remains that they probably were guilty of nothing.

The much-trumpeted FBI "feat" in tracking down the atom spies was actually a case of closing the barn door after the horse was gone and only retribution remained. Although post mortems at the time by press and politicians adroitly sidestepped the obvious question of why the watchdog had been barkless, the Bureau itself was apparently sensitive about it. In *The FBI Story,* Whitehead takes pains to point out that not until the Atomic Energy Act of 1946 was the FBI responsible in place of the Army for atomic security, thus implying that the theft of atomic secrets prior to 1946 was really none of the Bureau's business. This is nothing more than semantic nonsense. The theft was perpetrated by a Soviet espionage apparat, and the FBI had all along been responsible for violations of the Espionage Act of 1917—the act under which the Rosenbergs were prosecuted.

Conceivably, the G-men could have cracked the case earlier on the basis of information in their files on Fuchs, Gold, and Julius Rosenberg. The fact that the Canadian RCMP had, through Igor Gouzenko's disclosures, cracked a Soviet ring aimed at the atomic facility at Chalk River, Ontario—Dr. Allan Nunn May, like Fuchs a British physicist, had been a member—might have suggested the existence of a companion ring in the United States. But where the Bureau seems to have slipped up badly was in its surveillance of the American terminus of the transmission route to Moscow—the Soviet consulate in New York. Nominally a vice consul, Anatoli A. Yakovlev was the resident director of espionage who met with Gold and, perhaps, Rosenberg. Ordinarily, the FBI isolated such "legal" agents and tailed them to identify their contacts, but Yakovlev seemingly escaped detection. "The failure to shadow Yakovlev was a serious omission," opined former naval intelligence officer Ladislas Farago in his *War of Wits,* "since it is an established fact that almost all Soviet nationals among the intelligence personnel work under the cover of diplomatic and trade agencies abroad."

The G-men's inability to penetrate the atom spies ring during its period of activity was but one more sign that they were, after all, quite human. Yet the Bureau persisted in projecting a superhuman image. "Nine months after J. Edgar Hoover flashed the warning that atomic secrets had been stolen by agents of a foreign power," asserted *The FBI Story,* "the whole wretched story of espionage was known to the FBI."

This must rank as one of the most dangerously presumptuous boasts in the history of counterespionage. Four years after it was published, Hoover learned to his chagrin that a New York couple questioned by his agents in connection with the Rosenberg affair were actually top Soviet agents who belonged to the apparat of master spy Colonel Abel. After slipping the FBI net, they eventually landed in England, where they became key members of a ring whose target was British nuclear secrets. The head of that ring was another old FBI nemesis—Conon Molody.

On the face of it, Morris and Lona Cohen seemed unlikely prospects to confound the FBI. Born in Russia, Morris Cohen was brought to the Bronx in infancy. A borderline student, he excelled in football—his teammates dubbed him "Unc" because of his friendly solicitude for their welfare—and won a football scholarship to, of all schools, Mississippi State.

During the Spanish Civil War, Cohen fought with the Abraham Lincoln Brigade on the Loyalist side. Like other international volunteer units, the brigade was overseen by Soviet commissars who tapped likely recruits for espionage. The commissars demanded the passports for the brigade members, purportedly as a security precaution in the event of capture. But the passports were doctored and assigned to the proselytes (as of the 1960s some were still turning up in Africa, Vietnam, Laos, and Cambodia). When he returned to the United States in 1938, Morris Cohen was carrying a passport in the name of Israel Altman.

At this point, however, it does not appear that he was deeply involved in espionage. He made no effort to conceal his Communist Party affiliation, went to work for Amtorg, the Soviet government trading organization, and filled in as a guard at the Russian pavilion at the 1939 World's Fair. About 1940 he married Lona Petka, also a Party member. When the war broke out, Cohen was inducted into the Army and his wife got a job in a defense plant.

It was after the war that Morris Cohen disassociated himself from Party activity and joined a clandestine apparat. Colonel Abel arrived surreptitiously in the United States via Canada in 1948 and evidently linked up with the Cohens shortly thereafter. At the Cohens' 1961 trial in London's Old Bailey, Detective Superintendent George Smith of Scotland Yard's Special Branch testified that in early 1950 the Cohens apparently "gave a dinner party at which [Abel] was introduced as a wealthy English businessman." Smith said Abel was using the surname Milton, an Anglicized version of Emil, the first part of his pseudonym in the United States, Emil Goldfus. When the FBI ultimately arrested "Emil Goldfus," a photograph of the Cohens was found in his quarters.

In 1950, the Cohens were living in an apartment at 178 East 71st Street, and Cohen was fronting as a teacher. In midsummer, as the FBI zeroed in on Gold, Greenglass, and the Rosenbergs, the Cohens began escape preparations. The day after David Greenglass was arrested, they cashed in their bonds and closed their bank account. When the FBI learned that they were somehow associated with the Rosenbergs—there is an unverified report that the Rosenbergs paid their rent, which, if true, would have been a security lapse—Cohen was questioned. Glibly surviving the session, he and his wife vanished, leaving behind in their haste furniture, clothes, and personal articles.

By a circuitous route, the Cohens made their way to England, where, as Peter John Kroger and his wife, Helen Joyce, they set up an antiquarian bookseller's business in the London suburb of Ruislip. The choice of this village was not whimsical: the third U.S. Air Force Headquarters was nearby. But the principal objective of the ring operated by Conon Molody, alias Gordon Lonsdale, was the British submarine base at Portsmouth, in particular the H.M.S. *Dreadnought,* a nuclear vessel incorporating many features of the American *Nautilus* and *Skipjack.*

The Cohens seem to have served mainly as a communications center for the Molody ring. Following their arrest, their bungalow yielded an array of modern espionage accoutrements, including a high-powered radio tuned to Moscow, a coding device, microfilm and microdot equipment, four forged passports, and a generous supply of escape funds in U.S. currency.

Upon the arrest of Colonel Abel in 1957, the FBI had disseminated an alert for the Cohens among North Atlantic Treaty Alliance countries. Yet their downfall did not come until three years later, and then in the classic pattern of spy fiction. The Soviets had recruited a British naval petty officer posted to the Moscow embassy who had a prodigious capacity for liquor and women. When the officer was transferred to the Portsmouth base, the Russians placed him under the wing of Molody. But his lavish spending habits soon attracted attention, and British intelligence clamped him under surveillance. This led to Molody and, in turn, the Cohens. It was a shabby demise for the three veterans of Soviet espionage in the United States.

An espionage case that contributed immensely to the legend of the FBI as well as to the political agendas of Hoover and Richard Nixon was that of Alger Hiss in 1950. Hiss was a high-ranking State Department official who had law-clerked for Justice Oliver Wendell Holmes and accompanied Franklin D. Roosevelt to the Yalta Conference. A Communist Party defector named Whittaker Chambers alleged that Hiss had passed him classified documents that he in turn put in the hands of Soviet agents. A melodramatic touch was added when Chambers showed investigators a hollowed-out pumpkin in a patch in his yard, from which he retrieved hidden microfilms purporting to contain the documents, which became famous as the "pumpkin papers." Chambers also claimed that Hiss had typed document summaries on his Woodstock typewriter, which brought the celebrated FBI Laboratory into the picture to compare typewritten specimens.

During the Hiss trial Chambers, with his checkered past, was unconvincing and the other evidence flimsy, resulting in a hung jury. Hoover was so angry he censured four agents who worked on the case. For his part, Nixon, who was riding the case like a toboggan to preeminence as an anti-Communist crusader, was so furious he demanded that the trial judge be impeached.

But at a second trial Hiss was convicted of perjury, and Hoover

and Nixon celebrated their victory. It was not until the recent col-
lapse of the Soviet Union that information came to light indicating
that Hiss had been wrongfully sent to prison. General Dimitri Volka-
gnov, head of the Russian government's intelligence archives,
combed through the files and concluded, in October 1992, that Hiss
was "never a spy for the Soviet Union." It had taken forty-two years
for Hiss, who had stoutly maintained his innocence, to be vindicated.

•

There are two kinds of espionage agents—"legal" and "illegal." The
former enters the country legally as a member of a diplomatic or
commercial establishment that provides the cover for his clandestine
functions. The latter crosses a border by means of spurious documents or sneaks in, then synthesizes an identity and erects a cover.
"Gordon Lonsdale" and "Peter and Helen Kroger" are examples of
the illegal agent.

The FBI maintained permanent surveillance on the Russian
Embassy and other official establishments as well as those of the
Soviet-bloc nations, just as the KGB kept a close scrutiny on our
embassy in Moscow. The Bureau had "fisur" terms (a phonetic con-
traction of "physical surveillance") that tailed those suspected of
having intelligence functions. In his book *Spy in the U.S.*, defected
Polish military attaché Pawol Monet recounted the way he played
cat-and-mouse with these teams, trying to shake the tail in order to
carry out an espionage assignment. Monet claimed he usually didn't
have too much difficulty, but rated the agents of the Chicago office
as his most tenacious shadows.

At times the surveillances turned into a bit of gamesmanship.
On one occasion in Seattle I was tailing the cultural attaché of the
Romanian embassy in Washington, suspected of being a spy, on
foot in downtown Seattle. As it turned out he was in fact very tail-
conscious. At a triangular building he went down one side so I
decided to go down the other in order to be shielded from view for
a minute or two. The next thing I knew he came back around the
corner and we passed each other. He then crossed the street and
entered a movie theater lobby. When I entered he was just standing
around. So I bought a box of popcorn to avoid looking conspicu-

ous. At that he strode by, grabbed a handful of my popcorn, and went out the door. A cultural gesture that I had been "made."

The Bureau also kept electronic watch on the Soviets and their allies, who were well aware of the fact. In 1958, for example, Poland built a new consulate in Chicago. An FBI technician enlisted the cooperation of the American contractor so that bugs were imbedded in the walls during construction (the same thing that the Soviets did to the new U.S. embassy building in Moscow a few years ago). When the Poles moved in, agents in the monitoring plant listened in expectantly. They heard a thickly accented voice say, "Go back to Texas, FBI." There was a rush of static and the bugs went dead. Apparently the Poles had an image of FBI agents as cowboys in suits.

The merits of surveillance were illustrated in a case involving Vasili Zubilin, former third secretary of the Soviet embassy. Bibulous and overbearing, Zubilin expended considerable effort in cultivating the Hollywood producer Borris Morros for spy work. Vulnerable to the hostage ploy because of relatives in Russia, Morros gave evidence of going along with the game. FBI watchers observed the scenario and approached Morros to double for them, which he agreed to do. The affable movie man made several trips to the Soviet Union attended by a valet who in reality was an FBI agent. His performance was worthy of an Oscar. The ring Morros is credited with exposing was a large one under the direction of Jack Soble, who seems to have been Colonel Abel's predecessor as resident director.

Another case centered about Robert Glenn Thompson, a disgruntled GI who was recruited by the Russians in 1957 while he was stationed in Germany. Thompson was given a cram course in the trade in East Berlin, and when he was routinely transferred back to the United States was placed under Fedor Kudashkin, a Soviet translator at the United Nations. Among other assignments, Thompson cased the FBI residence agency at Babylon, Long Island. "I got them a layout of this office," he later bragged in a *Saturday Evening Post* article dated May 22, 1965. "My plan was so complete, if they didn't bug the office they was [*sic*] idiots not to."

Although Thompson, hardly a smooth professional, operated for seven years, the weak link was Kudashkin—bumbling, jittery, and, worst of all, a creature of habit. He always wore the same overcoat, Thompson complained, a "blue overcoat that looked like it came right out of the GUM department store on Red Square." On a spring night in 1963, Thompson realized that the G-men had caught on at last. While meeting with the Russian, he saw a red light blink inside a panel truck nearby. "It didn't have any marks on it that I remember," he said, "but it might as well have had 'FBI' all over it. I knew what they were doing. They were taking mine and Fedor's picture with an infrared light."

Most headline counterespionage coups stemmed from the day-in, day-out surveillance of Soviet legals, as in the Thompson case, or from the tips of persons approached for recruitment as spies. The latter was what happened in 1958 when a Chicago man informed the Bureau that he had been contacted to help supply data about the city's vital installations; in 1963 when a CIA employee of Eastern European origin divulged that he had been cajoled by a Russian embassy officer; and again in 1963 when electronics engineer John W. Butenko made one too many meetings with an attaché of the Soviet mission to the United Nations and was arrested for passing sensitive information.

The detection of illegals is a more exacting task, one the FBI may not be up to. To my knowledge, the only active Soviet illegal of recent times uncovered by the FBI wholly on its own was Kaarlo Tuomi (the story has been told in an earlier chapter).

Just how many Soviet illegals were operating in the United States was a question only Moscow could answer. Conon Molody put in his stint undetected. Tuomi was discovered only by an unusually alert and tenacious agent. Colonel Abel was compromised by a defecting subagent. These were fortuitous discoveries.

Colonel Rudolf Ivanovich Abel exemplified the professional Soviet spy. The hawk-faced Russian was urban, cool, well-spoken, multilingual, steeped in literature and the arts, skilled in "Trade-craft"—the quintessential espionage agent. A devoted family man, he had been a Soviet intelligence operative for thirty years when captured. It was about 1948 that he slipped across the border from Canada, opened a photographic studio within eyeshot of the Federal Courthouse in New York, and began his duties as resident director.

In his modest rented room were shortwave radios, cipher pads, cameras and film for producing microdots, and hollowed-out shaving brushes and cuff links. He also kept an assortment of hollow bolts, pens, pencils, batteries, and coins into which could be fitted microfilm messages to be left in "dead drops" for subagents.

The talented Abel might have operated for a much longer time had not Reino Hayhanen panicked. Hayhanen had entered the country aboard the *Queen Mary* in 1952 under the assumed identity of Eugene Maki, an Idaho native who had been taken to Estonia in childhood. As a spy, Hayhanen was a flop. A heavy drinker, he more than once attracted the attention of the police with boisterous conduct. In May 1957, Moscow ordered his return. Fearful that he was marked for liquidation, Hayhanen defected to the CIA in Paris, which under delimitations agreements handed him over to the FBI. He put the G-men onto Abel.

A slight oversight by the FBI almost cost Abel's conviction. At the trial, only Hayhanen's dubious word linked him to the colonel, who claimed he had never seen him before. Later, while Abel's property was being reexamined by the FBI prior to shipment to East Germany when the colonel was being exchanged for U-2 pilot Francis Gary Powers, an agent found a hidden compartment in his wallet that contained microfilmed rows of numbers in Hayhanen's code. Of this belated find, Abel's American attorney, James B. Donovan, commented: "There remains the fact that the most incriminating evidence against Abel was not discovered before the trial and introduced as evidence."

Abel himself added insult to injury. In 1966, after being repatriated, he asserted that he had disposed of a decoding device and taped radio message from Moscow under the very eyes of the arresting G-man. He had tricked them, he said, by using the tape to wipe off an artist's palette and flushing it and the decoder down the toilet.

Another facet of the Hayhanen-Abel saga raises further doubt about the FBI's ability to cope with the subtleties and nuances of the espionage game. In June 1953 a newsboy for the old *Brooklyn Eagle* dropped some change and was startled to see a nickel split apart. He gave it to a New York detective, who sent it on to the FBI. Inside was a cavity housing a tiny strip of paper with what seemed to be a coded message. Laboratory technicians concluded that the message had been typed on a foreign-made machine, but cryptographers were stumped by the code. I can recall an espionage desk supervisor telling us the story and soliciting our ideas. But for over four years the message kept its secret. Then Reino Hayhanen defected.

Hayhanen, in the course of being debriefed, was shown the message on the off change he might recognize the code. He did indeed. The message had been intended for him, but apparently he had lost or spent the nickel on one of his binges. "We congratulate you on a safe arrival," it read. "We confirm receipt of your letter to the address 'V' repeat 'V' and the reading of Letter Number 1." It went on to detail instructions for the transmittal of funds and information. The code? Well, said Hayhanen, it was based simply on Russian folk songs.

H. Montgomery Hyde, in his account of wartime counterespionage, put his finger on one of the basic deficiencies of the FBI. "Many of the FBI's troubles with double agents, whom they tried to run," Hyde wrote, "arose from their lack of understanding of the European mind and outlook, and from their inability to place in charge of a double agent an officer with background likely to win his sympathy and friendship."

In fact, the type of man who would make the best counterspy would never pass FBI muster or flourish in its anti-intellectual environment. Hoover might have looked down his nose at the "Harvard Yard liberals" and somewhat off-beat types employed by the CIA, but in the final analysis the machine-gun mentality didn't crack spy rings.

"In essence, the G-man is merely the prosaic, well-meaning, and, at times, pedestrian law enforcement officer of a democratic nation," wrote Nathaniel Wehl. "He is not selected or trained because of any special proficiency in combatting Soviet agents."

CHAPTER SIXTEEN
TAPS AND BUGS: WHOSE SECURITY?

> How often, or on what system, the Thought Police
> plugged in on any individual wire was guesswork. It was
> even conceivable that they watched everybody all the
> time. But at any rate they could plug in your wire
> whenever they wanted to. You had to live—did live,
> from habit that became instinct—in the assumption that
> every sound you made was overheard, and, except in
> darkness, every movement scrutinized.
>
> —*George Orwell in* 1984

Not long ago at a San Francisco cocktail party I had the strange sensation of recognizing a distinctively mellifluous voice from the past that I couldn't quite place. I studied the woman's face—it was unfamiliar. I went up to her and she introduced herself as Jessica Mitford, the noted author. Of course! Years earlier as an FBI agent I had monitored a wiretap on the home of Mitford and her husband, Robert Truehaft, a well-known civil liberties attorney. I had heard her voice on the phone so many times that I knew what brand of toothpaste she used. But I had never seen a photograph of her.

The tap on the Mitford-Truehaft residence was one of more than a dozen that the FBI had installed on a permanent basis in the San Francisco-Oakland area in the 1950s. All were supposedly in the interest of "national security"—Communist Party functionaries, the Party's organ *Daily People's World,* the California Labor

School, and the Yugoslav consulate, to name a few. They were monitored around the clock in two central plants that were alluded to as "the clubs." The one in San Francisco was in a small downtown building on Sacramento Street that fronted as a marine architect's office. Ships' blueprints on drawing boards cluttered the main floor, which could be seen from the street, but in the basement was the monitoring area with its jumble of wires and banks of amplifiers and recorders. The tapped and bugged conversations were fed into the room via lines leased from the telephone company under a fictitious business name. The lines, which ran from the target offices and residences, were obtained through the cooperation of telephone company special agents, who had to know what the purpose was. But the San Francisco police didn't have a clue. Noticing that an awful lot of lines funneled into one building, they conducted a raid one night thinking it was a bookie joint. When I flashed my FBI credentials and informed them that it was a special operation, they discreetly withdrew.

The Oakland plant was high up in an office building inside a suite with drawn blinds and a double-locked door; there was nothing but a number on the entrance door. It was from this lofty perch that I listened in on the doings in the Mitford household, which were more Murphy Brown than Moscow Red. In fact, during the countless hours I spent with the earphones on I don't recall one momentous breakthrough in protecting the national security.

At the time, the Smith Act trials were on and one objective of the taps was to try to overhear scraps of information that might lead to several defendants who had gone underground. We kept daily logs of all calls and recorded those that seemed important; once a day, the logs and records were taken to the main office, where they were reviewed by security squad agents.

In 1958, I became more deeply involved in electronic eavesdropping when I was sent to "sound school," a euphemism for a three-week course in the theory and practice of wiretapping, bugging, and lockpicking. The course was held in the attic of the Identification Building, far from the eyes of tourists taking the FBI tour. There was a jerry-built room, I recall, where we practiced planting bugs in the wall, a task that requires some skill in carpentry and plastering.

On Saturdays, when the Justice Building was practically deserted, we experimented with finding one particular wire out of the spaghetti maze traversing the conduits.

The most hush-hush subject on the sound school curriculum was lockpicking. We were given noninventory sets of lockpicking tools and instruction in their use, the purpose of which was assumed to be self-evident. "Don't forget," George Berley, the instructor who was the Bureau's top surreptitious entry man, smilingly warned me, "possession of burglar tools in the state of Washington can get you up to ten years."

Entry skills were needed, of course, in order to plant bugs inside premises. In FBI jargon, one of these official burglaries was called a "black bag job," after the equipment kit taken along. All possible precautions were taken to preclude surprise discovery. It was ascertained that the normal occupants were far from the premises, and a tail was put on them to make sure they didn't double back. An FBI agent sat with the police radio dispatcher to ensure that prowler calls from the target neighborhood were ignored. Just in case, the agents going on bag jobs carried no credentials and nothing that would connect them with the FBI. Those of us who carried out these missions often discussed what we would do if, despite everything, we were caught. The consensus was that we would act like a burglar by knocking the man out and fleeing.

On one break-in I nearly had to make that decision. My instructions were to plant a bug in the living room of a security subject's home in a quiet residential area. Further, the bug had to be positioned proximate to the telephone so that it would not only pick up room sounds but also one side of phone conversations. And it was not to be a transmitting bug, one whose batteries would have to be changed periodically, necessitating more break-ins. It was to be a "metallic connection" all the way back to the FBI monitoring plant through a line leased from the phone company.

The installation was made in two steps. The first was to replace the "drop wire" running from the pole outside to the house with one sent by the lab that had two fine wires imbedded in it. These wires would then be connected inside the house to the bug. So we began by borrowing a truck and hardhats from the local power company, which was only too willing to assist the FBI. I and a senior agent assigned as my driver sat anxiously on the crest of a hill awaiting the word to drive down to the house—that both occupants had arrived at their jobs and were under surveillance. The radio crackled with the go signal. With that, my nervous driver revved up the engine and let in the clutch—too suddenly. As we lurched forward there was a loud screeching noise punctuated by a thump. The transmission had fallen out.

But we came back another day, and this time step one went without a hitch. No one in the neighborhood seemed to notice that although I was working out of a power company truck, it was the phone line that I was busy with. A few days later we returned for step two. I picked the lock on a side door and, accompanied by another agent, entered. I immediately saw a problem in the form of a parakeet sitting in its cage right by the telephone where I was to hook up the bug. "Ed," I cautioned my accomplice in a whisper, "don't say 'pass the pliers' or anything else that this goddamn parakeet can repeat later."

It was when we were making the final splices in the basement that we heard the dread sounds of a door opening upstairs and footsteps moving from room to room. Had we been spotted? We froze. The footsteps started and stopped for what seemed an eternity but was only a couple of minutes. We braced for the sound of them coming down the stairs, but there was only the welcome noise of a door closing again. After a decent interval we strode purposefully out of the house and drove off in the truck, as if it was all in a Wichita lineman's day.

Most wiretap installations were routine. It was a simple matter of tapping the phone company special agents for data as to which wires in a polebox belonged to the target subscriber, leasing a line terminating next to them, and making a bridge with a short piece of wire. When I climbed a pole with phone-company issue climbing irons (spikes) and lineman's belt, no one had a clue that I was an FBI agent. In the Coors kidnapping case I put in a tap on the phone of the parents of suspect Joseph Corbett, Jr. (It turned out to be unproductive.) It took fifteen minutes.

But the break-ins weren't always for the purpose of secreting a listening device or two (on occasion two were placed to provide easy-listening stereo). Security squad agents pulled off black-bag jobs on the offices or residences of Communist Party secretaries to photograph membership lists and other documents. But some were an enigma. I have yet to figure out the purpose, for example, of a sneak attack on the Japanese consulate in Seattle in 1957, since Japan was supposedly a Cold War ally. The Bureau's burglar supreme, George Berley, flew out from Washington to mastermind the mission. He brought with him photos of the consulate staff obtained from the State Department so we could beat a hasty retreat should one show up in the middle of the night. At the time the consulate offices were on an upper floor of a downtown building, and we had gotten a key to the entrance from the building superintendent. The target was the contents of the safe. Berley brought along a slug of radioactive cobalt, which he taped to the rear of the safe. Then he placed a photographic film in front of the dial. After a couple of hours of this exposure, the film silhouetted the alignment of the tumblers. Berley spun the dial back and forth and the door swung open. Whatever documents Berley wanted, they were there. But before removing them he carefully measured their position in the safe so that they could be put back exactly. They were photographed with a document camera and we were out of there.

Although headquarters kept its hands clean of this kind of dirty work, it was quick to acknowledge the fruits of a successful bag job when submitted to Washington in carefully worded form. Cash awards in the amounts of $500 and $1,000 were not uncommon, and a few recidivist "badgeless burglars of the Bureau" made a steady supplemental income this way.

Years before, when wiretapping was not a violation of the law, Hoover had denounced it as a lazy man's tool and an obstacle to the "development of ethical, scientific and sound investigative technique." Then, in 1934, the Communications Act made it illegal. As war drew near, Hoover reversed his stand and pushed for authorization to wiretap in matters involving "the national security." Although the legislation was tabled, President Roosevelt gave executive authority for the attorney general "to approve wiretapping when necessary involving the defense of the nation."

Like many wartime measures, wiretapping didn't cease with the hostilities. Hoover took to announcing the number of taps—always around the modest 100 mark—in operation at any given time to thwart "espionage, sabotage and grave risks to internal security." Criticism of the tapping as lawless law enforcement met with the stock answer: there is no violation of the Communications Act because information is intercepted but not divulged—a key element in the act—outside the Justice Department. "The Act was directed against telephone company employees," a sound school instructor explained to us in a tone indicating the law wasn't meant for the FBI to obey.

Although the annual announcement of the number of wiretaps in operation helped to reassure the public that the FBI was not promiscuous in its practices, it only hinted at the actual scope of electronic eavesdropping. In the first place, there existed in the field what we called "suicide taps"—those not authorized by Washington that would have killed the career of any agent caught installing them. But what the Bureau didn't know—or didn't want to know—was that you cannot train and equip people for electronic intrusion and expect them to hold themselves in check. It is just too handy a shortcut for human nature to resist.

In the second place, what Hoover was referring to in his announcements was the wiretap, as opposed to the bug. My sound school notes stress that taps must be approved by the attorney general, but "Authority for mikes [bugs]: Bureau authority only." What this meant was that the Bureau was strictly on its own in bugging. Once, for example, I was instructed by headquarters to disconnect a wiretap whose allotment was needed in a more urgent case; in the next paragraph I was ordered to put in a bug in its place. Thus the books were primly in balance as far as the public—and the attorney general—were concerned: Hoover could state he had only so many taps in operation with at least half-truthfulness. But the under-the-table switch required that I pick a lock and sneak inside a private home in order to plant the bug, whereas the wiretap had been made on a pole box without surreptitious entry.

Yet in his 1966 row with Robert Kennedy over who had authorized the ill-fated bugs in the Las Vegas casinos, Hoover, in a letter to Representative H. R. Gross dated December 7, 1966, asserted: "Your impression that the FBI engaged in the usage of wiretaps *and microphones* only on the authority of the Attorney General is absolutely correct" [italics added]. Had the Director for some reason especially secured permission from Kennedy to plant microphones, or was he being disingenuous?

To back up his contention that Kennedy had done the authorizing, Hoover released two memoranda written by former FBI Assistant Director Courtney A. Evans in 1961, when he was serving as liaison man between the Director and his nominal boss. In one, Evans reported that he had discussed the possibility of using "electronic devices" against organized crime with Kennedy, who "stated that he recognized the reasons why telephone taps should be in defense-type cases and he was pleased we had been using microphone surveillances where these objections do not apply wherever possible in organized crime matters." In the other, Evans said he had talked to Kennedy about obtaining leased lines from the telephone company to use with microphone surveillances in New York City. But Evans himself maintained that he "did not discuss" the use of microphones with Kennedy—he knew that they need not be specifically approved—and did not "know of any written material" sent to the attorney general on the subject, a seeming reference to the lack of any specific requests for the Las Vegas bugs by the FBI.

Kennedy categorically denied that Hoover "ever asked me for authorization for any single bugging device, in Las Vegas, New York, Washington or anywhere else." As for the claim that illegal bugging had "intensified" under his regime, the senator retorted that the Director "never discussed this highly important matter with me, and no evidence exists supporting his recollection that we did."

The most likely explanation of the situation is that Hoover, under pressure to produce intelligence, had stepped up bugging activity under the carte blanche authority from the Department he had possessed all along, and that Kennedy knew generally that he was doing so and didn't object but also didn't specifically acquiesce to each installation. (Judging from the tactics he used against Teamster boss Jimmy Hoffa, Kennedy had no profound philosophical objections to electronic eavesdropping.) This had been implicit in the statements of Solicitor General (later Supreme Court Justice) Thurgood Marshall when he stepped before the Supreme Court some six months before, on July 13, 1966, to admit that Hoover was responsible for the bugging of the hotel suite of aerospace lobbyist Fred B. Black in 1963. According to Marshall, the FBI chief had on its own initiative expanded the scope of bugging for intelligence purposes beyond "national security" cases *without* the Department's knowing.

From my own experience, the Bureau began this expanded coverage some four years earlier, during the post-Apalachin Top Hoodlum Program. When I helped inspect the Los Angeles office in October 1959, I saw several bug installations on suspected organized crime figures.

The Marshall revelations were excruciatingly embarrassing to the FBI, so much so that on the day they were made the Bureau arrested an accused spy, gaining front-page coverage, in a case that had been on the back burner for years. Reportedly, Hoover argued vociferously against disclosure with then Attorney General Katzenbach, and it wasn't long afterward that Katzenbach was demoted from his cabinet position by LBJ and moved over to the State Department as undersecretary.

The admission of the Black bug opened a can of worms. There followed over the next few years dozens of courtroom concessions that defenders had been bugged, a string that culminated in the Dr. Martin Luther King, Jr., contretemps in the summer of 1969. This, of course, jeopardized the prosecutions, since the fruits of electronic eavesdropping and any leads derived from it are, theoretically, inadmissible in court. But one byproduct of the bugging was a windfall of intelligence on Washington sachems that kept Hoover tuned in on all kinds of high-level planning and plotting.

Consider the bug on Black: Acting on Hoover's orders, agents rented a suite adjoining Black's in the Sheraton-Carlton Hotel, drilled a hole through the common wall, and inserted a tubular microphone, a type of high acoustical quality. They listened from February 7 to April 25, 1963. In accordance with longstanding practice, daily logs were kept on what transpired in the target room, and seemingly germane conversations were tape-recorded. Summaries of Black's discussions, including privileged ones with his attorneys, were sent over to headquarters stamped "JUNE," a red flag that the information was obtained in a highly sensitive way.

An excerpt: April 1, 1963, seven P.M. Subject is on the telephone with an unknown party. "I had a call about an hour ago from [Senator] Mike Monroney's office, and he and [Representative] Carl Albert want to have breakfast with me Wednesday morning at eight A.M. at the Senate Office Building. Just the two of them. I accepted the date and thought you'd better know. The two of them are the big ones in Oklahoma. . . ." As a result of this interception, a subsequent report to Hoover informed, "WFO [Washington Field Office] made a discreet survey of the streets in the vicinity of the Senate Office Building for Black's car during the pertinent period with negative results. . . ." As it turned out, Black arrived by cab and discussed with Albert new aerospace plants for Oklahoma to be under construction before the 1964 elections.

On April 4, the bug picked up a conversation between Black and columnist Jack Anderson, who was interviewing him concerning contacts with Las Vegas casinos. Black admitted knowing Edward Levinson, one of the casino operators who was also bugged, although it wasn't known then. He maintained that it was a nonbusiness relationship, but that he was watched by the FBI every time he went to Las Vegas. "They're watching everyone with those people," said Anderson. "They think that you're some kind of bag man or something for them." "I represent legitimate companies," Black insisted.

On April 23, President James Kerr of the giant AVCO Corporation and company executive Earl ("Red") Blaik dropped by the suite to talk about a military contract the firm was attempting to negotiate and the role of House Republican leader Gerald Ford in the dealings. The next day, FBI agents called on the AVCO plant in Ohio that manufactured the equipment in question.

One of the FBI's more elaborate bugging setups was exposed in 1967 during pretrial testimony in a Springfield, Illinois, tax evasion case. The defendant was Frank Balistrieri, suspected by the FBI of being aligned with the Wisconsin crime syndicate. Using the fictious name "John A. Hansen," agents had rented an apartment across the hall from the Milwaukee apartment of Jennie Alioto, bookkeeper for several Balistrieri businesses. Not only did they monitor room sounds from a miniature bug-transmitter hidden in her apartment, they watched visitors through a peephole in their door. Downtown, agents had broken into the law offices of Dominic Frinzi, an attorney for Balistrieri, and concealed a microphone in a ceiling fixture. Wires were run from the mike to connect with a leased line that led to FBI headquarters in the Federal Building, where a monitoring room was in operation. Into this same room was fed a wiretap on Balistrieri's home telephone. And a transistorized mike-transmitter was buried in the wall of his jukebox sales agency, from which it broadcast to cars positioned nearby.

In a companion case in Kenosha, William ("Wheezer") Covelli was apparently under a similar electronic blanket. Frinzi was Covelli's lawyer, too, and John A. Holtzman, the retired SAC at Milwaukee, took the Fifth Amendment when questioned about trespasses committed to plant the bug in Frinzi's office (it had evidently been done in 1963). In addition, the Justice Department claimed executive privilege to justify the silence of agent Joseph E. O'Connell, who remarked that it "wasn't my position to question my superior."

Perhaps no other area of its operations contributed more to the FBI's credibility gap than electronic eavesdropping. The chronicle of deceit went back to 1949 to the Judith Coplon espionage case. During Miss Coplon's Washington trial for pilfering classified documents, a Bureau supervisor denied having ordered taps installed on her, and attorneys from the Department of Justice swore there had been none. She was convicted. However, at pretrial hearings in New York on a second charge of transmitting the documents to the Soviets, Justice Department attorneys admitted to the court with deep chagrin that there had been taps all along—on Miss Coplon's home and office phones and on her parents' phone. Moreover, the taps had remained in service through the Washington trial, and the FBI had overheard conversations with her attorney. The attorneys said that they had only discovered the existence of the taps when they asked FBI agents for affidavits swearing that they had not wiretapped and the agents balked.

When Federal Judge Sylvester Ryan delved deeper, it was

learned that some thirty FBI employees had participated in the eavesdropping, and that a high Bureau official had ordered the removal of all vestiges of the taps just prior to the New York trial. In a memorandum to an assistant director dated November 9, 1949, Inspector (later Assistant Director) Howard B. Fletcher wrote: "The above named informant [code named Tiger, the tap] has been furnishing information concerning the activities of the subject. In view of the immanency of her trial, it is recommended that this informant be discontinued immediately, and that all administrative records in the New York office covering the operations of this informant be destroyed."

The hanky-panky cost the Bureau the convictions, which were reversed on appeal.

History repeated itself in the August 1969 appeal of Teamster President Jimmy Hoffa on a jury tampering conviction. In the course of a Chattanooga hearing on the extent of bugging and wiretapping by federal agents, Department attorney Michael T. Epstein said he "had never heard" of a special FBI file on eavesdropping and contended the Hoffa people just wanted to "rummage in government records." But a few days later Charles Dolz, the FBI head of accounting and records, acknowledged on the stand that there was such a file—the June File.

The Martin Luther King, Jr., affair brought more prevarication. The FBI had stated it had discontinued the tapping of King on April 20, 1965, and both Nicholas Katzenbach and Ramsey Clark denied they had authorized any resumption of it. However, as an FBI agent testified under oath in 1969 hearings, the tapping was in fact continued up to the moment of King's assassination. Then it came to light that the Bureau, under orders to submit the original logs of the tapped conversations involving Muhammad Ali, had submitted a copy altered without the Department's knowledge.

There was a moment of panic in the FBI in 1965 when Senator Edward Long of Missouri geared up his Subcommittee on Administrative Practice and Procedure to explore government agencies' "armory of electronic snooping devices." If Long got too nosy the Bureau's illegal bugging, tapping, and black bag jobs might be exposed.

According to *Boss,* Cartha DeLoach moved to protect the FBI's family jewels by proposing that Long place in the record a Bureau statement absolving itself of any illegal electronic snooping. But Long's waspish counsel, Bernard Fensterwald, Jr., wouldn't buy into the plan, suggesting instead that an FBI official take the witness stand. No, DeLoach countered, that "might open a Pandora's box insofar as our enemies of the press [are] concerned." Fensterwald then floated the idea of calling me to testify on the basis of my FBI experience, which would in fact have opened the box. DeLoach went ballistic, denouncing me as "a first-class SOB, a liar, and a man who had volunteered as a witness only to get a public forum." Long, who had oh-so-discreetly been tipped by Hoover that his voice had been captured on tape in conversations with organized crime figures, backed off. Instead, the hearings were highlighted by private detective Hal Lipset's demonstration of a bug in a Martini olive.

Nominally, the Omnibus Crime Act of 1968 exerts controls over electronic surveillance—while at the same time legalizing it—by limiting it to organized crime and national security matters and then under court supervision only. Previously, the Johnson administration had clamped down on all bugging and tapping except in national security matters.

My own opinion is that electronic eavesdropping should be eliminated entirely. In the final analysis, it is a totalitarian tactic, the kind of end-justifies-the-means rationalization that leads inevitably down the path to a police state. The cavalier attitude of the FBI toward departmental and other interdictions made controls by the courts an empty safeguard. As the *St. Louis Post-Dispatch* editorialized on June 22, 1969, "The King case is a frightening example of how political police can misuse their powers with the help of electronic gadgetry and huge files." There is no reason to believe that the Bureau, given an inch, will not take a mile.

To be realistic, however, a total ban on electronic snooping was not in the offing. For one thing, there was no overwhelming public mandate to be rid of it. A Gallup Poll released on August 20, 1969, showed an even division: 46 percent for, 47 percent against, 7 percent undecided.

"National security" is too amorphous a term. Where does national security leave off and bureaucratic security begin? As Judge Heard sagely observed in the Coplon case, "You can point your finger at anybody and say for security reasons."

A glimpse at what public permissiveness for "law and order" in any form wrought was visible in Attorney General Mitchell's staggering claim to power above and beyond that granted by the Omnibus Crime Act. In a memorandum filed in a Chicago federal court in the case against eight persons accused in the demonstrations at the 1968 Democratic national convention, Mitchell held that Congress could enact no laws to abridge the president's eavesdropping edicts, and that his decisions were not subject to judicial review. In other words, the president—represented by J. Edgar Hoover—could perforce overstep the law and permit agents to bug and tap militant blacks and political radicals who happened to be involved in dissent. The Fourth Amendment? It didn't apply. Declared the *San Francisco Chronicle* with no feelings spared: this "Mitchell Doctrine" sought "to graft on American democracy the kind of absolutism with which Czars and the early Soviet autocrats were invested. And it could be taken as authority for an unrestrained invasion of privacy such as marked the police states of Adolf Hitler and many a lesser dictator."

The notion of a Hoover-Mitchell bugging tandem brought reactions from many quarters. Attorneys representing the Chicago Eight issued a statement that the attorney general's claim to power was "one of the most shocking lawless statement ever made by the highest law enforcement officer in the nation." Less self-serving and even more pointed was the question posed by a group of respected law professors: "If Martin Luther King, Jr., Black Muslim leader Elijah Muhammad and vigorous opponents of the Vietnam war are considered appropriate subjects for such gross violations of their rights, which group vigorously seeking change, whether radical, liberal, or conservative, is safe?"

A fair question, for it raised the specter of that barren suffocating world depicted by George Orwell where "you had to live—did live, from habit that became instinct—in the assumption that every sound you made was overheard."

CHAPTER SEVENTEEN
THE HOOVER U. ALUMNI ASSOCIATION

Part of [the FBI alumni society's] business meeting was given over to a sales message for miniatures of the bust of The Director which his graduates had given him on his 40th anniversary last May. Its sculptor said that this was the biggest thrill of his life and that he had "really enjoyed" an hour and a half with Hoover.

And the former agents all began to laugh. "He was one of the few that ever really enjoyed it," said former agent Harvey Foster from the chair. This may be one school whose graduates don't queue up to buy souvenir busts of the dear old dean.

—*Murray Kempton*
in the New York World-Telegram,
October 2, 1964

The Society of Former Special Agents of the Federal Bureau of Investigation, Inc., claimed close to five thousand members in the 1970s. There was possibly an equal number of former Feebees, as they were often referred to, who elected not to join the society. By any reckoning it was a goodly group and it made its impact felt. "There does seem to be an awful lot of ex-FBI men around," a Congressman stuck with their prevalence on Capitol Hill once remarked.

In fact, seven were in Congress in 1970, and Nixon's commissioner of the Internal Revenue Service, Atlanta lawyer Randolph Thrower, was a former G-man. So was Robert E. Lee, a commissioner of the Federal Communications Commission; in 1946, Lee made his mark by taking a leave of absence from the FBI to furnish the Taber committee with lists of "subversives" in government, the same lists that Joseph McCarthy would later exploit in his witch-hunts.

A few alumni went into journalism, a field that seemed to evoke their critical faculties. In a 1968 speech before the Commonwealth Club of San Francisco, *Life* publisher Jerome S. Hardy pooh-poohed Hoover's assertion that Communists were behind civil disorders with the words, "Once I worked for Mr. Hoover and he was saying the same thing then and that was twenty-five years ago." Investigative reporter Walter Sheridan of NBC News was an FBI agent before joining Robert Kennedy and heading the "get Jimmy Hoffa" crusade in the Justice Department. He quit the Bureau, he told *Newsweek* (October 23, 1967), because he felt uneasy participating in Hoover's brand of anti-Communism: "I was a cut liberal, and the FBI is a right-wing organization."

The sporting world was also peopled with former FBI sleuths. Joe Muaney, a G-man in the early 1950s, was coach of the Los Angeles Lakers basketball team. A former agent was hired by football commissioner Pete Rozelle to head up the league's investigative arm, and Joe Namath of the New York Jets tried to counter Rozelle's dim view of his Bachelors III bar habitués by retaining an ex-agent.

There were a surprising number of top business executives who prepped at Hoover's school: Harold M. Perry, president of the huge CIT Financial Corporation; William J. Quinn, president of the Chicago, Milwaukee, St. Paul and Pacific Railroad; Edwin J. Foltz, president of Campbell Soup Company's international division; John D. Stewart, vice president of American Express Company; and George V. Myers, executive vice president of Standard Oil Company (Indiana).

Possibly the largest single employer of former G-men was North American Aviation, with sixty-one, and another aerospace firm, Autonetics (a Ford division), had twenty-four.* The Ford Motor

---

*These figures were taken from the membership directory of the ex-agent's society, which means they were minimal.

Company ranked high, with thirty-two. One of its vice presidents, John S. Bugas, was SAC at Detroit until he moved over to Ford in 1944 as assistant to Harry Bennett, the notorious strikebreaker. Paul J. Shine, an executive in the company's legal department, was SAC at Cleveland and worked an interim period at the defunct Packard automobile plant. The airlines, especially American, had many alumni in key positions; Harvey Foster, a personable one-time SAC in New York, was a vice president of the line, and Robert E. Wick, formerly an FBI public relations officer, did similar PR duty with Pan American's Washington office. Sears Roebuck always welcomed resigned agents, and American Photocopy Equipment Company sought them out. Chairman Samuel G. Rautbord of APE told the *Wall Street Journal* of October 16, 1962, the reason: "We've found the FBI, along with teaching its men to shoot straight, develops in them an unusual ability to solve problems quickly, react intelligently in emergencies and get along with all sorts of people."

If the alumni in the executive world were making salaries well in excess of what the Bureau paid, those who moved laterally in government generally were not. There were, of course, the exceptions at the top: General Joseph F. Carroll, director of the Defense Intelligence Agency, and James Rowley, chief of the Secret Service. But the droves of FBI agents who moved to other federal agencies weren't lured by money—in 1970, the Bureau paid $11,626 to start, a comparative king's ransom above the Secret Service and IRS Intelligence Division starting scale of $6,981; well above the average starting salaries for lawyers in government, $8,462; and one grade above what the CIA offered to candidates with doctoral degrees.

In his book *The Real CIA,* former executive director Lyman B. Kirkpatrick, Jr., touched on the cross-traffic from the FBI to the CIA. At one point, he related, J. Edgar Hoover was invited over to discuss the "less than satisfactory relationship" between the two agencies. It turned out that a prime sore spot with the FBI chief was, in his words, "the former FBI men working for the CIA, who are continually proselytizing FBI men to join them, and criticizing the FBI." Kirkpatrick courteously dropped the matter without speculating on the reasons for the rush from Ninth and Pennsylvania to bucolic Langley, Virginia. In my opinion, the movement to the CIA and other agencies reflected not so much the positive appeal of those agencies as a desire to remain in government in less paranoid surroundings.

Prominent among the scores of ex-agents in local and state law enforcement were Edmund L. McNamara, police commissioner of Boston; Edward J. McCabe, a deputy commissioner of the New York police; E. Wilson Purdy, sheriff of Dade County (Miami) Florida; Joseph I. Woods, the Matt Dillon sheriff of Cook County (Illinois); and Peter J. Pitchess, the debonair sheriff of Los Angeles County. The late Arthur Cornelius, Jr., once SAC in Albany, was named superintendent of the New York state police in 1959 and brought with him a large contingent of Bureau alumni, including former Assistant Director John J. McGuire. This nepotism caused considerable resentment among the troopers. One complained to me about the surfeit of forms and paperwork since Cornelius had taken over, adding, "We even have Hoover's 'loyalty oath'"—the Elbert Hubbard poem.

The series of assassinations that struck down American leaders focused the spotlight on several alumni. Dallas District Attorney Henry Wade was one. Los Angeles District Attorney Evelle J. Younger, whose office prosecuted Sirhan Sirhan for the murder of Robert Kennedy, was another. The first lawyer for James Earl Ray, who at first pleaded guilty to killing Dr. Martin Luther King, Jr., and then tried to retract the plea, was Arthur J. Hanes, who had also been mayor of Birmingham, Alabama; in public statements, Hanes contradicted his former boss by contending that Ray was no more then a pawn in a political conspiracy.

Jim Garrison, the New Orleans D.A. who launched his own probe into a conspiracy in the assassination of John Kennedy, was also a former agent. Once president of the New Orleans chapter of the ex-agent's society, Garrison was the subject of a glowing article in the society's publication *Grapevine* in October 1962 following his upset election the previous spring. "Political patronage and political hacks have vanished from the office," it related, "new security measures have been adopted, the finest legal talent available has been brought into the office, and a full scale drive has been begun against narcotics sellers, armed robbers, and organized crime." No one's election, raved the *Grapevine,* "brought more cheers from fellow X-agents" than did Garrison's.

But somewhere along the line the mutual admiration vanished, for by 1965 he was no longer listed as a member. No matter, for his conspiracy theory in the death of JFK not only diametrically opposed the Director's lone assassin conclusion but involved another member of the ex-agent's society, the late W. Guy Banister. In 1963, Banister, who had retired as SAC in Chicago, was running a private detective bureau in New Orleans. It was located at 544 Camp Street, an address that Lee Harvey Oswald had stamped on pro-Castro literature he had handed out in the summer of 1963. Apparently the link between Banister and Lee Harvey Oswald was the strangely brilliant David W. Ferrie, who was a part-time investigator for Banister. Oddly, in view of Oswald's being a putative Marxist, Banister was a shrill racist affiliated with the paramilitary right-wing Minutemen, and his office was headquarters for some of New Orleans' most militant anti-Castroites. His office was a crossroads for anti-Castro militants and a CIA nerve center for the Bay of Pigs invasion.

The Wackenhut Corporation, a Florida-based investigative firm with a staff of thirty-five hundred (placing it just behind Pinkerton's and Burns in size), was headed by George R. Wackenhut, who turned in his FBI badge in 1954 after three years' service. The company discreetly advertised "Services for Management and the Professions," among which is lie detector testing. The crew-cut, granite-faced Wackenhut, who had a Hoover bust on his desk, was in the news when his firm was hired by incoming Florida Governor Claude Kirk for a privately financed "war on crime"—the arrangement was dropped when Kirk came under fire for using the Wackenhut men as a "private gestapo"—and when Wackenhut himself was depicted as a Birch Society sympathizer. "I'm not the extreme right-wing monster that I've been painted by certain people in the press," he demurred in *Newsweek,* May 1, 1967. "I am nothing more than a full-blooded, pro-American man." The firm's board of directors included other "patriots" such as General Mark W. Clark, former FBI Assistant Director Stanley J. Tracy, and Los Angeles lawyer Loyd Wright, long identified with ultraconservative causes (Wright was a Richard Nixon counsel). The firm put out a monthly *Wackenhut Security Review* that, in language as robust as

Hoover's, exposed the "threat of Communism" in such diverse movements as civil rights and Latin American reform.

Another security and detective firm run by former agents was Dale Simpson & Associates of Dallas, which numbered many oil firms among its clients. Still another, a franchise and information-sharing operation, was Fidelifacts. Billing itself as a "National Organization of Ex-FBI Agents," it had twenty-two offices throughout the country manned by two hundred former G-men. A New York City operative, Vincent W. Gillen, hit the front pages in 1966 when hearings before a government committee revealed that he had been hired by General Motors to spy on auto safety critic Ralph Nader.

The "security" or "industrial relations" departments of large corporations were prime employers of ex-FBI men. The American Society for Industrial Security estimated that one quarter of the 750,000 men in the business in 1970 had shifted over from the government. While Bureau alumni constitute only a small fraction of that vast army, they hold the top-layer positions. The security chiefs of Texas Instruments of Dallas, Lockheed at Sunnyvale, California, the giant Wynn-Dixie supermarket chain, and Reynolds Metals Company, to name only a few, were former Hoover minions.

The alumni were also well represented in Congress. Titular head of the delegation was Senator Thomas J. Dodd, and members included H. Allen Smith of California, William T. Cahill of New Jersey, Samuel L. Devine of Ohio, Ed Edmondson of Oklahoma, Omar Burleson of Texas, and Don Edwards of California. All were considered conservatives except Edwards, who was an officer of the Americans for Democratic Action and active in Senator Eugene McCarthy's presidential campaign. And all were members of the ex-agent's society—except Edwards. In 1963, Burleson, as chairman of the House Administrative Committee, locked horns with columnist Jack Anderson, the Drew Pearson partner, over allegations of congressional payroll padding. When Anderson insisted on protecting his informants, just as the Bureau did, Burleson abruptly adjourned the hearing. Smith is the Congressman who introduced the nepotistic bill that would have made it mandatory for the next FBI director to come from the inside, and the *Grapevine* enthusiastically endorsed it.

Probably the best-known of the right-wing propagandists among the alumni was Howard D. (Dan) Smoot of Dallas, who published *The Dan Smoot Report* and was heard and seen on a radio and television network reaching millions. Also prominent was W. Cleon Skousen of Salt Lake City, who wrote *The Naked Communist* and appeared frequently as a fire-breathing lecturer on the Birch Society banquet circuit.

The American Security Council (ASC), set up by ex-agents in 1955, did more than spout anti-Communist rhetoric. An ASC pamphlet boasted that it had "seven major files and libraries on Communism and statism. It has the largest private files on Communism in this country." Although ASC denied keeping files on individuals as such, it reportedly indexed the names of one million persons and groups suspected of leftist activity. This massive accumulation had been assembled by purchasing the files of *The American Vigilante,* a defunct anti-Semitic periodical; from the records of a number of corporations that went Red-hunting in their plants; and from the hearings of state and congressional "antisubversive" committees. Some idea of what activities arrested ASC's vigilant eye can be gained from the statement of President John W. Fisher, an FBI agent from 1947 to 1953; "Interest for or against the free enterprise system—that's the thing that starts our interest. If the situation is in line with the current Communist Party line, then it becomes of interest to us."

The ASC files actually served as a blacklist, for some twenty-nine hundred corporations assertedly subscribed to ASC's "services." A charter subscriber was Sears Roebuck, whose chairman General Robert E. Wood, a prime mover in the old *America First* isolationist organization and frequent supporter of radical right causes, helped ASC get started. Such industrial titans as Illinois Central Railroad, Motorola, Stewart-Warner, and United States Steel also subscribed. Other former G-men in the ASC hierarchy included Operating Director Jack E. Ison, Research Director William K. Lambie, Jr., and W. Cleon Skousen, who was a field director. Among the advisory officers were ex-agents Kenneth M. Piper, the senior vice president who was personnel director at Motorola; Stephen L. Donchess, a vice president who was a United States Steel executive; and Russell E. White, another VP who was an industrial security consultant with General Electric.

The fact that the overwhelming majority of the alumni didn't put in full careers with the most prestigious law enforcement agency in the world indicated some degree of disenchantment with Hoover and/or his organization. But scarcely any criticized either openly—it simply wasn't good business to knock the institution whose prestige could be converted into earning power. This was brought home to me when a retired SAC, Richard Auerbach, whom I had known telephoned. A group of former agents had been discussing my articles, he said, and while they agreed that the ones on police science were excellent, they disapproved of those critical of the FBI. "Why?" I asked. "Well," he replied, "the boys don't think you can hurt the Bureau, but you can hurt them." "How?" I wanted to know. "In the pocketbook," was the answer.

•

On the logo of the Society of Former Special Agents of the FBI are the words "Loyalty—Goodwill—Friendship." With a full-time staff at national headquarters in the Statler-Hilton Hotel in New York, the society strived to make this motto a reality for its nearly five thousand members.

Founded in 1937, the society achieved its most rapid growth in the 1960s. For a nominal ten-dollar initiation fee and a like amount in annual dues, it offered a number of advantages. There were the customary group insurance plan and group travel arrangements. There was the camaraderie afforded by local chapter meetings, the national convention each October, and the postconvention excursion to exotic resorts. And of course the slick *Grapevine* and a chatty newsletter.

There was also a committee called "Executive Services," which was a placement bureau with national facilities as well as local chairmen. It seemed to do well by its clients: the newsletter of July 18, 1969, reported that it had "placed 39 Society members with an average salary of $19,750." The Society Foundation, administered by a thirteen-man executive committee, pushed heartily for member contributions in order "to attract outside contributions from major corporations and foundations." In fact, it was suggested that members who found jobs through Executive Services "will want to make an extraordinary contribution to the Foundation."

Despite the levity over the miniature busts of Hoover procurable through the society, their sale was brisk, as was the sale of copies of *J. Edgar Hoover on Communism*, an anthology of the Director's monologues on the Menace. "Personally, I have received many thank you letters from men to whom I have given copies," the 1969 president of the society, a Los Angeles banker, told his fellow alumni. "Several of them have commented that it is an excellent source of quotations that they use in their speeches. For the reduced price of $2.75 each, we cannot afford to miss this book for our own library and it certainly is a valuable business development and/or community relations gift for any businessman or professional man."

The society was quite insistent that no iconoclasts violate its ranks. There were a few applicants, "involuntarily separated" from the Bureau, who were admitted, but their sins were not of heresy. The society selected on the blackball principle. A list of applicants was circulated among the membership with the instruction that members "carefully study" it and pass on "any information bearing adversely upon the character or reputation of any of the applicants which you believe would render them unfit for membership in the Society."

One of the society's most excruciating moments came in 1967, when one of its members in good standing, Norman T. Ollestad, wrote *Inside the FBI*. Like many members of the society, the young Californian had spent only a year in the Bureau before resigning. But the book was, as its dust jacket proclaims, one that "FBI agents will buy and read in secret, publicly disown and privately cheer." That is, it stripped some veneer from the legend. The society's duty was plain: Ollestad was expelled for writing a book "detrimental to the good name or best interest of the Society."

To Ollestad, a capable young attorney whose eyes were to the future, the expulsion may have been of no more import than being drummed out of the Book of the Month Club. In fact the FBI went further than its alumni, trying to block Ollestad's hiring by the Southern Pacific Railroad's legal department. Alan Furth, the SP's vice president-legal, told me that Bureau officials tried to interfere but he replied that he hired on the basis of capability.

But many of the older members who served in the headier days before World War II were quite nostalgia-stricken, and to them the legend was the reality.

They defended the legend as if any swipe at it were a call to arms. In 1964, *Life*'s reporter-at-large Loudon Wainwright questioned the ongoing value of the Hoover cult. "The trouble with this deification of Mr. Hoover is that the FBI gets lost in all the flack about its Director," he wrote, suggesting that neither the Bureau nor its boss "would suffer much from a separation. A new man might spend more time improving the FBI than praising or defending it."

This sacrilegious talk prompted a reply in the form of a letter to the editor over the signature of Emmett C. McGaughey, a Los Angeles advertising executive then president of the society. Attributing the low turnover rate to the inspirational leadership of the Director, McGaughey (who had been a seven-year man) rhapsodized:

> The amalgam that binds the agents of the FBI to the bureau is Mr. Hoover and his leadership. He is also the amalgam that binds the 4,600 members of our organization together in our devotion to each other, to the Federal Bureau of Investigation, and to Mr. Hoover, whose life is the fulfillment of the motto of the FBI: fidelity, bravery, integrity.

When I wrote an article for the March 1964 issue of *Saga* illuminating internal problems that may have kept the Bureau from preventing President Kennedy's assassination, including friction with the Secret Service, the magazine received a generally favorable response—with one searing exception. An angry Wichita, Kansas, man called the piece "nonsensical and irresponsible" and an "attempt to capitalize on a most unfortunate incident at the expense of the greatest law enforcement agency and the most outstanding law enforcement officer, Director Hoover." The sweeping superlatives seemed familiar. Although he didn't say so, the author of the letter had been an agent from 1937 to 1941 and was, predictably, a member of the society.

Taking up the cudgel was in fact a pattern among members of the society. When former agent Jack Levine loosed his broadside against Hoover and the Bureau in 1962, the society's Leonard R. Viner wrote an across-the-board rebuttal that was published in the *New York Times* on November 10 of that year. Although Viner, a Washington diaperwash executive, didn't say so, he hadn't been in the Bureau much longer than Levine, and at that had served during World War II, which newer agents who had fought in the war considered draft dodging.

In 1962, Edward Bennett Williams's book *One Man's Freedom,* in arguing for pretrial discovery, cited the Kathyrn Kelly case in which an exculpating report had been suppressed. One Lewis G. Bernstein wrote a published letter to the editor of the *Saturday Evening Post,* which had serialized the book, flatly declaring: "The FBI does not suppress evidence which it secures in its investigations but turns it over completely to the United States Attorney who will be prosecuting the case. If there was any suppression it was by the United States Attorney rather than by the Federal Bureau of Investigation." This, of course, begged the question of whether the USA ever even saw the FBI's report. Since Bernstein described himself merely as a New York attorney, giving the impression he was a neutral observer, I checked into him. It turned out that he had been an FBI agent from 1928 to 1931, three years before the Kelly case happened. He was also a founding member of the society. At the time his letter to the *Post* ran, he was also the author of an article in the *Grapevine* captioned: "G-Men Cut Gangsters Down to Size in Blazing 1920's." Reminiscing that the public had once held a perverse admiration for the gangsters, he related that the picture changed when "the FBI stepped in with brilliant detective work and undaunted courage under the matchless leadership of J. Edgar Hoover."

At that, Bernstein's version of history may eventually prevail, thanks in no small part to the energetic drum-beating of the Society of Former Special Agents of the FBI. Which shows that you can take the man out of the FBI, but you can't always take the FBI out of the man.

EPILOGUE 1970

Men born to freedom are naturally alert to repel
invasion of their liberty by evil-minded rulers. The
greatest dangers to liberty lurk in the insidious
encroachment by men of zeal, well-meaning but
without understanding.

—Justice Louis Brandeis

A recent Conrad cartoon in the *Los Angeles Times* showed a
bulldog tagged "J. Edgar Hoover" chasing a scrawny black cat
labeled "Black Panthers" past a window in which several
cigar-smoking large cats—organized crime—were looking on amus-
edly. The caption: "There are cats and there are fat cats. . . ."*

Author's note: This epilogue was originally Chapter Eighteen: The Future? of
the 1970 edition of *Hoover's FBI.* As in the Foreword to the 1970 edition, I
have not changed the tense. The speculations contained in this epilogue represent my concerns about the future of the Bureau before J. Edgar Hoover's death.

*On June 4, 1969, heavily armed FBI agents conducted a predawn raid on the
Chicago headquarters of the Black Panther Party, arresting eight persons.
Although the Bureau contended it was seeking a fugitive, no fugitive was found
and charges against the eight for harboring a fugitive were later dropped. On July
15, 1969, in his report on the previous fiscal year, J. Edgar Hoover declared that
of the militant black groups in the United States, "the Black Panther Party, without question, represents the greatest threat to the internal security of the country."
In December 1969, only days apart, the Chicago and Los Angeles police mounted
predawn raids against Panther headquarters in their respective cities. The raids
were marked by heavy gunfire, and in the Chicago raid two Panthers, including
Illinois leader Fred Hampton, Jr., were killed. The series of raids, coupled with the
fact that Hampton was shot while sleeping in bed, raised the specter of a concerted law enforcement pogrom against the Panthers. A number of moderate organizations, including black groups not sympathetic to the Panthers, demanded an
investigation, and an ad hoc commission of inquiry was set up headed by former
Supreme Court justice and United Nations ambassador Arthur Goldberg.

The cartoon graphically illustrates the false set of priorities Hoover has employed during his lengthy directorship. For nearly four decades, he stuck his head in the sand while the crime syndicates, plainly a federal problem, waxed fat. By the time Robert Kennedy forced him into action, the Bureau's belated and less-than-wholehearted efforts hardly fazed the organized crime moguls. So politically and economically entrenched had they become that the Nixon administration, in sizing up the administration, despairs of any clear-cut victory over them.

Yet there was always the Crime Menace. When Hoover caused the populace to cringe with warnings about the criminal "horde larger than any of the barbarian hosts that overran Europe and Asia in ancient times," and the "massive avalanche of crime," he was not talking about the organized fat cats but about the mean and petty criminals, the psychopaths, the desperate and the damned so well represented in our prison population. And while crime grew, so did the FBI. As the G-men set up one "Public Enemy" straw man after another and knocked it down, Hoover was St. George slaying the monstrous dragon.

On the subversion front, the Director's rhetoric has been equally lurid and doomsday. One specter after another materialized to imperil the Republic: the radical syndicalists and anarchists of the 1920s, the sly Reds and wild Wobblies of the 1930s, the Moscow-puppeted American Communist Party after the war, "interlocking subversion" in government during the McCarthy epoch, and then Communist infiltration of the civil rights and peace movements. Of late it has been the campus militants, epitomized by the Students for a Democratic Society, and the black nationalists, exemplified by the Black Panthers. But the country has survived Hoover's past "crises," and it will somehow survive the SDS and the Panthers.

It may not long survive the corruptive ravages of organized crime, however, nor the impetus toward a police state that has been supplied by Hoover in his overweening ambition. The words of Arthur S. Miller of the National Law Center, who sees a national police force "to be either in being or in the making," are worth repeating: "At some time the FBI will be recognized as a national police force—in fact if not in theory."

The trend is now so well established that it is doubtful whether even Hoover, if he were so inclined, could reverse it. The nucleus of any secret police is a collection of raw files concerning the private lives of hundreds of thousands of citizens, and this the Bureau has. And it is growing day by day, fed by personnel inquiries, electronic eavesdropping, and unsolicited gossip. Does the FBI scruple to use these files in underhanded ways? The whisper campaign against Martin Luther King, Jr., answers that with an emphatic no. In 1967, Senator Joseph S. Clark of Pennsylvania warned that the FBI posed a "major threat to the successful survival of American democracy." Speaking on the radio program "Reporter's Roundup," he declared that the danger was "evidence by recent disclosures in the newspapers of the FBI and the threat they pose to the privacy of the individual citizen and the further threat they pose by way of blackmail, direct or indirect, or anybody who has the effrontery to say anything unkind about Mr. J. Edgar Hoover."

It is inevitable that the FBI's massive dossier depository will eventually be automated, so that its contents will be available at the push of a button. A step in that direction is the FBI's National Crime Information Center, a computerized storage and retrieval bank storing data contributed by the nation's police departments. Gradually being tied into police networks around the country, its stated aims are, of course, beneficial. For instance, an officer in the field can determine by radio within a minute or two whether the man he has in custody is wanted anywhere else. But the ominous part is that the police and the FBI are prying more and more into the area of political dissent under the guise of "crime" investigation, so that what goes into this center, coupled with data in the raw files, may well spawn a national thought police.

The "seeds" of such a force were perceived by Louis M. Kohlmeier in the *Wall Street Journal,* October 15, 1968. "Even now, the FBI is elite and secretive," he noted. "If it isn't being used for suppression, it clearly is investigating dissent and potential insurrection," infiltrating not only militant groups but also "not-so-militant groups like the National Association for the Advancement of Colored People." as Kohlmeier saw it, the Bureau "is a police force, and it is national, even if spread rather thin. Its agents have badges, carry arms, and make arrests. Every county in the U.S. is assigned to one of the FBI's 58 field offices and their 500 'outpost' agencies."

Unfortunately, Congress as a whole seems not to have recognized what is happening and keeps adding more jurisdiction to that already possessed by the FBI. At present, the agency has the power to act under more than 170 statues and executive orders, a far cry from the tidy outfit Hoover began with. Despite his protests that he would have liked to see the FBI kept within limits, the Director hasn't yet petitioned Congress to relieve the Bureau of outmoded jurisdiction.

Just as it has increasingly fortified its position to this point, the FBI seems to be winning the fight to take over exclusively the training of local police, a step that will give it more effective control over the nation's police system. The 1968 Crime Control Act empowered the Bureau to train local and state police in any way and any place it wants, to expand the FBI National Academy, and, through its laboratory, to "develop new techniques, systems, equipment and devices to strengthen law enforcement." Concomitantly, of course, these new powers strengthen the FBI's hegemony over law enforcement. Already, a $15 million expansion program is under way at Quantico that will increase the capacity from two hundred to more than twelve hundred officers a year for the full course, and allow an additional one thousand officers a year to take shorter specialized courses. Further evidence of the FBI's increasing domination over local police forces came in 1967, when the Bureau distributed thirty-two thousand copies of its booklet *Prevention and Control of Mobs and Riots** (written by the military police). The same year, Hoover pushed harder to assume overall control in the field by inviting representatives from the major departments to attend a mob and riot control demonstration at Fort Belvoir, Virginia, under the direction of the provost marshal general; some six hundred attended, representing three hundred departments.

---

*In recognition of the army's role, Hoover in May 1967 presented a special award to Major General Carl C. Turner "in appreciation of his valuable assistance to the FBI." Since retired, Turner in 1969 came under fire during a Senate probe into alleged irregularities in the handling of service club funds and his selling of guns seized in the course of rioting.

For fiscal 1970, Hoover has asked for—and gotten, with the endorsement of President Nixon—a $233 million appropriation a hike of $13.2 million at a time when other agencies are being trimmed back. This whopping budget, over double that of 1960, has allowed the addition of 525 more agents and 336 more clerks, bringing the work force to a record 17,345.* Symbolizing the permanence of the rapid buildup is the huge new eleven-story FBI headquarters now under construction at Tenth and Pennsylvania. Asymmetrical in design, it will contain two million square feet of space and, in the FBI's words, "expanded tour facilities enabling an increasing number of visitors to tour FBI headquarters." When the structure is completed in 1973, FBI autonomy will be a physical as well as an administrative fact.

Is there any chance at this late date of disarming this incipient police-state apparatus?

The FBI monolith is Hoover's legacy, and it would be sheer folly to deed it in perpetuity to the "insiders" who for so long have been the instruments of his policies. Like the Director, most have had little or no experience in the field, with the result that they exercise tremendous power in a near-vacuum. Like him, most are law enforcement troglodytes, standing foursquare against enlightened progress. In 1967, Hoover, through Cartha DeLoach, brought pressure to bear on the President's National Crime Commission not to recommend the liberalization of marijuana laws and provide outside review of police conduct. After Chicago 1968, it was Hoover who declared Mayor Richard Daley's police blameless, the same Hoover who has always looked the other way when members of that force and others have been on the take from organized crime. As *Life* observed in an editorial on January 24, 1969, the FBI chief is part of the problem in that his "continuation symbolizes to many, particularly the young, official unresponsiveness to the challenges of today."

---

*Apparently the recruiting problems that have beset the FBI in recent years continue. In reporting the new authorized strength, the *New York Times* on July 8, 1969, said the "bureau has been searching also for language specialists and physical science majors, and earlier this year, three of the 23 teachers at the Winnemucca, Nev., High School were recruited."

But the appointment of a more responsive director from the out-side would be only a stopgap measure. It is the organization itself, benign of image on the one hand, fraught with dangerous power on the other, that must be redesigned. If we shed popular assumptions about the FBI and go back to the beginning, we find that the agency was designed simply to investigate those areas not specifically under the jurisdiction of other agencies. In other words, it was to be an auxiliary force. I believe it is time to revert to that original concept.

In considering this move, one discovers that there would most likely be collateral advantages in terms of efficiency.

In today's specialized world, the FBI is too inflexible and bureaucratic to handle with ease the multiplicity of duties now assigned to it. It is essentially a federal anticrime force, and its prime efforts might most profitably be directed toward cracking the orga-nized crime menace. With the twin objectives of streamlining its operation in this field and reducing its police-state potential, I would propose the following changes:

Police services. The centralization of police services in the hands of a federal agency is contrary to the traditional American principle of dispersion of police powers. The Identification Division should revert to the local police, who are, after all, its most frequent users. The fingerprint file could then be run as a separate entity by, say, the IACP, with operational funds supplied under the Law Enforce-ment Assistance Act. Similarly, police training and laboratory ser-vices should be placed under the collective management of the local departments, again with the help of federal funds. This would strip the FBI of its control over the nation's police system and place the Bureau in its intended auxiliary role.

Civil rights. As early as November 12, 1962, Dr. Martin Luther King, Jr., took note of the inherent conflict of interest faced by the Bureau in this field: "One of the greatest problems we face with the FBI in the South is that the agents are white Southerners who have been influenced by the mores of the community. To maintain their status, they have to be friendly with the local police and people who are promoting segregation." The same year the Southern Regional Council, composed of whites and blacks, issued a report sharply critical of the FBI's performance. The report's author, Dr. Howard

Zinn, a professor at Spelman College in Atlanta, commented that he had found "a considerable amount of distrust" of the Bureau among blacks, one of whom called the agents "a bunch of racists." Then he made the point: "Whether true or not, this is the feeling of many Negroes who have had contact with the FBI, and, even if distorted, it is a general reflection of the efficacy of the FBI's role in the area of civil rights."*

In July 1964, shortly after the three civil rights workers later found slain had disappeared, Hoover threw Deep South blacks a sop by opening a field office in Jackson, Mississippi. But the Director, who personally presided over the opening ceremony, made it very clear that not much would change. His guests were not black leaders, but Mississippi Governor Paul B. Johnson and a gaggle of state and local officials. And he commented, "We most certainly do not and will not give protection to civil rights workers. In the first place, the FBI is not a police organization. It is purely an investigative organization." Protection, he said, was strictly the prerogative of local authorities.

On August 24, 1965. Joseph L. Rauh, Jr., vice chairman of Americans for Democratic Action, proposed that a special agency be created to take over from the FBI in civil rights investigations. Rauh contended that the FBI was inadequate, alluding to public statements made by Hoover that were "replete with hostility toward the civil rights movement." I would second the motion, for reasons broader than Rauh's. Civil rights violations are not limited to the South, as an incident during the Patterson riots of 1967 shows. A citizens' committee produced evidence that during the height of the disturbances, eight Patterson police officers had wantonly damaged black-owned business property. The committee could not interest the local FBI in the matter, and indictments against the eight were obtained only after the evidence was taken directly to the Department of Justice Civil Rights Division in Washington.

---

*Emblematic of such distrust was a cartoon in *Student Voice,* a publication of the SNCC, showing a man in a snap-brim hat and carrying a briefcase captioned, "J. Edgar Standby (Federal Officer)." The man is asking: "Well, murder in this case is a local matter. Would you like to contend that the sheriff denied this Negro his civil rights in killing him?"

Moreover, there is the ageless and compelling question of who will police the police, in this case the FBI. At present, the Bureau may not be above reproach, but it is beyond recourse. Take as an example the case of Anthony Polisi, owner of a Brooklyn motel. On September 30, 1965, FBI agents arrested two men registered at the motel and charged them with belonging to a bank robbery ring. The agents also questioned Polisi, who had no criminal record and denied any knowledge of the men's activities. On October 4, Polisi claimed, four FBI agents picked him up at his motel and drove him to a secluded area:

> The agent in the front passenger seat turned around and kneeling on the seat grabbed my tie and pulled it tight choking me, he said, "You ——, you'll talk today or you're a dead man" while he was pulling my tie, the agent on my left held my left hand and was pulling my hair, they said, "Give us the information or we'll kill you." They kept asking about guns and where did I have them. Every time I told them I didn't know anything about any guns they put more pressure on my fingers and pulled tighter on my tie. I asked them if they knew what they were doing, that I had a heart condition, the agent in front who was holding my tie said, "Good, we'll give you an attack right now" and started to punch me in the area of my heart. . . . I told them they had made a mistake and had the wrong man and begged them to stop before they had a corpse on their hands, when I said this he again punched me three or four times in the same spot, the agent on my left punched me in my face with his left.
>
> . . . The agent on my left took his gun out and put it to my temple, said "Tell us where the guns are or you're a dead ——," the agent on my right still bending my fingers back said, "If you want to see your grandchildren again you better talk." I told them the only thing I could say was that I was being tortured as much as Jesus Christ, the agent on my left said "What kind of Catholic are you?" and again punched me in the face. . . . The driver kept saying to let him do it his way, let me get out and run away so they could shoot me trying to escape. . . . They said "Oh you

won't get out huh, we'll get you out" the agent on my right
opened the door and started to pull me out while the agent
on my left pushed, the agent in front was pulling me by my
tie towards the door. I tripped over the floor hump and they
dragged me out onto the ground, told me to get up and run,
they were punching and kicking me while I was lying there.
Someone tried to pick me up by my hair while two others
took my arms, after standing they were pushing me away
from the car telling me to run, they were pointing their guns
at me. By this time I was completely terrorfied [sic] and
begged them to leave me.

. . . They pushed me back into the car, and started back
towards the hotel. They told me that if I said anything to
anybody about what happened they would put me and my
son in jail for life, my grandchildren would have a father
and grandfather in prison, and we would never see them or
our wives again. They said that they would get us one way
or another even if they had to plant something in the hotel
or put a sack of dope in my pocket. . . . They pushed me out
of the car and drove away fast. . . . I had severe pains in my
chest and blacked out, the next thing I remember is hearing
my son calling for an ambulance.

A Jamaica Hospital emergency report shows Polisi's injuries to
have been the classic ones of a man "worked over." After being
released from the hospital, he reported the alleged beating to the
106th precinct. In a letter to the Queens County Attorney, Polisi's
attorney protested that the detective to whom the matter was
reported advised the next day that "the FBI denies any knowledge
or implications on any assault of him and that *his complaint should
be lodged with the FBI*" [italics added].

The attorney demanded, properly, that the district attorney rectify this ludicrous situation by investigating and prosecuting "an
alleged felony in your county." There was no reply. But two days
later, the FBI obtained two indictments charging Polisi and his son
with purportedly conspiring with the two motel guests to commit
bank robbery. Polisi was convicted on the testimony of the actual

robbers, whose stories were replete with perjury. He was sentenced to fifteen years, and went to prison still protesting both the beating and his innocence.

Did FBI agents severely beat Polisi? Did they then protect their own groin by throwing a "cover charge" (in this case conspiracy) at him, a common police practice in the United States? The frightening aspect of the case is that no one in authority—and Polisi appealed to the mayor, the governor, and just about every other police official—would dare to investigate his serious allegation of lawless law enforcement on the part of the FBI. And I doubt that officials of other states in a similar situation would be any more courageous.

Hence the dire need for an independent federal agency that will not only vigorously probe civil rights complaints, but will police our federal police.

Security and counterespionage. The United States is the only major power that places both criminal and security responsibilities under a single roof. The FBI was shaped as a criminal investigative force and that it should remain. But its strong ideological bias and lack of sophistication rendered it eminently unfit for the delicate task of conducting antisubversion inquiries in a democracy. Again, the creation of a separate agency, with no political axe to grind and no penchant for overblowing menaces to enhance its own importance, is the logical answer. This same agency could assume counterspy functions, a natural collateral to security inquiries that requires a much lighter hand and more finesse than the Bureau has displayed.

Finally, there is the matter of outside inspection. Only the FBI and the CIA are immune from the quizzical eye of the General Accounting Office, and Congress has never really exercised its duty to look searchingly at the agency's operations and policies. Congressman T. J. Dulski once quipped, "The FBI is like a convent—we don't know what's going on in there for sure." A sorry pass, and one that must be remedied.

Back during the Coolidge administration, when J. Edgar Hoover took over, no one envisioned the FBI of today. No safeguards were installed, no effective checks were put on the Director's ambitions. The only solution now is to turn back the clock, conceptually speaking, to 1924. If we do not, the FBI may soon advance us to *1984*.

EPILOGUE 1993

On April 30, 1972, I completed a lecture tour on *Hoover's FBI* with a stop at the State University of New York at Cobleskill. When I went to bed that night at the local hotel I tossed and turned. So I arose before dawn, drove to Albany, and caught the first plane out headed in the direction of home. When I got in my car at the San Francisco airport a radio news bulletin announced, "Flags in Washington are at half-staff for"—I wondered what celebrity had died—"J. Edgar Hoover." He had died in his sleep that night. It was, ironically, May Day, the international Communist holiday.

My first emotion was relief, the kind of lifting of the spirit that comes with the end of an oppressive regime. The second was apprehension that someone as hard-line as Cartha DeLoach would be named Director. In fact there were press pundits who bet even money that Richard Nixon would name DeLoach. When DeLoach had retired two years earlier at the minimum age of 50 he moved to a cushy post at Pepsi-Cola, which was headed by Nixon's longtime ally Donald Kendall. Some even thought that DeLoach was in a holding pattern at Pepsi, so he could land in the Director's office as a kind of inside-outer. It was a nightmarish thought. Even conservative columnists Rowland Evans and Robert Novak had been moved to observe, on June 14, 1970, that had "DeLoach ever succeeded Hoover (as seemed quite probable a few years ago), the charges against him of right-wing bias and blatant opportunism would have racked and possibly wrecked the FBI."

But President Nixon appointed an outsider, L. Patrick Gray III, a retired Navy submarine commander who was personally loyal to him. Gray immediately began reforms. The first woman agent came on board. Blacks became agents in fact, not mannequins in Hoover's store window. Other minorities were admitted. The dress and grooming code was modified to fit the times. Weight rules were laxed. Gray visited every field office except Honolulu and conversed with ordinary agents, a refreshing contrast with Hoover's pomposity.

As soon as the new openness became apparent, agents and even their wives barraged Gray with accusations of impropriety against top officials on their own enemies list. Their letters were actually signed—the days of the anonymous letter were gone. Gray ordered an investigation, and before long John Mohr and Thomas Bishop, who had succeeded DeLoach as head of Crime Records, were out the door. Nor were the more detested field officials spared. SACs Robert Kunkel of the Washington Field Office and Richard Rogge of Honolulu were replaced, and Wesley Grapp of Los Angeles was forced into retirement.

The ousting of Grapp was especially satisfying to the agent corps. Gray's inquiry determined that he had bugged his own agents and had dispatched an agent whose sideburns were deemed too long on a nonsurveillance into the Mohave Desert in summer without an air-conditioned car. Gray busted Grapp from SAC and transferred him to Minneapolis as an ordinary agent. Roger "Frenchy" LaJeunesse, a senior Los Angeles agent, called ahead to find out what preparations had been made for Grapp's arrival. "Don't worry, Frenchy," his Minneapolis counterpart told him. "When Grapp gets here he's being sent on a long road trip to North Dakota. It's cold as hell now and his car won't have a heater." Evidently aware of the fate that awaited him, Grapp never showed up; he had his attorney negotiate an early retirement. But when he tried to join the Society of Former Special Agents of the FBI, he was blackballed. His old Bureau rabbi John Mohr lobbied to get him admitted, but the door stayed closed.

L. Patrick Gray didn't last long, becoming, after only fifty-four weeks, a collateral-damage victim of Watergate. He remained intensely loyal to Nixon, burning the contents of Howard Hunt's safe and otherwise thwarting the Watergate probe. But at his Senate confirmation hearing he developed a case of loose lips that started unraveling the cover-up, and, as counsel John Dean was heard to say on White House tapes, "Let him twist slowly, slowly in the wind." The dumping of Gray was cheered by the FBI old guard, who had dubbed him "Tattletale Gray" because of his modest reforms and had missed no opportunity to torpedo him.

In seeking a successor Dean asked W. Mark Felt, who had been Gray's Associate Director, what the reaction would be should William Sullivan be named. The feisty Irish egghead had had a rollercoaster career as the Bureau's resident expert on Communism. He had composed the notorious anonymous letter to Martin Luther King, Jr., suggesting he commit suicide. On the other hand he flatly told Hoover that the Ku Klux Klan was much more a threat to the domestic tranquillity of the country than the Communist Party, which wasn't exactly music to the Director's ears. Close to the Nixon administration, Sullivan was on standby when in July 1971 Nixon summoned Hoover with the intention of firing him. Assistant attorney general Robert Mardikian recaptured the moment for Sullivan: "Goddamn, Nixon lost his guts. He had Hoover there in his office, he knew what he was supposed to tell him, but he got cold feet." At this point the Bureau was not big enough for both Hoover and Sullivan, who in a confrontation told the FBI chief, "I think you'd be doing the country a great service if you retired." It was the kind of straight talk Hoover wasn't used to hearing, and he labeled Sullivan a Judas. "I'm not a Judas, Mr. Hoover," Sullivan shot back, "and you certainly aren't Jesus Christ."

For Dean to have solicited Mark Felt's opinion on Sullivan was like asking George Bush what he thinks of Saddam Hussein. The handsome Felt had been Hoover's Golden Boy with a reputation as his number-one hatchetman in the last years. Felt had his own designs on the directorship. So when Dean approached him, he savaged Sullivan as a director who would create "chaos" in the Bureau.

If by chaos Felt meant that Sullivan would clean house, he was undoubtedly correct. Sullivan had changed from the man who a few years earlier had reacted angrily at Cornell University when his speech on the Communist menace was interrupted by students chanting, "We want Bill Turner." After he left the Bureau he declared, in one of several conversations with me, "You know, Bill, the way these big corporations are corrupting this country would make a socialist out of you." (On the early morning of November 9, 1977, Sullivan was shot to death near his rural New Hampshire home by the son of a state police official who said he mistook him for a deer.)

Sullivan didn't get the nod—but neither did Felt. Nixon appointed another outsider, former EPA chief William Ruckelshaus, as acting Director. He arrived at his desk to find a copy of a telegram to the president in which all the Bureau brass and SACs except one urged the appointment of someone from "within the organization." The telegram had been engineered by Felt, who hoped to be its beneficiary. When Ruckelshaus summoned the 59 SACs to Washington and laid down his policies, Felt immediately caucused the group, making no secret of his contempt for the new Director and comparing him unfavorably with Hoover.

When Ruckelshaus caught Felt leaking stories to the press promoting his own candidacy, there was a clash that ended with Felt submitting his resignation. To his surprise Ruckelshaus accepted it. But after only two months Ruckelshaus, unsullied by Watergate, submitted his own resignation to advance his political career.

This time Nixon appointed Clarence Kelley, who had been an FBI agent for 21 years before becoming Kansas City police chief. I had known Kelley, a square-jawed Dick Tracy type, in Seattle, and regarded him as decent and capable. But there was a question of whether he had the will and savvy to deal with the old guard of top-level executives, bureaucrats, and senior field officials who had been personally selected by Hoover because they fit his mold. Kelly's first move was hardly encouraging. He elevated Nicholas P. Callahan, a charter member of the "Mohr clique," to second in command. Soon word spread that while Kelley was busy mending fences with the media to try to restore the FBI image, Mohr was actually running the Bureau by remote control, consulting with Callahan almost daily by phone.

The old guard's intractability was illustrated when a press aide whom Kelley had brought along from Kansas City, William Ellingsworth, was ostracized and subjected to a whispering campaign. Ellingsworth resigned with a blast at the Hoover loyalists, saying, "They wanted a public-relations program. I wanted a public-information program." Then Kelley's naïveté surfaced. He confidently told a Senate committee that the FBI kept no dossiers on members of Congress, only to have the news break afterwards that there were scores of dossiers amounting to what the *Washington Post* called "a pile of cancer."

And on an ABC television documentary aired in 1975 he suggested that a file cabinet labeled "Security Index" spotted by ABC people in the FBI building might have something to do with criminal matters. But what the cabinet actually contained were the names of some fifteen thousand American citizens to be rounded up as subversives in the event of a national emergency. That wasn't all. Kelley steadfastly maintained that FBI burglaries ceased in 1966 on Hoover's orders, only to find that they had continued into his directorship. "I was lied to," Kelley fumed, conceding he could not guarantee that the burglaries were not still going on.

During Kelley's watch the Church committee discovered a raft of rogue-elephant abuses, illegalities, and immoralities committed by the FBI, and set about installing checks so that they would not be repeated. In a speech on the subject, Kelley acknowledged that "these activities were clearly wrong and quite indefensible." Although he was merely stating the obvious, the hardcore Hooverites holding sway in the Society of Former Special Agents of the Federal Bureau of Investigation created such an uproar that Kelley felt compelled to issue a "clarification." They had of course a commercial interest in preserving a myth, but there were also some true believers. "These guys have lived the lie so long," a dissenting ex-agent griped, "they actually believe it."

Since Kelley retired in 1978 the post of Director has been held by two former federal judges, William Webster and William Sessions. Both are no-nonsense men of probity and commitment, but certainly not visionaries. They have had no need to empire-build because there is now a term limit of ten years to prevent the rise of another Hoover. But vestiges of Hooverism remain. In 1988 it was revealed that Webster, encouraged by the Reagan administration's softening of Church committee guidelines, authorized the investigation and surveillance of more than a thousand individuals and organizations opposed to Reagan's aid to the *contras* in Nicaragua and propping up of the "death squad" regime in El Salvador. The targets included the Maryknoll Sisters, the United Auto Workers, and the National Council of Churches.

Under Sessions a lawsuit filed by Hispanic agents to open up promotional opportunities was settled to the advantage of the plaintiffs, but a vicious campaign against a black agent remains an ugly scar. Racist agents in the Chicago office forged the signature of Donald Rochon on a death and dismemberment policy, pasted a photo of an ape over his son in a family portrait, drowned a black doll in effigy, and ordered delivery of unwanted merchandise to his home. When Rochon complained, he was censured. And when one of the harassing agents confessed and was suspended for two weeks, his colleagues took up a collection to cover his salary loss. As Rochon's attorney Patricia Motto put it after repeatedly failing to get the FBI to do anything but wrist-slap the offending agents, "You start to feel like you're fencing with Hoover's ghost."

The Hoover wraith. It still stalks the corridors of the fittingly monolithic J. Edgar Hoover Building. Although his old guard has faded away, their progeny live on. As of now there is a bit of schizophrenia: those who dream of a neo-Hoover regime, those who want to exorcise forever the Hoover legacy.

Personally, I am encouraged that the Hoover legacy can be finally put to rest. An assistant director under Hoover, Charles Bates, invited me to lunch to deplore the excesses that the FBI had indulged in against me. Scores of former agents have contacted me to give the thumbs-up sign. A current SAC publicly called me "a very fine gentleman," which is in counterpoint to Hoover's "rat, vermin, jackal" and other zoological impossibilities.

"Who will people remember a hundred years from now," Joe Pyne asked, "Bill Turner or J. Edgar Hoover?"

J. Edgar Hoover, again, of course. He will have gone down as the most dangerously ambitious bureaucrat in modern American history.

APPENDIX

Editor's Note
On the following pages are photographic copies of actual FBI memorandums, all relating to material appearing in the text. If they appear to be less than brightly legible, it is because these are photographic copies of Xerox copies of original memorandums or reports.

Laboratory Report

CAA:AFP.

Case: GEORGE R. KELLY, Fugitive, et al, Kidnaping.   Number:
    Specimen: Letter to Oklahoma newspaper with envelope and letter to Charles
F.Urschel with envelope; also letter written by Kathryn Kelly addressed to Mr.
and Mrs. R. G. Shannon as normal specimen her handwriting.
    Examination requested by: Oklahoma City office.

Date received: 9/22/33.
Examination desired: compare handwriting.

Date of Report: 9/23/33.
Result of examination: Examination by: C.A.Appel.

The handwriting on the letters to the Oklahomian and to Urschel is not
identical with that of Mrs. Kelly. There are a great many similarities
which on casual examination would lead one to think that these handwriting
are the same. However, detailed analysis indicates that Mrs. Kelly did not
write these letters. The handwriting in the letters is not to any great
extent disguised or changed from normal as far as I can tell, and the same
is true of the handwriting of Mrs. Kelly.

A comparison of the signatures of George R. Kelly on three fingerprint
cards with those on these letters indicates that he may have written these
letters. I do not consider the signatures sufficient to definitely state
that he did write the letters but they are sufficient to indicate that he
might have done so. If additional specimens of George R. Kelly's handwriting are obtained, further comparison may be made. The original letters are being examined for latent fingerprints.

7-6-845

- 4.

*Suppressed FBI laboratory report that tends to exculpate Kathryn Kelly,
convicted with her husband George "Machinegun" Kelly in famous 1933
kidnapping case.*

SAC, OKLAHOMA CITY (7-6)

GEORGE KELLY BARNES, aka,
ET AL.;
KIDNAPING

ReBulet to Oklahoma City, 10/7/59.

Information concerning the testimony of handwriting expert D. C. PATTERSON, who appeared as a Government witness during the trial of GEORGE and KATHRYN KELLY, was brought to the attention of the Bureau in order that these circumstances and their potential as a source of embarrassment to the Bureau might be fully evaluated and considered prior to the time that any action was taken by this office to inform the U.S. Attorney. PATTERSON was a private handwriting expert presumably hired by the U.S. Attorney at Oklahoma City. He is now deceased.

As has been pointed out previously, it is KATHRYN KELLY's contention in her motion for vacation of sentence that she was denied the opportunity to engage the services of a handwriting expert to refute the Government's testimony that she had written certain ransom notes. Although the transcripts of the proceedings establish that there was no attempt by the Government to prove that KATHRYN KELLY or any other individual defendant wrote the ransom notes in this case, the transcript of the record of the second trial in 1933 does establish that she was identified by a Government witness, D. C. PATTERSON, as the writer of the two letters mailed from Chicago, Illinois, on 9/18/33 during the course of the first trial involving her mother, ORA SHANNON, and others. It should be borne in mind that the transcript of the second trial, which involved only GEORGE and KATHRYN KELLY, was not available at the time of the hearings on the motion in June, 1958, and it was not then known exactly what handwriting testimony might have been used against these persons.

Should action be taken at this time to acquaint the U.S. Attorney with these circumstances, it is not improbable he might take the position that he was obligated to acknowledge to the Court and the defendants at this time that the testimony

KEC
CTA:de
(3)

REVIEWED BY
AGENT

7-6-3454

Memorandum from SAC Wesley G. Grapp, Oklahoma City, October 15, 1959, reccommending that the exculpating laboratory report not be made known to the U.S. attorney due to "potential embarrassment to the Bureau."

of the Government witness on this particular point of evidence was possibly based on an erroneous conclusion, even though it did not relate to actual ransom notes as alleged by KATHRYN KELLY in her motion. As was indicated in earlier communications to the Bureau, it was clearly brought out during the hearings in June, 1958, that the ransom notes were typewritten and that the Government had not sought to establish their origin through handwriting testimony in either of the 1933 trials.

The FBI file and the USA's file in this case do not indicate that the USA's office was ever made aware of the fact that the two letters mailed from Chicago on 9/18/33 had been submitted to the FBI Laboratory in 1933 for a handwriting examination or that the FBI Laboratory conclusion was contrary to that of PATTERSON. There is not any information indicating the USA's office was informed of the results of any examination other than that made by PATTERSON. To disclose the results of the earlier examination by the Bureau to the U.S. Attorney now, could be the basis of some embarrassment to the Bureau, and would probably result in a request from him for a re-examination to resolve any conflict.

As the Bureau is aware, the attorney for the defendants on 9/15/59 filed notice with the U.S. Supreme Court, appealing from the decision of the U.S. Circuit Court of Appeals, 10th District, on 7/27/59. By the latter decision, the matter was remanded to the District Court for further hearing on the motion to vacate sentence. Should the pending appeal result in a continuation of the hearings on the motion, it is entirely possible that this particular phase of the case might not be further pursued since it was covered by testimony offered prior to the time hearing was discontinued. On the other hand, should the counsel for the defendants reopen this phase of the case in the hearings in view of the information now shown by the transcript, it would appear that further handwriting examinations would be requested since Mr. PATTERSON is now deceased. On the basis of such re-examination, any error in Mr. PATTERSON's conclusions would be brought out and could thus be considered by the Court without raising any question regarding the possibility of any earlier examination by the Bureau.

In the event the pending appeal should result in a new trial, it would, of course, be the decision of the U.S. Attorney as to what items of evidence and testimony he

The Bureau further instructs that no individual should be recommended who fails to possess outstanding potential.

In addition to the above, the Bureau will now again consider outstanding graduates of a four-year resident college, who have a degree in accounting and three years of practical accounting or auditing experience.

The Bureau has instructed that each office recruit at least one Agent for each of the scheduled classes and for those which will be scheduled at later dates.

For your information, the classes scheduled are as follows:

June 12
July 17
August 14
September 18

In your day-to-day contacts, you must be alert for qualified recruits who possess not only the above qualifications by also the present qualifications with respect to law training, language ability, and degree in the various sciences.

I am confident that under the present qualifications, we will successfully recruit a minimum of one Agent for each of the scheduled classes, if each Agent takes a personal interest in this matter.

INDEX